ZOHAR

Bereishit I

◆

Selected, translated and annotated

by

Rabbi Moshe Miller

Published by Fiftieth Gate Publications and Seminars, 24 Tikvah Way, Morristown, NJ 07960.
www.fiftiethgate.com
e-mail: fiftiethgate@yahoo.com.
Call toll-free: (877) 848-1611

ISBN 0-9700894-0-6 (cloth)
Library of Congress Card Number: 00-104115

Includes bibliographical references and glossary

10 9 8 7 6 5 4 3 2 1

Dedicated to

Ze'ev ben Beilah
Mira bat Tamar
Tal bat Mira
Ilan ben Mira
Noam ben Mira

with love

Golan Ben-Oni

In Appreciation of

Felix and Veronica Kestenberg

for your many years of help and support

◆

In Loving Memory
of
Our Dear Parents

Tzvi Hirsch ben Reuven
and
Mir'l bas Yosef HaLevi

whose life-long love, devotion and sacrifice for each other,
and for us, remain our inspiration

Menachem Mendel ben Tzvi Hirsch
and
Raizel bas Yaakov
Sklar

In Loving Memory of

Yosef ben Shmuel
and
Donna bat Yosef

◆

Blessings and Best Wishes For The Success of

Moshe Menachem ben Tzippa Rachel
Fruma bat Chaya Sarah
Avraham ben Donna
Bracha bat Fruma
Dovid Yitzchak ben Aidel
Dina Raizel bat Bracha
Shneur Zalman ben Dina Raizel
Sholom Dovber ben Dina Raizel

with love

Avraham ben Donna
Bracha bat Fruma

Dedicated to My Beloved Children

Bebesh Batia
Jennifer Chaia
Joseph Ariel

May Hashem bless you with light and mazel tov

Liora bat Moluk Batia

FOREWORD AND APPROBATION

RABBI DR. J. IMMANUEL SCHOCHET
Rabbi of Toronto's Kehilat Kielcer Congregation,
Professor of Philosophy Humber College, Toronto

The *Zohar* is popularly known as the "Bible of the Kabbalah." Its pre-eminent place in Jewish mysticism does not derive from its antiquity. Other basic works of the Kabbalah, like *Sefer Yetzirah* and *Sefer Hababir*, are of earlier origin. The *Zohar's* importance must rather be attributed to its comprehensiveness, becoming the source for practically all the later authoritative Kabbalistic teachings of the school of R. Isaac Luria and others.

Authorship of the *Zohar* is traced to Rabbi Shimon bar Yochai (known by the acronym Rashbi), the second-century *Tanna* who is the central master in the *Zohar*. This does not mean that Rashbi actually wrote the *Zohar*. In fact, he had a scribe, Rabbi Abba, who recorded his teachings.[1] Moreover, the *Zohar* itself attributes its disclosure of the Torah's mysteries to R. Shimon bar Yochai and his *Chevraya*, i.e., the group of his close associates:[2] his son R. Eleazar; his scribe R. Abba; R. Yehudah; R. Yossi ben Yaakov; R. Yitzchak; R. Chizkiyah; R. Chiya; R. Yossi; and R. Yaakov bar Idi.[3]

Early sources state that the composition of the *Zohar* extended over the period of Rashbi, his disciples and their disciples.[4] The present form of the Zohar, in order of the *parshiyot* of the Torah, is of a much later date, i.e., most likely from the period of the *Geonim*, and there are some interpolations from these late editors.[5]

1) *Zohar* II:123b. See also ibid. III:287b and 296b.
2) *Tikunei Zohar* 1a; *Zohar Chadash, Tikunim*, 93d.
3) *Zohar* II:152b; ibid. III:127b and 287b. See R. Abraham Azulay, Foreword to *Or Hachamah*, p. [2d]. See there also for a list of other authorities cited in the *Zohar*.
4) R. Abraham Zaccuti, *Sefer Yuchassin*, ed. Philipowski, s.v. R. Shimon ben Yochai, p. 45a; cited by R. Abraham Azulay, ad loc. cit.; and see also R. Yechiel Heilperin, *Seder Hadorot*, s.v. R. Shimon ben Yochai.
5) R. Abraham Galanti (disciple of R. Moshe Cordovero), commentary on *Zohar* I:168a, in *Or Hachamah, Bereishit*, p. 159b. Note R. Shalom Buzaglio, *Mikdash Melech*

The *Zohar* was concealed for many centuries, as the study of the Kabbalah was restricted to a select few qualified individuals. It became revealed only in the thirteenth century, with the approach of the period the mystics regarded to be *ikveta deMeshicha*, the period preceding the Messianic era.[6] Thus it was stated already in the *Zohar* itself that Rashbi and his *Chevraya* were permitted to reveal the mysteries of the Torah, but that these would not be disclosed until the approach of the Messianic era. Indeed, the disclosure and study of the *Zohar* would be the catalyst to hasten and bring about the Messianic redemption.[7] As of that period of time it was not only permissible but also obligatory to study *pnimiyut haTorah*, the esoteric dimension of the Torah.[8]

Moreover, the mystics ascribe special potency to the study of the *Zohar*: it effects a nullification of evil decrees, eases the *galut*, hastens the redemption, and draws forth Divine effluence and blessings.[9] There is great merit even in the mere recitation of the sacred texts of the *Zohar* even though one does not understand them.[10]

Ideally an effort is to be made to understand and comprehend the texts.[11] The language of the *Zohar*, however, is not easy, aside of the difficulty of its mystical principles and ideas. The greater part of the *Zohar* is written in Aramaic. This led to various attempts to translate

on *Zohar* III:247a, s.v. *vedibura kadma'ah*. Cf. also R. Abraham ben R. Eliyahu, Rav Pe'alim, s.v. *Zohar*; and R. David Luria, *Kadmut Sefer HaZohar*, sect. III and IV.

6) See R. Abraham Azulay, Introduction to *Or Hachamah*, p. [1c], dating this to the year 5250 (end of 15th century).

7) *Zohar* III:124b; and see also ibid. 68a; *Tikunei Zohar* 1a, and ibid. 6:24a; *Zohar Chadash, Tikunim*, 94a-b. See R. Shalom Buzaglio, *Kissei Melech* on *Tikunei Zohar*, Introductions.

8) R. Chaim Vital, *Sefer Hagilgulim*, ch. 32; R. Abraham Azulay, ibid.; R. Shneur Zalman of Liadi, *Tanya, Igeret Hakodesh*, sect. 26. See at length my "The Mystical Tradition," pp. 115-148.

9) See R. Abraham Azulay, Foreword to *Or Hachamah*, p. [2d]. Note the analogy of the *Zohar* to the saving ark of Noah in *Zohar* III:153b and *Zohar Chadash, Tikunim*, 94a.

10) R. Chaim David Azulay, *Moreh Be'etzba* II:43.

11) R. Shalom Buzaglio, *Hadrat Melech* on *Zohar* III:124b; idem, *Kissei Melech* on *Tikunei Zohar* 6:23b; R. Menachem M. Schneerson of Lubavitch, *Likkutei Sichot*, vol. VII, p. 206ff.

the *Zohar* into Hebrew. We know of several old translations, such as one by the renowned R. Israel ibn Al-Nakavah in the fourteenth century[12] and by one R. Berachiel, apparently around the sixteenth century.[13] R. Chaim Vital, the principal disciple of R. Isaac Luria, refers to a Hebrew translation[14] that may possibly be one of these two.

In the past century, Rabbi Yehudah Rosenberg composed a Hebrew translation, as did also later on Rabbi Shemuel Kipnis. Both of these rearranged the contents of the *Zohar* in order of the Scriptural verses and omitted the more difficult mystical passages, thus leaving the greater part of the *Zohar* untranslated. Most recently there is an excellent translation by Rabbi Yehudah Ashlag, following the complete text of the *Zohar*, with the insertion of his own commentary.[15] [There is also an English translation published by the Soncino Press, however it is not only incomplete but also oftentimes incorrect.]

The various translations obviously intended to make the *Zohar* accessible to a wider audience unable to cope with the Aramaic text. In this same context we have the present translation by Rabbi Moshe Miller. It, too, is an anthology in the order of the Scriptural verses, though much more comprehensive than that of his predecessors.

Rabbi Miller's work in translating the *Zohar*, and adding helpful explanations generally culled from the classic commentaries, is most impressive. It is quite obvious that great effort went into composing this book, and he is to be commended for allowing so many more people to taste from the "Tree of Life," the inestimable treasure of

12) Cited in R. Abraham Azulay's introduction to *Or Hachamah*, p. [2b]. Note that R. Israel cited the *Zohar* numerous times in his *Menorat Hama'or*, mostly in Hebrew translation.

13) The manuscript is found in the Oxford Library. The first part, to the end of *parshat Bereishit*, was published, Petach Tikvah 1946.

14) *Derech Emet* on *Zohar* I:34b.

15) Rabbi Ashlag translated the *Zohar* and the Biblical parts of *Zohar Chadash*. His disciple Rabbi Yehudah Tzvi Brandwein continued his work by translating the addenda to the *Zohar* and the *Tikunei Zohar* up to folio 68b, and the remainder of *Tikunei Zohar* was translated by Rabbi Mordechai Scheinberger.

the very soul of the Torah. It is our sincere hope that the next volumes will appear in the not too distant future.

No doubt but that the present work will contribute greatly to the dissemination of the teachings of the *Zohar*, the very spring-wells of *pnimiyut haTorah*, and their illuminating and inspiring insights. This will surely contribute to transforming our world into a better place, thus hastening the coming of Mashiach speedily in our days, as stated by R. Shimon bar Yochai.[16]

Rabbi J. Immanuel Schochet
Toronto, Ont., Menachem Av 5760

16) See above note 7; and see the Baal Shem Tov's letter appended to R. Yaakov Yossef of Polnoy's *Ben Porat Yossef* (also prefacing *Keter Shem Tov*).

APPROBATION

RABBI YITZCHAK GINSBURGH

Kabbalist, Rosh Yeshivah *Od Yosef Chai*

ג	ל	ע	י	נ	י
ו	א	ב	י	ט	ה
נ	פ	ל	א	ו	ת
מ	ת	ו	ר	ת	ך

Gal Einai **גַּל-עֵינַי**

ת.ד. 545, רחובות 76100. טל: 5947-936 (08); פקס: 3843-947 (08)
P.O. Box 545, Rechovot 76100, Israel;
tel: +972-8-936-5947; fax: +972-8-947-3843
E-mail: inner@inner.org **Web page**:
http://www.inner.org

בס"ד

12 Iyar 5760

Rabbi Moshe Miller

Shalom uvrachah!

I was most pleased to see that you have undertaken to translate and explain the major sections of the holy *Zohar*, the central and seminal text of the inner dimension of our holy Torah. As you know, the *Zohar* itself states that through studying this work of Rabbi Shimon bar Yochai, we, the Jewish people, will merit to be mercifully redeemed from our bitter exile. This will happen, the *Zohar* tells us further, when we have internalized its teachings of to the extent that we are "sustained" by them, which, as the Lubavitcher Rebbe points out, implies that we understand and comprehend them. And as the Rebbe has pointed out further, the teachings of Kabbalah are most fully explained and made relevant to daily life by the teachings of *Chassidus* in general and *Chabad Chassidus* in particular.

Moshiach told the Ba'al Shem Tov—when his soul ascended to the heavenly chambers on *Rosh HaShanah* of 1746—that *Moshiach*'s coming is dependent upon the dissemination of the wellsprings of *Chassidus*. Your translation will surely aid in this holy endeavor.

With esteem and blessing,

Rabbi Yitzchak Ginsburgh
Kefar Chabad

CONTENTS

בס"ד

Translator's Preface

"There shall be light. And there was light" (*Bereishit* 1:3). But this light was not the same light that shall be, for the original light of creation was concealed within the Torah.[1] The *Zohar* (which means *radiance*) was composed in order to uncover this light. It is for this reason also that the *Zohar* is sometimes referred to as *Midrash Yehi Or* – "The Treatise of There Shall Be Light."

The *Zohar* is one of the classic texts of the *Kabbalah*, which means "received tradition," for the teachings of *Kabbalah* were handed down from master to student, from generation to generation (see Introduction). But "*Kabbalah*" also means "parallel," from the Hebrew word "*hakbalah*," because *Kabbalah* in general, and the *Zohar* in particular, draws parallels between things which have no apparent connection whatsoever. The *Zohar* does this by examining the spiritual root of things above, and finding that ultimately everything is connected in and through their original source.

The *Zohar* in its present form is almost as large as the entire Talmud, and equally complex, if not more so. Facing the daunting task of providing an accurate, authentic, yet understandable translation of the *Zohar*, it occurred to me that selections from the *Zohar* arranged according to the order of the verses as they appear in the Torah might make it more accessible. Several leading kabbalists, foremost among them Rabbi Menachem Mendel Schneerson, the revered *Rebbe* of Chabad-Lubavitch, concurred with this view. This work has thus been arranged as a verse-by-verse Biblical commentary – something which has not been done before in English. Furthermore, explanations from the classical commentaries have been woven into the original text (in a smaller font size to distinguish them from the text of the *Zohar*), together

---

1. *Zohar Chadash, Ruth* 85a. See also *Bereishit* 8a. *Zohar* vol. I, 264a; vol. II, 149a.

with cross-references and further explanation in footnotes – also the first time this has been done in English.

This volume covers stories which will probably be very familiar to the reader – the creation of the world, the creation of man, the story of Noah and the flood, and the life of Abraham, until the binding of Isaac. These verses also provide insight into some of the passages most representative of the *Zohar's* world-view and present us with a glimpse into the inner-dimensional realm of *Kabbalah*.

I have used the traditional names of the various Bibilical books transliterated into English. Thus *Genesis* is rendered as *Bereishit*, *Exodus* as *Shemot*, *Leviticus* as *Vayikra*, *Numbers* as *Bamidbar*, *Deuteronomy* as *Devarim, Joshua* as *Yehoshua*, and so on, as listed in the Glossary. I have also transliterated the Hebrew names of the Prophets and Sages, rather than using the anglicized version. Modern Hebrew pronunciation has been used throughout.

I would like to take this opportunity to thank my family for their encouragement throughout this project, as well as all those who have provided the support that made this work possible, especially my good friends Golan Ben-Oni and Michoel Livshin.

Lag BaOmer, the day of Rabbi Shimon bar Yochai's passing, 5760.

Moshe Miller.

INTRODUCTION

– I –

Historical Background

The Written Torah and the Oral Torah

The prophetic experiences of the ancestors and founders of Judaism – Abraham, Isaac, and Jacob – are recorded in several important Biblical passages. Their intimacy with God gave them wisdom and insight, which they passed on to their descendants, the twelve tribes of Israel. Some of this tradition was committed to writing;[1] the remainder was transmitted orally from generation to generation.

The legacy that was handed down from generation to generation, gained the status of Divine Law when Israel stood at the foot of Mount Sinai and witnessed the Revelation. This in essence laid bare the hidden core of Divine knowledge. Until that time only a select few had managed, by virtue of their sanctity, to pierce the barrier between heaven and earth and attain this enlightenment. At Mount Sinai God revealed to Moses the entire complex of Divine wisdom and law[2] that is called Torah.[3]

The *Gemara*[4] explains that just prior to the giving of the Torah an argument ensued between Moses and the angels about whether it

---

1. Maimonides, *Yad, Avodah Zara* 1:3: "Abraham... wrote books on the subject [of theology.]"
2. Maimonides, *Yad*, Introduction. See also *Yerushalmi, Pe'ah* 2:4; *Megillah* 4:1; *Sifri, Ha'azinu* (32:2).
3. This term sometimes used to signify the Written Law found in the Pentateuch, and at others, as a generic term including the entire body of Jewish religious literature and oral law.
4. *Shabbat* 88b-89a. *Gemara* is one of the sections of the Oral Law, as will be explained below.

was appropriate that God's "hidden treasure" should be revealed at all to mere mortals.[5] The angels argued that the heavens were a worthier place for the lofty Torah, "since Torah in essence speaks about the higher worlds, and only hints to matters in the lower world."[6] It is apparent, however, that Moses presented a convincing case, for the Torah was given to him and the Jewish People on Mount Sinai in the year 2448 in the Hebrew calendar – 1,313 years before the Common Era.[7] According to the account given in the *Gemara*, it is clear that until this point in time, the Torah was concealed on high.[8]

When the Torah was given to Moses as the Written Law, it was accompanied by the Oral Law – the interpretation and rules of application of the Written Law. However, it was strictly prohibited for anyone to commit the Oral Law to writing for publication – "You have no permission to transcribe that which is transmitted orally."[9] Although it is evident that many of the sages committed sections of the Oral Law to writing, this was generally only for their own private use, as a reminder of the contents of the laws.[10] These written documents were therefore referred to as "*megillot s'tarim*" – "concealed documents."[11] In several passages, for example, the Babylonian Talmud reports that the famous sage Rav, nephew[12]

5. Elsewhere the Talmud (*Pesachim* 54a; *Midrash Tanchuma* 90:12) explains that the Torah actually preceded the world by 2,000 years. Some comment that this cannot be meant in a chronological sense, since time was created together with the rest of creation, but rather in the sense of spiritual gradations. Hence, the Torah is 2,000 spiritual levels above the world and is therefore too spiritual to be revealed here, other than to select individuals of superior spiritual stature..

6. *Asarah Ma'amarot,* Rabbi Menachem Azarya of Pano, *Ma'amar chikur HaDin,* section 3, chap. 22; *Shnei Luchot HaBrit* 13b ff.

7. *Seder Olam Rabbah*; *Seder HaDorot.*

8. The fact that Abraham Isaac and Jacob also observed the entire Torah even before it was given (*Yoma* 28b) was due to their unique spiritual prowess; not to the intrinsic nature of Torah as revealed law.

9. *Gittin* 60b.

10. Rambam (Maimonides) *Yad*, Introduction.

11. *Shabbat* 6b, 96b; *Bava Metzia* 92a.

12. *Pesachim* 4a.

and secretary[13]of Rabbi Chiyya (one of the most important sages of the *Zohar*), found such *megillot s'tarim* in his uncle's house.[14]

It was only due to extraordinary circumstances, i.e. fearing that the entire oral tradition would be lost in the military conquests and attendant travails that beset that era, that Rabbi Yehudah HaNassi (the thirty-fourth generation recipient of the Torah from Moses) and other sages of his generation decided to commit the germinal form of the Oral Law to writing.[15] Rabbi Yehudah occupied himself with this task and brought it to completion in the year 189 of the Common Era, the year in which he passed away. He arranged the vast body of Oral Law into the six orders of the Mishnah:

> From the days of Moses until the Holy Rabbi [Rabbi Yehudah HaNassi] no written work had been compiled from which to teach the Oral Torah publicly. Rather, in every generation the head of the Rabbinical Court, or the Prophet who lived in that generation, wrote for himself, as a reminder, all that he had heard from his teachers. He then taught the public orally. Similarly, each according to his ability, wrote for himself the explanation of the Torah and its laws as he heard them. In addition, [they also wrote down] those laws which each generation had derived by way of deduction. . . . rather than by way of direct tradition. And so it was until the days of the Holy Rabbi.[16]

The style and language of the Mishnah is incredibly compact, and it had to be accompanied, again, by oral explanation, called *Gemara*.

As the generations continued, and the adversities and calamities facing the Jewish people increased, Rabbi Yochanan, one of the great Talmudic sages living in Israel, resolved to commit the rudiments of the oral explanation and commentary on the Mishnah

---

13. *Bava Kamma* 99b.
14. *Shabbat*; *Bava Metzia* ibid.
15. *Gittin* ibid.; Rambam ibid.
16. Rambam idid.

to writing. This was called the Jerusalem Talmud, or *Talmud Yerushalmi*, which was completed approximately one hundred years after the redaction of the *Mishnah*, or about three hundred years after the destruction of the Second Temple. Over one hundred years later, Rav Ashi and Ravina, two Talmudic sages living in Babylon, produced another version of the Talmud, a more comprehensive and complete one, known as the Babylonian Talmud, or *Talmud Bavli*. The latter was completed in the thirty-ninth and fortieth generations after Moses had first received the Torah, around the year 427, which coincides with Rav Ashi's passing. Many other sages also wrote halachic (Jewish legal) and Midrashic works prior to the completion of the *Talmud Bavli*.[17]

Jewish mystical teachings were always an integral part of the Oral Law – transmitted together with the rest of the Oral Law by Moses to Joshua, and so on, through the era of the Prophets, and the Men of the Great Assembly, until the time of the redactors of the Talmud. The Five Books of Moses and the other Prophetic Books describe numerous mystical prophetic visions and experiences, but do not explain them or the methods used to achieve them. There is no doubt that explanation and the methods of achieving prophecy were expounded in an oral tradition, just like the rest of Torah. However, because of their esoteric nature, these mystical teachings were not published together with the remainder of the Oral Law.[18] Moreover, it was forbidden even to transmit these teachings on a broad scale: "One may not expound. . . . *Ma'aseh Bereishit* [the Work of Creation] to more than one student [at a time]; the *Ma'aseh Merkavah* [literally, Work of the Chariot, see below] not even to one student – unless he is wise and can understand these matters by himself" (*Mishnah Chagiga* 2:1). The *Gemara* explains: Rabbi Chiyya taught, "[One may not expound the *Ma'aseh Merkavah* to any student] but one may give him the

17. Rambam ibid.
18. Although they may have been part of the 600 orders of Mishnaic teachings prior to their redaction by Rabbi Yehudah HaNassi. (*Shem HaGedolim* מערכת ספרים s.v. זהר.)

'chapter headings,'" [i.e., the fundamentals, without lengthy explanation]. Rabbi Zeira added, "And then only to the Head of a Rabbinical Court, or to those who are properly wary." Some maintain that Rabbi Zeira said, "And then only to the Head of a Rabbinical Court, and only if he is properly wary." The *Gemara* then goes on to list various other conditions and limitations relating to the transmission of this esoteric wisdom (*Chagiga* 13a).

Several different definitions have been given of *Ma'aseh Bereishit* and *Ma'aseh Merkava*:

Rambam (Maimonides) explains[19] that *Ma'aseh Bereishit* is knowledge of the natural realm (as distinct from the supernatural), and *Ma'aseh Merkavah* is divine knowledge, that is, knowledge concerning the existence of God and the Divine Names and descriptions used for Him; the categories of angels, the nature of the soul, and so on. Rabbi Menachem ben Shlomo Meiri (c. 1249-1315) describes *Ma'aseh Merkavah* as the knowledge of the angelic realm and the existence and unity of God.[20]

Rabbeinu Nissim[21] (*Ran*, c. 1290-1380) explains further that although *Ma'aseh Bereishit* refers to knowledge of the natural realm this does not mean "science" in the regular sense of the word, for it is not gleaned by scientific inquiry and observation, which merely studies matter; but rather by examination of the true form of things, which can only be known through Torah. *Ma'aseh Merkava*, however, is the knowledge of how these forms derive from Divine Names.

Rabbi Ovadiah Bartenura (c. 1445-1524) explains that *Ma'aseh Merkavah* is the practical use of Divine Names to enable the Kabbalist to view the angels in their various levels.

---

19. *Moreh Nevuchim* part 1, Introduction; *Yad, Yesodei HaTorah* chaps. 1-4.
20. Commentary to *Chagiga* 11b.
21. *Drashot HaRan Derash* 2.

The *Tosafot Yom Tov*[22] (R. Yomtov Lipman Heller, 1579-1654) explains that both *Ma'aseh Bereishit* and *Ma'aseh Merkavah* refer to the practical use and methods of application of each of these branches of knowledge.

Several facts can be gleaned from the above: 1) That there was a secret mystical tradition in the time of the *Mishnah*, handed down from Moses via the Prophets, until it was recorded by Rabbi Yehudah HaNassi; 2) that there were two aspects of the mystical tradition as mentioned in the *Mishnah* – *Ma'aseh Bereishit* and *Ma'aseh Merkava*; 3) that the contents of this mystical tradition was a tightly guarded secret and was transmitted to only extremely select individuals in each generation.[23]

The *Zohar*

The *Zohar* first came to light some time in the last third of the thirteenth century. One of the leading kabbalists of the day, Rabbi Moshe de Leon (1238-1305), had discovered or had somehow come to possess ancient manuscripts, purported to have been written by the Second Century Tanna[24] Rabbi Shimon bar Yochai and his circle of disciples. Rabbi Moshe began disseminating copies of the text to other leading kabbalists.

It was conjectured that Rabbi Shimon bar Yochai, one of the teachers of Rabbi Yehudah HaNassi,[25] and his disciples had committed the esoteric tradition to writing for the same reasons that

---

22. Rabbi Yom-Tov Lipman Heller in his commentary on the *Mishnah Chagiga* 2:1.

23. It is interesting to note that the very same Rabbi Chiyya who was reported to have possessed various *megillat s'tarim* teaches us in *Gemara Chagiga* about the transmission of the mystical tradition. Although we cannot **automatically** conclude that he had written documents pertaining to the secret tradition, it is nevertheless a reasonable assumption, and might well be worth further examination, especially since his name appears in literally hundreds of places in the *Zohar*.

24. Sage of the *Mishnaic* era.

25. Rambam *Intro.* Ibid.

Rabbi Yehudah HaNassi had committed the Mishnah to writing. These texts were subsequently handed down to Rabbi Shimon's successors and the leaders of his Kabbalistic circle. However, unlike the Mishnah, these writings were not intended for publication, nor even for widespread dissemination, in keeping with the esoteric nature of the Kabbalistic tradition. Instead, they were passed down in each generation to a mere handful of carefully selected disciples until they reached Rabbi Moshe de Leon. Some believed that the Ramban (Rabbi Moshe ben Nachman 1194-1270, himself a renowned Kabbalist) had sent them from Israel by ship to his son in Catalonia, but the ship had been diverted and the texts ended up in the hands of Rabbi Moshe de Leon.[26]

Others explained that these manuscripts had been hidden in a vault for a thousand years and had been discovered by an Arabian king who sent them to Toledo to be deciphered. Some maintained that Spanish conquistadors had discovered the manuscripts of the *Zohar* among many others in an academy in Heidelberg.[27] Other explanations have also been offered.

However the texts came to be in the possession of Rabbi Moshe de Leon, according to traditional Jewish sources and authorities, there is no doubt that the *Zohar* was authored by Rabbi Shimon bar Yochai and his circle of disciples.[28] Many of the teachings of the *Zohar* have been incorporated into Jewish law and philosophy.

---

26. *Shem HaGedolim*, Chida *Sefarim, Zayin*, 8.
27. *Shem HaGedolim, ibid.*
28. The translator is currently occupied with writing a series of articles which examine the various theories of authorship in depth, refuting those which maintain that Rabbi Shimon did not write the *Zohar*. In brief, the claims of those who maintain that the *Zohar* was written by Moshe de Leon remain largely unsubstantiated.

Rabbi Shimon bar Yochai and his circle

Rabbi Shimon bar Yochai was one of the great Tannaitic sages who lived during the era of Roman persecution (2nd century). He was one of the foremost students of Rabbi Akiva, who had said to him, "Let it be sufficient that I and your Creator know of your powers."[29] He was also one of the teachers of Rabbi Yehudah HaNassi,[30] as mentioned above.

Rabbi Shimon was well-versed in miracles, and was therefore sent by the leaders of the Jewish people to Rome to attempt have the ban on Jewish observance officially lifted by the emperor of the time (Antoninus Pius). The Talmud tells that the daughter of the emperor was possessed by a demon, which Rabbi Shimon exorcised. The ban was subsequently abrogated.[31] However, around the year 149 C. E. Rabbi Shimon himself was forced to flee from the Roman authorities. An acquaintance of his had privately praised the Romans for their efforts in initiating and organizing aspects of commercial and social life in Israel. Rabbi Shimon countered that they had done so merely out of self-interest. Word of this discussion reached the Roman authorities, who declared that Rabbi Shimon be put to death. He fled and hid in a cave for thirteen years together with his son Rabbi Elazar, where they studied Torah day and night. They were miraculously sustained by the fruit of a carob tree and water from a spring until the emperor died and the sentence upon them was annulled.[32]

During his stay in the cave, Rabbi Shimon apparently wrote the main body of the *Zohar*, which was described as "the First *Mishnah*."[33] The remainder of his teachings was passed on orally to his disciples and to their disciples, and they committed many of his teachings to writing, probably over a period of several generations.

---

29. *Yerushalmi Sanhedrin* 6b.
30. Rambam *Intro.* Ibid.
31. *Me'ilah* 17a-b.
32. *Shabbat* 33b.
33. *Chabura Kadmaa* mentioned in *Zohar III*, p. 219a.

Kabbalah

These secret mystical traditions came to be known as "Kabbalah," from the Hebrew word *kabeil* – "receive," signifying the transmission of the esoteric tradition which was received by the leaders of the generation from the leaders of the previous generation. This tradition was interpreted and expounded in both its theoretical and practical aspects.

We have spoken above of *Ma'aseh Bereishit* and *Ma'aseh Merkavah.* Another useful (albeit more modern) classification of Kabbalistic wisdom distinguishes between its theoretical and practical aspects, or *Kabbalah Iyunit* ("contemplative Kabbalah") and *Kabbalah Ma'asit* ("practical Kabbalah").[34]

The Contemplative Tradition[35]

Kabbalah Iyunit, the category to which the majority of Kabbalistic texts in circulation today belong, sets out to explain the process whereby the created realm came into being as a finite, tangible existence through the will of the infinite Creator. *Kabbalah Iyunit* also analyzes the nature of the relationship between the creation as it proceeds toward the fulfillment of the purpose for which it was created, and the Divine source from which it emerges. On a deeper level, *Kabbalah Iyunit* explores the complex nature of Divine reality itself – in particular, the paradox of God's simultaneous transcendence and the consequent inability of human thought to grasp Him at all, together with His immanence and active and reactive relationship with Creation and humanity.

An additional aspect of the contemplative tradition is the use of various meditative techniques to ponder the Divine, the manifestations of Divinity and the esoteric underpinnings of the material world. These include the contemplation of Divine Names,

---

34. See *Tiferet Yisrael's* commentary to the *mishnah* in *Chagiga* op. cit.
35. For a more detailed analysis of the following, see Rabbi Yitzchak Ginsburgh's teachings, published by *Gal Einai* – www.inner.org.

of Hebrew letter permutations and of the ways in which the *sefirot* (supernal Divine forces, see below) harmonize and interact. Some ancient forms of Kabbalistic meditation produced a visionary experience of the supernal "chambers" and the angelic beings who occupy them. This is known as the *Heichalot* tradition.

These techniques are also sometimes used as a means of rectifying imperfections in the soul, rather than producing spiritual knowledge or elevation.

The Practical Tradition

The practical tradition of Kabbalah involves techniques aimed specifically at altering natural states or events – techniques such as the incantation of Divine names or the inscription of such names, or those of the angels, upon amulets. On occasion, these methods have been used to fashion a *golem* (humanoid) or some other creature.[36] However, *Kabbalah ma'asit* is meant to be employed by only the most saintly and responsible of individuals and for no other purpose than the benefit of man or implementation of God's plan in creation.

Even in the era of the great kabbalist, Rabbi Isaac Luria, known as the holy Ari (mid 16th century), there are indications of these techniques being abused by unfit practitioners. The holy Ari himself admonished his disciples to avoid the practical arts of Kabbalah, as he deemed such practice unsafe so long as the state of ritual purity necessary for service in the Holy Temple remains unattainable.

In essence, however, there is no clear demarcation separating the contemplative elements of Kabbalah from those aimed at influencing or altering existence. Just as *Kabbalah Iyunit*, through its system of *kavanot* (guided meditations), can influence the configuration of Divine forces impinging upon our reality, so too is

---

36. Cf. *Sanhedrin* 65b; R. Yaakov Emden's *Megilat Sefer*, p. 4 and *Mitpachat Sefarim*, p. 45a.

the efficacy of "practical Kabbalah" predicated upon the knowledge of Kabbalistic theory and doctrine.

Kabbalah and the *Zohar*

Kabbalah Iyunit has thus been characterized as a descriptive "anatomy" of the Divine reality.[37] Kabbalah is concerned with the technical identities and "locations" of, and relationships between, the worlds (planes of reality), the *sefirot* (Divine emanations), and the order in which they evolve from one another and affect one another in the vast chain of being known in Kabbalah as the *seder hishtalshelut* – the process by which Divine energy (or "light," in Kabbalistic terminology) devolves from higher spiritual planes to lower ones, eventually to become manifest in this physical plane of existence.

Of course, the ultimate intention of Kabbalah (including *Kabbalah Iyunit*) is practical – to reveal the Divinity manifested in the *sefirot* on each of the planes of reality, rather than merely describe the emanations themselves. The ultimate intention of kabbalah is to bring the individual, and then the entire world – all the planes of reality – into harmony with the Divine purpose for which they were initially created.

Within this scheme, the *Zohar* is regarded as the primary Kabbalistic text on which much if not most of later kabbalah is based.

---

37. The following is a paraphrase and adaptation of translator's footnote to *On the Essence of Chassidus*, Rabbi M. M. Schneerson, *Kehot*, 1986, transl. by R. H. Greenberg, p. 34.

– II –

The Structure of the *Zohar*

Although the *Zohar* is generally referred to as a single multi-volume work, it comprises several books which may be further sub-divided into approximately twenty main sections.[38] These are:

1) The main bulk of the *Zohar*, sometimes also called *Midrash HaZohar*, written as commentary on sections and passages of the Torah.

2) *Sifra d'Tzniuta*, or "Book of Concealed Matters." This is a commentary on *Bereishit* – the first section (*parsha*) of the Book of Bereishit (*Zohar II*, 176b-179a).

3) *Idra Rabba*, or Greater Assembly. In it Rabbi Shimon bar Yochai reveals the mysteries of the extremely recondite passages of the *Sifra d'Tzniuta* to his disciples (*Zohar III*, 127b-145a).

4) *Idra Zuta*, or Lesser Assembly. Here the passing of Rabbi Shimon bar Yochai, and the teachings which he revealed just prior to his death, are described. The methodology of the *Zohar's* redaction is also described briefly (*Zohar III*, 287b-296b). We will discuss this point at length shortly.

5) *Idra de-bei Mishkana*, the Assembly in which the section of the Torah dealing with the Tabernacle is discussed (*Zohar II*, 127ab-146b).

6) *Razin d'Razin*, the "Secret of Secrets," or "Mystery of Mysteries" discusses *chochmat ha-partzuf* (the "wisdom of the countenance" – i.e., how to "read" a person's character etc. from his facial features) and *chochmat ha-yad* (palmistry) (*Zohar II*, 70a-78a; *Zohar Chadash* 35b-37c).

---

38. This division is somewhat arbitrary; some of the sections may be subsumed under others, or may be further sub-divided. See e.g., Shalom, *Major Trends* p. 159 ff.

7) *Heichalot*, a description of the seven chambers of light perceived by the mystic during prayer, or by a righteous person as his soul passes away from this world and ascends on high (*Zohar I*, 38a-45b and *Zohar II*, 244b-268b).

8) *Matnitin* and *Tosefta*, are brief statement of Kabbalistic principles which are explained more fully in the sections which follow them. (These are spread throughout all three volumes of the *Zohar* and are also found in several places in the *Zohar Chadash*. See below).

9) *Raya Mehemna*, "the Faithful Shepherd," a Kabbalistic exposition of the commandments and prohibitions of the Torah (scattered throughout vols. 2 and 3. The bulk of the *Raya Mehemna* can be found in *Zohar II*, 114a-1121a, III 97-104, 108b-112a, 121b-126a, 215a-259b, 270b-283a).

10) *Sitrei Torah*, "Secrets of the Torah," a mystical interpretation of certain passages of the Torah (found in *Zohar I*, 74a-75b, 76b-80b, 88a-90a, 97a-102a, 108a-111a, 146b-149b[39]).

11) *Midrash HaNe'elam*, "Hidden Midrash," on various sections of the Torah (*Zohar Chadash* 2b-30b; *Zohar I* 97a-140a; *Zohar II*, 4a-5b, 14a-22a) and on *Shir HaShirim* (Shir HaShirim)

12) *Sava d'Mishpatim*, the wisdom of an old man who reveals the secrets of reincarnation and transmigration contained in the section of the Torah dealing with the laws governing the Hebrew slave (*Zohar II*, 94b-114a).

13) *Yenuka*, "The Child." The discourse of a young child who reveals mysteries of the Torah (*Zohar III*, 186a-192a).

14) *Rav Metivta*, a description of a journey through the Garden of Eden, and a discourse on the destiny of souls (*Zohar III*, 161b-174a).

---

39 . According to some, the section of *Zohar I*, 15a-22b is the *Sitrei Torah* on *Bereishit*).

15) *Zohar* on *Shir HaShirim*, a Kabbalistic exposition of the Shir HaShirim (*Zohar Chadash* 61d-75a).

16) *Kav HaMiddah*, "The Measuring Rod." Mystical insights into the *Shema Yisrael* prayer (*Zohar Chadash* 56d-58d)

17) *Sitrei Otiot*, "Mysteries of the Letters." An exposition of the secrets of the Hebrew alphabet (*Zohar Chadash* 1-9).

18) *Tikkunei Zohar* and addenda. Discussing seventy permutations of the first word of the Torah – *Bereishit*, and commentaries on various other sections of Scripture.

19) *Zohar Chadash*, commentary on the Torah and on *Shir HaShirim*, *Ruth*, *Eichah* (Lamentations). The section on *Shir HaShirim* is actually part of the *Midrash HaNe'elam*.

– III –

Mystical concepts in the *Zohar*

The Oneness of God

There is One Infinite Creator, the Cause of causes and the Producer of effects. He is not one in a numerical sense – since He is not subject to change, definition or multiplicity – but rather in the following figurative sense: The number one signifies an independent unit and is the basis of all numbers, and in this sense contains all numbers in potential; it is also actually contained in all numbers. Similarly, the Creator is actually within everything, and everything is within Him, in a state of potential. And He is the Beginning and Cause of everything. We attribute these qualities to the Creator, since He does not change – one cannot add or subtract from Him.

Moreover, His existence is necessary existence (i.e. it is not contingent upon anything else), just like the number one is a necessary for the existence of any other (whole) number. If the number one would cease to be, every other number would also cease to exist. However, if other numbers disappeared, one would continue to exist. These are properties of the number one. Similar qualities apply to the Creator. He brings into being, creates everything, and sustains the existence of everything. Even if the act ceases to be, the One who acted remains. Since His existence is not contingent upon the existence of anything else; were they to cease existing, His existence would continue, for He is completely independent of anything else.[40]

---

40. *Or Ne'erav*, Rabbi Moshe Cordovero, part 6.

The *Or Ein Sof*

Prior to creation, there was only the infinite revelation of God which filled all existence. This is called the *Or Ein Sof* – the Infinite Light – which is not God Himself, only His Infinite Revelation of Himself. Within this infinite revelation, limited beings could not possibly exist. Accordingly, there was a progressive lessening and constricting of the *Or Ein Sof*, making room for limited existence.

This progressive constriction, called *tzimtzum*,[41] brought about various planes of reality – called in Kabbalah the five worlds. Each "world" is a certain level of concealment of Godliness, of the *Or Ein Sof*. From highest to lowest (i.e. from greater to lesser revelation of the *Or Ein Sof* they are: The world of *Adam Kadmon* which is the primordial world, or the first level of somewhat finite revelation; the world of *Atzilut*; the world of *Beriah*; the world of *Yetzirah*; and the world of *Asiyah*. The entire physical universe is the lowest aspect of the world of *Asiyah*. In each of the worlds there is an increasingly dim revelation of the Infinite light as it descends further and further and becomes more and more concealed. It is important to note that these worlds do not occupy different geographical places. They are not geographical at all, but descending planes of reality.

41. The concept of *tzimtzum* is essentially Lurianic. However, it is based on an abstruse section of the *Zohar* (cf. *Zohar Chadash, Midrash Hene'elam, Bereishit*, מאמר יקוו המים).

The Planes of Reality – the Worlds

Adam Kadmon

The highest of the five worlds is called *Adam Kadmon*. "*Adam*" means "in the likeness of," or "in the image of," from the word דומה (*domeh*) in Hebrew. And "*Kadmon*" means primordial, or primary. So, *Adam Kadmon* is the primordial world which is "in the likeness of" the Infinite Light which preceded it and which was concealed in the process of creation. This means that even though *Adam Kadmon* is a world, that is to say it comes into being through the concealment of the Infinite Light; nevertheless, it is such an elevated plane of reality that it is "in the likeness of" the Infinite Light, the *Or Ein Sof*, which precedes (*kadam*) the world of *Adam Kadmon*.

Thus, although the world of *Adam Kadmon* is a world, it is a level so sublime, pure, and transcendent that it is almost imperceptible. It cleaves to and mirrors the original *Or Ein Sof*.

In Kabbalah the world of *Adam Kadmon* represents the transcendent will of God. The desire that God has that there should be a creation, and what kind of creation it will be are planned out in one broad, all-encompassing overview, without separation into specific details. This is called the *machshava kedumah*, or "primordial thought" of *Adam Kadmon*. The primordial thought functions as the blueprint for all of creation.

In the world of *Adam Kadmon* everything is seen in one broad overview, but the exact details are not yet separated and ordered into the categories of reality. All the details of creation, from the beginning of space to the end of space, and from the beginning of time to the end of time – are all superimposed in this one thought, for in *Adam Kadmon* there is no concept of space and time whatsoever. There is as yet no inside and no outside, no up and no down, no before and no after. There is only a potential for these limitations. Everything is undefined, unified, and simultaneous. Here lies the root and source of all the other planes of reality which descend from *Adam Kadmon*.

It is clear that the succeeding levels of creation, i.e. the series of worlds which descend from *Adam Kadmon*, particularly the lowest world, cannot possibly exist within the parameters of the existence of *Adam Kadmon*. Everything in *Adam Kadmon* is undefined, unified, and simultaneous, superimposed in a single primordial thought, which contradicts the very idea of worlds in the sense that we understand them, as limited being which presupposes separation and division. Subjectively, in terms of our awareness of God, the world of *Adam Kadmon* parallels the highest source of consciousness in man. It is the awareness of total unity with the Infinite Light.

The first step in bringing about the separation and division necessary for creating the lower worlds, is by "breaking" the unity of the light as it is in *Adam Kadmon*. As the light descends from *Adam Kadmon*, it breaks up into ten individual qualities or attributes (*sefirot*, *sefirah* in the singular), which act as separate independent points of light. Each of these points is an extremely powerful concentration of light as it descends from *Adam Kadmon*. These are called the *sefirot* of *Tohu*, which means chaos or disorder. The world of *Tohu* is not included in the scheme of the five worlds mentioned previously, by virtue of the fact that it shattered and does not exist as a stable plane of reality.

It will be explained later that *sefirot* generally constitute the inner structure of each of the worlds, somewhat like the bones give shape and form to the body. However, in *Tohu* this is precisely what is absent. The *sefirot* of *Tohu* are absolutely independent of each other, and form no inter-relationships with each other. Thus there is no order and no structure. Moreover, each *sefirah* in *Tohu* is the manifestation of one absolute and quintessential aspect of the light of *Adam Kadmon*, and therefore it does not interact with the other *sefirot*, since they have nothing in common. A consequence of this lack of interaction is that none of the *sefirot* of *Tohu* are able to limit the activity and expansion of any of the other *sefirot* to a level in which all the *sefirot* can function together. Therefore none of the *sefirot* can endure the activity of any of the other *sefirot*. This results in the disintegration, or "shattering" of the *sefirot* of *Tohu*. Scripture hints at this process in describing the succeeding kings of Edom: "These are the kings who ruled in the land of Edom before any king ruled over the Israelites [representing the rectification of *Tohu* as will be explained shortly]. Bela son of Beor became king. . . .. died and was succeeded as king by Yoav. . . . Yoav died, and he was succeeded as king by Chusham. . . . Chusham died, and he was succeeded. . . . etc." (*Bereishit* 36:31-39). Rabbi Yitzchak Luria explains that this refers to the *sefirot* of *Tohu*, each of which rules exclusively, and then shatters and "dies".

Nevertheless, the shattering of the *sefirot* of *Tohu* is no coincidence, nor does it signify a flaw in the creative process. On the contrary, it serves a very specific and important purpose, which is to bring about a state of separation or partition of the light into distinct qualities and attributes, and hence introduce diversity in creation. However, since the ultimate purpose of creation is not to remain in a state of separation and diversity, but to achieve unity and harmony, the separateness brought about by the shattering of *Tohu* is rectified in *Tikkun* (rectification, restitution, or reformation), which signifies the synthesis and re-unification of the diversity and fragmentation introduced by the shattering of the vessels of *Tohu*. The nature and specifics of the rectification that takes place in *Tikkun* will be discussed more fully below.

Atzilut

The next plane of reality, the highest and most perfected level of *Tikkun*, is called the world of *Atzilut*, the world of emanation. The word "*Atzilut*" in Hebrew derives from the word אצל meaning "close to" or "near," for the world of *Atzilut* is also "close to" the Infinite Light, even though it is not united and identified with it to it to the same degree as the world of *Adam Kadmon*.

The word "*Atzilut*" also means "to set aside," or "take from" and to "draw down," for the light of the world of *Atzilut* is, so to speak, taken from and drawn down from the world above it, the world of *Adam Kadmon*. But is it already a step lower.

At every stage of devolution of the *Or Ein Sof* an additional factor of limitation is added. The dimension and limitation that is added in the world of *Atzilut* is the aspect of inner structure. Whereas everything in *Adam Kadmon* is unstructured and is so tightly bound together that it is impossible to distinguish top and bottom, inside and outside, beginning and end; in *Atzilut* the dimension of internal structure is added. In fact, the entire concept of internalization, of immanence – as opposed to transcendence – is first evident in the world of *Atzilut*.

Atzilut is thus the first plane or world of immanence, of structure. In the world of *Atzilut* there is a distinction between lights and vessels – called *orot* and *kelim*. This is not a **separation** between the lights and vessels, for the lights and vessels of *Atzilut* are integrally bound up with each other. But nevertheless there is a distinction between them. One aspect is recognizable as light and another is recognizable as the vessels which contain and limit the light.

A simple analogy could be used: in an initial flash of insight, the "eureka" of sudden inspiration, one has not yet had the time to analyze and interpret the original flash of insight, and sort it into the appropriate categories of thought and understanding. The inspirational idea is felt, it is present, and the potential to analyze and interpret and understand the inspiration is in some way included in the inspiration, but it hasn't been conceptualized yet. In our analogy, the world of *Atzilut* corresponds to the structuring of the idea, and the process of understanding it, or, in more technical language, this is the forming of vessels to contain the original unformed light. Obviously, how much light is revealed depends on the capability of the vessels to receive it, just as the degree to which a person understands an idea is dependent on his intellectual capabilities. And so, the original idea (an analogy for the light), and the understanding of it (an analogy for the vessels), are integrally connected – for the idea is grasped only according to the level of understanding. The light fits the vessel perfectly. But they are, nevertheless, two distinct things. It could be that the person doesn't understand the idea. Accordingly, what he doesn't understand remains in a transcendent state, beyond his intellectual capabilities. The idea is grasped (i.e., internalized or made immanent) only according to the ability of the person to understand. The light is grasped (i.e., internalized or made immanent) only according to the ability of the vessels to receive it. In other words, the quality of light drawn down corresponds directly to, and is dependent on, the receptivity of the vessels. In the world of *Atzilut* the correlation between lights and vessels is about as perfect as it can be without the vessels actually disappearing, as they do in *Adam Kadmon*. The vessels in *Atzilut* exist – but they are nullified to the light.

This is how we would define the world of *Atzilut* – there is internal structure, and the light becomes immanent; i.e. the light drawn down from above becomes structured and ordered. In our analogy – the idea becomes understood perfectly.

This is why the world of *Atzilut* is called the world of *tikkun*, which means rectification and order. This is because the light becomes ordered and structured according to the capability of the vessels to receive it. The vessels of *Atzilut* are as capable of receiving light as vessels can be before disappearing into oblivion. Thus it follows that structure in the world of *Atzilut* is neither a hindrance to, nor an obscuring of the light, as it is in the lower worlds. In this sense, the world of *Atzilut* is still a world of non-being, a world of thought, since the vessels are nullified to the light.

This concept of structure will be explained further when we discuss the *sefirot*, the emanated lights and vessels below. And we will explain later that actual existence comes about through the vessels, not through the lights.

Beriah

The next plane of reality, the next level down, is called the world of *Beriah*, the world of creation. It is a tremendous step down from the world of *Atzilut*.

Beriah, or creation, implies limited reality, or bringing into being a limited existence. The dimension, the limitation, which is added by the descent of the light into the world of *Beriah* is the very concept of "being," as opposed to the "nothingness" of *Atzilut*. The world of *Atzilut* is a world of non-being, because the structuring of the light by the vessels is not a hindrance or an obscuring of the light, as it is in the world of *Beriah*. In the world of *Beriah*, however, the vessels begin to obscure the light and thereby create limited being. This can be understood by way of an analogy: if you were to go out on a very bright day – so bright that you would not be able to see anything if you kept yours eyes wide open, so that in order to see you have to almost close your eyes. But you still can't see properly, even with your eyes half closed – you can only make out vague shapes. So you put on a pair of sunglasses. Now you can see better – you can see things clearly. This is like the world of *Beriah* – the clear form and existence of things only becomes apparent when the light is sufficiently dimmed and obscured. Of course the analogy is imperfect since the objects which one sees with sunglasses were always separate, individual objects – which is not entirely true in the world of *Atzilut*.

The previous analogy we used, that of understanding a thought, can be used here, too. But here, in the world of *Beriah*, we move one step lower. Now we talk about explaining the thought to another person. And between the way you understand something and your ability to explain it to someone else, there is a tremendous gap. A story which is told about Rabbi Yitzchak Luria, better known as the Arizal,[42] one of the greatest kabbalistic masters who ever lived, will help us understand this. One day – a Sabbath afternoon – the Arizal fell asleep. One of his students, Rabbi Chaim Vital, saw that his master's lips were moving and when the master woke up he asked him, "what were you dreaming about?" The Arizal answered him, "I ascended to the supernal academy, and there I heard an explanation of the story of Balak and Bilaam. But what I saw in that moment would take me eighty years to explain.

Now, as yet, in the world of *Beriah*, we are not even talking about actually explaining an idea to another person. We are still talking about planning in one's mind **how** one would explain it to another person before actually doing so. In the world of *Atzilut*, the structuring of the original flash of inspiration, the original idea, was only in one's own understanding. And your grasp of the idea is proportionate to your own ability to comprehend. In the world of *Beriah*, there is an additional factor. The teacher who wants to explain an idea to his student now has to measure out the capability of his student to understand, and the teacher has to tone down and limit the idea accordingly. In fact, although for his own understanding it is not necessary for him to break the idea down into various simpler components, for the understanding of his student he must do so. For the student is, as yet, unable to grasp a vast complexity of ideas all at once. First he needs to understand all of it simpler components, one by one, until he is ready to piece

---

42. An Acronym for ***A**doneinu* (our Master) **R**abbi **I**saac, *zichrono livracha* (may his memory be a blessing).

together the entire idea. So in order for the teacher to communicate his ideas to his students, he must break down and simplify the original idea, as it is in his understanding, so that it can be grasped by someone with lesser capabilities.

Another definition of the word *beriah* in Hebrew signifies "outside of." This implies a new level of separation – it is considered to be outside of the realm of the Infinite Light. That is to say that the Infinite Light, the *Or Ein Sof*, is concealed to such an extent that this plane of reality is considered as separated from the *Or Ein Sof*, even though, as we pointed out before, there is no place devoid of the *Or Ein Sof*. An analogy is used in Kabbalah to explain the relationship between *Beriah* and *Atzilut*. The light of *Atzilut* is like the light of a candle in a room. And the light of *Beriah* is like the light of the candle as it is seen on the other side of a curtain which closes off the room.

In a subjective sense, the awareness of separation implies that one is aware of one's existence as a separate (albeit dependent) entity.

Yetzirah

The next plane of reality, the next world down, is called the world of *Yetzirah*, the world of formation. The limitation that is added by the descent into the world of *Yetzirah* is that of dimension itself. Formation is essentially a spatial concept, and Kabbalah also discusses the nature of space. It is important to know that the Kabbalah views time and space as created conditions, and not as intrinsic qualities, as will be discussed shortly. That is to say, until the descent of the light to the world of *Yetzirah*, the light is not limited by dimension. And even in the world of *Yetzirah* dimension is still spiritual and has not yet become the physical limitations of space.

Physical space has six dimensions which limit and define it. These are: above and below, right (south) and left (north), in front (east) and behind (west). In Kabbalah each of the directions derives from a spiritual quality, one of the six dimensions of the world of *Yetzirah*, i.e. the spiritual dimension or quality of the world of *Yetzirah* devolves in the world of *Asiyah* into actual spatial dimension. These six dimensions as they are in the world of *Yetzirah* are called the six *middot*, or the six *sefirot* which are revealed primarily in that world. The word *middah* in Hebrew means dimension, limitation, measurement. This is the primary characteristic of the world of *Yetzirah*; that light which descends to that world is limited and measured.

One of the characteristics of dimension or measurement is that it requires at least two reference points – where something starts and where it ends. This is because the world of *Yetzirah* is the first plane of existence where polarity and duality (the opposite of unity and oneness) come into being. Thus, here is the beginning of relationship, i.e. where each thing is defined in reference to something else, rather than in terms of its own intrinsic qualities. However, this duality is still spiritual, and therefore the dimensions of the world of *Yetzirah* are beyond the limitations of **physical** space. When the surface reality of the world is stripped away, the inner dimension is seen.

Spatial dimension in the world of *Yetzirah* can be understood in the following way: "Above" is the active reaching out of light and life force (analogous to sunlight streaming down from above), which descend to the vessels which are waiting and ready to receive them (to continue the analogy – like plants or trees which absorb the sunlight). "Below" is the receiving by the vessels. The more light the vessels receive, the more they expand and grow (south, toward the path of the sun, toward the light), and consequently, the more elevated they become (advance toward the origin of the light). Conversely, if the vessels do not receive light from above, being too immature and constricted, or because something obstructs the light and prevents it from reaching the vessels, they contract. They do not grow, and they may even face away from the sun and the source of light, and retreat, like a plant shriveling and dying in our analogy. This is the inner dimension of physical space. If we could watch this process we would not see merely the surface of things but their inner dynamic processes.

In the analogy we used earlier, if the original idea and its expansion in understanding represents the world of *Atzilut*, and thinking how to explain the idea to another person represents the world of *Beriah*; then the actual explanation of the idea to another person represents the world of *Yetzirah*. In explaining an idea to someone else, there is bound to be a limit as to how much of your understanding you can transmit in speech. Some have more success at this than others, but even the best teacher cannot communicate his own exact understanding to his student. The student has to work on this himself. Thus, speech is much more limited than thought. So too, the descent of the light into the world of *Yetzirah* defines and limits the light so that it can be absorbed by the lower level vessels of the world of *Asiyah*. In so doing the light becomes much more hidden and much more limited. In this way each vessel becomes separated from the other, because each receives the light and absorbs and expresses it in a different way. Thus there is division and diversity.

Asiyah and the Physical World

The most limiting feature of all is the limitation of time. The limitation of time means that one object cannot be here and somewhere else simultaneously. Moreover, the concept of time is bound up with change. This means that when one thing ceases to be and another thing begins to be, a change has occurred. Change can only take place where the unity and infinity of God are hidden, where the continuity of being is not evident.

Time is created from the process of the extension and retraction of the light and life force as it reaches out to the vessels below and returns to its original place. The "gap" between the reaching and returning of the light and life-force, as it pulsates continuously from above, creates time. From moment to moment the light and life force is extended downward, and then retracted, returning to its original place. That which it activated or vitalized "dies," so to speak, as soon as the life force is withdrawn, and then when it reaches down once again, it creates a new being. This change is the origin of time, for time is a measure of change. This process is analogous to a motion picture. Light shining through the constantly changing frames of the strip of film appear to create a continuous scene. But in reality each frame in the strip of film is different from, and separated from the previous one – it is only because the movement of the frames through the projector is fast enough for the human eye to be unaware that these are separate frames. Thus the scene appears to the eye to be continuous. So too is it with the pulsating of the life-force into the physical world – the "gap" between one pulse and the next is so minute, that the scene appears to be continuous.

This reaching out and returning, or pulsating, of the life force from above is mirrored in the advance and retreat of the life-force below. The pulse which you can feel in your wrist and the heart-beat which you can hear is the result of this process. Each time you feel the thump of your pulse or your heart-beat, it indicates that a different "permutation" of the light and life-force is enlivening you, and therefore you change from moment to moment.

In Kabbalah, this continuous pulsation or fluctuation is manifested in the world of *Asiyah*, or the world of action. The essence of the world of *Asiyah* is action. The story of creation concludes with the words "that God made to do [or to rectify]". The word *la'asot*, to do, is derived from the same word as *Asiyah* – action. This world is created for the sake of action, which means rectification. The just about perfect rectification of the world of *Atzilut* needs to be drawn down to this world too. This world is created "incomplete." What it is "lacking" is the revelation of

Godliness that is found to greater or lesser extent in all the other worlds or planes of reality, and the rectification of this world is the revelation of Godliness in this world through the actions of man. The Jewish sages therefore recommend that every person say to himself "for me the world was created."[43] This does not mean one should regard oneself as the center of the universe and everything was created to serve one's ego. Quite the contrary. "For me the concealment of God was created," in order that I should reveal Godliness in this world and thereby rectify the world. This is the task God set us – to reveal the inner dimensions, the Godliness, of this world (and the other worlds). Thus, the world of *Asiyah*, the world of action, is really the ultimate purpose of creation. For here, more than anywhere else, Godliness is hidden. And God can be revealed here just as much as in the world of *Atzilut* and even more so, as will be explained later on.

43. *Sanhedrin* 37a.

The Structure of Reality – the *Sefirot*

In the previous section we discussed the various planes of reality which are called the five worlds. We explained that the higher the world or plane of reality, the greater the unity and infinity of God that is revealed or manifested there. Nevertheless, since all worlds are the result of a constriction and lessening of the Infinite Light (the *Or Ein Sof*), they are all, in one sense or another, limited and defined. That is to say, the revelation of God is less or more limited, depending on which world is referred to. Therefore the word for "world" in Hebrew, "*olam,*" is etymologically related to the word "*he'elem,*" meaning hiddeness, or concealment – referring to the concealment of God's Infinite Light, so that in the higher worlds the Infinite Light is more revealed, and in the lower worlds the Infinite Light is less revealed.

The light is revealed in each world by what Kabbalah calls the *sefirot.* These are Divine emanations by which God reveals Himself to man, and by which He conducts the worlds, as the introduction to the *Zohar* states, "You are He who brings forth ten. . . . *sefirot.*

The *sefirot* are not distinct entities, or intermediaries, which would imply duality or plurality in the Infinite Light or in God. Quite the contrary – they are nothing other than various phases and levels of God's revealing Himself to man. Thus the *sefirot* are called *bli-mah,* without substance, in *Sefer Yetzirah.* The *sefirot* constitute the inner structure of each of the worlds, somewhat like the bones give shape and form to the human body. How, and to what degree, the *sefirot* reveal the Infinite Light in each world gives each particular world, each plane of reality, its individual character. Furthermore, the *sefirot* account for the dynamic interactions that take place in each of the worlds.

Now, even though the *sefirot* in all of the worlds bear the same names, it is nevertheless self-understood that the quality and power of the *sefirot* in the world of *Atzilut*,[44] for example, are incomparably greater than the quality and power of the *sefirot* in the world of *Asiyah*, for in the world of *Atzilut* the Infinite Light is revealed through the *sefirot* to a much greater extent and in a much more elevated way than in any of the worlds below it.

The origin of the word "*sefirah*" is explained in four ways in the classical texts, and one of these four explanations or derivations corresponds to the *sefirot* as they are in one of the four worlds of *Atzilut, Beriah, Yetzirah* and *Asiyah* :

1) Regarding the *sefirot* of the world of *Atzilut*, the world of emanation, the word *sefirah* is explained as deriving from the word " *sapir*" – a diamond or sapphire in Hebrew. Just as the beauty and value of a sapphire is determined by its clarity and purity, that is to say how perfectly and flawlessly it reflects light, so too, the *sefirot* of *Atzilut* are characterized by the flawlessness and purity with which they reveal and manifest the Infinite Light, the *Or Ein Sof*.

2) Regarding the *sefirot* of the world of *Beriah*, the world of creation, the word *sefirah* is explained as deriving from the word "*sippur*," meaning a story, as is mentioned in the verse in Psalms, "the heavens tell of (*mesaprim)* the glory of God." A good story describes an event clearly and succinctly to someone who did not see the event himself, and the person listening to the story can then picture the event in all its details in his mind. Nevertheless, one who hears the story experiences the event only second hand. It is obviously not the same as experiencing the event oneself. This is therefore the proper explanation of the word *sefirah* as it applies to the world of *Beriah*, since the *sefirot* of *Beriah* do not reveal and manifest the Infinite Light, the *Or Ein Sof*, to a degree comparable to that of *Atzilut*. They only "tell the story," so to speak.

---

44. The concept of *sefirot* as lights and vessels applies only in the world of *Atzilut* and below.

3) Regarding the *sefirot* of the world of *Yetzirah*, the world of formation, the word *sefirah* is explained as deriving from the word "*sfor*" meaning boundary or border. This is very much the characteristic of the world of *Yetzirah*, as explained in the previous lecture. The light that descends into the world of *Yetzirah* is given form and dimension. Borders (in a spiritual sense, of course) signify a **qualitative** limitation. This means that the light is now limited, in a qualitative sense, to a certain range, just as the natural limitations of the power of sight or of hearing in a human being are limited to a certain range of physical light or sound which the person can see or hear, whereas other creatures are able to focus on a much greater range of light or sound.

4) Regarding the *sefirot* of the world of *Asiyah*, the world of action, the word *sefirah* is explained as deriving from the word "*mispar,*" meaning number. Numbers signify a **quantitative** limitation, stressing the idea of finitude. That is to say, the extent of effect or power the light will have is severely limited by its descent into the world of *Asiyah*.

Although we just now explained that the ten *sefirot* of the world of *Atzilut* are very different from those of *Beriah*, and the ten *sefirot* of *Beriah* from those of *Yetzirah*, etc., nevertheless, in a certain way the *sefirot* of all the worlds are similar to each other. The reason for this is quite simple. The ten *sefirot* of the world of *Asiyah* derive (or "devolve") from the ten *sefirot* of *Yetzirah*, and those of *Yetzirah* derive from *Beriah* and those of *Beriah* from the *sefirot* of *Atzilut*. Or, in the language of Kabbalah, within the ten *sefirot* of Asiyah are the ten *sefirot* of *Yetzirah*, and within the *sefirot* of *Yetzirah* are the *sefirot* of *Beriah* and within them are the ten *sefirot* of *Atzilut*, in which abides the light of the *Ein Sof*. Therefore, keeping in mind that each individual *sefirah* that we are about to discuss can be placed in the context of any of the four worlds, only that in *Yetzirah* the *sefirot* are more abstract and refined than it in *Asiyah*, and in *Beriah* much more so than in *Yetzirah* and so on. So, by a process of increasing abstraction, delving deeper and deeper into the essence of these divine manifestations, one can come to some understanding of the inner structure of the increasingly elevated planes of reality, and to ever-increasing awareness of God's revelation of Himself to man through the attributes which He emanates.

The ten *sefirot* are called *keter*, *chochmah*, *binah*, *chesed*, *gevurah*, *tiferet*, *netzach*, *hod*, *yesod*, and *malchut*. In certain Kabbalistic texts an additional *sefirah* is mentioned. In reality, there are only ten *sefirot,* not eleven. However, sometimes *keter* is counted in the ten, and at other times *da'at* is counted instead of *keter,*[45] depending on whether we are looking at them from the point of view of the Creator, or from the point of view of the created. In the process of creation, in which the *sefirot* are emanated from above, i.e. from God to the physical world, *keter* is counted, and not *da'at*, since it is the first emanation, the manifestation of the Divine Will, whence all other emanations derive, as will be explained. But when the process is from below to above, man elevating himself from level to level in his desire to cleave to God, *da'at* is counted and not *keter*, since the latter is a level so sublime that it is in general beyond the scope of the average individual's ability to internalize or comprehend.[46] In the discussion of the *sefirot, keter* will be discussed, and in the discussion of the soul powers, *da'at* will be discussed.

Keter

The first and highest *sefirah* then is called *keter* or "crown," in which there are two main aspects – the inner aspect of *keter*, which is called *atik* or *atik yomin*, and the outer aspect, called *arich anpin*. Due to its loftiness *atik yomin* is sometimes referred to as *temira d'chol temirin* (the most concealed of all)[47] and as *ayin*

---

45. *Eitz Chaim* 25b.
46. See *Hadrat Melech* on *Patach Eliyahu* (Introduction to *Tikkunei Zohar*).
47. *Zohar I,* 49a, 147a; *vol. II*, 234b.

(nothingness).[48] The infinite light of *Or Ein Sof* illuminates *atik* without any separation.[49] This aspect is the source of the Torah, which is referred to as "God's delight,"[50] and is revealed primarily in the esoteric teachings of the Torah, i.e. in kabbalah.[51]

Arich Anpin is essentially the expression of God's **will**. It is also the expression of God's purpose in emanating that plane of reality. In other words, the outer aspect of the *keter* of *Atzilut* is the expression of God's will and purpose in emanating *Atzilut*, and the outer aspect of the *keter* of *Beriah* is the expression of God's will and purpose in the creation of *Beriah*, and so on.

This can be understood better by comparing this *sefirah* to certain aspects of a human being.[52] The will of a human being is the most all-encompassing power of his soul, since it gives rise to and motivates all of the other powers of the soul. If a person has a will for something he begins to invent ways in which to achieve his will, his goal. Once he has discovered a theoretical method of achieving his goal he starts to plan out how to achieve this in reality, etc. From there he initiates the action. As long as he has not yet achieved his desire his will drives him onwards until he does so.

Similarly, *keter* contains within it the ultimate goal which it seeks to attain. The goal or the aim of every plane of reality is to reveal the *Or Ein Sof*, the Infinite Light appropriate to that plane of reality. Thus *keter* contains within itself the end-point which it desires to achieve. And when it has achieved that desired end-point, it ceases to drive further. This is the meaning of the statement of the Sages in *Sefer Yetzirah* (1:7), "the end is wedged in the beginning, and the beginning is wedged in the end." *Keter* is wedged in the lowest *sefirah*, *malchut* – for the purpose of the

48. *Zohar III*, 256b.
49. See *Eitz Chaim, sha'ar* 16, chap. 1.
50. *Proverbs* 8:30; *Zohar I*, 5a, 47a; *vol. II*, 93b; *vol. III*, 35b, 67b.
51. *Zohar III*, 166b.
52. As will be explained below in the section titled "Powers of the Soul."

emanation of the *sefirot* which is expressed in *Keter* – is to unfold the level of Infinite Light appropriate for that plane of reality, all the way through the various stages of development (i.e. through the various *sefirot*) to the final revelation and manifestation of that light in the *sefirah* of *malchut*. The will of *keter* drives onward until it achieves its final aim. And *malchut* is wedged in the highest *sefirah*, *keter*, for it is the end-point which fulfills the purpose of the entire emanation.

Thus *keter* is the generator and activator of all the other *sefirot*. For in order to achieve the end-point – the fulfillment of the will of the Creator in bringing into being that plane of reality – the entire range of emanation from its highest point to its lowest is emanated and generated and unfolded from *keter* until the desired goal (the revelation of the Infinite Light) is achieved.

But, just as a person's will is transcendent, it envelops all of him, and there is no organ or limb which is the seat of the will. Rather his will envelops all of his organs and limbs and transcends them. So too, the will and purpose of the Creator in producing that plane of reality is transcendent and envelops the entire inner structure of that world. There is no level of revelation, and no level of manifestation which is outside of the Will of God as manifested in the *keter* of that world. Thus *keter* is the all-encompassing and transcendent *sefirah* of every world and is generally beyond human comprehension. The process of immanent, or in-dwelling, and comprehensible revelation of the Infinite Light appropriate for that plane of reality only begins with the next *sefirah*, the *sefirah* of *chochmah*.

Chochmah

The *sefirah* of *chochmah* may be explained in several ways, because it has several aspects, each corresponding to a different relationship of the *sefirah* of *chochmah* to the other *sefirot*:

1) The *Zohar*[53] breaks up the word *chochmah* itself into two words: כח (*koach*) and מה (*mah*). *Koach* means "potential," and "*mah*" means "what is." Thus *chochmah* means "the potential of what is," or, "the potential to be." This aspect of *chochmah* describes the state of *chochmah* in relation to the *sefirah* of *keter*. As *chochmah* emanates from *keter*, the first dawning of the *Or Ein Sof*, it "appears" in an obscure and undefined state. It is only potential being. It is virtually non-being. Thus the verse states, "and *chochmah* emerges from nothingness" (*Job* 28:12).[54] In other words it is in a state of constant flux between being and non-being, between revelation, the first point of immanent being, and non-revelation as it returns to its state of potential and merges in its source in *keter*. *Chochmah* flashes in and out of existence. The light of *Ein Sof* thus becomes unified in the world of *Atzilut* through clothing itself first in the *sefirah* of *chochmah*.[55]

2) The second aspect of the *sefirah* of *chochmah* is that it is the first of the immanent or in-dwelling *sefirot*. This is why it is called the beginning. One of the verses in *Tehillim* (111:10) states ראשית חכמה, *reishit chochmah* – *chochmah* is the first, the head, that is to say the first of the immanent *sefirot*, the beginning and root of immanent being. Whereas *keter* is the all-encompassing *sefirah*, **from which** all other *sefirot* are generated, *chochmah* is the first *sefirah* **to be** generated.

3) The third aspect of *chochmah* is that it is called the life-force of all creation. The account of the creation at the beginning of the book of *Bereishit* (Genesis) begins with the word "*Bereishit*" – "in the beginning." One of the Aramaic translations of the Torah, *Targum Yonatan* renders the word *Bereishit* as *b'chuchmata* – "with *chochmah*," for this *sefirah* is also the instrument of creation.

---

53. *Vol. III*, 235b, in *Raya Mehemna; Tikkunei Zohar* p. 111a, 112b.

54. The literal reading of the text is: "From where shall wisdom be found?" However, this is the interpretation given in *kabbalah*. See *Zohar II*, 121a, *Zohar III*, 290a, commentaries

55. *Note in Tanya* chap. 35 (p. 44b) regarding a passage in *Eitz Chaim*.

That is to say, it permeates all of creation. This is the meaning of the verse כולם בכחמה עשית, "You made everything with *chochmah*" (*Tehillim* 104:24). In this sense Scripture refers to *chochmah* as the life-force of all creation (as opposed to *keter* which is the expression of purpose and motivation of all of creation), as in the verse: והחכמה תחיה בעליה, "and *chochmah* enlivens (or vitalizes) all that possess it" (*Kohelet* 7:12). Similarly, ימותו ולא בחכמה, "They will die but not with *chochmah*" (*Iyov* 4:21), that is to say, when they are without *chochmah*. This is the aspect of *chochmah* in its relation to all the other *sefirot*.

Thus, in brief, we could define *chochmah* as the germinal, highly condensed revelation of Godly Light on its highest level of immanence that is the life force of all of creation.

Binah

The word *binah* is related to the word לבנות, (*livnot*) to build. For this is the essential quality of *binah*. The abstract, non-dimensional, incomprehensible point that represents *chochmah* is expanded and built into a three-dimensional structure, sometimes compared to the physical dimensions of length, breadth, and depth. In the context of *sefirot* they signify three aspects of *binah*, each aspect corresponding to a different relationship of the *sefirah* of *binah* to the other *sefirot*.

1) The "depth" of *binah* is that aspect of *binah* which expresses its relationship to it source in *chochmah*. The depth of *binah* derives from *chochmah*. And thus *chochmah* and *binah* together are called "the two beloved friends that never part," for where there is *chochmah*, *binah* invariably follows. The *Zohar*[56] therefore symbolizes *chochmah* and *binah* and their relationship as "the supernal point (*chochmah*) within its palace (*binah*)."

---

56. *Zohar I,* 6a.

2) The "breadth" of *binah* signifies the aspect of expansion which is the definitive characteristic of *binah*. In this connection the sages of the Talmud (*Chagiga* 14a) describe *binah* as המבין דבר מתוך דבר (*hameivin davar mitoch davar*) – "understanding one thing from another." In other words, what is contained within one concept (the word תוך in Hebrew means "within"), in *chochmah*, is expanded into an entire conceptual framework of inter-related ideas in *binah*.

3) The "length" of *binah* describes its relationship to the *sefirot* below it. The extent to which *binah* reaches down in affecting the other *sefirot* is called its "length." Obviously, the further down *binah* has to reach in order to effect even the lowest *sefirah*, the more powerful it must be in its original state.

Thus, *binah* could be defined as the expansion of the initial point of *chochmah* into a full-blown and comprehensible revelation of the Divine Light.

An analogy is used in Kabbalah to describe the relationship of *keter*, *chochmah* and *binah*: From the great depth of waters – called in Hebrew the *tehom rabbah* – which reside under the earth (this signifies *keter*), a spring of water spurts out. The spring represents *chochmah*. It is connected by hidden channels to the great depth of waters, and the spring is their first revelation. The bubbling spring forms a trickle, and the trickle becomes a stream and the stream becomes a mighty river. The river represents *binah*. The source or depth of the river is the spring of *chochmah*, and corresponds to the power of the outflow from *chochmah*. The breadth of the river is the amount that the river expands over a wide area. The length of the river is the distance from its original source, via many levels and stages (signifying the other *sefirot*), until the river eventually flows into to the sea, which represents *malchut*, as will be explained.

There is another analogy used to explain the relationship of *chochmah* and *binah*. A drop of semen, which potentially contains the life of hundreds, and even hundreds of thousands of people, is analogous to *chochmah.* And the womb which receives the drop of sperm is analogous to *binah,* which expands and develops and builds that single drop of potential life into a fully developed person with all the necessary limbs and faculties.

A further analogy: Imagine that you are walking in a unfamiliar place on a very dark night. Suddenly, a flash of lightning illuminates the whole area, and for an instant you can see everything with absolute clarity. But, a moment later, the night is just as dark. Now you have to reconstruct what you saw in that momentary flash of lightning, in order to find your way home. The lightning flash is akin to the activity of *chochmah,* which flashes in and out of existence. Reconstructing what it was that was revealed when the darkness was briefly illuminated is akin to the functioning of *binah.*

Again, *binah* is the expansion and extension of the initial point-like revelation of God into a comprehensive system.

The remaining seven *sefirot* are called the seven *middot* (singular: *middah*). The word "*middah*" in Hebrew means a measurement or an amount. This is precisely the function of these seven *sefirot* – to distribute the light and life force of a particular plane of reality, a particular world, according to its proper measure. They are also called in Kabbalah the seven days of Creation, for it is essentially through them that structure of each of the planes of reality is built. If *binah* is analogous to the builder, or to the process of building, as explained previously, then the seven *middot* are analogous to the edifice itself.

Each one of these seven *sefirot* also corresponds to one of the seven days of creation. The *sefirah* of *chesed* corresponds to the first day of creation, the *sefirah* of *gevurah* to the second day, and so on, until the seventh *sefirah, malchut,* which corresponds to the Sabbath. The nature of each of these *sefirot* can be understood by examining the seven days of creation as a paradigm of the activity and interaction of these *sefirot*.

Chesed

The word *chesed* means kindness or benevolence. It denotes the unbounded loving-kindness with which God created the worlds, and with which all of creation is permeated, as the verse explains: עולם חסד יבנה – "The world is built with *chesed*" (*Tehillim* 89:3). Kabbalah explains that kindness was in fact the reason for the creation. Since the "nature" of God, so to speak is absolute benevolence and loving-kindness, He created the worlds so that He would have on whom to bestow His kindness – "It is the nature of He who is good, to do good."[57]

Light was created on the first day. Light is revelation, as explained previously. This light was infinite, as our Sages say, "The light that was created on the first day shone from one end of creation to the other." Or, in the language of Kabbalah, "In the beginning, an infinite, uncompounded light filled all of creation."[58] This is the light of *chesed* which permeates all of creation, and through which all of creation is built.

Gevurah

However, since the *chesed* of God is infinite and unlimited, while the creatures on whom it is intended to be bestowed are finite and therefore unable to absorb infinite kindness and yet remain in physical existence, the attribute of *chesed* is controlled and restrained, or concealed and limited, by the aspect of *gevurah*. *Gevurah* means restrictive power, the power to limit and conceal

---

57. *Emek HaMelech, sha'ar Sha'ashuei HaMelech*, chap. 1.
58. *Eitz Chaim, Otzrot Chaim*, beginning.

the Infinite Light so that each creature can receive according to its capacity. Thus, *gevurah* is also an aspect of God's kindness, for if the outpouring of infinite kindness were to remain unrestricted, finite creatures would become instantly nullified in the infinite revelation of Divine Love. Therefore the *sefirah* of *gevurah* is the manifestation of God's power to restrict and conceal the Light which He emanates, in order that His creatures will be able to receive His loving-kindness according to their capacity.

On the second day of creation, separation of the higher waters from the lower waters was introduced. This is called the firmament (*rakia*) in the Torah. In Kabbalah water signifies kindness, *chesed*. The separating of the waters means that the infinite *chesed* of God, referred to as the higher waters, is separated from the lower waters, signifying finite *chesed* which can permeate creation.

Tiferet

Tiferet (from *pe'er* – beauty) represents the harmonious blending of varying colors and forms, producing a work of great beauty.[59] The harmonizing and blending of *chesed* and *gevurah*, so that a proper mixture of the two will result in a bearable revelation of *chesed* to finite created beings is brought about by the attribute of *tiferet*. In other words, *tiferet* is the attribute which blends the benevolent outflow of *chesed* and the restrictive severity of *gevurah* so that each creature will receive its proper measure of Divine Light and life-force. This is why *tiferet* is also called compassion or mercy, for it enables *chesed* and *gevurah* to balance each other so that God's benevolence can be absorbed by the limited world without its ceasing to exist.

On the third day of creation, water and land were separated, and the vegetable kingdom was created. The third day sets a balance between water and land, so that the vegetable kingdom (and thus the animal and human kingdoms also) can be sustained by both of

---

59. *Tikkunei Zohar, tikkun* 70, p. 133b; *Pardes, sha'ar* 8, chap. 17.

them, when there is a proper balance between them, each plant according to its needs.

Netzach and *Hod*

Whereas *chesed* and *gevurah* signify unbounded loving-kindness, and the limitation and concealment thereof, respectively, so that finite creatures can receive according to their ability; *netzach* and *hod* are the two *sefirot* which define the ability of the **recipient** to receive. In addition they perform together as the "joint distribution committee," which decide how, and in what measure, each recipient will get its due.

Let us give an analogy. A professor wants to teach his student calculus, let us say. Of course, the professor wants to teach his students as much as possible in the shortest possible time, so that the students can go on to other subjects in math (this is the attribute of *chesed*, the desire to give more and more). But the professor is well aware that his students present level of understanding is insufficient to grasp the entire theory of calculus in a single lesson. So he divides up the subject into several lectures, explaining only one section of the theory at a time (this is the attribute of *gevurah*, limiting and dividing the outflow of benevolence). When the professor actually explains the subject, he takes into account the individual abilities and limitations of each of his students, and he explain the subject accordingly (this signifies the functioning of the attributes of *netzach* and *hod*).

On the fourth day of creation the sun and the moon and the stars were created. Even though light was created on the first day, this light was infinite and too sublime to be of use to the finite worlds. Thus on the fourth day, a finite, usable form of light was apportioned. On the fifth day birds and sea-creatures were created, the first recipients of God's benevolence and the first created beings able to fulfill the commandment *pru u'rvu*, be fruitful and multiply.

According to Kabbalah the powers of prophecy and Divine inspiration derive from the *sefirot* of *netzach* and *hod* – for they actually receive the efflux of Godly light.

Yesod

Just as the *sefirah* of *tiferet* harmonizes and balances *chesed* and *gevurah*, so too, *yesod* harmonizes and balances *netzach* and *hod*. However, there is an additional unique aspect of *yesod* – it acts as the **channel** through which *malchut*, the recipient, receives its proper measure of light and life force. In the previous analogy: whereas *netzach* and *hod* distribute the Divine efflux and measure the amount the recipients will receive, and in what way, *yesod* is the actual distribution point. Thus *yesod* functions as the connector between all of the *sefirot* which precede it, and the recipient, *malchut*, below it.

In order for the distribution to reach its intended destination, there must be a proper channel of communication between the giver, *yesod*, and the receiver, *malchut*. To continue with the previous analogy: the distributor (*yesod*), must be able to identify the recipient (*malchut*) in order to match each portion with its intended recipient. This is why *yesod* is also called אמת – (*emet*) "truth" in Kabbalah. *Yesod* makes sure that the light and life force reaches the proper destination.

But the "identification" process does not only mean that the recipient fulfills the necessary conditions that must be met in order for it to be able to receive. Much more than this, there must be an **internal bond** between *yesod* and *malchut*, between giver and receiver – a bond of love and understanding. *Yesod* arouses the desire to receive in *malchut*, and *malchut* in turn arouses in *yesod* the desire to give. In this way, *yesod* unites itself with *malchut* in complete empathy, so that the "giving" is direct, face to face, and not indirect, back to back, as it were.

Thus, *yesod* could be defined as the divine attribute which joins God to His creation in a bond of empathy and love. This is why the *sefirah* of *Yesod* is also called "*tzaddik,*" as in the verse צדיק יסוד עולם (*tzaddik yesod olam*) "a saint is the foundation of the world" (*Mishlei* 10:25). A *tzaddik*, or saint, arouses mankind to seek God. At the same time he draws down God's compassion and goodness into the world. Thus he is the foundation of the world.

On the sixth day of creation the animal kingdom was created, and also the first man and woman, Adam and Eve, who were created in the Divine Image. Both animals and man are also told "be fruitful and multiply;" which also means to use God's benevolent kindness to grow and expand in consciousness of Him. But an additional duty is given to man. Be fruitful and multiply, and rule over the animals and the birds and the fish. In other words, be **over** and above them, and not among them. Transcend your limited nature, transcend that part of yourself which is simply natural, like the animal world, and become the Divine Image in which you were created. The drive to do this is initiated by the power of *yesod*, the *tzaddik*.

Malchut

The tenth and final *sefirah* is called *malchut*. *Malchut* contains two completely opposite qualities, called התנאשות (*hitnasut*) meaning "exaltedness," and its opposite שפלות (*shiflut*) – "humility." When we explained the *sefirah* of *keter*, it was pointed out that *keter*, the beginning, is wedged in *malchut* – the end. The reverse is also true – *malchut* is wedged in *keter*. We explained there that this means that the final product, *malchut*, is the original intention of the entire process of emanation. When *malchut* is still contained in the original intention (that is, in *keter*), it is in a state of exaltedness. And when it descends to its place as the last of the *sefirot*, it is in a state of humility. However, it is not the case that *malchut* is in one state or the other; it is in both states simultaneously.

On one hand, *malchut* receives all that it has from the other *sefirot*, and is described in Kabbalah as "having nothing of her own."[60] Thus the *Zohar* compares *malchut* to the moon which has no light of her own;[61] while on the other hand *malchut* is the final revelation of the Divine Light for which the entire process was begun. It was for the purpose of *malchut* that all the *sefirot* were emanated. Thus *malchut* is both the receiver and the consummation of giving.

In a previous analogy, we explained that *keter* was symbolized by the great depths of water hidden under the earth, the *tehom rabbah. Chochmah* was symbolized by the well-spring, from which flows a small quantity of pure water, and *binah* was symbolized by a broad and mighty river which begins from its source in the well-spring of *chochmah. Malchut* signifies the sea into which the river flows. It is the actualization of the entire revelation which began as a single tiny point of trickling water. Whereas *chochmah* is the potential to be, *malchut* is the actual being, the final manifestation, which was the original intention. It is for this reason that *malchut* is also called " *Shechinah*" – the Divine Indwelling Presence, the immanent revelation of God. And so the sea returns to the *tehom rabbah*, as the final revelation fulfills the original purpose.

The seventh day of creation, the Sabbath day, is therefore a cessation of work. The Sages say, "he who works prior to the Sabbath, will eat on the Sabbath." That is to say, all the six days of creation which precede the Sabbath must do their work if the culmination of creation is to be revealed on the Sabbath day. The *Zohar* (*III,* 92b) states, "Each day does its work." By fulfilling its function each day's purpose is consummated. Again the *Zohar*[62] expresses this perfectly – "from the Sabbath day all other days become blessed." This applies both retroactively and proactively. As the Torah states at the completion of creation: "And the work was complete. . . . and God blessed the seventh day and sanctified

60. See *Eitz Chaim, sha'ar* 6, ch. 5; *shaa'r* 8, ch. 5.
61. Vol. I, pp. 249b, 251b; vol. II, p. 245b.
62. Vol. *III,* 144b.

it." Thus the *Zohar* states: "the supernal crown [*keter elyon*] is the crown of kingdom (*keter malchut*)." The first, highest of the Divine emanations, *keter*, is thus linked to the last, *malchut*.

The Arrangement and Interaction of the *Sefirot*

The *sefirot* represent the various stages of the creative process whereby God generated the progression of created realms which culminated in our finite physical universe. As a coexisting group, the *sefirot* constitute the interacting components of a single metaphysical structure whose imprint can be identified at all levels, and within all aspects, of Creation.

The *sefirot* exist not only as individual qualities, but also (and primarily) in configurations which are depicted in *Kabbalistic* texts as having the structure of the human body, which is called the *tzelem Elokim* (supernal "image of God"). Just like the body, the *sefirot* are arranged in vertical arrays along three parallel axes, each representing a mode of Divine influence within Creation. Hence each *sefirah* is associated with the particular limb or organ that corresponds to its position in the anatomical *sefirotic* structure. This configuration is also referred to in the literature as a *sulam* ("ladder"), or an *eitz* ("tree").

The interaction among the various *sefirot* takes place through a network of connecting *tzinorot* ("channels") which carry the flow of Divine energy throughout Creation. These connections suggest various sub-groupings of the *sefirot,* each reflecting a certain dynamic amongst the *sefirot* which they include. The loftiest triad of *sefirot* identifies comprises *keter, chochmah* and *binah* (or alternatively *chochmah*, and *binah* and *da'at*). This sub-grouping defines a cognitive dynamic; the following triad comprises *chesed*, *gevurah*, and *tiferet* – these are the primary emotions; the final grouping comprises *netzach, hod* and *yesod* – the instinctual and pragmatic forces. *Malchut* may be viewed as either an appendage of this last sub-grouping, or as an independent entity receiving and manifesting those energies that precede it.

Another way of dividing the *sefirot* is into *partzufim* ("visages" or "profiles"). A *partzuf* is a metaphorical figure of human likeness, used to represent the expansion of a *sefirah* (or group of *sefirot*) into an independent configuration with ten *sefirot* of its own. According to Kabbalah, the *sefirot* of *keter, chochmah, binah* and *malchut* each possess two interrelated *partzufim*; whereas the six *sefirot* from *chesed* through *yesod* form their own common and independent pair of *partzufim*.

In the configuration of the *sefirot, keter* appears at the top of the middle axis, and corresponds in the *tzelem Elokim* to the skull.

The *sefirah* of *keter* develops into two *partzufim*. Its outer *partzuf*, is referred to as *Arich Anpin*, and its inner *partzuf* is referred to as *Atik Yomin.*

Chochmah appears in the configuration of the *sefirot* at the top of the right axis, and corresponds in the *tzelem Elokim* to the right hemisphere of the brain. In its fully articulated form, *chochmah* possesses two *partzufim*: the higher of these is referred to as *Abba Ila'ah* ("the higher father"), whereas the lower is referred to as *Yisrael Sabba* ("Israel, the Elder"). These two *partzufim* are referred to jointly as *Abba* ("the father").

Binah appears in the configuration of the *sefirot* at the top of the left axis, and corresponds in the *tzelem Elokim* to the left hemisphere of the brain.

In its fully expanded form, *binah* also possesses two *partzufim*: the higher of these is referred to as *Imma Ila'ah* ("the higher mother"), whereas the lower is referred to as *tevunah* ("comprehension"). These two *partzufim* are referred to jointly as *Imma* ("the mother").

The union of *chochmah* and *binah* ("the higher union," in Kabbalah), the "father" and the "mother" (the right and left hemispheres of the brain) is continual, and is referred to in the *Zohar* as "two companions that never separate." This union is necessary for the continual re-creation of the world (beginning with the birth of the seven attributes of the heart, corresponding to the seven days of Creation, from the womb of "mother," *binah*).

Da'at is the third and last conscious power of intellect in Creation. Generally, *da'at* is only enumerated among the *sefirot* when *keter* is not, as explained above. This is due to the fact that *da'at* represents the reflection of (the inner dimension of) *keter* itself within the realm of consciousness. Hence *da'at* appears in the configuration of the *sefirot* along the middle axis, directly beneath *keter*; and, corresponds in the *tzelem Elokim* to the cerebellum (posterior brain).

In the *Zohar*, *da'at* is referred to as "the key that includes six." The "key" of *da'at* opens all six attributes of the heart (the emotions) and fills them with life-force.

Chesed appears in the configuration of the *sefirot* along the right axis, directly beneath *chochmah,* and corresponds in the *tzelem Elokim* to the "right arm."

Gevurah is the fifth of the ten *sefirot,* and second of the emotive attributes in Creation. *Gevurah* appears in the configuration of the *sefirot* along the left axis, directly beneath *binah,* and corresponds in the *tzelem Elokim* to the "left arm."

Tiferet is the sixth of the ten *sefirot,* and the third of the emotive attributes within Creation. *Tiferet* appears in the configuration of the *sefirot* along the middle axis, directly beneath *da'at* (or beneath *keter,* when *da'at* is excluded), and corresponds in the *tzelem Elokim* to the upper torso (in particular, the heart).

Netzach is the seventh of the ten *sefirot,* and the fourth of the emotive attributes within Creation. It appears in the configuration of the *sefirot* along the right axis, directly beneath *chesed,* and corresponds in the *tzelem Elokim* to the right leg.

Hod is the eighth of the ten *sefirot,* and the fifth of the emotive attributes within Creation. It appears in the configuration of the *sefirot* along the left axis, directly beneath *gevurah,* and corresponds in the *tzelem Elokim* to the left leg.

The two *sefirot* of *netzach* and *hod* are referred to as "two halves of a single body." This is so because more than with respect to *chesed* and *gevurah* (the right and left arms), *netzach* and *hod* (the right and left legs), can only perform their function in unison – walking together.

Netzach and *hod* are also referred to in the *Zohar* as "the scales of justice." *Netzach* merits while *hod* concedes ("acknowledges" or "confesses"). As the two hips of the body they are responsible for the general state of equilibrium of the body.

Yesod is the ninth of the ten *sefirot,* and the sixth of the emotive attributes within Creation. *Yesod* appears in the configuration of the *sefirot* along the middle axis, directly beneath *tiferet,* and corresponds in the *tzelem Elokim* to the procreative organ (in the male; in the female, to the womb).

The six *sefirot* from *chesed* to *yesod* join and develop to form the *partzuf* of *Zeir Anpin. Zeir Anpin* (or *z"a* in Kabbalistic shorthand) receives its "head" or "brain-power" (the three higher *sefirot* of *chochmah, binah* and *da'at*) from the higher *partzufim* of *Abba and Imma.*

Malchut is the last of the ten *sefirot,* and the final emotive attribute within Creation (or, more precisely, the manifestation of what is contained above it in a potential or latent state, as explained above). *Malchut* appears in the configuration of the *sefirot* at the bottom of the middle axis, directly beneath *yesod,* and corresponds in the *tzelem Elokim* to the "crown" of the procreative organ (the corona in the male; the labia in the female). *Malchut* also corresponds to the mouth, and is often referred to as "the world of speech," insofar as the spoken word represents the essential medium of self-expression, allowing one to not only reveal himself to outer reality but to guide and influence that reality as well. Hence, speech allows one to exercise authority and "kingship," the literal meaning of *malchut*.

Malchut also serves as the means for establishing an identification with outer reality. Analogously, exercising kingship requires utmost sensitivity to the needs of the realm which one seeks to rule. Conversely, every individual creation must accept Divine authority, for only then can the ultimate good of the mundane realm be assured.

In its meditation of Divinity, the soul can only perceive and ascend to the higher *sefirot* through the "pane" and portal of *malchut*. "This is the gate to God, the righteous shall enter through it" (Psalms 118:20). In one's devoted service to God this means receiving upon oneself, in total commitment, "the yoke of the kingdom of heaven." When this is not done, the result is *galut haShechinah* – the exile of the Divine Presence.

The Structure of Consciousness – the Soul –

The divine soul is an indivisible essence inseparably bound to God,[63] as the verse states, "For part of God is His People" (*Devarim* 32:9), and as Rabbi Shimon bar Yochai states about himself: "My soul is one with Him, as one flame, cleaving to Him."[64] Nevertheless, as it emanates from the *Ein Sof* – the Infinite One – eventually to be clothed in the physical body, the soul descends via the five worlds mentioned above, leaving a root in each of the worlds,[65] until it is clothed in a physical body. Thus there are five levels of soul, or levels of God-consciousness, corresponding to the various planes of reality, or levels of Divine revelation/concealment manifested in each of the worlds.[66]

The soul enclothed within the body is a reflection of the Divine Form, called the *tzelem*, or *tzelem Elokim*. This *tzelem Elokim* may be described as the human mold of man's physical form, linking his body and soul. This mold derives from the configuration of the *sefirot* which structure of the worlds through which the soul descends on its journey down into the body.

At the same time that the soul's outer dimension reflects the configuration of the *sefirot*, the inner dimension of the soul reflects the Infinite Light which illuminates the *sefirot*. This reflection is called the *demut Elokim* (the Image of God).[67] Thus man includes all of creation within him, from the loftiest spirituality to the most mundane physicality.[68]

---

63. See *Zohar II*, p. 5b, 96a, ; *Zohar III*, p. 94a; *Pardes, sha'ar* 4, chap. 7.

64. *Zohar III*, p. 292a.

65. See R. Chaim Vital's *Sha'arei Kedushah*, part 3, chap. 5; ד"ה יונתי בחגוי הסלע in *Likutei Torah, Shir Hashirim*, Rabbi Shneur Zalman of Liadi.

66. See *Tikkunei Zohar* p. 132b; *Pardes, sha'ar* 31, chap. 2.

67. See *Zohar I*, 37a, b; *Zohar II*, 70b; *Hashmatot* p. 265a; *Pardes, sha'ar* 31, chap. 4.

68. *Pardes, sha'ar* 4, chap. 10.

Viewed from the point of view of man's service of God, these levels of soul may be described as five ascending levels of awareness of, and communion with, God. They are called (in ascending order) *nefesh, ruach, neshamah, chayah* and *yechidah.*[69] Regarding these levels of soul, the *Zohar*[70] states that when a person is born, he is given a *nefesh* from the world of *Asiyah*, the lowest world, representing the greatest concealment of God. If, through his divine service and proper action, he makes himself worthy, he is then given *ruach* on the plane of *Yetzirah.* With greater effort, he can earn the revelation of *neshamah*, paralleling the world of *Beriah.* If he purifies himself greatly, he may be able to attain the level of *chaya* paralleling *Atzilut*, and even *yechidah* – the God-consciousness of the level of *Adam Kadmon* and beyond. ("Beyond," because the level of soul called *yechidah* in essence transcends all the worlds, since it is never separated from God. It is described as being "truly part of God above,"[71] and as "a spark of the Creator clothed within a spark of the created."[72])

Nefesh

Nefesh, the lowest level of consciousness, is awareness of the physical body and the physical world, the world of *Asiyah* – the world of action. However, this awareness of the physical body is not awareness in a passive sense; it is merely an observation of the facts. On the contrary, the nefesh is in fact the **life-force** of the body, and it is precisely because it is the life-force of the body that the nefesh has an awareness of the body. This physical awareness is a result of the enmeshing of the *nefesh* with the body. Now, although the *nefesh* is the life-force of the body, this does not mean that the *nefesh* creates the body. The body was and is created by God, just like everything else. After God created Adam's body

69. *Zohar II, Raya Mehemna,* p. 198b; *Hashmatot* p. 267a.

70. See vol. II, p. 94b; vol. III, p. 24b-25a, 70b; vol. I, p. 62a, commentaries; *Pardes, sha'ar* 31, chap. 3.

71. *Job* 31:2, *Tanya* chap. 2.

72. *Eitz Chaim sha'ar* 42, chap. 1.

"from the dust of the earth," He blew into Adam the breath of life (see *Bereishit* 2:7). This is the *nefesh* – the life-force – that was blown into the body.

It is this part of the person which dies and goes to the grave with the body.[73] Just as in the world of *Asiyah malchut* is the dominant *sefirah*, so too in the *nefesh*, which corresponds to the world of *Asiyah*, the attribute of *malchut* – action – is the dominant characteristic of the soul.[74]

The divine service associated with the level of *nefesh* is acknowledgment of, and submission to, the supreme authority of God, particularly in reference to the fulfillment of the Commandments. It is therefore called "accepting the yoke of Heaven" – *kabbalat ol malchut shamayim.*"[75]

Ruach

Ruach is the next level of soul – a higher plane of consciousness than the rank of *nefesh*. The world (i.e., level of revelation of Godliness) corresponding to *ruach* is the world of *Yetzirah*.[76] The primary manifestation of *ruach* is in the emotions, just as the primary activity of the six *sefirot* of *Zeir Anpin* (from *chesed* to *yesod*) is in the world of *Yetzirah*. In terms of Divine service this entails arousing the emotions of love and awe of God.

Love and awe of God are aroused by contemplating the divine energy which forms and maintains the world of *Yetzirah*, and by observing the tremendous self-nullification of the angelic beings which inhabit it.[77] Although the intellect may be used extensively on this level of soul; nevertheless, the primary focus of the intellect here is contemplation in order to arouse the emotions. The

---

73. *Pardes, sha'ar* 31, chap. 2.
74. *Zohar I,* 81a, b; *Zohar III,* p. 46b.
75. See *Zohar III, Raya Mehemna,* p. 29a. See at length *Kuntreis HaAvodah,* by Rabbi Shalom DovBer Schneersohn, chap 1.
76. *Zohar II,* 94b.
77. *Zohar ibid.*

Talmudic sages therefore refer to it as "the toil of the heart," through which one comes to love God with all one's heart.[78] Nevertheless, this is a lower level of love, since it is generated by contemplating lower levels of God's creative energy.

Neshamah

The primary activity of *neshamah* is in the conceptual grasp of the intellect, as the verse states, "and the soul (*nishmat*) from the Almighty gives them understanding"[79] The level of *neshamah* contemplates the manifestation of Divine energy in the world of *Beriah.*[80] Just as in the world of *Beriah* the primary *sefirah* is *binah,* so too in the soul – the primary activity is understanding. Unlike the world of *Yetzirah*, the world of form and relationship, the world of *Beriah* is nascent divine energy. It is the notion of coming into being from nothingness, rather than structured, quantified existence. Thus one of the primary meditations of the *neshamah* is the concept of continuous creation (the coming-into-being) and sustenance of life and existence.

Neshamah analyzes underlying principles abstracted from the categories of thought imposed upon them by the human mind and human experience.[81] It seeks to pierce through to the essential rather than the ephemeral. One of the signs that a person is on this level of consciousness is that when the mind is clearly focused on an appropriate Divine concept, all of the senses become temporarily nullified. Subsequently, due to the abundance of spiritual light one experiences at this level, the emotions of love and awe are automatically aroused, and to a much greater extent than in the previous level, where effort was expended in arousing the emotions. This is referred to in Kabbalah as "the rapture of the

---

78. *Devarim* 6:5; *Zohar I,* 178b; vol. *II* 134a, 162b; *Ta'anit* 2a.
79. *Job* 32:8.
80. *Zohar II*, 94b.
81. *Kuntreis HaAvodah* chap. 1.

heart" (*re'uta d'libah*).[82] Here the heart truly desires Godliness, and love is revealed in its fullness in the heart. This is referred to in the verse as loving God "with all of your soul."[83] This may therefore be described as communion with God as the Creator of the worlds.

Chayah

The aspect of the soul called *chayah* gazes upon the Divine energy of the world of *Atzilut*.[84] Whereas the primary activity of the level of *neshamah* is to use intellectual comprehension in order to come to communion with God as the Creator of the worlds, the level of *chayah* communes with God as He transcends the worlds. Here the soul's knowledge is not in the immanence of Divine attributes which identify the nature of the Divine energy manifested in creation, but rather with knowing what God is not – i.e. how He is not limited or defined by the finite universe. Thus the soul merges into a state of complete nullification of the ego. There is no self-seeking and no self-identity outside of God, and is called loving God "with all one's being."[85] This is knowledge of the absolute truth of things.

Yechidah

Corresponding to *Adam Kadmon* is the level of soul called *yechidah.* Just as the sublime, pure and transcendent world of *Adam Kadmon*, cleaves to and reflects the original *Or Ein Sof*, so too the level of *yechidah.* This is the essence of the soul which is naturally and immutably bound to the Holy One. In the words of Rabbi Shimon bar Yochai,[86] "Throughout the days of my connection to this world, I was bound to the Holy One blessed be

---

82. *Zohar II*, 93b, *III* 22b, in *Raya Mehemna*; *Tanya* chap. 39.
83. *Devarim* 6:5. *Zohar II*, 163a, 198b in *Raya Mehemna.*
84. *Zohar II*, 94b.
85. *Devarim* 6:5. *Zohar II*, 198b, in *Raya Mehemna.*
86. *Zohar III*, 288a in *Idra Zuta.*

He with a single knot. . . . at one with Him." This is the level of soul revealed at the moment of self-sacrifice or martyrdom for the sake of God, His Torah, or His people.[87]

Powers of the Soul

From the ten *sefirot*[88] described above the soul derives its corresponding ten soul-powers,[89] which have names identical to the *sefirot*. The soul is expressed and manifested through its powers, of which there are two general categories – the transcendent or encompassing powers, and the particular, or immanent powers (corresponding to the transcendent *keter*, and the remaining immanent *sefirot*). The transcendent or super-conscious powers of the soul are called delight (*oneg*) and will (*ratzon*), corresponding to the inner and outer dimensions of *keter* mentioned above.

The particular or immanent powers are further subdivided into intellect and emotions. The three intellectual powers are *chochmah*, wisdom or creative intellect; *binah*, understanding or developmental intellect; and *da'at*, which is knowledge or conclusive, synthesizing intellect.

Chochmah

Chochmah is the creative and generally unpredictable power of the soul which is manifested in spontaneous insights or inspiration – an intuitive flash of intellectual illumination which has not yet been processed or developed by the understanding power of *binah*.

---

87. *Kuntreis HaAvodah* p. 30.
88. *Tikkunei Zohar, Introduction – Patach Eliyahu.*
89. *Pardes, sha'ar* 31, chap. 1.

The creative power which illuminates *chochmah* derives from the concealed level of *keter* – "and *chochmah* emerges from nothingness" (*Job* 28:12), that is, from the hidden *keter*.[90] The reason that *chochmah* is able to act as a receptacle for the flash of Divine revelation is that in its inner essence is also "nothingness." That is, the inner essence of *chochmah* is self-nullification (*bittul*). This is why the *Zohar* characterizes the nature of *chochmah* by one of the permutations of the word *chochmah* itself – *ko'ach mah* (חכמה = כ"ח מ"ה) – the potential to be "what," i.e. undefined and therefore boundless.[91] In this state of *bittul*, a person will not experience his own being as an independent creation. Rather, his consciousness is focused on God's omnipresence.

Binah

Binah, usually translated as understanding, is the cognitive faculty that develops and articulates the seminal energy of *chochmah*, so that the latter becomes known, in a detailed conceptual way, through *binah*.[92] *Binah* is also the inductive and deductive faculty of "understanding (or deducing) one thing from another,"[93] thus expanding the point of *chochmah* into a multi-dimensional conceptual system. The *Zohar*[94] therefore symbolizes *chochmah* and *binah* and their relationship as "the supernal point (*chochmah*) within its palace (*binah*)." However, *binah* is not merely an adjunct to *chochmah*, it involves as well the ability to intuit a more inclusive reality that than encoded within *chochmah* itself.[95]

---

90. *Zohar II,* 121a, *Zohar III,* 290a, commentaries. A literal reading of the text is rendered as "From where shall wisdom be found?"
91. *Zohar III*, 235b, in *Raya Mehemna; Tikkunei Zohar* p. 111a, 112b.
92. *Tikkunei Zohar tikkun* 22, p. 63b.
93. *Chagiga* 14a; *Zohar Chadash* 4a.
94. *Zohar I,* 6a.
95. *Anatomy of the Soul*, Rabbi Yitzchak Ginsburgh (ed. Rabbi Yechezkel Anis), *Gal Einai* Publications, Jerusalem 1995, p. 53.

Binah is also the ability to explain the concept to another person, thus "reproducing" it. In this sense *binah* is referred to as "the mother of children" (*Psalms* 113:9).[96]

Da'at

Da'at (knowledge) is the third faculty of the intellect. It is the ability to integrate and harmonize diametrically opposed views or states of being. As mentioned above, when *keter* is counted, *da'at* is not, and vice versa. In terms of the soul powers, *da'at* in fact plays a dual[97] role: On the one hand, *da'at* is the power which binds together the powers of *chochmah* and *binah*. In this capacity it is called *da'at elyon* (higher *da'at*), which generally remains in a state of concealment. As such it is identified with *keter*.[98] On the other hand, *da'at* serves as the bridge between the opposing domains of the intellect and the emotional attributes of the soul. In this capacity it is called *da'at tachton* (lower *da'at*). *Da'at* is not merely another stage of intellect; it enables one to convert understanding into the vitality and inspiration of the emotions and actions. In this sense, the *Zohar*,[99] refers to *da'at* as "the key to the six [emotions]."

A person who possesses *da'at* will therefore exhibit rational, mature behavior, whereas one who lacks *da'at* is emotionally immature and will probably be plagued by inner emotional conflict.

Chesed

Chesed (love, kindness) is the first emotional attribute of the soul. Its motivating force is love and benevolence. *Chesed* is also sometimes[100] called *gedulah* (largesse), for it nurtures the other

96. See *Zohar I,* p. 154; *vol II,* 84a..
97. See *Tanya, Iggeret HaKodesh* chap. 15, end.
98. *Zohar III*, 291a in *Idra Zuta.*
99. *Zohar III*, 220b.
100. E.g. *Zohar II,* 59b; 132a, based on the verse in *I Chronicles* 29:11.

attributes of the soul into full development and maturity. The *Zohar*[101] therefore refers to it as "the first day [i.e., the first attribute] which accompanies all the other days [of creation]."[102]

Of the three Patriarchs, Avraham embodied the qualities of *chesed*, as the verse states, "Give. . . . *chesed* to Avraham" (*Michah* 7:20). He is also referred to as "Avraham, My loving one" (*Yeshayahu* 41:8).

Gevurah

Gevurah (fortitude, restrictive power), associated with the force of *din* (severe Divine judgment) restricts the benevolent expansiveness of *chesed*. As a soul-power it represents the emotional attribute of awe or fear.[103] Whereas *chesed* dictates that one give generously and unconditionally, without concern for the intended recipient's worthiness to receive, *gevurah* argues against doing so, for fear that the recipient is not worthy, or will misuse what he has been given. Accordingly, every opportunity to shower goodness upon someone is assessed in terms of the recipient's merit.

On the other hand, *gevurah* is just as influential in motivating one courageously to uphold another's rights to the rewards which are legitimately his, even in the face of stiff opposition. Should Divine justice dictate that someone be extended a particular benefit, the fear of Heaven impels one to do everything within one's power to facilitate it. Since *gevurah* is concerned with maintaining proper measure and proportion within Creation, it works to defend the boundaries of the law, be they to one's advantage or disadvantage, requiring courage or trepidation.[104]

---

101. *Zohar I*, 46a.
102. The seven days of creation correspond to the seven lower *sefirot*.
103. *Tikkunei Zohar* p. 18a; *Zohar, Hashmatot*, p. 264a; *Zohar Tosafot* p. 302a.
104. Anatomy of the Soul, Rabbi Yitzchak Ginsburgh, p 61.

As complimentary forces, *chesed* and *gevurah* actually work together, establishing the rigorous standard of merit that endows subsequent overtures of *chesed* with genuine value and meaning for the recipient.[105]

Gevurah corresponds to the Patriarch Yitzchak,[106] as in the verse "The One whom Yitzchak fears. . . ." (*Bereishit* 31:42, 53).

Tiferet

Tiferet (compassion) is the attribute of the soul which blends and harmonizes the two polar opposites of *chesed* and *gevurah*. *Tiferet* is also referred to as the attribute of truth, for it depends to some extent on the merit of the recipient[107] Nevertheless, ideally, *tiferet* tends towards *chesed*,[108] and is therefore known as *rachamim* (compassion or mercy).[109]

Tiferet corresponds to the Patriarch Yaakov.[110]

Netzach

Netzach has many meanings, referring to different aspects in the soul. It implies "victory" (*nitzachon*), "eternity" (*nitzchiyut*) and "orchestration" (*nitzuach*). Common to all these ideas is a sense of the initiative and persistence necessary in order to overcome the resistance to bringing thought and feeling into positive action. "Victory" assumes initiative; "eternity" implies persistence; and "orchestration" indicates a creative plan that deploys the other qualities in an intelligent way.[111]

---

105. Anatomy of the Soul, Rabbi Yitzchak Ginsburgh, p 61.
106. *Zohar I*, 90b; *Zohar, Tosafot* 276a, 302a.
107. *Zohar Chadash, Toldot*, p. 26c; *Yitro*, p. 31b.
108. *Pardes, shaa'r* 8, chap. 2; *sha'ar* 9, chap. 3.
109. *Zohar Chadash, Yitro*, p. 31b.
110. *Zohar, Tosafot*, 276a, 302a.
111. See *Anatomy of the Soul*, p. 63.

The quality of *netzach* in the soul is dependent upon the degree of confidence one has that he is doing what God wants of him.

Hod

Hod (surrender, acknowledgment) is the complementary soul-power to *netzach.* Whereas *netzach* thrusts forward, overcoming the barriers between the outflow of benevolence (from *chesed*) and the intended recipient; *hod* (a quality derived from *gevurah*) ensures that the person's success is predicated on his acknowledging the Divine source of his power and might.[112] *Hod* therefore represents sincerity and innocence. The *Zohar* refers to this complementary relationship as "two halves of one body, like twins."[113]

Yesod

Yesod is the quality which coalesces all the qualities which precede it into a single creative act binding the giver and the recipient into a single unit. In technical terms, *yesod* binds the higher *sefirot* to *malchut*, or heaven to earth.[114] In the soul this represents a person's ability to bind himself to God's will and thus bring about the implementation of God's plan for creation. *Yesod* also represents the *Tzadik* (saintly person), regarding whom it is said, "The *Tzadik* is the foundation (*yesod*) of the world" (*Mishlei* 10:25), for it is he who dedicates himself to fulfilling God's will and actualizing His plan for creation.[115]

---

112. See *Devarim* 8:18.

113. *Zohar III*, 236a.

114. As in the verse (*I Chronicles* 29:7): To You, O God, is the *gedulah* and the *gevurah*...**for all** that is in the heavens and the earth is Yours." The words "for all" (*ki kol*) have the numerical value of *yesod* (80).

115. See *Zohar I,* 45b.

Malchut

In terms of the powers of the soul, *malchut* represents receiving upon oneself the yoke of God's sovereignty, and acting in accordance with it, as a slave towards his master. *Malchut* thus experiences itself as a state of lowliness, for it possess nothing of its own – it is aware that it receives all of its qualities from the other powers of the soul. At the same time, *malchut* also represents royalty and sovereignty. Only when a king humbly takes upon himself the yoke of Heaven, is he able to find the strength and wisdom to rule properly.

When man does good, his soul disseminates God's abundant goodness and reveals His greatness. Through man's good deeds, certain *sefirot* prevail. For instance, if a person displays compassion towards others, he causes *tiferet* to prevail. Thus, for example, Abraham represents kindness and love, which derive from the *sefirah* of *chesed,* as explained above, for his deeds were concentrated in this direction.[116]

116. See *Pardes, sha'ar* 31, chap. 1; *Eilimah Rabbati* pp. 1, 43.

Angels

Maimonides[117] writes that everything which God created may be divided into three categories: Those things which are a composite of mutable substance and form; those of immutable substance and form; and those creatures which are form without substance. The latter are the angels. They are not bodies nor physical beings, but rather forms which are separated from one another by the principles which they represent. Thus "form" in this case does not mean dimensional structure, but rather a clearly defined spiritual principle, or permutation of Divine energy.

Angelic beings fall into two general categories – those which were created during the six days of creation[118] (referred to as the "ministering angels") and those which are created on a day-to-day basis to fulfill various missions in this world.[119] The names of the angels change in accordance with their mission.[120]

When angels are sent down to this world as emissaries of the Holy One to carry out a specific mission,[121] they become clothed in a body[122] formed from the element of air[123] or of fire.[124] Angels may also appear in human form.[125] Once they have completed their worldly duties, they divest themselves of their bodies and return to their former spiritual state.

---

117. *Yad, Yesodei HaTorah,* 2:3.
118. *Bereishit Rabbah* 1:4. On which day of creation is the subject of a dispute among the sages: R' Yochanan says that they were created on the second day; R' Chanina – on the fifth.
119. *Zohar II,* 11a; *Eichah Rabbah,* 3:5.
120. *Tikkunei Zohar, tikkun* 57, p. 91b.
121. See *Zohar I,* 127a; vol. *III,* 68b.
122. *Zohar I,* 144a; vol. *III,* 152a.
123. *Zohar I,* 101a.
124. *Zohar I,* 40b; *Zohar Chadash, Ruth* 99a.
125. *Zohar I,* p. 81a.

There are angels which inhabit each of the four worlds: *Ofanim* in the world of *Asiyah*;[126] *chayot* in the world of *Yetzirah*;[127] *serafim* in the world of *Beriah*.[128] There are also angels in the world of *Atzilut*.[129]

The angels are further subdivided according to the *sefirah* from which they derive.[130] The angels are thus divided into "camps" according to the division of the *sefirot*. The angel Michael and his "camp," for example, derive from the *sefirah* of *chesed*,[131] and the angel Gabriel and his "camp" derive from the *sefirah* of *gevurah*,[132] and so on.

Evil and Impurity

Evil and impurity are often referred to in the *Zohar*[133] as "the other side" (*sitra achra*), meaning the side distinct from, and opposed to holiness. Evil is also referred to as *kelipah*,[134] literally, shell or bark. The *kelipah* conceals within it a spark of holiness, which is the vital force by virtue of which the *kelipah* exists, analogous to a fruit surrounded by a shell or peel. In order to release the holy spark the encumbering shell must be removed.

---

126. *Eitz Chaim, sha'ar* 40, chap. 15.
127. *Eitz Chaim, sha'ar* 40, chap. 13.
128. *Ibid.*
129. *Eitz Chaim, sha'ar* 28, chap. 1; *sha'ar* 40, chap. 13; *Sha'ar HaGilgulim* chap. 19.
130. *Eitz Chaim, sha'ar* 40, chap. 13.
131. *Zohar I*, 235a; *Tikkunei Zohar, Introduction* (p. 12a).
132. *Tikkunei Zohar, tikkun* 55 (p. 89a); *tikkun* 57 (p. 91b).
133. E.g., *vol. I*, 12a, 12b, 13a.
134. E.g., *vol. II*, 108b, 141a.

The *Zohar* distinguishes among four *kelipot*, three of which are entirely evil.[135] The fourth, *kelipat nogah*, is the shell which actually envelops the spark of holiness. It thus has direct contact with holiness and is not entirely evil. The other three *kelipot* surround *kelipot nogah* and are therefore further removed from holiness.

All matters pertaining to the prohibitions of the Torah (the forbidden objects, actions, utterances, thoughts, etc) derive from the *sitra achra,* from the three impure *kelipot*. Those matters which are permitted by the Torah (but do not pertain to the commandments of the Torah) derive from *kelipat nogah*.

---

135. *Zohar II*, 131a, 203a-b.

Bereishit

In the Beginning

1:1 בראשית – In the Beginning

The Holy One blessed be He created the world and all created beings through the Torah. Regarding the Torah, the verse states, "God made me (the Torah) as the beginning (ראשית) of His way, the most primal of His works from the outset of time" (*Mishlei* 8:22). With this beginning, the Torah, He created the heavens and the earth, and He sustains them through Torah.

(*Zohar I*, 24a)

Rabbi Chiyya taught: "Who can express the power of God, and acclaim all His praises?" (*Tehillim* 106). When God chose to create the world, He looked into the Torah and created the world with it. With every single act of creation God looked into the Torah again, and created that detail of creation, as the verse states, "I will be An instructor (אמון – *amun*) to Him, I will be His delight day by day!" Do not read אמון, an instructor, but אומן (*uman*), a workman. However, when He chose to create man, the Torah questioned if man should be created, for if he would sin, God would judge him, and the creation of man would be in vain, for none can withstand God's retribution. God replied that He had already allocated repentance for this purpose, even before the world was created. Moreover, at the time of man's creation, God declared that the world could only exist by virtue of the Torah, and for this reason He created man who could occupy himself with Torah. But if man would not do so, He would return the creation to a state of chaos. Hence, the world exists by virtue of man. This is the meaning of the verse, "I made the earth, and I created man upon it" (*Yeshayahu* 45:12) i.e., the creation of man upon earth is for the sake of its continued existence. Therefore, any person who occupies himself with Torah sustains the world, and keeps every aspect of the world in its proper order.

(*Zohar* vol. I. 134a ff)

The following section of the Zohar discusses the process of creation of the world. The world was created in such a way that it can endure as a created world, and also fulfill the purpose for which it was created. This purpose, the Zohar explains elsewhere[1], is that "the creation must recognize God." The following section explains that God implanted this potential to know Him within creation, by virtue of the letter with which He chose to begin the creation. All the letters but one are rejected for the purpose of beginning the creation because they would have created a world which would have been inherently defective, or would not have fulfilled its stated purpose, or because it would not have allowed man to seek God.

Rabbi Hamnona Sabba explained: When it arose in the Will[2] of the Holy One blessed be He to create the world, all the letters of the Hebrew alphabet were in a concealed state. For two thousand years prior to the actual creation of the world, the Holy One blessed be He gazed upon the letters and delighted in them. Then, when the Holy One blessed be He chose to actually create the world,[3] all the letters came before Him in reverse order, from *tav* to *aleph*:

ת: The letter *tav* was the first to claim the privilege of beginning the creation, because it is the concluding letter of the word "truth" (אמת), which is called the Seal of God.[4] Since God is also called אמת, it would be proper for Him to create the world with letters of this word, beginning with ת. However, God replied that even though the letter *tav* is a good and honest letter, nevertheless, it would not be suitable for beginning the creation, since it would be used in the

---

1. vol. 2, 42a, b.
2. See *Sha'ar HaClalim 1:6;* Damesek Eliezer.
3. The world was created with the "speech" of God, as our Sages explain, "With ten utterances the world was created" (*Avot* 6:1). These ten utterances include all the letters of the Hebrew alphabet.
4. See *Shabbat* 55a, Rashi.

future for a different purpose – to mark the foreheads of men of faith[5] who had fulfilled the Torah from *aleph* to *tav*, from beginning to end. With the letter *tav* on their foreheads, they would pass away from this world.[6] In addition, the letter *tav* is also the final letter of the word מות, death; hence it would not be proper to use it in creating the world.

ק, ר, ש: Then the letter *shin*(ש) came before the Holy One blessed be He and claimed that it would be fitting for God to use it to create the world, for ש is the initial letter of the holy Name ש-ד-י and it would be appropriate to create the world using this holy name. But God replied that although the letter *shin* would be an eligible choice, being a good letter and a true letter, nevertheless, it would not be suitable for creating the world, since the letters *kuf* and *reish*, which are the letters of deception and untruth, need the *shin* together with them, so that שקר (falsehood) can exist. From this we learn that when a person wants to deceive others, he introduces his lies with a true statement, followed by untruths, just as the word שקר begins with a *shin*, a letter of truth which is associated with the Patriarchs,[7] and it is followed by the letters of deception, *kuf* and *reish*. But in order to endure, the letters ק and ר take the ש between them, forming the word קשר – a (permanent) knot. Since all three

5. See *Yechezkel* 9:4.

6. See *Shabbat* 55a. Several explanations of this are found among the commentaries: The Gemara (*Shabbat,* ibid.) explains that the letter *tav* was written in *ink* on the foreheads of the righteous to protect them from the Angel of Death, and in *blood* on the foreheads of the wicked as a sign that they must die. However, the attribute of severity argued that the righteous were also deserving of death since they did not admonish the wicked. Hence, they also died (*Or Yakar; Or Hachamah; Matok miDvash)* and the letter *tav* is therefore associated with death. According to *Damesek Eliezer*, "they would pass away from this world" refers to the wicked, not to the righteous, i.e. that the letter *tav* on the foreheads of the righteous indicated that the wicked would die, unlike the righteous who observed the entire Torah, from *aleph* to *tav*. nevertheless, the letter *tav* is associated with death.

7. The three arms of the *shin* represent the three Patriarchs, Avraham, Yitzchak, and Yaakov (*Or Yakar; Damesek Eliezer; Matok miDvash.*

letters are associated with falsehood, they are not appropriate for beginning the creation.

צ: The letter *tzaddi* then came before the Holy One blessed be He and claimed that it would be fitting for God to use it to create the world, for this is the sign of saints (*tzaddikim, tzaddik* in the singular). God too is called *Tzaddik*.[8] Hence, He is inscribed within this letter. However, God replied that although this letter is indeed saintly, it must remain hidden, and should not be revealed to such a large extent,[9] in order to avoid giving the world an excuse for remaining imperfect.[10] Why should it remain hidden and not be revealed? The letter צ is comprised of two other letters: it itself is a נ (*nun*), and a י (*yud*) from the eternal four-letter[11] Name of God became attached to it, and united with it. In the scribal art of writing the Hebrew letters, according to *Kabbalah* the letter *tzaddi* is formed by first producing a נ so that the head of the *nun* leans over to the left and down, towards its foot: Then a letter *yud* י is joined to it, though facing the opposite direction, thus forming the letter *tzaddi*. This is the secret of the creation of Adam, whom the Holy One blessed be He created with two aspects male and female.[12] For this reason, i.e. since the letter *tzaddi* represents these two aspects, which are joined only back to back, the *yud* faces the opposite way to the *nun*, and they do not face each other. Rather the *yud* faces upward, which the *nun* faces downward. Therefore, since the letter *tzaddi*, at present, represents two opposing forces, which is called a union back to back, had the world been created by means of the *tzaddik*, it would necessarily be incomplete and imperfect, which would have the given the world an excuse not to seek completeness and perfection, and the forces of evil would prevail.[13] In addition, the Holy One, added that although in the future He would separate these two aspects from one another, and then join them face to face and therefore the letter would be in a state of completeness and perfection, nevertheless, the letter *tzaddi* would then exist on a

8. *Tehillim* 11:7.
9. As it would be if it began the creation of the world.
10. See *Or Yakar*.
11. See *Or Yakar*.
12. See *Bereishit* 1:27, Rashi.
13. *Or Yakar*.

different much more elevated plane which is too sublime to be revealed. Therefore it could not be used in creating the world.

ע, פ: The letter *peh* (פ) then came before the Holy One blessed be He and claimed that it would be fitting for God to use it to create the world, because the redemption (פדות) begins with the letter *peh*. And the advent of *Mashiach* signals an end to sin and evil.[14] But God replied that although the *peh* is indeed a good letter, nevertheless it is the initial letter of the word פשע – deliberate transgression, which is done in secret. Therefore the shape of the letter פ is like that of a snake which has its head curled up into its body, like a sinner who hides his head – in humility, a sign of righteousness[15] – while stretching out his hands to sin.[16] [An alternative explanation: The sinner hides his head in shame and repentance while stretching out his hands in prayer, begging for forgiveness.[17] But, in either case, the *peh* is associated with sin]. The same applies to the letter *ayin*, which is associated with עון – transgression. And even though the *ayin* is also the first letter of ענוה – humility – which is the gateway to repentance, and because of this quality it would be fitting to create the world with the letter *ayin*,[18] nevertheless, the Holy One blessed be He said that He would not use it to begin the creation of the world.

ס: Then the letter *samech* came before the Holy One blessed be He and claimed that it would be fitting for God to use it to create the world, because it begins the words סומך נופלים- supporting those who are about to fall[19] as the verse states, "God supports all those who are about to fall" (*Tehillim* 145:14). But God replied, this being so, you are needed where you are and you may not move from your place. For if you do, what will happen to those who are about to fall, and are dependent upon you?

---

14. *Or Yakar.*
15. *Or Yakar.*
16. *Or Yakar.*
17. *Damesek Eliezer.*
18. R. Avraham Galanti; *Or HaChamah.*
19. Not those who have already fallen, for if this were the intention, the verse would have said, "raising or lifting the fallen" – *Damesek Eliezer.*

נ: Then the letter *nun* came before the Holy One blessed be He and claimed that it would be proper for God to use it to create the world, for it begins the words which proclaim the awe-inspiring majesty of God, who is נורא תהלות – "Awesome to praise."[20] Moreover, the righteous delight in singing beautiful praises and hymns to God – לישרים נאוה תהלה.[21] נאוה, which signifies both delight and beauty , also begins with a נ. The righteous and the upright comprehend the glory and the majesty of God, and this inspires them to sing His praises.[22] Hence the purpose of creation, to know God, can be fulfilled through the letter *nun*. But God replied, "*Nun,* return to your place. Because of you, the letter *samech* was sent back to its place, and you are what the *samech* supports. *Nun* is the initial letter of נופלים – "those who are about to fall,"[23] alluding to those who are not yet perfectly righteous, and to the fallen Temple during the time of exile.[24] Hence the letter *nun* was found to be unsuitable. Immediately, the *nun* returned to its place, leaving God's presence.

מ, ל, ך: The letter *mem* (מ) came before the Holy One blessed be He and said that it would be appropriate for God to use it to create the world, for it is the initial letter of the word מלך – "king," and because of it, the Holy One blessed be He is called "King". Since this indicates the submission of all creation to God's authority, the purpose of creation will have been fulfilled, as the verse regarding the future states "And God will be King" (*Zechariah* 14:9).[25] "This is certainly true," God replied. "Nevertheless, I will not use you to create the world, since the world needs a king." Had the world been created with a *mem*, the entire creation would have been imbued with the glory and majesty of God, so that every creature would have felt itself to be a king, and there would be no fear of Heaven. In addition, man would not have had to serve God by consciously submitting himself to God's authority. Since the continued existence of the physical world is dependent on man accepting the yoke of Heaven, accepting the

---

20. *Shemot* 15:11.
21. *Tehillim* 33:1, Ibn Ezra, Metzudot.
22. See *Metzudat David* to *Tehillim* ibid.
23. See *Tehillim* 145:14.
24. *Damesek Eliezer*.
25. *Or Yakar*.

King, this letter is unsuitable for beginning creation.[26] The *mem* is then told to return to its place, and to join together with ל (*lamed*) and ך (final *caf*), making the word מלך (king), representing an earthly king, whose duty it is to guide the world in the service of God, for it is not good for the world to be without a king.[27]

כ: At that moment the letter *caf* descended from the throne of Glory, כסא הכבוד (*kisei hakavod*) and stood before the Holy One blessed be He and said: "Master of the worlds. It is fitting that You begin the creation with me, for I am your כבוד, your glory." Since the world was created for the purpose of glorifying God, as the verse states, ". . . .For My glory, I created it. . . ." (*Yeshayahu* 43:7), it would be proper to create the world with the letter *caf*.[28] In addition, the *caf* (=20) has the advantage of being numerically equal to two *yuds*, one representing the Jew's service of God, by which he elicits a corresponding response for God[29] Thus, this letter possesses the inherent potential to know God, but only according to man's depth of service. This fulfills the purpose of creation. But, when the *caf* descended from the Throne, 200,000 worlds began to totter, and the Throne began to shake. Thus, the descent of the *caf* caused the Glory (כבוד) of God to be diminished.[30] The Holy One blessed be He told the *caf* to return to its place – i.e. to the Throne of Glory.[31] It would not be used to initiate creation, for it is also the first letter of כליה – total destruction.

י: The letter *yud* came and said, "Master of the Worlds. It is fitting that you use me to create the world, for I begin Your Holy Name י-ה-ו-ה. The *yud* symbolizes the *sefirah* (supernal emanation – see Introduction) of *chochmah*, the wisdom of God. Hence, by way of the *yud* the Wisdom of God will be revealed in the world. But God replied that it is sufficient for the *yud* that as the initial letter of His Name, it is engraved

---

26. See *Nezer Yisrael.*
27. See *Zohar Chai; Damesek Eliezer; Derech Mitzvotecha* מצוות מנוי מלך. See *Chinuch*, 497.
28. *Zoharei Chama.*
29. *Or Yakar.*
30. *Nezer Yisrael; Damesek Eliezer.*
31. *Or Yakar.*

and etched within Him, and that all of His Will is initiated through it. Will, or *Arich Anpin* (see Introduction) is first revealed in *chochmah*.[32] Accordingly, it would not be proper for the world to make use of this letter, since this would entail being separated from the essential Divine Name which is too lofty for creation. As we see, the name *Elokim* is used in creating the worlds, not the Tetragrammaton.[33]

ח, ט: The letter *tet* (ט) rose up and said, "It is proper that You initiate the creation with me, for I begin the verse, טוב וישר ה׳ – "God is good and fair"[34] and God created the world in order to reveal His kindness.[35] But God replied that the goodness of this letter must remain hidden, until the advent of the World to Come,[36] as the verse states, "How great is Your goodness, which you have hidden away for those who fear You."[37] Moreover, the goodness that is within this letter will sink into the ground with the doors of the Holy Temple, when that edifice will be destroyed, as the verse states, טבעו בארץ שעריה – "Her gates will sink into the ground"[38] and the Jewish people will go into exile, so that God's goodness will not be manifest. In addition, ט may be joined to the letter ח which follows it, forming the main body of the word חטא – "sin." And therefore it would not be suitable to use it in creation. For this same reason, these letters are not found in the names of the twelve tribes of Israel to show that all of Yaakov's sons were righteous.[39]

ז: The letter *zayin* rose up and said to the Master of the Worlds that He should use this letter to initiate creation because it alludes to the Sabbath ז is the seventh letter from א, just as the Sabbath is the seventh day of the week, about which the verse states, "Remember the Sabbath, to keep it holy".[40] And since the Sabbath sanctifies and sustains all

---

32. *Sulam; Nezer Yisrael.*
33. See *Nezer Yisrael.*
34. *Tehillim* 25:8.
35. R. Avraham Galanti.
36. Regarding the concept of the World to Come, see *Introduction.*
37. *Tehillim* 31:20.
38. *Eichah* 2:9.
39. See *Pesachim* 56a.
40. *Shemot* 20:8.

of creation,[41] it would be appropriate to initiate creation with this letter. However, God replied that since the word *zayin* also means "weapon" it would not be proper to create the world using it. The *zayin* departed immediately.

ה, ו: Then the letter *vav* came before Him and said, "it is fitting to create the world through me, since I am one of the letters of Your Name. Although the letter *yud* made the same claim, and was rejected, nevertheless, the letter *vav* has an advantage over the *yud*. It does not begin the Tetragrammaton, and hence is not on the same lofty level. Together with the *heh* (ה) of the Tetragrammaton, they would be in the correct proportion to initiate the creation.[42] However, God replied that both letters must be satisfied with remaining concealed within His Name for if they were inherent within creation, they might reveal more than is desirable. Moreover, since the soul of man as enclothed in his body derives from these letters; if the world would be created through them, the body could not be a vessel and vehicle for the soul, since it would be on the same spiritual level.[43]

ג, ד: The letters *dalet* (ד) and *gimmel* (ג) then arose and they too made the same request. But He replied, "It must suffice for you to be together, for the poor (דל - *dal*) require acts of loving kindness (גמילות חסדים), and one must not become separated from the other. Nevertheless, they cannot both operate in creating the world, for since the *dalet* refers to those who are poor, it alludes to the exile, hence it is unsuitable to be used in creation. And the *gimmel*, which bestows loving kindness upon the *dalet* must not abandon it.[44]

ב: The letter *bet* then came before the Holy One blessed be He and claimed that it would be fitting for God to use it to create the world, because it is the initial letter of the word ברכה, "blessing," and with it the Holy One is blessed both above and below. This is the purpose of creation – that all of creation will recognize God's kindness, and that He has blessed them with His abundance and prosperity. Then they will

41. *Beitzah* 17a.
42. *Or Yakar; Sulam.*
43. *Or Yakar.*
44. *Nezer Yisrael.*

acknowledge Him and bless him.[45] The Holy One blessed be He said to the letter *bet*, "I will certainly create the world with you. You will be the first letter of creation."

א: Only the letter *aleph* remained, and it did not rise up before God. The Holy One blessed be He said, "*Aleph, aleph,* why did you not come before Me like all the other letters?" It replied, "Master of the Worlds. I saw that all the letters came before You, but gained no benefit from it. What could I accomplish there? Moreover, You have given the letter *bet* this great privilege, and it is not proper that the Supernal King should revoke the gift He gave to one servant, and give it to another." Then the Holy One blessed be He replied, "*Aleph, aleph*, although I will create the world with the letter *bet*, you will be the first and the head[46] of all letters, and My uniqueness will be expressed only through you – *aleph* is the initial letter of the word אחד, which expresses the uniqueness of God. And you will be the first of all numbers (א = 1), and all unity of disparate entities will be through you, *aleph* – for it is the initial letter of the word אחדות, meaning unity.

(*Zohar I,* 2b ff)

The world was created in the month of Tishrei[47] בתשרי in Hebrew. The name of this month has the identical letters to the word בראשית however the א is missing. The א of בראשית alludes to Adam אדם in Hebrew, who was created on א (the first of) Tishrei. But because the earth was to be cursed on account of Adam, the א withdrew from ראשית, leaving בתשרי. Hence the Torah begins with a ב, rather than an א, since it is the initial letter of ברכה, "blessing," so that the earth can be blessed, and rid itself of its curse.[48]

(*Tikkunei Zohar, Tikkun* 35, 77b)

---

45. R. Avraham Galanti.
46. *Sulam*.
47. See *Rosh HaShanah* 10b – R. Eliezer.
48. See *Yerushalmi Chagiga* 2:1; *Bereishit Rabbah* chap. 1.

1:1 בראשית ברא אלקים את השמים ואת הארץ – In the beginning God created the heaven and the earth

Our Sages explain that the world was created with ten utterances[49] *which were spread over six days of creation. Although there appear to be only nine utterances, the Sages conclude that the word* בראשית *("In the beginning") is also an utterance, even though it is not preceded explicitly by the words,* ויאמר אלקים *– "And God said. . . ."*[50] *The following extract explains these ideas.*

Rabbi Abba said: The higher world is concealed, and everything associated with the higher world is also concealed, because they are all part of the sublime mystery of the day in which all other days are contained – i.e. all nine utterances, spread over the six days of creation, are included in the first utterance, בראשית, "In the beginning."[51] At this stage, creation is not yet manifest as material being. However, when the Holy One blessed be He brought the creation into manifest existence, he emanated the six days of creation,[52] during which the physical creation came about. Then each of the nine utterances through which creation came about are preceded by, "And God said." But, since the higher world is concealed, and everything that is associated with it is also concealed, the verse merely states בראשית, and it is not preceded by "God said." That all the six days of creation are contained in the word can be seen from this word itself, which can be broken down into two words: ברא – "He created," שית – "six."[53] Nevertheless, while the six days of creation are still contained within the word בראשית the verse does not mention who created them, because this refers to the concealed higher world which remains hidden from the created beings of the lower worlds[54] and therefore, בראשית, "In the beginning" is not preceded by "And God said."

---

49. *Avot* 5:1.

50. *Rosh HaShana* 32a; *Megillah* 21b; *Zohar* 15a, 30a.

51. *Zohar, Hashmatot* p. 256b; *Zohar, Midrash HaNe'elam, Bereishit.* See also *Avot* ibid. and commentaries; *Rashi, Bereishit* 1:14; *Ramban, Bereishit* 1:1.

52. *Mikdash Melech.*

53. This is explained in numerous places in the *Zohar*, e.g. *Zohar* vol. I 15b, 24a, 56a; *Tikkunei Zohar, Tikkun* 11, *Tikkun* 69, etc.

54. *Or Hachama.*

Afterwards, when He chose to reveal and articulate the remaining nine utterances through which the world was created during the six days of creation, the verse states who created them, ברא אלקים את השמים ואת הארץ – "*God* created the heaven and the earth," for this refers to the revealed worlds. And therefore the verse states אלקים ברא– His name, Elokim, is revealed.[55] However, the higher world alluded to in the word בראשית, which precedes material creation, remains concealed, and who created it is not specified, because it refers to the concealed higher world. The lower world is revealed, so that the deeds of the Holy One blessed be He always comprise two planes – hidden and revealed. This is the mystery of the Holy Name, which is both hidden and revealed. The intention is to show that everything in the revealed world is preceded by, and depends on, the higher world, their source.[56]

(*Zohar* vol. I 39b)

55. Note that this name signifies the attribute of limiting and diminishing the Infinite Light (the *Or Ein Sof*) so that a physical world can exist. *Zohar, Midrash HaNe'elam, Noach, מאמר דור המבול*. See Introduction.
56. *Or HaChama.*

1:2 הארץ היתה תהו ובהו – The earth was inconceivably void

God built worlds and destroyed them. He said, "These please Me, and those do not please Me."[57] The verse, "God created the heaven and the earth," refers to those worlds which pleased the Holy One blessed be He whereas, regarding those worlds which did not please the Holy One blessed be He the verse states, "The earth was inconceivably void." Some maintain that He did not actually build them, but only thought about building them. This is the world of *Tohu*.

(*Hashmatot* to section 29 in *Zohar* vol. 1, 262b)

At those times when the Jewish religion is threatened, if a person does not martyr his soul, his life, or his possessions out of love of his Master, it is as if he reverted the entire world to an inconceivably void state. For this reason, this verse follows the verse, "In the beginning, God created. . . ."

(*Tikkunei Zohar,* Introduction, 10b)

1:2 ורוח אלהים מרחפת על פני המים – The Sovereignty of God hovers over the surface of the waters:

The previous verse, "the earth was inconceivably void. . . ." refers to an era prior to our time, for this is the rule with *kelipah* – negative forces which block the Divine Light – they precede the light, just as a peel or a shell precedes the fruit.[58] "The Sovereignty of God hovers over the surface of the waters" – this is the spirit of *Mashiach* (the Messiah) which hovers over the waters of Torah, and this is immediately

---

57. See also *Bereishit Rabbah* 3:7; 9:2. This is not to be understood as implying that there was some accidental flaw in the world of *Tohu*. Rather, the flaw inherent in the world of *Tohu* was deliberately formed in order to allow for the possibility of evil and thus provide man with the possibility of choosing between good and evil. See *Etz Chaim* 11:6; *Shaar HaHakdamot* p. 228 ff.

58. See *Derech Emet.*

followed by the redemption, alluded to in the following verse: God said, "There shall be light."

(*Hashmatot siman* 29 – *Zohar* vol. I, 263a)

ורוח אלקים – "The Sovereignty of God hovers": This refers to the spirit of *Mashiach* – the Messiah[59] – of which the verse states, "And the spirit of God will rest upon him" (*Yeshayahu* 11:2).

(*Tikkunei Zohar, Tikkun* 26, 71b)

Each day of the Holy One blessed be He equals one thousand years.[60] Now the verse states פני המים in the plural, literally, "the *facets* of the waters," signifying two facets of Torah – positive commandments and negative commandments, which are called white (corresponding to *chesed* – kindness), and red (corresponding to *gevurah* – severity or limitation. See Introduction), or right and left.[61] And the two thousand years of *Mashiach* are alluded to in the verse, "God said, 'There shall be light,' and there was light." This does not contradict the previous explanation, for "the Sovereignty of God *hovers* refers to the era prior to the eternal Kingdom of God, i.e. to the two thousand years of Torah, before the sovereignty of God is properly established. The final era, when the Kingdom of God will be fully established, will be ushered in by *Mashiach*. This is referred to in the verse, "God said, 'There shall be light,' and there was light."

(*Tikkunei Zohar, Tikkun* 36, 77b)

---

59. cf. *Bereishit Rabbah 2:4.*

60. *Sanhedrin* 97a. As the verse states, "For one thousand years in your eyes is like yesterday" (*Tehillim* 90:4) i.e. one day. And the week of creation is therefore six supernal days i.e. six thousand years. The first are two thousand years of chaos, the next two thousand years are the era of Torah, and the last two thousand years are the days of *mashiachap.* Two thousand years of chaos are alluded to in the verse, "The earth was inconceivably void." Two thousand years of Torah are alluded to in the verse, "The sovereignty of God hovered over the surface of the waters," for "water" always signifies Torah. See *Taanit* 7a.

61. See *Introduction to Tikkunei Zohar,* ה פתח אליהו"ד. Chesed is the right arm and severity the left.

1:3 ויאמר אלקים – God said

Our Sages explain that the world was created by means of Asarah Ma'amarot (ten utterances)[62] *as mentioned previously. This section of the Zohar explains the correlation between the Asarah Ma'amarot and the Aseret Hadibrot (Ten Commandments)*

Rabbi Shimon bar Yochai taught: Regarding the gifts which the heads of the tribes of Israel donated to the *Mishkan* the verse states עשרה עשרה הכף – "each incense bowl weighed ten sanctuary shekels" (*Bamidbar* 7:86). Why עשרה עשרה twice, literally, "ten ten?" Once, to allude to the work of creation, and once to allude to the Torah. There are ten utterances in the creation of the world, and corresponding to them, ten utterances in the Torah – the ten commandments, which God communicated to the Jewish people. What does this tell us? That the world was created for the sake of Torah, and as long as the Jewish people occupy themselves with Torah, the world will continue to exist. But if the Jewish people abandon Torah, the verse declares, "If not for My Covenant i.e. the Torah,[63] I would not have set day and night, and the bounds of heaven and earth." (*Yirmeyahu* 33:25, Rashi).

The Zohar now explains how the ten utterances parallel the Ten Commandments

The first commandment, instructing us to have faith in God, states: I am the Lord your God. . . ." (*Shemot* 20:2ff). Regarding creation the verse states: "There shall be light, and there was light."[64] From the verse ה' אורי וישעי ממי אירא – "God is my light and salvation, whom

---

62. *Avot* 5:1.

63. *Or Yakar*.

64. Note that this passage in the *Zohar* does not regard the word בראשית as the first utterance, as explained previously. Perhaps this is according to the view that the verse, "I am the Lord your God" also expresses belief in God Himself, which is not a commandment, but *precedes* all commandments. (See view of *Ba'al Hilchot Gedolot* in Ramban's *Hasagot* to *Sefer HaMitzvot*, Aseh 1; view of R. Chasdai in *Rosh Amana* (Abarbanel) chap. 4. And בראשית corresponds to this prior belief. Nevertheless, in the light of other passages in the *Zohar* this seems unlikely.

shall I fear?" (*Tehillim* 27:1), we learn that faith in the Holy One blessed be He is also called "light". Hence, light and faith in God, the first commandment, correspond.

It is written in the second commandment: "You shall have no other Gods before Me," and the corresponding verse regarding creation states, "There shall be a firmament between the waters, and it shall divide between water and water."

"There shall be a firmament," refers to the Jewish people who are part of God Above (*Iyov* 31:2),[65] for they are attached to that plane which is called שמים (Heaven, or firmament).

"Between the waters," – among the words of Torah which is called water, as our Sages explain.[66]

"And it i.e. the Jewish people, shall divide between water and water" – between the Holy One blessed be He who is called "the Source of Living Water" (*Yirmeyahu* 2:13),[67] and false deities which are called "broken wells" (*Yirmeyahu* ibid) containing bitter, putrid and stagnant water. . . . Thus, the division between water and water is dependent on the Jewish people learning Torah.

The third commandment states: "Do not take the name of God in vain," and the third utterance of creation states: "The waters below the firmament shall be gathered into one place. . . ." Do not cause a separation in the unity of the waters, referring to the *Shechinah* – the indwelling Divine Presence[68] by uttering a false oath.

---

65. See *Tanya* chap. 2.

66. *Bava Kama* 17a.

67. Note that the present version of the *Zohar* states באר מים חיים, not מקור מים חיים. However, since the latter is the same verse which is quoted shortly, perhaps the text should be amended.

68. See *Chagiga* 14b regarding the advice of R. Akiva to the Sages who entered the *Pardes:* Do not say, 'Water, water"." (i.e. cause a separation between the waters); *Pardes Rimonim* s.v. שיש.

The fourth commandment states: "Remember the Sabbath to keep it holy," and regarding creation, the fourth utterance states, "The earth shall sprout vegetation. . . ." When does the earth become fertile and become covered with vegetation? On the Sabbath, when the bride i.e. the Sabbath unites with the King – the Holy One blessed be He.[69] This brings forth vegetation and blessing for the world. Every weekday provides its food by virtue of the blessing it receives from the Sabbath.[70] This was also witnessed in the *manna* which came down only during the week, but by virtue of the Sabbath.[71]

The fifth commandment states: "Honor your father and mother," and regarding creation, the fifth utterance states, "There shall be luminaries in the expanse of the sky. . . ." This means that the luminaries are your father and mother – the sun is your father, and the moon your mother, alluding to the Holy One blessed be He your father, as the verse states, "For the sun and its sheath are God, the Lord"[72] (*Tehillim* 84:12). The verse makes an association between God – who is the ultimate source of all "light" – in the sense of Divine revelation – and the sun, the source of physical light. And the moon refers to *Knesset Yisrael* the collective soul of the Jewish people, as the verse states regarding Israel, "Your moon shall never disappear" (*Yeshayahu* 60:20). Although the *Zohar* does not state this explicitly, it appears that the intention here is that our "father and mother" (God, and the collective Jewish soul) are honored by the Torah which the Jewish people learn in this world, as our Sages explain, "There is no honor other than Torah."[73]

The sixth commandment states: "Do not murder," and regarding creation, the sixth utterance states, "The waters shall teem with living creatures." Do not kill a man, who is also called "a living creature"

---

69. Technically, this refers to the unification (*yichud*) of *malchut* and *zier anpin* – Commentaries.

70. *Zohar* vol. II, p. 88a.

71. *Zohar* ibid.

72. The Names used in this verse are ה-ו-ה-י, the Tetragrammaton, denoting the transcendent revelation of God as He is in Himself, and אלקים, God as He is within creation.

73. *Avot* 6:3; *Zohar* vol. III, p. 81b.

(*Bereishit* 2:7). And do not be like fish, the larger of which swallows the smaller.

The seventh commandment states: "Do not commit adultery," and regarding creation, the seventh utterance states, "The earth shall bring forth living creatures. . . .in their species." From this we learn that a man should not approach a woman who is not his soul-mate. For this reason the verse states, "in their species." For a woman must not bear children from one who is not her "species" i.e. her soul mate.

The eighth commandment states: "Do not steal," and regarding creation, the eighth utterance states, "I have given you every seed-bearing plant on the surface of the entire earth." i.e. that which I have given you, and allowed you to use, is yours. Do not steal that which belongs to someone else.

The ninth commandment states: "Do not testify as a false witness," and regarding creation the ninth utterance states, "We shall make man with Our image, of Our likeness." Do not testify falsely against one who bears the Divine image. And if one testifies falsely, it is as if he blasphemed.

The tenth commandment states: "Do not be envious of your neighbor's wife. . . ." and regarding creation the tenth utterance states, "It is not good that man is alone. I will make him a helper to match him." This refers to each person's soul-mate who matches him perfectly. Hence, "Do not be envious of your neighbor's wife. . . ."

These are the ten utterances of creation, which parallel the Ten Commandments, and therefore the verse states, עשרה עשרה הכף – "Each incense bowl weighed ten sanctuary shekels," for they weigh the same, and by virtue of this the world survives and maintains equilibrium. . . .

(*Zohar* vol. III, 11bff)

1:3 ויאמר אלקים יהי אור – God said, "There shall be light"

Rabbi Chiyya taught: The Holy One blessed be He foresaw that the world could not exist without a foundation. What is the foundation of the world? A *Tzaddik*[74] a saint, or righteous person as is stated in the verse, "A *Tzaddik* is the foundation of the world." (*Mishlei* 6:25). And a *Tzaddik* is referred to as "light", as the verse affirms, "Light is sown for the righteous" (*Tehillim* 96:11). Also, this may be learned by comparing the next verse, "God saw that the light was *good*," with another verse which states, "Praise the *Tzaddik*, for he is *good*." (*Yeshayahu* 3:10). This is the second of Rabbi Yishmael's rules of expounding the Torah, by which an identical expression appearing in two verses shows an inherent link between them.

(*Zohar Chadash, Bereishit* 7b)

"There shall be light": This refers to the light which the Holy One blessed be He created before He created the world. . . . It is the light which He revealed to Adam, by which he was able to view the beginning of the world to its end.[75] And this is the same light which the Holy One blessed be He revealed to King David, and he praised God and said, "How great is the good which you have concealed for those who fear You" (*Tehillim* 31:20). And this is the same light which the Holy One blessed be He revealed to Moshe *Rabbeinu*, by which he saw from one end of the land of Israel, Gilead, until the other end, Dan. But God foresaw that there would be three generations of sinners; the generation of Enosh who began serving idolatry,[76] the generation of the flood, about whom the verse states, "The world was corrupt before God, and the land was filled with immorality (*Bereishit* 6:9), and the generation which built the Tower of Babel.[77] Therefore He concealed this light, so that they would not be able to utilize it;

74. cf. *Chagiga* 12b; *Bereishit Rabbah* chap. 3.
75. See *Chagiga* 12a.
76. *Bereishit Rabba* 19:13; *Shir HaShirim Rabbah* 5:1, and commentaries.
77. See *Bereishit* 11:1 ff.

but He allowed it to be used for Moshe during the first three months after his birth, as the verse states, "And his mother hid him for three months." (*Shemot* 2:2). Moshe was born three months premature, and thus, for three months, his mother managed to evade Pharaoh's decree that all newborn boys were to be cast into the Nile (*Shemot* 1:22). Since he was shrouded in this light, which the wicked are not able to use, he remained invisible. After this, when Moshe was adopted by Pharaoh's daughter, who found him floating in a box in the Nile, and was taken to Pharaoh's palace,[78] this light was withdrawn until he stood on Mount Sinai to receive the Torah. Then it was returned to him-[79] and he used it throughout his life.

(*Zohar* vol. I, 31b)

1:3 יהי אור ויהי אור – There shall be light, and there was light

Wherever the word ויהי ("there was") appears, it alludes to this world and the World to Come.[80] יהי אור – "There shall be light" in this world; ויהי אור "There was light." Was – because it was subsequently hidden, as explained above – to be revealed[81] in the World to Come. (See also commentary to the next verse).

(*Zohar* vol. I, 30b, 31b)

Rabbi Yose said: This light was completely concealed, and will only be revealed to the righteous in the World to Come, as the verse states, "Light is sown for the righteous" (*Tehillim* 97:11). Rabbi Yehudah said: Had it been completely concealed, the world would not continue to exist for even one moment. However, it is concealed and sown like a seed which produces plants which in turn generate more seed and more plants. In this way the world is sustained. Not a day passes without some of this light being emitted

---

78. See *Shemot* 2:2 ff.
79. See *Shemot* 34:29 ff. – Moshe's face shone with a brilliant light.
80. Regarding the concept of the World to Come, see *Introduction*.
81. See *Zohar* vol. I, p. 45b; vol. III, p. 93a.

to the world so that it can continue to exist. And this is how the Holy One blessed be He nourishes the world. In every place that Torah is studied at night, a thread of this light is drawn down upon those who study it.

(*Zohar* vol. II, 148b ff)

1:4 וירא אלקים את האור כי טוב – God saw that the light was good

This light shone, and illuminated the world from one end to the other, and through it the world was created, But the Holy One blessed be He foresaw that in the future there would be wicked people, so He concealed it in the World to Come for the righteous. Now you may ask, "Since He was going to conceal it, why did He create it?" And the answer is, that He utilized it in creating the world. And even today, although it is concealed, the world exists by virtue of it. Anyone who achieves understanding of the secrets of Torah, i.e. the wisdom of *Kabbalah*, will attain this light, as is written, "And the Torah is light" (*Mishlei* 6:23), and it is also written, וירא אלקים את האור כי טוב – "God saw that the light was good." The words "that the light [was good]" – אתהאור in Hebrew – has the numerical value of 613: א = 1; ת = 400; ה = 5; א = 1; ו = 6; ר = 200. This corresponds to the number of *mitzvót* (commandments) in the Torah (613 altogether) and therefore alludes to the Torah, which is the concealed light.

(*Zohar Chadash, Bereishit* 8a)

1:4 ויבדל אלקים בין האור ובין החשך – God separated the light from the darkness

Rabbi Bunn asked: What is the meaning of the verse יוצר אור ובורא חשך – "He *formed* light and *created* darkness"[82] i.e. why does the word "formed" apply to the light, but the word "created" apply to the darkness? He answered: Light has substance, and therefore it is appropriate to talk about *forming* the light, whereas darkness has no substance,

82. *Yeshayahu* 45:7.

and therefore it is called *created.* The English equivalents do not express the difference between בריאה and יצירה. The former refers to the creation *ex nihilo* of a primordial substance, or *chomer hiyuli*, sometimes translated as "ether" (see discourse of Rabbi Abba, above, *Ramban's* commentary on *Bereishit* 1:1), whereas the latter refers to the mere *formation* of existing matter. Thus the verse states, "He formed mountains, and created the wind." (*Amos* 4:13).

(*Zohar* vol. I, 263a – *Hashmatot, siman* 31)

"From the darkness" refers to false prophets whom the Holy One blessed be He separated from the true prophets – "the light." As explained above, "light" alludes to the righteous.

(*Tikkunei Zohar, Tikkun* 40, 80a)

The Holy One blessed be He separated good synonymous with light – as this verse itself affirms, "God saw that the light was good" – from evil which is synonymous with dark – "and so God separated the light from the darkness." This is the secret of the curtain in the *Mishkan* or Tabernacle, which separated the Holy of Holies from the rest of the *Mishkan*. See *Shemot* 26:33.

(*Tikkunei Zohar, Tikkun* 67, 98b)

1:5 ויקרא אלקים לאור יום ולחשך קרא לילה – God named the light "Day" and the darkness He named "Night"

The following section of the Zohar explains that the secret of Divine Providence, which is fundamental to Jewish thought, is contained in this verse. When one witnesses events that have no rational explanation – know that nothing is incidental. God oversees every detail of creation, and everything is known, foreseen and planned. Moreover, each thing achieves its proper spiritual level.[83] *As an example of this, the Zohar explains why Yitzchak (Isaac) became blind in his old age, whereas Avraham (Abraham) retained his sight.*

Rabbi Shimon bar Yochai taught: It is written "God named the light "Day," and the darkness He named "Night." Come and see[84] from this verse that all the deeds of the Holy One blessed be He are absolute truth, and contain supernal secrets. Moreover, every word of the Torah can be relied upon absolutely, and every word is fully illuminated with supernal secrets. The narratives of the Torah are not intended to merely narrate historical events, but rather to reveal Divine secrets.[85] The Torah informs us that with age, Yitzchak became blind (See *Bereishit* 27:1). Rabbi Shimon asks, was Yitzchak less worthy than Avraham, who did not become blind? How could this have happened? Yitzchak was a "pure offering" and a perfect saint, hence it was certainly not sin that caused him to become blind.[86] However this is a supernal secret, a secret of faith which is contained in the secret of the verse, "God named the light 'Day.'" This alludes to Avraham whose light grows, and shines, and becomes stronger just like the light of day. We see this association of Avraham with dawn and progression of day from the verse, "Avraham rose early in the *morning*"[87] – to serve God. Therefore, the verse states, "And Avraham was old, advancing in days" (*Bereishit* 24:1) i.e. advancing in the illuminating light. And he became old, in the sense of "Shining more, and more, until the height of day." (*Mishlei* 4:18). This is the meaning of the verse, "God named the

---

83. See R. Chaim Vital, quoted in *Or HaChamah's* introduction to this section.
84. תא חזי in Hebrew. This is a common expression in the *Zohar,* usually before citing a verse as proof for a thesis. I have sometimes translated it as "look."
85. *Or Yakar*.
86. R. Chaim Vital, quoted in *Or Hachamah*; *Matok MiDevash*.
87. *Bereishit* 22:3.

light ‘Day’“, i.e. He named the attribute to which Avraham cleaved “day”. And therefore, Avraham retained his sight. “And the darkness He named ‘Night’“ This is the attribute of Yitzchak, night, which becomes progressively darker. The association of deepening night with Yitzchak is seen in the verse, “And Yitzchak went out to the fields *toward evening*, to pray.” (*Bereishit* 24:63). For Yitzchak’s type of Divine service is practiced at night. Therefore, when he became old, it is written, “When Yitzchak grew old, sight faded from his eyes” (*Bereishit* 27:1). This is the proper situation – that Yitzchak should become blind by cleaving to his attribute. Hence, the more Yitzchak cleaved to his attribute, the darker his vision became. And therefore “And the darkness – the attribute to which Yitzchak cleaved – He named ‘Night.’”

(*Zohar* vol. I. 141a ff)

1:5 ויהי ערב ויהי בקר יום אחד – There was evening, and there was morning, one day

Rabbi Yehudah taught: Why is it that regarding each day of creation the Torah states, “There was evening, and there was morning?” This is to inform us that there is no night without day, and no day without night. Moreover, they are not called one until they are combined. Hence, it is not proper to view them as separate entities. Since darkness and night generally allude to severity and evil, whereas light and day generally allude to kindness and goodness, as explained previously, Rabbi Yehudah teaches that one should not therefore conclude that there are two divinities.[88] Rabbi Yose explained that the light which was produced on the first day accompanies all the days of creation; therefore, “There was evening, and there was morning” is written on each occasion. Rabbi Shimon bar Yochai explained that this teaches us that the first day accompanied all the other days, and all the other days are contained in the first day, to show that there is no division in the Holy One blessed be He.[89]

(*Zohar I*, 46a)

---

88. *Ziv HaZohar*.
89. cf. *Bereishit Rabbah* 3:8; Rashi, *Bereishit* 1:4.

1:6 ויאמר אלקים יהי רקיע בתוך המים ויבדל בין מים למים – And God said: There shall be a sky in the midst of the waters, and it shall separate between water and water

Rabbi Yose bar Chalafta said to Rabbi Shimon bar Yochai, "Why isn't the phrase, 'that it was good' mentioned on the second day," in stark contrast to all the other days of creation where it is mentioned? He replied, "because the work was not completed on the second day, and something that is unfinished is imperfect, and therefore cannot be called good. But when it was completed on the third day, the verses[90] state, "it was good" twice, the first time corresponding to the completion of the work of the second day, and the second for the completion of the work of the third day.[91]

(*Midrash HaNe'elam, Zohar Chadash* 9a)

Once, when they were traveling through the desert, Rabbi Yitzchak said to Rabbi Elazar, "I would like to ask you one question. . . . Would it not have been preferable for the Torah to state, 'and God saw that it was good' before the act of creation, because by saying it after the act, there is an implication the He did not know prior to the act what the nature of the act would be, what form it would take, and its benefit? But when the act was completed, it implies that God examined it, and only then declared that it was good, as is written, 'and He saw,' and only then does it state, 'and it was good!'" Rabbi Elazar replied, "This should be interpreted homiletically – as a lesson to man, as Rabbi Yehudah explained: When a person learns the work of creation, regarding each day's work, he should not ask 'why was this action done in this way, and in this form, whereas another was done in a different way?' For he has been told why: 'God saw that it was good' to do so in that way! Furthermore, this is also a warning and an instruction to man regarding the proper way to comport oneself: The nature and benefit of an act is known and revealed to Him before it is

90. *Bereishit* 1:10, 12.
91. See Rashi, *Bereishit* 1:7.

performed, and yet He did not wish to declare that it was good before it was finished. Similarly, it is not proper for a person to praise a thing until it is completed, for something may be found deficient, and then he will be regarded as a fraud.

(*Midrash HaNe'elam, Zohar Chadash* 12d)

1:9 יקוו המים מתחת השמים אל מקום אחד – The waters beneath the heaven shall be gathered into one place, that the dry land may appear

In the commentaries this verse is treated allegorically. Since the entire creation was brought into being for the sake of the Jewish People and for the sake of the Torah,[92] the entire process of creation can be viewed from this perspective.

The Holy One blessed be He wished to give the Torah to the nations of the world[93] in order to rectify the "shattering of the vessels" of *Tohu* (see Introduction), by giving them the commandment of circumcision. This would have provided the necessary basis for the revelation of the Torah,[94] but they refused to accept it. Thus, the earth remained desolate and parched – devoid of Torah, which is compared to water. . . . This is the meaning of "The waters beneath the heaven shall be gathered into one place, that the dry land may appear." "The waters shall be gathered" – this is the Torah.[95] "Into one **place**" – this refers to the Jewish People, for the souls of Israel are drawn from that place of which it states, "Blessed is God from His **place**" (*Yechezkel* 3:12).

(*Zohar* I, 25a)

Rabbi Tanchum began interpreting this verse on the basis of another verse: "The *Tzaddik* (a righteous, saintly individual) perishes, and no

---

92. *Pesikta Zutrata, Bereishit* 1:1. See also Rashi's commentary ad loc. See also our commentary to this verse.

93. See *Devarim* 33:2, Commentaries.

94. *Sulam*, ad loc.

95. As in the verse, "All who are thirsty go to water" (*Yeshayahu* 55:1), i.e., Torah (Rashi).

man takes it to heart. Men of kindness are removed, and none understand that the *Tzaddik* has been withdrawn because of the evil to come" (*Yeshayahu* 57:1) – here we learn that when the Holy One blessed be He looks at the world and sees that man is not worthy, and there are many wicked people around in the world, then He passes judgment upon the world. Rabbi Tanchum added: The Holy One blessed be He made the generation like a body and soul. Rabbi Yitzchak asked, "How so?" He replied: As in this case – *Tzaddikim* (plural of *Tzaddik*) are the soul, and the unworthy are the body. When the Holy One blessed be He looks at the world and sees that man is not worthy, He removes the soul, and the body remains as putrid flesh. What does He remove? He removes the souls of the righteous, and the body of the unworthy remain. This is the meaning of, "The waters shall be gathered" – these are the righteous, who are withdrawn to their world, "into one place" – the place that is set aside for them because of their elevated spiritual level. When they have been gathered in to the World to Come (Paradise) then "the dry land appears" – these are the wicked who are without good deeds to their credit, and they are left without anyone to protect and shield them.

(*Midrash HaNe'elam, Zohar Chadash* 12c)

1:14 תדשא הארץ דשא עשב מזריע זרע עץ פרי עשה פרי למינו – The earth shall sprout vegetation, plants bearing seed, and fruit trees, each producing its own kind of fruit

Rabbi Yitzchak began his discourse with the following verse: "Awake, O north wind, and come, south wind. Blow upon my garden, so that its spices flow forth. Let my Beloved come into His garden, and eat its choicest fruits" (*Shir HaShirim* 4:16). In another section of the *Zohar*,[96] this verse is interpreted as follows: The "north (*tzafon*) wind" refers to the holiest sacrifices which were performed in the north of the Temple Courtyard. These correspond to self-judgment of the hidden depths (*tzfunei*) of one's heart. The "south wind" refers to the peace-offerings which were performed in the south of the Temple Courtyard, and correspond to a person's

96. Part III, p. 11a.

faith in God, which brings his divine service to completion. "Spices" refers to the incense, and corresponds to joy. The Holy One blessed be He delights in these offerings and comes into His garden to partake of these – its choicest fruits. Rabbi Yitzchak then quoted the interpretation of Rabbi Abohu who said: A person[97] must reflect to a great extent upon his deeds, the "fruits" mentioned above, and examine them daily to ensure that they are the choicest of fruits) because the Holy One blessed be He gave him a holy soul by virtue of which he can come to know and recognize his Creator, and gaze upon the wondrous deeds He does every day.

(*Midrash HaNe'elam, Zohar Chadash* 13a)

1:14 יְהִי מְאֹרֹת בִּרְקִיעַ הַשָּׁמַיִם לְהַבְדִּיל בֵּין הַיּוֹם וּבֵין הַלָּיְלָה – There shall be luminaries in the expanse of the sky to separate between the day and the night

"Luminaries" in the plural refers to the Written Torah and the Oral Torah, which reveal the light of God, thus separating between day (good) and night (evil).[98]

(*Tikkunei Zohar, tikkun* 44)

1:16 אֶת שְׁנֵי הַמְּאֹרֹת הַגְּדֹלִים אֶת הַמָּאוֹר הַגָּדֹל לְמֶמְשֶׁלֶת הַיּוֹם, וְאֶת הַמָּאוֹר הַקָּטֹן לְמֶמְשֶׁלֶת הַלַּיְלָה – The two great luminaries, the greater luminary to reign by day, and the lesser luminary to reign by night

Why does the verse refer to the sun and moon as the **great** luminaries, but subsequently refer to them as the "greater luminary" and the "lesser luminary?" Rabbi Yitzchak said: The Holy One blessed be He made the luminaries and placed them in the sky so that they could reign over earth, and be used by the created beings. When He created them,

---

97. The word used here to denote a person is אדם (Adam) – a cognate of the word אדמה (*adamah* = earth), since man was fashioned from earth, as verse 2:7 below states explicitly.

98. See *Tikkunei Zohar, Tikkun 67 p. 98b.*

He created them equal – each of them was a **luminary** – the light of the moon was equal to that of the sun. But the moon said to the Holy One blessed be He "It is not proper for You to use[99] two equal crowns." What did the Holy One blessed be He do? He reduced[100] the light of the moon, so that its light is no longer equal to that of the sun. The explanation is as follows: God's intention in creating the world was that He should come to be revealed to His creation.[101] However, this divine revelation (referred to here as the "crown"[102]) can come about in two ways:[103] 1) God reveals Himself to man in this world by way of the Divine light which transcends creation. Technically, this refers to *Zeir Anpin*,[104] which is symbolized by the sun; and 2) God reveals Himself to man through the light which He used in creating the world, and which was later concealed.[105] Technically, this refers to *malchut*, which is symbolized by the moon.[106] Initially, both forms of revelation were equal.[107] However, the moon argued that this situation is untenable, for if the revelation of God on earth would equal that of the higher worlds, evil could not exist, and man would have no free choice between good and evil, and he would be unable to achieve recognition of God by his own efforts.[108] Accordingly, the revelation of God within creation must be reduced drastically, so that the moon has no light of its own.[109] This argument is accepted,[110] and the situation which allows for the existence of evil is achieved by the vessels of the world of *Tohu* shattering,

---

99. Other versions (e.g. *Tikkunei Zohar, Tikkun* 21, p. 59a) state: "It is not possible for two kings to use one crown."

100. Other versions state: He told the moon, "Go and reduce yourself." See *Chullin* 60b; *Bereishit Rabbah* 6:3.

101. This is the purpose of the world's creation according to *Zohar II* 42a, b – as explained above in our commentary to *Bereishit* 1:1.

102. See R. Meir Ibn Gabbai in *Avodat HaKodesh* part 4, chap. 8.

103. See *Torat Shmuel*, Discourses 5627, p. 399 ff.

104. See *Pardes, Shar Arachei Hakinuim,* s.v. שמש; *Sulam* and other commentaries. See Introduction.

105. See our commentary to Bereishit 1:3, 1:4.

106. See *Pardes, Shar Arachei Hakinuim,* s.v. ירח; *Sulam* and other commentaries. See Introduction.

107. Cf. *Bereishit Rabbah* 19:13 – "The chief aspect of the Divine Presence (the *Schechinah*) was in the **lower** worlds."

108. Cf. *Midrash Tanchuma, Nasso* 16.

109. *Zohar I*, 181a, 249b, 251b; vol. *II*, 245b, and several other places.

110. This is apparently the view of the *Zohar* as cited by R. Moshe Cordovero in *Pardes, Shaar* 18, chap. 2: According to this the moon **requested** to be allowed to reduce itself to a lower level than the sun, and its request was granted. In *Avodat HaKodesh* part 4, chap. 1, R. Meir ibn Gabbai offers the Talmudic view – that this was a punishment.

causing sparks of holiness to become embedded within creation.[111] The revelation of God now comes about by way of extricating these holy sparks from their entanglement in evil, and by refining and elevating them. When the process of refining has been completed, then *Malchut* will be equal to *Zeir Anpin*, as will be explained below.

The *Zohar* now continues. . . . Rabbi Yose, the son of Rabbi Shimon ben Lakunya came to visit his son-in-law, Rabbi Elazar, the son of Rabbi Shimon bar Yochai. Rabbi Yose's daughter came out to greet him. She took his hands and kissed them. He said to her, "Go and humble yourself before your husband, Rabbi Elazar, for he is a holy man." Rabbi Elazar overheard this and commented, "This reminds me of a valuable teaching regarding the moon: We learned that the Holy One blessed be He told the moon to go and reduce itself. The *Zohar* thus indicates that the relationship of a husband and wife is a reflection of spiritual dynamics, and fulfills God's purpose in creation.

(*Midrash HaNe'elam, Zohar Chadash* 14a)

This verse alludes to the commandment to give charity: "The greater luminary" is the secret of the wealthy, and "the lesser luminary" is the secret of the poor. Just as the moon borrows from the sun, and has no light other than that which it is given by the sun,[112] so too, the indwelling Divine Presence (the *Shechinah*) says to the Jewish People, "Borrow from Me – give charity generously[113] – and I will repay you." This is also the explanation of why Joshua received his gift of prophecy from Moses,[114] as it is said[115] Moses' face was like the

111. Tzemach Tzedek *Or HaTorah Bereishit,* p. 80-2. The concept of the "shattering of the vessels" (*shevirat hakelim)* is found in several places in the *Zohar* (II, 176b; III 128a, 135a-b, 142a-b). The *Zohar* explains that God originally built a primordial world called *Tohu*, which He then destroyed (see our commentary to 1:2 above). Fragments of the substance of that world fell from their elevated level and became embedded within the various levels of creation. Man's task is to extricate, refine and elevate these sparks, restoring them to their original level of sanctity.

112. See *Zohar I*, 181a, 249b, 251b; *II,* 245b; *Tikkunei Zohar, Tikkun* 44, p. 82b. See also *Eitz Chaim, sha'ar* 6, chap. 5, and *sha'ar* 8, chap. 5.

113. *Kisei Melech.*

114. See *Bamidbar* 27:18-23

115. *Bava Batra* 75a; *Sifri, Pinchas* 27:20; *Zohar I* 28a; *Zohar II* 215a.

sun, and Joshua's face – like the moon. Similarly, all the prophets compared with Moses are like the moon and planets before the sun, for they have no light of their own – only that which they receive from the sun as we see clearly regarding the seventy elders who received their spirit of prophecy from Moses.[116]

(*Tikkunei Zohar, Tikkun* 44)

1:17 להאיר על הארץ – To give light on earth

Rabbi Yitzchak said: It is written, "The light of the moon will be like the light of the sun; the light of the sun shall be sevenfold the light of seven days" (*Yeshayahu* 30:26). Rabbi Yitzchak now asks: Which "seven days" are these? He answers: The seven days of creation. According to this view, the verse from *Yeshayahu* explains that the light of the moon which will be revealed in the future[117] will equal the light of the sun now, whereas the light of the sun will be seven times greater than the light which was revealed during the seven days of creation. Accordingly, the moon will still be subservient to the sun. However, Rabbi Yehudah said: This refers to the seven days of inauguration (מילואים) of the First Temple. Accordingly, in the future, the light of the moon will **equal** the light of the sun, and both will be sevenfold the light that was revealed during the inauguration of the First Temple. Accordingly, the moon will not need to receive its light from the sun, for it too will be a luminary. The *Zohar* continues: Certainly the verse refers to the seven days of inauguration, for then the world will be completely rectified and the moon will return to its fullness without blemish, just as it was in the days of the First Temple.[118] (Note that the word מילואים literally means "fulfillment"). And when will this be? At the time of which it is written, "He will destroy death forever" (*Yeshayahu* 25:8) and life will be eternal. Of that time it is also written, "On that day God will be One and His Name One" (*Zechariah* 14:9).[119]

---

116. See *Bamidbar* 11:25.

117. See *Zohar I,* p. 45b; *III,* p. 93a.

118. As the *Zohar Sitrei Otiot, Bereishit; Zohar, Sitrei Torah, Yitro* states regarding the era of King Solomon who built the First Temple: "The moon remained in its fullness."

119. The above interpretation is based on *Or Yakar*, and seems to be supported by *Zohar I,* p. 45b.

(*Zohar I,* 34a)

1:20 ישרצו המים שרץ - The waters shall teem with living creatures

Rabbi Elazar said: This refers to the waters below i.e., waters in the literal sense of the word, referring to rivers and seas, which teem with species of living creatures, just like the spiritual waters above which teem with the souls of those types of righteous *tzaddikim* who are called נוני ימא– "fish of the sea,"[120] because they are always united with their Source Above, and because their ways are hidden from man, just like those below – fish, which are totally enveloped in their medium, which is the source of their life,[121] and are thus hidden from man. Rabbi Chiyya said: The upper waters brought forth a living soul – in the singular. Accordingly, it must refer to one specific soul. Which is this? This is the soul of Adam, as it is written, "Man became a living soul" (*Bereishit* 2:7).

(*Zohar I,* 34a)

Since the world was created for the sake of the Jewish People and the Torah, as explained above, there is a necessary correspondence between the commandments of the Torah and the Ten Utterances through which the world was created.[122]

The preceding verses all allude to the relationship between man and God:[123] "In the beginning," corresponds to awe of God; "there shall be light, "corresponds to love of God; "the waters shall be gathered, "corresponds to acknowledging God and His dominion; "there shall be luminaries in the sky. . ."corresponds to knowing that God is One. This verse, however, concerns man himself. Three commandments are alluded to in the verse, "The waters shall teem with living creatures" – 1) To occupy oneself with Torah; 2) To concern oneself with propagation; 3) To circumcise a male child on the eighth day, removing the foreskin.

---

120. See *Zohar III,* 174a; ibid. *Raya Mememna* 42a. Explained in *Likkutei Torah* (R. Shneur Zalman of Liadi), *Tzav* 14b.
121. See *Avodah Zara* 3b.
122. *See our commentary to verse 1:3 above.*
123. *Zohar* I, *11b ff.*

To occupy oneself with Torah: [124]

This includes reviewing the written Torah, probing the Oral Torah (*Talmud*) deeply, and daily increasing one's practical knowledge (*Mishnah*), reviewing it over and over so that nothing will be forgotten. In this way, the bidding of our Sages[125] to divide one's learning into three parts – Scripture, *Talmud* and *Mishnah* – is fulfilled. In addition to rectifying one's *nefesh* and *ruach*, the two lowest levels of the soul through acquiring awe of heaven and fulfilling the commandments, when a person occupies himself with Torah, he acquires another, higher level of soul – the holy *neshama,*[126] as is written, "the waters shall teem" – i.e. shall give birth to a **living** soul, the literal translation of נפש חיה, a soul with holy life-force, as stated in the verse, "But you who cleave to the Lord your God – you are all **alive** today" (*Devarim* 4:4). For when a person does not occupy himself with Torah, he does not acquire a holy soul, and supernal holiness does not rest upon him. However, when he does strive in Torah, he merits a living soul, and becomes as exalted as the holy angels. . . .

To concern oneself with propagation:

Everyone who concerns himself with propagation as the verse states, "Be fertile and produce many offspring" (*Bereishit* 1:28) causes that river – the outflow of divine energy from above[127] – to flow constantly and steadily,[128] so that the sea – the reservoir of divine energy assigned to animate this world[129] – becomes filled from all sides – i.e., to animate the worlds, and to produce new souls which were originally part of Adam, but split off from him due to the sin of the Tree of Knowledge.[130] These now issue forth from that Tree – the Tree of Life.[131] Many angels are produced above, together with these holy souls, in order to protect them from harm. This is the meaning of the verse, "the waters shall teem with living

---

124. The following interpretation is from *Or Yakar*.

125. *Kiddushin* 30a.

126. For an explanation of the levels of soul mentioned here, see *Introduction*.

127. Technically, the *sefirah* of *yesod* (*Or Yakar*).

128. *Or Yakar*.

129. Technically, the *sefirah* of *malchut* (*Or Yakar*).

130. Tree of Knowledge, Tree of Life – see *Introduction*.

131. See *Raya Mehemna, Zohar* II, p. 117a; *Sulam*.

creatures" – it refers to the holy covenant – when the commandment of circumcision has been fulfilled, the river flows forth, and its waters increase, generating a multitude of these living souls which are then drawn down to those who are worthy of them. . . . But one who withholds himself from being fertile and multiplying – it is as if he reduces the Divine Image, which includes all images – the image in which man was created[132] – and does not allow that river of Divine energy to flow downward, thus blemishing every aspect of the holy covenant[133] – regarding both the life-force of the worlds, and the generation of new souls in this world.[134]

To circumcise on the eighth day:

The third precept alluded to in this verse is the commandment to circumcise a boy on the eighth day, thus removing the defilement of the foreskin, for the sake of the living soul which is the eighth level – the attribute of *binah* when counting from *malchut* upwards.[135] That soul which derives from it – from the attribute of *binah* – must ascend to this level on the eighth day, since it is the eighth level, in order to drive away the forces of evil and externality, and allow the soul to receive its full illumination from this level. . . . This is the meaning of, "the waters shall teem with living creatures...." – the waters of holy seed will be imprinted with the image of the living soul.

(*Zohar I,* 12b-13a)

---

132. *Bereishit* 1:26-7.

133. According to the commentaries, this apparently refers to the covenant of circumcision, the purpose of which is to bring holy souls into this world, and educe holy Divine energy for the benefit of the world. See also *Zohar II*, 204b ff.; *III* 80-82; *Zohar Chadash – Bereishit*, p. 11.

134. *Or Yakar; Sulam.*

135. See *Sulam.*

1:20 ועוף יעופף על הארץ על פני רקיע השמים – And flying things which flitter about over the earth, in the expanse of the sky

"And flying things which flitter about over the earth" – these are the supernal messengers (angels) which are revealed in human form to man. This is understood from the fact that "over the **earth**" is written, implying that there are others which are not revealed in human form, but only in ethereal form, according to human comprehension. For this reason, here "the various kinds of winged birds" is not written in regard to them, whereas it is written in regard to others, in the following verse (1:21). The two verses therefore refer to two categories of angels: "The various kinds" refers to those angels which never change – these were created on the fifth day – whereas the others, regarding whom it is not written, "the various kinds" are created for the necessities of the moment, as supernal messengers, etc.[136]

(*Zohar I,* 34a)

1:21 את התנינם הגדלים – The great water-creatures

Rabbi Shimon said: This is the secret of the leviathan and its mate. However, the word **התנינם** is written in the defective form (i.e., instead of התנינים), because the Holy One blessed be He killed the female and removed it, and set it aside for the righteous. The explanation is as follows:[137] The leviathan and its mate have their root in extremely elevated levels of holiness, and are called "great" because they are the first to receive the divine energy flowing from the uppermost levels of the *sefirot.*[138] Elsewhere[139]

---

136. See *Zohar III,* 187a.

137. *Sulam*, based on *Chullin* 67b, that the leviathan is a *kosher* fish, interprets the entire passage in a positive sense – as referring to extremely elevated levels of holiness. The *Mikdash Melech*, however, interprets the entire passage in a negative sense – referring to the foremost levels of *kelipah.* We will explain this passage according to the former, positive, interpretation.

138. *Zohar III,* 39b. Technically, from *binah.* See *Pardes, Arachei Hakinuim* s.v. תנינים.

139. *Tikkunei Zohar, Tikkun* 21 (42b); *Zohar III,* p. 279a (*Raya Mehemna*). See also *Avodat HaKodesh*, R. Meir ibn Gabbai, part 4, chap. 9.

we learn that this refers to the greatest among the righteous. Moreover, the righteous are referred to as "leviathan" because this word signifies unification and integration[140] in the Oneness of God. However, this comprises two aspects, corresponding to the male and female leviathan – merging into the Oneness of God Above, and manifesting this Oneness in the world below.[141] However, it was God's intention that man have free choice, and achieve self-surrender and communion with Him by his **own** choice, and not as the result of divine "compulsion."[142] Accordingly, the Holy One blessed be He killed the female, thus preventing the righteous from openly manifesting His Oneness in the world. If one asks why then were they both created in the first place, the answer is that the female (i.e., the revelation of God below, through His righteous ones) was not killed in the usual sense of the word, but was simply **elevated** to a level which does not influence man below.[143] The *Zohar* now continues: Until the Holy One blessed be He killed the female (in the sense mentioned above), "the earth was inconceivably void,"[144] i.e., void of divine revelation – because the "vessels" (recipients) of the tremendous revelation of God revealed below by the female aspect of the leviathan, could not contain the revelation and shattered.[145] But after He killed it, it is referred to as *Bohu*[146] – which can be read as a compound word בו הוא (*bo hu*) – "He (God) is within it,"[147] albeit in a concealed way – and it began to have continuity. However, since Godliness was now concealed, "there was darkness upon the surface of the depths"[148] (*Bereishit* 1:2) for the limited and measured light which could be received by the creation did not illuminate the darkness until the words, "There shall be light" were uttered.

(*Zohar II,* 34a-b)

---

140. *Zohar II,* 11b. See also *Likkutei Torah, Nasso* 22a.
141. See *Pardes, Arachei Hakinuim* s.v. לויתן .
142. Cf *Shabbat* 88a – the Holy One, blessed is He, hung Mount Sinai over the Israelites like a barrel (a metaphor for the revelation of His infinite love for them – *Likkutei Torah, Re'eh* 22a). This "forced" them to agree to accept the Torah, but the agreement is regarded as a "מודעה רבה לאורייתא" – an agreement made under coercion. Only much later on, in the days of Mordechai and Esther, did the Jewish People actually accept the Torah of their own free choice (see *Esther* 9:27) – *Shabbat* ad loc.
143. .*Sulam*.
144. *Bereishit*, 1:2.
145. Explained in note 104 above.
146. *Bereishit* ibid.
147. See *Sefer HaBahir* chap. 30 (*Zohar II, Hashmatot* p. 263a).
148. *Bereishit* ibid.

1:24 תוצא הארץ נפש חיה למינה – The earth shall bring forth living creatures, each according to its kind

Rabbi Abba said: From the words נפש חיה (literally "living soul," in the singular, rather than in the plural) you see that all souls in the world above initially incorporate both male and female. But when they issue forth, i.e., when they are born into this world, they go as either male or female, and then go their separate ways – the male soul in a male body, and the female soul in a female body.[149] If they are worthy, they will unite in marriage. Then the female soul is referred to as the man's soul-mate, and they join together to form a single unit in every way – soul and body. This is the meaning of the verse, "The earth shall bring forth למינה נפש חיה" – literally, "living soul each according to its kind." What does "each according to its kind" mean? That it unites with that soul with which it was originally coupled. And what is the meaning of "**the earth** shall bring forth" in the verse? The meaning is as another verse states: "I was constructed in the lowest parts of the earth" (*Tehillim* 139:15) – referring to the attribute of *malchut*,[150] the lowest of the ten *sefirot*. The latter verse thus clearly parallels, "the **earth** shall bring forth," for it from this attribute that the living soul issues forth. This we have explained, "the living soul" refers to the soul of Adam. Due to Adam and Eve's sin of the Tree of Knowledge of Good and Evil, which brought evil into the world and caused separation where none existed before,[151] when souls issue forth from above, the male and female aspects become separated – until the Holy One blessed be He sees fit to reunify them. However, this depends on the person himself. If he is worthy, his soul-mate is given to him. If not, they are separated, and she is given to another man, and they give birth to children who are not fitting.

(*Zohar III,* 43b)

---

149. *Sulam.*

150. *Sulam.* See *Introduction.*

151. This will be explained below.

1:26 נעשה אדם בצלמנו כדמותנו – We shall make man with Our image, of Our likeness

The Zohar explains why the plural form "we" is mentioned only in regard to the creation of man

"We shall make man": After each workman (each of the *sefirot*) had completed its work, the Holy One blessed be He said to them, "I have one more activity to do, which requires the participation of all of us. All of you join together, each one of you doing your part, and I will join in and give My part – his soul." This is the meaning of the verse, "We shall make man with our image, of our likeness."[152] Image (*tzelem*) is the human mold of the man's physical form, which links his body and his soul. This mold derives from the configuration of the *sefirot*. The likeness (*demut*) of man refers to the soul clothed in the body, which reflects the *Atzmut*, or Infinite Light (*Or Ein Sof*), which illuminates the *sefirot*.[153] Our Sages explain that "man" refers only to Israel, as it is written, "But you, My flock, the flock of My pasture, are men, and I am your God. . . ." (*Yechezkel* 34:31). That is, only those to whom I am God are men, but not idolators.[154] And therefore "Israel rejoices in his Maker" (*Tehillim* 149:2) – meaning that everyone who is of the seed of Israel should rejoice in the joy of God who delights in His dwelling in the lower physical worlds, which become a vessels for His Oneness through His people.[155]

(*Raya Mehemna – Zohar III,* 238b)

Rabbi Abohu began explaining the words, "with Our image, of Our likeness," by citing another verse, "What is man, that You are mindful of him, and the son of man that You pay attention to him? Yet You made him little less than the angels!"[156] (*Tehillim* 8:5-6).

Rabbi Tanchum said: The words, "We shall make. . . ." can be explained as follows: When the Holy One blessed be He decided to create man,

---

152. *Or Yakar*.
153. *Pardes Rimonim, sha'ar* 31, chap. 4; *Shnei Luchot HaBrit, "Beit Yisrael,"* p. 6c; *Nefesh HaChaim, sha'ar* 1, chap. 1. See Rashi, *Bereishit* 1:26.
154. See *Yevamot* 61a; *Baba Metziah* 114b; *Zohar I*, 20b.
155. See *Tanya* end of chap. 33.
156. אלקיםhere is rendered as "angels" by Rashi, Ibn Ezra, *Metzudat David*.

He consulted with the angels which surround His throne, and said to them, "Shall we make man?" They replied: "Master of the Universe, what is he worth? What is man, that You are mindful of him?"

Another interpretation of "We shall make man": Rabbi Buta said in the name of Rabbi Bo: We reviewed the entire Torah, and did not find anywhere that the Holy One blessed be He took counsel with the angels regarding any matter which He intended doing. Moreover, we find that none among them, whether above i.e. the angels of the higher worlds, or below i.e., the angels of the lower worlds can grasp the intention of the Holy One blessed be He. When they run to comprehend as the verse states, "The *Chayot* (a category of angels) ran" (*Yechezkel* 1:14) – they immediately retreat from their perception, as the verse continues, "and returned" like a fledgling bird which tries to fly, but drops back to its original place.[157] So too, the angels make every effort to comprehend God's intentions, but to no avail, until they return to their own level and declare, "Blessed is God from **His** place" (ibid. 3:12). Accordingly, "We shall make man" cannot mean that God took counsel with the angels.

Rabbi Buta cites a further proof that the verse cannot mean that God took counsel: We find that the Holy One blessed be He created the first light (i.e., the light which was created from the utterance, "there shall be light," not from the utterance "there shall be luminaries"), and from it He created everything else that serves Him.[158] Now, since He did not take counsel with the first light He created, when He wanted to produce all the other hosts of heaven from it, how much more so would He have no need to take counsel when creating man, who is regarded as a mere puff of air, as verse 2:7 below states, "God. . . . **blew** into his nostrils a living soul."

---

157. *Nitzotzei Zohar*.
158. See *Zohar II,* 148b ff, according to R.Yehudah.

RabbiYitzchak said: Leave Rabbi Buta alone i.e., do not challenge his words, for he lives together with the masters of the *baraita*[159] – i.e., he is on their level. Rabbi Buta replied: I am not worthy of living together with them, but this question is theirs,[160] and we have also heard an answer to it – Rabbi Bo said: This is comparable to a king who rules over everyone in his kingdom. He wished to show that all are included in him, and he is everything, as our Sages declare, "the leader of the generation is (like) the entire generation."[161] Thus when he refers to himself he does so in the plural – the royal "we" – "We shall." So too regarding the Holy One blessed be He. Since He wanted to show that the entire world is His, and everything is under His dominion, He spoke in the plural in regard to Himself, thus demonstrating that He is everything.

Rabbi Yitzchak said: If I would have heard this from on high, and not from Rabbi Bo, I would have said that it is a good answer. However, as it is, it does not satisfy me, for although this **could** be the case, there is no proof that it is **in fact** so.

Rabbi Shimon bar Yochai came to Tiberias to purify the market place of spiritual impurity.[162] When Rabbi Pinchas, Rabbi Bo, and RabbiYitzchak saw him, they said, "How long do we have to sit in one spot, without being able to move?" They did not wish to proceed in their studies until they had answered this question to the satisfaction of all of them. "One of the masters of the *Mishnah,* Rabbi Shimon bar Yochai, is here," they said. "Let's ask him."

Then Rabbi Abohu arrived. He said to Rabbi Shimon, "If we do not receive an answer to the question regarding this verse, there is an opening for heretics to claim that there are **two** dominions."

---

159. The *beraita*, similar to the *mishnah,* are teachings authored by the Tannaim, but were not included by Rabbi Yehudah HaNassi in the six orders of the *Mishnah* which he compiled. After the *mishnah, beraitot* have supreme authority in Jewish law.

160. See *Bereishit Rabbah* 8:4.

161. *BamidbarRabbah* 19:17. See also Rashi, *Bamidbar* 21:21.

162. See *Yerushalmi Shevi'it* 9:1.

Rabbi Shimon said: It is written, "Hear, deaf ones, and look, blind ones, that you may see" (*Yeshayahu* 42:18). Did the Torah really address itself to the blind and the deaf? No, this is not the verse's intention. Rather "blind ones" refers to those who are blind in Torah, for they have a straight path before them, and yet they blunder about in crooked ways like the blind, and do not get to the root of the matter. We have learned this verse, "We shall make man," as follows: When the Holy One blessed be He created the world, initially everything was water; and from water He developed the world. He made three craftsmen to do His work in this world – heaven, earth, and water. With these, He created everything in this world. He bid each of these three to produce the creations that were necessary for the world. He bid water to produce earth from beneath it, and commanded the waters to gather into one place so that dry land should appear. The water did as it was commanded as it is written: "The waters shall be gathered. . . ." (*Bereishit* 1:9).

He then called upon the earth to produce its creations – animals and living creatures, and so on as it is written, "The earth shall bring forth living creatures, each according to its kind" (ibid. 1:24), which it immediately did.

He then called upon the heavens to make a separation between the upper water and the lower water, which it immediately did, as it is written, "God positioned the sky so that it separated the water below the sky from the water above in the sky" (ibid. 1:7).

He then called upon the earth to produce vegetation, plants, crops and orchards. What is written immediately afterwards? "The earth brought forth vegetation, plants bearing their own kind of seed. . . ." (ibid. 1:12).

He then called upon the heavens saying, "There shall be luminaries and lights i.e. stars suspended within you to illuminate the earth, as it is written, "There shall be luminaries in the expanse of the sky" (ibid. 1:14). He also called upon the water to produce swarms of fish and birds and their like, as it is written, "The waters shall teem with living creatures" (ibid. 1:20). Thus, it was by way of these three – the heavens, the earth, and water, that He wrought the entire creation, each thing according to its type – i.e., some are sky creatures, some are earth creatures and some are water creatures.

With the advent of the sixth day on which man was created all three elements sky, earth and water were ready to continue producing creatures at God's command, as on the previous days. But the Holy One blessed be He said to them, "None of you is able to produce this creature man alone. All of you must unite, and I too will join you. Together, "We shall make man," for even all of you together cannot create him on your own. His body will be the product of all three of you, and his soul, Mine." Therefore, when the Holy One blessed be He called upon them to create man, He said, "We shall make man," I and you. I will provide the soul, and you, the body. And so it was – the body is composed of these three, the "craftsmen" of creation, and the Holy One blessed be He gave the soul, thus joining with them in creating him.

(*Midrash HaNe'elam, Zohar Chadash* 16a-b)

"We shall make man with our image, of our likeness" – so that he will incorporate six sides – the six directions of space: north, south, west, east, up and down.; One hand to the north, the other to the south; his head above, his feet below; his face to the east and his back to the west[163] – which include everything, matching those Above – the six *sefirot* of *ze'ir anpin* in the world of *Atzilut.* And for this reason man is called "Adam" (אדם), since he is like (דומה) the One Above.[164] Thus, his 248 limbs will be arrayed in the mystery of *chochmah,* entirely according to the supernal order. Two explanations of "the mystery of *chochmah*" may be given: 1) The 248 limbs of the human body correspond to the 248 positive

---

163. *OrYakar.* Commentaries explain that mystically this refers to six of the soul's powers -kindness, severity, compassion, trust, sincerity, attachment, corresponding to the six *sefirot – chesed, gevurah, tiferet, netzach, hod, yesod.* See *Introduction.*

164. These words are actually etymologically related – cf. "I will be compared (*adameh*) to the One Above" (*Yeshayahu* 14:14).

commandments,[165] which are referred to in the *Zohar*[166] as the "248 limbs of the King." When a person fulfills the commandments, his physical body becomes a vehicle for God's Supreme Will vested in the commandments[167] of the Torah which is called *chochmah*. 2) The 248 limbs of the human body correspond to the 248 letters of the first paragraph of the *Shema* prayer,[168] so that when he recites it with the proper concentration and intention, he merges his physical being, as well as his soul, into the unity of God. This ability to nullify oneself and merge into the unity of God is also referred to as "the mystery of *chochmah*."[169]

"We shall make man" – this is the mystery of male and female as verse 27 below states, "male and female He created them" with all holy supernal wisdom in such a way that man is able to partake of the Godliness which is manifested in this holy supernal wisdom[170] for Godliness resides only where there is completeness and perfection,[171] and man must therefore incorporate both male and female aspects.

"With our image, of our likeness": So that one complements the other – again, image (*tzelem*) is the human mold of the man's physical form, which links his body and his soul. and derives from the configuration of the *sefirot*. Likeness (*demut*) refers to the soul clothed in the body, which reflects the Infinite Light (*Or Ein Sof*), which illuminates the *sefirot*.[172] Thus "image" complements "likeness," for it makes manifest the Infinite Light which illuminates the *sefirot*. Accordingly, man is unique in the world, for only he has this quality, and therefore the ability to reveal the Oneness of God in this world, "One within one."[173] And so he was given dominion over everything, as our verse continues and informs us that man "shall rule over the fish. . . . the birds. . . . the animals, and over all the earth" by virtue of the fact that He partakes of the Divine Image and Likeness.

(*Zohar I*, p. 47a)

165.For a listing of some of the correspondences see R.Elazar Azikri's *Sefer HaChareidim*.

166. *Tikkunei Zohar, Tikkun* 30.

167. *Tanya*, Rabbi Shneur Zalman of Liadi, chap. 23.

168. See *Zohar Chadash, Ruth, m'amar kriat Shema*; ibid. *Midrash HaNe'elam, Acharei, parshat HaShemot*.

169. See *Tanya*, chap. 47, and note on p. 44b.

170. See *Tanya*, note on p. 44b.

171. See *Zohar I*, 216b, explained in *Tanya* chap. 32.

172. *Pardes Rimonim, sha'ar* 31, chap. 4; *Shnei Luchot HaBrit, "Beit Yisrael,"* p. 6c; *Nefesh HaChaim, sha'ar* 1, chap. 1. See Rashi, *Bereishit* 1:26.

173. *Zohar II*, 135a.

The following section explains that although the utterance through which man was created is similar in structure to the utterances which brought the rest of creation into being, it must, nevertheless, be interpreted differently.

It is written, "God said, 'We shall make man with our image, of our likeness, and they shall rule. . . ." The *chevraya* (Rabbi Shimon's circle of disciples and colleagues) requested clarification of the verse: It is clear that the Holy One blessed be He spoke to His supernal Hosts, and took counsel with them regarding the creation of man, like a king among his courtiers. However, we wish to clarify whether this verse, concerning the creation of man, is the secret of the higher worlds where the Name *Elokim* is known as *Elokim Chaim* – the Living God, technically, the *sefirah* of *binah* – i.e., the mystery of the higher world, or whether the Name *Elokim* here is the mystery of the lower world – technically, the *sefirah* of *malchut* i.e., the Divine power through which the world was created and continues to exist.[174] Nevertheless, *malchut* "has no light of its own" – its light is entirely from the nine *sefirot* above it,[175] and it is therefore termed a "female" or receptive, attribute. Accordingly, how must we understand the words "We shall make man. . . ." on each level?

Rabbi Shimon answers: In fact, the entire matter may be explained according to one mystical teaching. Man comprises all aspects, and this is his secret, which derives from the mystical secret of the Name *Elokim*, and not from any of the other Divine Names. Note that the Divine Names do not denote different "personages" (in which case there would be plurality in God, which is absolutely anathema to Judaism), but different actions or activities, as the *Midrash*[176] explains: "I am called according to My **deeds**." And this is why it subsequently states, "***Elokim*** created man with His image – with the image of ***Elokim*** He created him" (1:27). Now, why does the verse repeat the words "with His image". . . . "with the image?" What are these two images? The explanation is this: One signifies the male aspect of man, and the other, the female

---

174. See also *Menachot* 29b.

175. *Zohar I,* 249b, 251b; *II,* 245b; *Tikkunei Zohar, Tikkun* 44, p. 82b. See also *Eitz Chaim, sha'ar* 6, chap. 5, and *sha'ar* 8, chap. 5.

176. *Tanchuma, Shemot* 20.

aspect of man. . . .[177] "With His image" signifies the male aspect *zeir anpin* and "with the image of God," the female aspect, *malchut.* (Because malchut "has no light of its own" – its light is entirely from the nine *sefirot* above it[178] – it is therefore termed a "female" or receptive, attribute). As we explained previously, the "image" (*tzelem*) of man is the human mold of his physical form, which links his body and soul. Since the purpose of the *tzelem* is to link two complete opposites, the soul and the body, it must have some affinity to each of them. This is the reason for the verse alluding to **two** images – "With His image" – the higher world; "with the image of God" – the lower world. The verse thus continues and states, "Male and female He created them." Nevertheless, at this stage, they form a single unit although later on these two aspect are divided as we will see in the commentary to verses 2:21-22.

(*Midrash HaNe'elam, Zohar Chadash* p. 73b-c)

177. *Sulam.*

178. *Zohar I,* 249b, 251b; *II,* 245b; *Tikkunei Zohar, Tikkun* 44, p. 82b. See also *Eitz Chaim, sha'ar* 6, chap. 5, and *sha'ar* 8, chap. 5.

The following extract also discusses the subject dealt with in the previous selection, but from a more technical point of view. Note that this extract interprets the words נעשה אדם *as a question – **"Shall we make man?"***

Regarding the creation of man, it is appropriate to cite the verse "God's secret is for those who fear Him" (*Tehillim* 25:14) – for this secret is revealed to only very few.[179] A hoary-headed elder[180] addressed Rabbi Shimon bar Yochai: "Shimon, Shimon![181] Who is it that said, 'We shall make man?' Doesn't the verse state, 'And *Elokim*[182] said. . . .?' just like all the other verses describing creation, and therefore the verse should presumably have said, "**I** shall make man," or, "Let **Me** make man," in the singular. Who is the "us" to whom the verse refers here?" The one who posed the question[183] disappeared, and Rabbi Shimon could not see him. As soon as Rabbi Shimon heard that he had been addressed as "Shimon," and not as "**Rabbi** Shimon," he said to his colleagues: "Without doubt it was the Holy One blessed be He who just spoke, for of Him it is said, 'The Ancient One sat. . . .'" (*Daniel* 7:9). God is referred to as "the Ancient One" or "the Ancient of Days" because He **precedes and transcends** all of creation.[184] He "sat" is a metaphor for God's revelation of Himself to the righteous, as the verse (*Tehillim* 113:6) states, "Who **lowers** Himself to **reveal** Himself in the heavens and on earth."[185] Thus, Rabbi Shimon had just experienced a divine revelation of a very elevated level. Rabbi Shimon continues: Now is the time to reveal the secret of the verse, "We shall make man," for this is undoubtedly a secret which we did not have permission to reveal until now. But now since the question has

---

179. *Sulam.*

180. Literally, "a grandfather of grandfathers" said to Rabbi Shimon. This refers to a very elevated level of *Keter* – namely, *Atik Yomin* – literally, "the Ancient of Days" *(Mikdash Melech).* In terms of man's soul this indicates a revelation of the level of soul called *yechidah* (*Sulam*). See *Introduction.*

181. Our Sages point out (*Bereishit Rabbah* 30:4, 38:12; *Shemot Rabbah* 2:6) that anyone whose name is doubled (as in "Abraham, Abraham" – *Bereishit* 22:1; "Moses Moses" – *Shemot* 3:4) has a portion in this world and in the world to come – *Damesek Eliezer.*

182. One of the seven Divine Names which may not may not be erased (see Maimonides, *Code, Yesodei HaTorah* 6:2). See *Introduction.*

183. Literally, "the old man flew off."

184. Technically, this refers to the level of *Keter called Atik Yomin*, as above.

185. This is the interpretation of the verse given in *Zohar 1,* p. 195a.

been raised from on High it appears that permission has been granted to reveal it. It is obvious that the question was addressed to Rabbi Shimon so that he could clarify the matter to his students, not because the answer was not known Above.[186]

Rabbi Shimon begins explaining by way of a parable: A king had many buildings to construct. He had a workman who would do nothing without the king's permission, as the verse states, "I was a faithful worker at His side"[187] (*Mishlei* 8:30). He now explains that the parable may be interpreted in two ways: The "king" denotes supernal *chochmah ila'ah*,[188] which is also referred to as *Abba* – "father," and also signifies the middle column, *ze'ir anpin* (the six *sefirot* from *chesed* to *yesod*) – called the king below. The Name *Elokim*[189] (אלקים) is the supernal "workman" in the parable, signifying *imah ila'ah* also referred to as *binah* – "mother." However the Name *Elokim* also signifies a workman below, which is the *Shechinah* (*malchut*) – Godliness revealed within creation. Thus, just as there are two interpretations of the "king" in the parable, *chochmah* and *ze'ir anpin*, so too there are are two interpretations of the "workman:" the name *Elokim – imah*, and *Shechinah*. The relationship between them is this: *Chochmah's* "workman" is *binah-imah*, whereas *ze'ir anpin's* "workman" is *Shechinah-malchut*.[190]

Now we can understand the two questions addressed to Rabbi Shimon by the elder who disappeared. The first question was this: All of the utterances through which creation came into being begin with the same words, "And *Elokim* said. . . ." – indicating a "communication" or transfer of divine energy from the king to the workman, i.e., from *abba* (*chochmah*) to *imah* (*binah*). However, the verse, "**We** shall make man," implies that the king himself (*abba-chochmah*) also participated in the work, which seems inappropriate. This is what the elder asked: Who is it that said, "We shall make man?" It cannot have been *abba-chochmah*, for this level does not participate in the actual work of creation.[191] Who then does "we" refer to?

---

186. Cf. *Damesek Eliezer*.
187. Interpreted according to *Targum Yonatan*, and *Zohar I*, p. 134a.
188. Literally, "the higher level of *chochnmah*."
189. We have pointed out in the previous extract that the Divine Names do not denote "persons" but actions.
190. *Sulam*.
191. *Sulam*.

The second question was this: All instances of the Name *Elokim* mentioned throughout the creation signify *imah-binah*. However, this cannot be the intention here, since the soul of man does not derive from this level, but from the union of *ze'ir anpin* and *malchut*. Accordingly, what does the Name, *Elokim* signify here?

Rabbi Shimon answered by way of the parable of a king who wished to construct a palace using the skills of his workman. He points out that the parable may be interpreted on two levels – as the relationship between *abba* and *imah* – a king and his workman above, in the higher worlds; or as the relationship between *ze'ir anpin* and *malchut* – a king and his workman in the lower worlds. He now clarifies the parable to his disciples:

A woman may not do anything without her husband's permission.[192] The relationship between the *sefirot* may be compared to the relationship between a husband and wife. Thus, in our allegory, *binah* "asks" *chochmah*. The entire construction of the uppermost world, the world of *Atzilut,*[193] was by *abba* "saying" to *imah* – i.e., the transfer of divine energy from *abba* to *imah,* referred to by our Sages as an 'utterance'[194] – "It shall be like this or like that." Once the command was given by *abba* to *imah* (once the energy had been transferred) it was immediately actualized in *imah*, in the world of *Atzilut.* There is no separation between the level of *chochmah-abba,* and its actualization[195] in the level of *binah-imah.*[196] This is why the verse states. . . . "There shall be light," and **immediately**, "there was light." Rabbi Shimon now explains that the words ויאמר אלקים mean that He – signifying *chochmah,* spoke to *Elokim* – signifying *binah,* the builder,[197] saying, "There shall be light," and this was immediately actualized in *binah*. So too regarding the construction of the entire *Atzilut.* He said, "There shall be a sky," "There shall be luminaries," and these immediately came into being. All of the above applies to the world of *Atzilut*, which is suffused with God's Oneness,[198] and in

---

192. Cf. *Tanna d'Vei Eliyahu* 9.

193. See *Introduction.*

194. *Avot* 5:1.

195. See *Pardes shaar* 11, chap. 3; *Derech Mitzevotecha* p. 57a ff.; Discourses 5666, p. 5 ff.

196. *Tikkunei Zohar, Tikkun* 69 (p. 112b); *Tikkun* 61 (p. 93b).

197. Note that *binah* (בינה) is a cognate of בונה– build.

198. As stated explicitly in *Tikkunei Zohar, Introduction,* p. 3b. Explained at length in *Igrot Kodesh* chap. 20 (*Tanya* part 4).

which there is no separation between thought and deed, between potential and actuality.

However, when it came to the creation of the world of separation, i.e., the world of *Beriah* and further down,[199] where the Oneness of God is not manifested in a revealed way, it is not the king who **commands** the workman, but the workman who **asks** the king, "Shall we make man with our image, of our likeness?" – in the image and likeness of *Atzilut*? This is in clear contrast to the creation up until this point, for until now the Torah has dealt only with the world of *Atzilut,* where divine energy is transferred from *abba* to *imma*, without any separation between them, and therefore the expression of plurality, "Shall **we**," has no place. Moreover, we see here that the workman speaks to the king, whereas in *Atzilut*, the king spoke to the workman. Thus the creation of man signifies a new stage – the world of *beriah*, where God's Oneness is not manifested in a revealed way, allowing for the possibility of separation.[200]

The king – *chochmah* of *Atzilut* – replied, "It is certainly a good thing to create man, but he will sin against you in the future, for he is a fool, as it is written, 'A wise son (*zeir anpin* of *Atzilut*) makes his father happy, and a foolish son (*zeir anpin* of *Beriah*) is the grief of his mother' (*binah* of *Beriah*) (*Mishlei* 10:1). Accordingly, it is better not to create him."

But she (*binah* of *Atzilut*) replied: "Since his sin concerns only his mother – for repentance is on the level of *binah*[201] – and not his father, as the words, "the grief of his **mother** (exclusively)" imply, I wish to create him in the world of *Beriah* with **my** image only, as it is written, "And *Elokim* created man with his image. . . ." (below, 1:27), without *abba* participating.

Accordingly, as regards the latter level the world of *Beriah* it does not have image (*tzelem*), that which links his body and his soul, deriving from the configuration of the *sefirot*; **and** likeness (*demut*) – the soul as it reflect the

---

199. *Damesek Eliezer, Sulam. Mikdash Melech* interprets this as referring to our physical world.
200. *Damesek Eliezer.*
201. *Damesek Eliezer*, based on *Zohar III,* 123a. Explained in *Tanya, Iggeret HaTeshuvah* chap. 4 ff.

Infinite Light (*Or Ein Sof*), which illuminates the *sefirot,*[202] but only image, as we see from verse 27: "*Elokim* created man with his image – with the image of *Elokim*, He created him." Male and female he created them."

(*Zohar I,* 22a-b)

1:26 בצלמנו כדמותנו – With Our image, of Our likeness

The ninth commandment[203] as listed in the Introduction to the *Zohar,* is to show the poor grace, and provide for their needs, as it is written, "We shall make man with our image; of our likeness." Thus, man is commanded to emulate his Creator and strive to reflect His image and likeness, based on the verse, "You shall go in His ways" (*Devarim* 28:9; 11:22). *Sifri* (*Eikev*) explains, "Just as the Holy One blessed be He is called 'Gracious,' you should be gracious; just as the Holy One blessed be He is called 'Righteous,' you should be righteous. Expounding the verse, "Follow the Lord your God. . . ." (*Devarim* 13:5), the Gemara[204] derives the practical implication of this concept: "Emulate the attributes of the Holy One blessed be He: Just as He clothes the naked. . . . so should you; just as He visits the sick. . . . so should you. . . ."

"With our image" – refers to the wealthy, since the Holy One blessed be He endowed man with the human mold (the *tzelem*) which derives from the ten *sefirot*, and by virtue of which he is human. However, "of our likeness" refers to the poor – because we have not been granted the revelation of the Infinite Light which illuminates the *sefirot* (the *demut*), as we deduce from the following verse, "God created man with His image." – with His **image**, but not of His **likeness**. Rather, the latter level must be **earned**, by eliciting it from Above through the practical performance of the precepts. This is called charity, for the *tzelem*, which is connected to the human body, endows the *demut* with a revelation of Infinite Light.

(*Zohar I,* 13b)

---

202. *Pardes Rimonim, sha'ar* 31, chap. 4; *Shnei Luchot HaBrit, "Beit Yisrael,"* p. 6c; *Nefesh HaChaim, sha'ar* 1, chap. 1. See Rashi, *Bereishit* 1:26.

203. This is also one of the positive commandments as listed by Maimonides in *Sefer HaMitzvot, aseh* 8; *Code, De'ot* 1:5, and by *Sefer HaChinuch, mitzvah* 611.

204. *Sotah* 14a.

Man was also[205] created through the Torah, as it is written, "God said, 'We shall make man'" – the Holy One blessed be He said to the Torah, "I wish to create man." But the Torah replied, "Man will in the future sin and anger You. If You are not tolerant and forgiving, how will he continue to exist?" Then He said, "I and you together will support and sustain him – not for nothing am I called *erech apayim*[206] tolerant. Rabbi Chiyya said, "The Written Torah and the Oral Torah establish man in this world, as it is written 'We shall make man with our likeness referring to the written Torah, which is on the level of *zeir anpin* – of our image – the Oral Torah, *malchut*.'"[207]

Rabbi Yose said, "From this we understand why the verse states, 'that which has already been done **by them**' (*Kohelet* 2:12) is in the plural, for this refers to image (*tzelem*) and likeness (*demut*). "Image" – the male aspect; "likeness" – the female aspect. And therefore, the Torah begins with the letter ב – which is the second letter of the Hebrew alphabet, and has the numerical equivalent of 2, alluding to these two aspects, male and female.

(*Zohar III,* 35b)

1:27 ויברא אלקים את האדם בצלמו – God created man with His image

Rabbi Eliezer and Rabbi Akiva were traveling together. Rabbi Akiva said, "My master, explain to me why after the verse, "We shall make man," it does not state ויהי כן – "This immediately took place" or "and it was so?" On all the other days of creation, when the Holy One blessed be He voiced one of the ten utterances through which the world was created[208] it states right afterwards, "This immediately took place" or "and it was so." Here, however, after it states, "We

205. The previous paragraph of the *Zohar* explains that the world was also created through the Torah. See the commentary to verse 1:1above.

206. *Shemot* 34:6.

207. See *Patach Eliyahu, Intro. Tikkunei Zohar.*

208. *Avot* 5:1.

shall make man," it is written "God created man. . . ." Shouldn't it have stated, "This immediately took place?"

"Akiva," Rabbi Eliezer replied, "Is this the only instance throughout the creation where an utterance is not followed by the statement, "This immediately took place?" Is it not written, "God said, 'There shall be sky between the waters. . . ." (above, 1:6) – and it does not subsequently state, "This immediately took place," but rather, "God made the sky" (1:7). Similarly, regarding the utterance "There shall be luminaries in the expanse of the sky. . . . giving light upon the earth" (1:14-15), it should also have said, "This immediately took place." Instead it is written "God made the two great luminaries". (1:16). However, this is to inform you that regarding anything which does not have the aspect of being emanated from Above, it states "This immediately took place," for the earth brought them forth as soon as they had been completely formed, and there was no need to wait for an emanation from Above to complete its formation. But anything which the earth produced, whose existence was not complete, had to wait until the power from Above would establish it and complete it. So too here in our verse regarding man – the earth produced whatever it could, and it remained that way until He gave what only He can give. For this reason the verse does not say right afterwards "This immediately took place," for there was a delay until the Holy One blessed be He gave him life from above, thus bringing him into being.

(*Midrash HaNe'elam, Zohar Chadash* 16d)

The following selection explains the apparent contradiction between the two verses, "We shall make man with our image, of our likeness," and "God created man with His image."

Rabbi Shimon the holy lamp asked *Raya Mehemna*[209]: Since verse 26 states, "We shall make man with **our** image. . . ." what is the

---

209. Rabbi Shimon bar Yochai is often referred to as "the holy lamp." *Raya Mehemna* is the soul of Moses to whom R. Shimon addressed many questions (*Ziv HaZohar*).

meaning of what it states in verse 27, "God created man with **His** image?"[210] He replied, "As the masters of the *Talmud* have explained it – some angels said, 'Let him be created,' and others said 'Let him not be created.' But the Holy One blessed be He alone, created him, as it states, '**God** created man with His image.' And He created him replete with all powers, i.e. embracing all the powers which derive from the ten *sefirot*, whereas each angel derives from one *sefirah* only and He set him to rule over everything. Had each one of the angels granted man the aspect which each of them possessed, had they become angry with him, each of them would have taken back his aspect. However, the Holy One blessed be He created man with His image, which is the holy attribute of *malchut*,[211] which is the representation of all of the nine *sefirot* which precede it, because all of them pour their light into *malchut*.[212] Regarding it the verse states, "At the image of God he gazes" (*Bamidbar* 12:8 – referring to Moses). For it was upon this image which God Himself gazed and then created the world, together with all the creations in the universe. And He included the higher worlds and the lower worlds within it, without any separation at all. It is that which binds all together, and is the completion of everything, and through it is fulfilled, "His kingdom – *malchuto,* a derivative of the word *malchut* – is over all dominions" (*Tehillim* 103:19).

Rabbi Shimon said: "Certainly no one can remove his aspect from man, for no created being gave him anything. Rather, he was created by the First Cause alone.[213] And upon Him alone does man's reward and punishment depend,[214] not on any of the categories of angels. For this reason the masters of the Talmud have said that one who mentions the Name of Heaven in conjunction with something

---

210. Explained according to *Ziv HaZohar.*

211. The tenth and final *sefirah*, identified with the *Shechinah*, the immanent aspect of the Divine Presence, and the source of all souls. See *Introduction.*

212. *Ziv HaZohar.* See *Zohar I,* 181a, 249b, 251b; *II,* 245b; *Tikkunei Zohar, Tikkun* 44, p. 82b. See also *Eitz Chaim, sha'ar* 6, chap. 5, and *sha'ar* 8, chap. 5.

213. This subject is discussed at length in *Tanya – Igeret HaKodesh* chap. 20.

214. See the eleventh of Maimonides' *Thirteen Principles of Faith.*

else is uprooted from the world.[215] Happy is the lot of he who makes every effort in this final exile to cleave to the holy *Shechinah*, to give the Divine Presence honor by fulfilling the *mitzvot*. He experiences distress, but nevertheless remain faithful to God.

(*Raya Mehemna – Zohar III,* 238b; *Hashmatot* 252a)

1:28 ויאמר להם אלקים פרו ורבו – God said to them: Be fertile and produce many offspring

This is a commandment to occupy oneself in this world with producing offspring; that is, to give birth to descendants who will fulfill the task of spreading the knowledge of God's Holy Name in every direction (for this is the purpose of man's existence[216]) by gathering souls from their source above and bringing them down to this world. In this way, the glory of God is revealed both Above and below. Conversely, anyone who does not occupy himself with this precept reduces the image (*tzelem* – the divine mold which connects his soul and body) of his Master, by preventing it from being manifested in this world. Thus he prevents the *Shechinah* the immanent revelation of Godliness within this world from dwelling in this world. For according to the increase in souls in this world, so is the honor of the King increased, as it is written, "In the multitude of people is the King's glory, but in the lack of people is the downfall of the prince" (*Mishlei* 14:28). "The King's glory" is drawn down into this world as divine radiance when this commandment is fulfilled, whereas "the downfall of the prince" indicates a reduction of the King's *tzelem* in this world, and also Above. This divine radiance does not descend when conception is avoided or prevented, and one who does this (who avoids or prevents conception) is regarded as if having spilled blood.[217] Therefore, man is obligated to occupy himself with producing offspring in order to manifest the Divine *tzelem*.

(*Raya Mehemna – Zohar I, Hashmatot* para. 38)

---

215. *Sukkah* 45b; *Sanhedrin* 63a.
216. *Zohar II,* p. 42a, b.
217. See *Bereishit* 38:7 ff., regarding Er and Onan.

1:31 וירא אלקים את כל אשר עשה והנה טוב מאד – God looked over all that He had made, and indeed it was very good

Rabbi Shimon said: The verse states, "**Everything** that He had made," without qualification. This implies that everything is included in the statement – even snakes, scorpions and mosquitoes, and even those creatures which appear to be harmful for the world. Regarding all of them it is written, "and indeed it was very good." All of them have their purpose in this world; and in the way this world is conducted, even though man is not aware of it, as the *Zohar* states elsewhere,[218] "the Holy One blessed be He did not create a single thing for nothing". Moreover, "Everything which the Holy One blessed be He created, He created for His glory."[219]

(*Zohar III*, 107a)

Rabbi Akiva said: Everything which the Holy One blessed be He does is so that we can learn great wisdom from it, as it states, "All that God has made is for His sake" (*Mishlei* 16:4) – i.e., for the sake of knowing Him. This is the purpose of man's existence,[220] as explained previously. Rabbi Elazar derived this from our verse, as it is written, "God looked over all that He had made, and indeed it was very good." What is the meaning of "**very** good?" That it is beneficial to learn supernal wisdom from it. Commentaries[221] explain that by meditating on the infinite variety of created beings, as the verse states, "How manifold are Your works, O God" (*Tehillim* 104: 24), and that each created being has its source in a higher spiritual level, and each higher level in turn, derives from an even higher level, and so on. As the verse states, "How great are Your Works O God" (*Tehillim* 92:6), a person can come to a deep appreciation and understanding of the Creator.[222]

(*Zohar II,* 15b)

---

218. *Zohar I,* 23a. See also *Shabbat* 77b; *Bamidbar Rabbah* 18:18.
219. *Shemot rabbah* 17:1; *Shir HaShirim Rabbah* 3:10.
220. As stated explicitly in *Zohar II*, 42a-b.
221. *Or Yakar*; *Or HaChamah.*
222. Cf. Maimonides, *Code, Yesodei HaTorah* 4:12.

The following extract gives two additional reasons for the words "very good."

"And indeed it was very good" – "God saw that it was good" was not said on the second day of creation, because that is when death was created. However, this fact was now rectified, by the verse stating that "it was **very** good" – which refers to death, according to the interpretation of the *chevraya* (Rabbi Shimon's group of colleagues and disciples). Accordingly, the statement "it was good," is appropriate for the second day as well, even though death was created on that day, because on the sixth day it was revealed that death is not only good, but **very** good.[223] Why so? Because everyone knows that they will die eventually and return to dust. And many repent and return to their Master, and are afraid to sin before Him, due to the fear of death. Many fear the King because this strap hangs before them, and it makes them into good and upright people, and they mend their ways properly. Therefore, death is called **very** good.

The following secret, veiled in mystery, we learned from the "holy lamp" – Rabbi Shimon bar Yochai:[224] "And indeed it was good" – this is the angel of life; "**very** good" – the angel of death, who is even more important than the angel of life.[225] Why so? Because when the Holy One blessed be He created the world, everything was created flawless before man, the king of this world, came along. When man was created, he was also established in the way of truth, as it is written, "God created man upright i.e., righteous, but they sought out many schemes" (*Kohelet* 7:29) – He made him untainted, but then man sinned, and was driven out of *Gan Eden* (the Garden of Eden). What is the Garden of Eden? *Gan Eden* on earth was among those things which the Holy One blessed be He planted, as it states (*Bereishit* 2:8): "The Lord God (ה' אלקים) planted a Garden in Eden of old." "Planted" in this context may be understood metaphorically – signifying God's instruction to Adam[226] when He placed him in *Gan Eden* – "to

223. *Sulam.*
224. *Ziv HaZohar.*
225. *Sulam.*
226. See *Zohar I,* 216a.

work it and guard it" (ibid. 2:15), referring to the positive and negative commandments – "work it" and "guard it," respectively,[227] so that it would grow and produce fruits.[228] He planted it with His complete Name ה' אלקים – the former of the two Names, the four-letter Tetragrammaton, signifies the eternal, transcendent revelation of God, incorporating past, present and future. The latter signifies the immanent revelation of God within creation,[229] so that *Gan Eden* on earth is like *Gan Eden* Above, in the higher worlds, since all the supernal formations of the *sefirot* in the higher worlds are also woven and depicted in *Gan Eden* below. That is where the *Keruvim* ("cherubs" – a category of angels which guard the entrance to *Gan Eden)* are. Now these are not the man-made *Keruvim* on the Ark (see *Shemot* 25:18) formed of gold or of some other substance. Rather, they are all entirely supernal illuminations engraved and formed in a skillful interlacing of the letters of the complete Name of God. Everything i.e., every created being in the world below is engraved there. All forms and representations[230] in this world are all depicted, engraved and carved out there, just the way are here below.[231] Now this place *Gan Eden* is the dwelling place of holy souls, whether those which have already descended to this world, or those which do not descend to this world, as well as those which will descend to this world in the future. All of them are souls which are clothed in "garments" and "bodies" which have "countenances" just like in this world. Elsewhere,[232] the *Zohar* explains that these "garments" and "bodies" which have "countenances" are formed by the precepts a person performs in this world – they enwrap his soul before it enters *Gan Eden*. By virtue of this "body" or "garment" souls enter the Divine Presence and gaze upon the glory of their Master, until they descend to this world. As soon as they leave that place, in order to come to this world, those souls divest themselves of the "body" and "garment" of *Gan Eden*, and are clothed in a body and garment of this world – the physical body, regarding which it states, "You

---

227. *Zohar II*, 165b.
228. Cf. *Zohar II*, 4a.
229. See *Pardes, sha'ar* 19, 20. See our *Introduction*.
230. The inhabitants of the lower worlds are merely reflections and representations of spiritual formations in the upper worlds. See *Introduction*.
231. Since this world is a reflection of the world above.
232. *Zohar II*, 210a-b, 229a-b; *III*, 169a. See also *Pardes, sha'ar* 31, chap. 7; cf. *Bereishit Rabbah* 19:6.

have clothed me in skin and flesh" (*Job* 10:11). They then make their dwelling in this world in this garment and body that comes from a putrid drop.[233]

When the time comes for the soul to leave this world, it does not depart until the angel of death strips off this garment and body of flesh and blood. As soon the body is stripped away from the soul by the angel of death, the soul is clothed in the other garment in *Gan Eden*, of which it was stripped when it descended to this world. The soul has no joy other than when it is in its spiritual garment in *Gan Eden*, and it delights in the fact that it has been stripped of the worldly body, to be clothed in the other complete body in *Gan Eden*. By way of this spiritual body it goes and gazes upon the Divine Presence to learn the supernal mysteries, which it cannot know and gaze upon in this world in the physical body. Now when the soul becomes clothed in the spiritual garment of that world – *Gan Eden* – what pleasure and delight it has there. And who caused the soul to become clothed in its spiritual "body" in *Gan Eden?* The one which stripped it of the garments of this world – the angel of death. Accordingly, the angel of death is **very** good! The Holy One blessed be He does His creatures a kindness by not stripping man of his worldly garments until he has provided other better and more precious garments for himself in *Gan Eden*.

(*Zohar I*, 47a; *II*, 149b-150a)

"God looked over all that He had made, and indeed it was very good." The words "looked over" imply that God saw that they were good only after He created them. Accordingly, we must ask did He not see them previously even before He created them? The answer is that of course the Holy One blessed be He saw everything before He created it and afterwards also. Nevertheless, the verse states, "God looked over all that He had made" to inform us that this includes all generations that would follow afterwards, as well as everything which would be brought anew into the world in every generation, even before they came into being in this world. "That He **had** made," in the past tense, refers to the

233. A drop of semen. Cf. *Avot* 3:1.

entire work of the six days of creation – during these six days the foundations and roots of everything which would be brought into the world anew at some point in the future were already created. For "there is absolutely nothing new under the sun" (*Kohelet* 1:9). The basic foundations for everything which would ever exist were created during the six days of creation, and any apparently new being is simply a new combination of these basic elements, which were created by God according to His decision as to what would exist at any time in the future.[234] For this reason, the Holy One, blessed it He, looked over the entire creation before it existed and prepared everything during the six days of creation.

(*Zohar I,* 47a)

Since the entire creation was for the sake of Israel and the Torah, the laws of nature may be suspended for them.

Everything which the Holy One blessed be He created was created conditionally. On the first day He created the heavens on condition that they would raise the Prophet Elijah aloft in a whirlwind as he passed away from this world. So it was, as is written, "And Elijah soared aloft by a whirlwind into heaven" (*II Melachim* 2:11). On that same day He created light on condition that the sun would be completely obscured for three days during the plague of darkness which struck Egypt, as it is written, "And there was thick darkness upon all the land of Egypt for three days" (*Shemot* 10:22).

On the second day He created the firmament to divide between water and water. The Holy One blessed be He made this conditional; as long as water would also separate between spiritual impurity and purity. And so it was. . . .

On the third day, He brought forth dry land from the water, and gathered the waters together. From the waters which were gathered into one place He made the sea. But He made a pact with the sea that it would allow the Israelites to pass through on dry land and drown the Egyptians who tried to do likewise (*Shemot* 14:15 ff). So it was, as is written: "The sea returned in full force (לאיתנו)" (ibid. 14:27).

---

234. *Ziv HaZohar.*

Do not read "in full force" (לאיתנו) but, "to its pact" (לתנאו) which the Holy One blessed be He made with the work of creation. He also made a pact with the earth; that it would open up and swallow Korach and his entire company when they mutinied against Moses. So it was, as is written, "The earth opened its mouth and swallowed them. . . ." (*Bamidbar* 16:32).

On the fourth day He created the sun, the moon and the stars. He made a pact with the sun that it would stand still in the middle of the sky in the days of Joshua, as it is written, "And the sun stood still in the middle of the sky" (*Yehoshua* 10:13). He also made a pact with the stars to wage war against Sisera, as is written, "the stars in their course fought against Sisera" (*Shoftim* 5:20).

On the fifth day God created the fish of the sea and the birds of the sky. He made a pact with the birds that crows would feed Elijah when the land was wracked by drought and famine because rain and dew had not fallen for a long time as it is written, "I have commanded the ravens to sustain you there" (*I Melachim* 17:5-6) "I **have** commanded" in the past tense, i.e., at the beginning of creation. Likewise He made a pact with the fish of the sea that a fish would appear to swallow Jonah, and then spit him out (*Yonah* 2:1 ff).

On the sixth day He created man and made a pact with him that a woman would be formed from him who would provide for Elijah's needs, as it is written, "See, I have commanded a widow there to provide you with food" (*I Melachim* 17:9). "I **have** commanded" in the past tense – from the day the world was created! So too, regarding every event that takes place in the world – the Holy One blessed be He planned it from the day the world was created.

(Zohar II, 198b ff)

1:31 יום הששי – The sixth day

What is different about the sixth day in that it states, "**the** sixth day" (הששי), with a *hei* prefix (..ה), indicating the definite article, whereas on all the other days it does not state "**the** first day, the second day, etc.?" Elsewhere,[235] the *Zohar* explains that the letter *hei* represents the *sefirah* of *malchut*, i.e., the Divine power through which the world was created and continues to exist.[236] Nevertheless, malchut "has no light of its own" – its light is entirely from the nine *sefirot* above it.[237] It is therefore termed a "female," or receptive, attribute. Here on the sixth day, when the world was completed, the female pairs with the six male *sefirot* of *zeir anpin* to form one unit[238] – *hei* with *vav* (the numerical value of *vav* is six, signifying the six *sefirot* of *zeir anpin*). For this reason, the following verse (2:1) states, "The heavens (*zeir anpin)* and the earth (*malchut*). . . . **were completed** (ויכולו)." They were completed to perfection and everything, i.e., all of creation, was now finished. The word ויכולו ("they were completed") has three interpretations: The **entire** process of creation was finished, in such a way that each created being **incorporated** every other being, and in this way together they formed a **perfect whole**.[239]

(*Zohar I,* 47a)

Why does הששי have an additional *hei* indicating the definite article? Because wherever a *hei* is written it alludes to *Knesset Yisrael*, the collective souls of the Jewish people, which come to attach themselves to

---

235. See *Zohar III, Raya Mehemna,* 122a; *Tikkunei Zohar, Tikkun* 19, p. 40b; *Zohar Chadash*, p. 11a.
236. See also *Menachot* 29b.
237. *Zohar I,* 181a, 249b, 251b; *II,* 245b; *Tikkunei Zohar, Tikkun* 44, p. 82b. See also *Eitz Chaim, sha'ar* 6, chap. 5, and *sha'ar* 8, chap. 5.
238. See *Introduction.*
239. *Or Yakar.*

their "Husband," the Holy One blessed be He which takes place on the Sabbath day as will be explained further on.

(*Zohar I, Hashmatot* 257a)

2:1 ויכלו השמים והארץ וכל צבאם – The heavens and the earth and all their profusion were completed

The following extract interprets the word ויכולו *as meaning "perfection."*[1]

"The sixth day. . . . the heavens and the earth. . . . were completed." The passive voice here implies that became complete automatically, with the conclusion of the process of creation. If you ask, doesn't it state (below, 2:2) "**God** completed the creation on the seventh day?" i.e., that they were not, in fact, complete until **God** completed them this is certainly the case for although all of the individual acts of creating the entire world were finished, the world as a whole was not **perfect** until the seventh day came. When the seventh day came, then all the work was complete and perfect, and with it – the Sabbath – the Holy One blessed be He perfected[2] the universe. That is why it states, "**God** completed His work on the seventh day." Thus we learn that nothing in creation was **perfect**, even though it was **complete**, until God perfected it, since "You are the perfection of all things."[3]

(*Zohar II,* 222b)

"Were completed" – the work above, of constructing the higher worlds, and the work below, of constructing the lower worlds, which are called "the heavens" and "the earth" respectively was complete.[4]

Rabbi Shimon explained that the word "heavens" alludes to the completion of the Written Torah;[5] the word "earth" alludes to the completion of the Oral Torah; and the words "and all their profusion"

---

1. See *Or Yakar* vol. 2, 94a
2. Ibid. 97b
3. See *Patach Eliyahu, Tikkunei Zohar, Introduction*: "אנת הוא שלימו דכלהו".
4. *Sulam*.
5. Cf. "From the heavens He made you hear His voice" (*Devarim* 4:36).

allude to the details of the Torah, the facets of the Torah, i.e., the accepted interpretations of the Torah, which are called "the seventy facets of the Torah."[6] "Were completed" – each established and perfected the other, for the Oral Torah gives the explanation and instruction in the practical application of the Written Torah. "The heavens and the earth" – a specific case followed by a general rule,[7] and just as when a specific case is followed by a general rule,[8] the general rule embraces only that which is embraced by the specific case, so too, there is nothing on earth other than that which is in the heavens, and everything on earth is merely a replica of what is found above in the heavens.[9] "And all their profusion" – the secrets of Torah.

(*Zohar I,* 47b)

The following extract also interprets the word ויכולו *as meaning perfection*

Rabbi Elazar began speaking: "How great is Your goodness which "You have set aside for those who fear You, which You have made for those who trust in You in the full view of other men" (*Tehillim* 31:20). See how the Holy One blessed be He created man in this world, and set him up in such a way that he can serve Him in every way, and make his ways just and righteous. All this is only out of His goodness so that man will merit the supernal light which the Holy One blessed be He concealed for the righteous,[10] as it states, "No eye other than Yours has seen what God will do for those who wait for Him" (*Yeshayahu* 64:3, Commentaries). How will they merit this light? With the Torah, for everyone who applies himself to Torah-study daily will be worthy of receiving a portion in the World to Come. It will be regarded as if he had built the world, for the worlds were built and perfected through the Torah,[11]

---

6. See also *Zohar III,* 20a, *Raya Mehemna; Bamidbar Rabbah* 13:15.
7. The fifth of Rabbi Yishmael's Thirteen Rules by means of which the Torah is expounded (see *Sifra*, Introduction).
8. "A general rule" = כלל, a cognate of ויכל. *Or HaChama.*
9. *Ziv HaZohar.*
10. See *Zohar I,* 31b, cited above in the commentary to *Bereishit* 1:3.
11. See *Zohar I,* 134a ff.

as it is written with reference to the Torah,[12] "God founded the earth with wisdom and established the heavens with understanding" (*Mishlei* 3:19). . . . and the more he strives in it, the more he perfects the world and sustains its existence. Rabbi Elazar's intention here is to explain that all the upper and lower worlds were created only for the sake of man. However, one may ask, "Is there a workman anywhere who builds vessels from many bars of iron only for the sake of a single pin?" Accordingly, Rabbi Elazar explains that the existence of the world is **dependent** upon man studying Torah and fulfilling the precepts, and therefore it is proper that the entire creation should be subject to his authority, as verse 1:27 states, ". . . . fill the earth and have dominion over her." Thus, He created man with a number of superior qualities, which are not found in all the rest of creation: 1) God Himself participated in man's creation: "**We** shall make man. . . . ;" 2) All the other creatures were created in their species, whereas man was created uniquely single; 3) Man was created last, when everything else had been created, so that it would all be ready for him; 4) God created man with free choice, so that he is able to fulfill the purpose of his creation – to serve God of his own free will; 5) God commanded only man to make his ways just and righteous, and not any other creature.[13]

(*Zohar I,* 47a)

2:1 ויכל אלקים ביום השביעי מלאכתו אשר עשה – With the seventh day, God had completed all His work

*Note that we have translated the word ביום as, "**With** the seventh day. . . ." not as it is usually rendered: "**On** the seventh day. . . ." or, "**By** the seventh day. . . " The explanation follows.*

Grammatically, the letter ב can have several meanings: with, on, by, in. However, in our verse, the word ביום undoubtedly means, "**With** the seventh day, God had completed." For, although each of the acts of creation were finished prior to the seventh day the existence of the world was not yet complete until the seventh day came. When the seventh day came, then all the acts of creation were completed. Thus the Holy One blessed be He perfected the world by way of the seventh day therefore the verse states, "**With** the seventh day. . . ."

(*Zohar II*, 222b)

---

12. See *Zohar I,* 207a; *II*, 221a.
13. *Or Yakar* vol. II. p. 95a-b.

2:3 ויברך אלקים את יום השביעי ויקדש אותו – God blessed the seventh day and sanctified it

Rabbi Yitzchak said: It is written here, "God blessed the seventh day," and regarding the manna which descended from heaven during the Israelites' forty year journey through the desert, it is written, "Six days you shall gather it, but the seventh day is Sabbath. On it there will be none" (*Shemot* 16:26). Rabbi Yitzchak now asks: Since food was not found on that day, in what way is it blessed? Blessing does not reside on an empty table – there must be some vessel upon which the blessing can descend, as the *Zohar* explains below.[14] He answers: We have learned as follows – all blessings above in the higher worlds and below in this world are dependent upon the seventh day, since "the Divine Presence (the *Shechinah*) rests only where there is wholeness and completeness."[15] The seventh day is the completion and perfection of the entire process of creation, as we saw from the verses and commentary above. Why was no manna found on that day? Because all the six supernal days, i.e. the six attributes above, *chesed, gevurah, tiferet, netzach, hod, yesod*, referred to as "supernal days,"[16] are blessed by it, the final *sefirah* – *malchut* and each of them receives its sustenance down below in this world from the blessing with which the seventh day is blessed.

For this reason, a person of faith must set his table and prepare a meal for Friday night, so that his table will be blessed all six days of the coming week, for blessing is not found upon an empty table.[17] Accordingly, one must set the table on Friday night with bread and food in order to draw down blessing for all six forthcoming days.

Rabbi Yitzchak said: One must **set** the table with bread and food on the Sabbath day also. According to both these opinions, **setting** the table elicits

---

14. See also *Metzudat David, Radak* on *II Kings* 4:2, 3.
15. *Zohar I*, 216b.
16. *Sitrei Torah – Vayeishev* in *Zohar Chadash*, p. 29b.
17. See also *Zohar II*, 155a.

blessing from Above,[18] similar to the laying of the show-bread on the Golden Table in the Temple,[19] not actually partaking of the meal.[20]

Rabbi Yehudah expressed a third view:[21] One must delight in that day, and **eat** three Sabbath meals.[22] This view maintains that the Sabbath loaves are not like the show-bread – it is a *mitzvah* to **eat** them., as the verse states, ". . . . and you shall call the Sabbath 'delight'" (*Yeshayahu* 58:13). The Sages of the *Talmud* explain that one delights in the Sabbath with food and drink.[23] Why should one eat all three Sabbath meals? So that by way of that day, delight and plenty will be found in the world. . . . The Sages of the *Talmud* explain[24] that the amount of a person's bread and sustenance for the entire year is set on *Rosh HaShanah,* the Jewish new year, excluding that which he consumes on the Sabbath or Festivals, for the more he spends to provide for those days, the more he will be given. However, since the Sabbath is the source of blessing, the more he delights in the Sabbath, the more its blessing will flow plentifully into the week ahead. This is the meaning of "by way of that day, delight and plenty will be found in the world."[25]

Rabbi Shimon said: As regards one who has three meals on the Sabbath – a voice comes out and announces,[26] "Then you shall delight in God" – this refers to the first meal. . . . "I will make you ride on the high places of the earth" – this refers to the second meal. . . . "I will nourish you with the heritage of Yaakov (Jacob) your father" – this refers to the third meal. . . . For this reason, the Sabbath is more precious than any other time or Festival, for everything is found in it. This is not so at other times or Festivals.

---

18. *Or HaChamah.*
19. *Shemot* 25:23-30; *Vayikra* 24:5-19.
20. It is not a **commandment** for the Kohanim (priests) to eat the show-bread – it is merely part of their reward for serving in the Temple (see *Chinuch siman* 97; *Smag, aseh* 196).
21. *Or Hachamah* explains that all three views maintain that one should partake of three Sabbath meals, and their disagreement is only in regard to what elicits blessing and plenty for the coming week.
22. This is also the view of the *Talmud* (*Shabbat* 118a), and the view accepted by the *Tur* and *Shulchan Aruch* (*Orach Chaim* 291).
23. *Shabbat* 118a; Maimonides *Code, Shabbat* 30:7.
24. *Beitzah* 16a; *Bava Batra* 10a.
25. *Or HaChamah.*
26. The following quotes are from *Yeshayahu* 58:13-14

Said Rabbi Chiyya: For this reason, the seventh day is mentioned three times here (in verses 2-3): "With **the seventh day**, God had completed His work;" "On **the seventh day** He refrained from all work;" "God blessed **the seventh day**."

(*Zohar II,* 88a)

The Zohar[27] *points out in several places that the verse (Shemot 20:11, 31:17) states, literally, "God made the heavens six days (ששת ימים)," and not "**in** six days (בששת ימים)." The verse therefore alludes to the six attributes, or sefirot*[28] *above. The seventh day, the Sabbath,*[29] *is the completion and culmination of all the days, and surpasses them all, for God's Oneness is revealed on that day.*[30]

Just as they the six supernal days, in the higher worlds merge above in the One and are nullified within the Infinite Light (the *Or Ein Sof*)[31] in absolute unity, so she – the seventh *sefirah, malchut* of *Atzilut*[32] – unites the six weekdays below in the lower worlds, by illuminating them from above with a radiance of *Or Ein Sof,* as the Sabbath day commences. Consequently all the workdays, and indeed, all the work that was done during those workdays, also become nullified and united[33] in the mystery of oneness. The sparks of holiness which are imbedded within creation and have been elevated by using them for Torah and *mitzvot* during the six workdays, now become elevated in the mystery[34] of oneness[35] on the Sabbath day where no work is allowed. Through this lower level of unity, the lower worlds become elevated to the level of **absolute** unity, as in the higher worlds, so as to be with them above – the days below are elevated to a higher level. Thus, the unity of the lower worlds,

---

27. Vol. *II,* 89b, 90a; vol. *III,* 94b, etc.
28. I.e., *chesed, gevurah, tiferet, netzach, hod, yesod.* See *Introduction.*
29. Corresponding to the *sefirah* of *malchut.*
30. In many communities it is customary to recite the first two of the following three paragraphs during the Friday evening service.
31. Rabbi Shneur Zalman of Liadi's *Siddur With Chassidic Commentary* p. 168a.
32. Ibid., p. 168c.
33. Ibid.
34. It is referred to as the **mystery** of oneness because it is a lower level of oneness than the oneness of the higher worlds, where God's Oneness is not a mystery, but **revealed**.
35. See *Introduction.*

parallels the unity of the higher worlds.[36] The Holy One blessed be He who is One above does not take His seat upon His Throne of Glory – this is a metaphor for God's revelation of Himself, as the verse (*Tehillim* 113:6) states "Who **lowers** Himself to **reveal** Himself in the heavens and on earth."[37] This refers to His revelation in the lower worlds, which does not take place until she – *malchut,* the seventh day – rises up and enters into the mystery of oneness, as the completion and consummation of creation, similar to His, so that oneness in the lower worlds corresponds to Oneness in the higher worlds. This, as we have stated,[38] is the esoteric meaning of the verse: "God is One prior to creation and His Name the life-force which brings all of creation into being and sustains it[39] is One" (*Zechariah* 14:9). The explanation of this follows:

The mystery of Shabbat is this: On the Sabbath she the seventh day, and the seventh *sefirah, malchut*[40] is united within the mystery of Oneness, so that the supernal mystery of Oneness of the higher worlds may rest upon her. This takes place during the evening prayer of the Sabbath eve, for then the holy Throne of Glory – the life-force which brings all of creation into being and sustains it – merges into the mystery of Oneness, and is ready for the holy transcendent King to rest upon it – i.e., for the transcendent revelation of God to be illuminate the lower worlds. As the Sabbath arrives, she merges into Oneness, and is separated from the "other side" – the side of unholiness, and all strict judgments are severed from her. She remains in unity with the holy light, and crowns herself with many crowns for the holy King. Then all powers of negativity[41] and all adversaries flee from her and vanish, and no other power reigns in any of the worlds. Her countenance is

---

36. *Siddur With Chassidic Commentary* p. 168d.
37. This is the interpretation of the verse given in *Zohar I,* p. 195a.
38. *Zohar II,* 134a.
39. See *Patach Eliyahu – Tikkunei Zohar, Intro. II*: "Within... is the Name, which is ... the watering of the Tree (the *sefirot*) with its arms and branches just as water irrigates a tree and it grown by that irrigation.... You water the Tree through that fountain, and that fountain is as the soul to the body, which is the life of the body." See also *Tanya, Shaar Hayichud v'HaEmunah* chap. 1 ff.
40. *Or Yakar.*
41. Literally, "wrath, anger," a metaphor for the negative forces of the "other side."

irradiated with a supernal light, the light of *chochmah*, as the verse states, "the *chochmah* of a person illuminates his countenance" (*Kohelet* 8:1). This illumination from *chochmah* is the revelation of God's Oneness,[42] which is now revealed because all the powers of severity and negativity, which prevented her from being irradiated, have been removed[43] and she crowns herself here below with the holy people, all of whom are crowned with new souls – the mystery of the additional soul[44] which every Jew acquires on the Sabbath.

Then the commencement of the prayer is to bless her with joy and radiant countenance and say, "Bless God who is blessed" (ברכו את ה׳ המברך). The word את – indicating something in addition to the main subject – referring to the Sabbath eve, which is also blessed. "Blessed is God who is blessed" (ברוך ה׳ המברך) is that which elicits the blessings from the source of life, and the place from which all streams – the life-force which brings all the worlds into being, and illuminates all of the *sefirot* – issue forth to irrigate all things. And because it is the source, the mystery of the "sign" the Sabbath is referred to as "an eternal sign" between God and the Jewish People[45] it is called "the blessed" (המברך). It is the stream of the wellspring the outflow of life-force from the Source Above into the worlds. And since they the blessings reach there, they all flow for all eternity. And this is the meaning of "Blessed is God who is blessed for all eternity" (ברוך ה׳ המברך לעולם ועד).

(*Zohar II,* 135a-b)

God created seven supernal days,[46] upon which He planted and built worlds, and that is why it is written *states, literally,* "God made the heavens six days" (ששת ימים) (*Shemot* 20:11, 31:17), and not "**in** six days" (בששת ימים). Corresponding to these seven supernal days He created seven righteous men – men of truth, who sustain these days and illuminate them – each corresponding to his supernal day. And He planted each one of these seven – in the generation that was

---

42. See *Tanya*, chap. 35, in note on p. 44b.
43. *Or Yakar.*
44. *Beitzah* 16a.
45. *Shemot* 31:17.
46. The sefirot above.

fitting for him. They are the Forefathers of the world, Avraham, Yitzchak, Yaakov, Yosef, Moshe, Aharon and David. Note that these seven saintly men have been listed in chronological order. However, corresponding to the *sefirot*, the *Zohar* arranges them as follows: Avraham (*chesed*); Yitzchak (*gevurah*); Yaakov (*tiferet*); Moshe (*netzach*); Aharon (*hod*); Yosef (*yesod*); David (*malchut*).

(*Zohar Chadash, Toldot,* 26c)

2:3 אשר ברא אלקים לעשות - which God had created to do

Rabbi Yitzchak said: When all the work of creation had been completed, God blessed them each creation and prepared them for fulfilling their allotted tasks in the world. He commanded each and every one of them never to change that which it had been prepared for, from its appointed task. He further commanded each and every one of them to produce its proper offspring, from then onward for all times. This is the meaning of the verse, "which God had created **to do**" – what does "to do" mean? To bring forth and produce according to its own type.

(*Midrash HaNe'elam, Zohar Chadash* 17a)

The Dynamics of Creation

2:4 אלה תולדות השמים והארץ בהבראם ביום עשות ה׳ אלקים ארץ ושמים – These are the products of the heaven and the earth which were created on the day that God made earth and heaven

Rabbi Elazar said: The entire universe and all of its descendants were created in one moment, in one hour, in one day, as it is written "These are the products of the heaven and the earth which were created **on the day** that God made earth and heaven." On the very same day, and at the very same hour, and at the selfsame moment everything was created.

(*Midrash HaNe'elam, Zohar Chadash* 2d)

Rabbi Yehudah bar Shalom said: On the very same day that heaven and earth were created, they produced their descendants, so that they were not deficient in any way. Although their descendants were only contained within them *in potentia*, as is clear from the continuation, nevertheless, whatever would be produced in the future was already "built in" to the creation from the very first day thereof – "In the beginning of God's creating the heavens and the earth" (above 1:1). This is implied by the verse, "These are the products of the heaven and the earth. . . ." When were these products created? "**On the day** that God made earth and heaven" – i.e., on the very same day, all the world's necessities were created. Afterwards, at a later stage, they were revealed each creation on its appropriate day on each of the days of creation.

(*Midrash HaNe'elam, Zohar Chadash* 13d)

The following extract from the Zohar explains why the letter ה *of* בהבראם *is smaller than the other letters of the same word*

The entire universe was created with the letter *hei* (ה)[47] – the final letter of the Tetragrammaton י-ה-ו-ה the *sefirah* of *malchut*,[48] and by way of it the heavens, the earth, the seas and all living things which were created are sustained, as it is written "These are the products of the heaven and the earth which were created (בהבראם). . . . "i.e., בה' – with the letter *hei*, He created them – בראם. And since the letter ה is the life-force of the worlds, if it becomes distanced from the world through man's sin for even a moment, everything would be instantly destroyed and nullified, and the universe would cease to exist.

(*Zohar III*, p. 123a, *Raya Mehemena*)

---

47. See also *Menachot* 29b.

48. As the prior paragraph in the *Zohar* states explicitly, and as found in numerous places in the *Zohar*.

If not for the attribute of kindness (*chesed*) the world could not continue to exist, even for an hour, before the severities which are aroused by those who transgress the commandments of the Torah. This is the meaning of the verse, "These are the products of the heaven and the earth which were created (בהבראם) on the day." Do not read בהבראם "which were created," but, באברהם – "with Avraham." The latter word has the identical letters of the former, but in a different order. For the world is sustained through the influence of Avraham, who personifies the attribute of *chesed*. When the attribute of Avraham is aroused in the world, all those severities. . . . are pushed away and cannot remain before him.

(*Zohar III,* 31a)

Rabbi Yochanan said: The Holy One blessed be He sealed a covenant with the world that He would create it only on condition that Avraham would live, and then the world could continue to exist in his merit as mentioned above, do not read the verse "which were created," but, באברהם "with Avraham." At the moment that He sealed the covenant with Avraham in fire, at the covenant between the pieces (*Bereishit* 15:9 ff), as the verse states, "there was a smoking furnace and a torch of fire which passed between the pieces" (ibid. 15:17), at that moment the world became stable. This is alluded to in the first word of the Torah בראשית which may be broken down into two words which have the identical letters but in a different order ברית אש, "a covenant of fire." God created the heavens and the earth so that the covenant of fire, which is the Torah, as the verse states, "From His right hand, a fiery law. . . ." (*Devarim* 33:2) could be established. Elsewhere,[49] our Sages explain that the era of Torah began with Avraham.

(*Midrash HaNe'elam, Zohar Chadash* 4d)

Before the Torah was given to the Jewish people, all creatures in the world were dependent upon the heavenly constellations (*mazalot*),[50] even children, health and wealth.[51] Essentially, the

---

49. *Avodah Zarah* 9a, Rashi; see also *Rosh HaShanah* 31a; *Sanhedrin* 97a.

50. *Mazalot* – plural, *mazal* – singular.

formations of the stars in constellations are merely a physical manifestation of the various constellations of the *sefirot* which act as channels for the life-force of this world. However, after the Torah was given to the Jewish People, they were exempt from the influence of the stars and constellations as our Sages state[52] explicitly "Israel has no *mazal*." This we learn from Avraham, for his future descendants, i.e., the Jewish People, received the ה from Avraham. Originally, Avraham's name was **Avram** (אברם), but later God added the letter *hei* to his name, which thus became **Avraham** (אברהם) (see *Bereishit* 17:5). The letter *hei* has the numerical value of five, alluding to the five books of the Torah, for the Jewish People were given the Torah in the merit of Avraham.[53] Regarding the Torah it states, "These are the products of the heaven and the earth which were created (בהבראם). . . ." – בה' בראם – He created them with the letter *hei.* He said to Avraham, "Because of the *hei* which I will add to your name, the heavens, along with all the stars and constellations which shine by virtue of the letter *hei,* since the life-force of all creation flows from it, are beneath you, and have no influence upon you. . . .

For this reason, anyone who occupies himself with Torah-study is absolved from any influence of the stars and constellations as long as he studies it in order to fulfill its commandments. However, if he does not learn Torah in order to fulfill the commandments, it is as if he did not occupy himself with it at all, and the influence of the stars and constellations upon him is not nullified.

(*Zohar III,* 216b, *Raya Mehemena*)

2:5 וכל שיח השדה טרם יהיה בארץ וכל עשב השדה טרם יצמח – All the trees of the forest were not yet upon the earth, and all the plants of the meadow had not yet sprouted

Rabbi Chagai asked Rabbi Dostai: It states "The earth brought forth vegetation, plants bearing their own kind of seed, and trees

---

51. Contrast with *Mo'ed Katan* 28a, which states that these three are dependent upon a person's *mazal* even after the Torah was given to the Jewish people.
52. *Shabbat* 156a.
53. *Shemot Rabbah* 28:1.

producing fruit, each with its own kind of seed within it" (above, 1:12). Since the earth brought forth trees and fruit, implying that it had **already** brought forth; what is the meaning of, "All the trees of the forest were **not yet** upon the earth, and all the plants of the meadow had **not yet** sprouted. . . .?"

This is indeed so," Rabbi Dostai replied, "the earth **brought forth** trees and fruit, but they did not have the ability to propagate at that point in time. Why not? "For God had not brought rain upon the earth" (2:5), and there was no mist rising up from the earth (see 2:6). Had it been so, i.e., if there was rain from above, and moisture rising from below, they – the trees and plants – would have had the power to propagate; but because rain had not yet fallen, etc. the earth did not have the power to produce plants and fruits.

(*Midrash HaNe'elam, Zohar Chadash* 13d)

The Purpose of Creation

2:5 ואדם אין לעבוד את האדמה – There was no man to work the ground

The following sections discuss the central role of man within creation.

R Chiyya began speaking: "The blossoms are seen on the earth, the time of the song bird has come, and the sound of the turtledove is heard in our land" (*Shir HaShirim* 2: 12). "The blossoms are seen on the earth" – when the Holy One blessed be He created the world, He implanted in the world everything which was necessary for it to fulfill its function as a physical world, which could but still reveal Godliness.[54] Everything was already on earth, but nothing brought forth progeny until man was created. As soon as man was created, everything was

54. See commentary to *Bereishit* 1:1.

revealed in the world – the earth brought forth its fruits through the powers with which it was endowed.

Similarly, the heavens did not give potency i.e., rain and dew[55] to the earth until man came along, as it is written, "All the trees of the forest were not yet upon the earth and all the plants of the meadow had not yet sprouted, for God has not yet brought rain upon the earth, and there was no man to work the ground." All those progeny were concealed and not revealed, and the heavens were restrained from bestowing rain upon the earth, because "there was no man. . . ." He was not there for he had not yet been created **on earth**, although his supernal form "the image and likeness of God" had already been created,[56] and everything was held in suspension for that reason. As soon as man appeared, immediately "the blossoms are seen on the earth," and all the concealed powers with which it was endowed became revealed. "The time of the song bird has come:" The activity of prayer (singing God's praises) was established, which was not the case prior to the creation of man in this world.[57] "The sound of the turtledove is heard in our land:" This refers to the words of the Holy One blessed be He i.e., the Torah,[58] and the words of the Prophets[59] which were not found in this world until man was created. As soon as man existed, everything was there.

(*Zohar I*, 97a)

Rabbi Abba said: Everything that was created in the entire universe was created only for man, and everything continues to exist only for his sake. Moreover, they were not revealed in the world even though they were needed by man, but were held in suspension until the one named "Adam" – so named because he was created in the likeness (*demut*) of the One Above – came along. This is what is written in the

55. *Damesek Eliezer.*
56. *Or HaChamah.*
57. Note that Rashi offers a similar interpretation of this verse.
58. *Damesek Eliezer.* קול התור (the sound of the turtledove) has the same letters as קול תורה (the sound of Torah).
59. *Or Yakar; Or HaChamah.*

first part of this verse, "All the trees of the forest were **not yet** upon the earth, and all the plants of the meadow had **not yet** sprouted" because the supernal form the arrangement of the *sefirot* which are reflected in man[60] had not yet appeared. This is why it states, "There was no man to work the ground" – i.e., everything was held up until that form appeared on earth.

(*Zohar III*, 48a)

2:6 ואד יעלה מן הארץ – A mist rose up from the earth

Man's submission to God, particularly through prayer and the fulfillment of His commandments, is metaphorically viewed as a stream rising from man to God. Technically, this is called העלאת מ"ן *– the elevation of the "female waters." The response from Above – i.e., the outflow of Divine benevolence, symbolized by "rain," is called* המשכת מ"ד *– the outflow of "male waters."*

Why had God not yet brought rain upon the earth? Because the activity of "rising up from the earth" did not exist as yet. The response from Above, "rain," is dependent upon the extent to which man seeks God. Accordingly, "from the earth," means from the earth below as a result of man's actions, the response is aroused Above. Come and see a practical example of this: Mist, i.e. water vapor ("female waters") first rises up from the earth, and this stimulates the clouds. Afterwards, the two (water from below- mist, and water from above – the clouds) combine, forming a single unit – the cycle of mist-rain-mist, which is necessary for life on earth. And so it is Above – the awakening must begin from below, from man seeking God. This elicits the appropriate response from Above, bringing the entire process to its consummation.

(*Zohar I*, 35a)

60. *Or Yakar*.

2:7 ויצר ה' אלקים את האדם עפר מן האדמה – The Lord God formed man of dust of the earth

וייצר has two *yuds* because God created man with two inclinations:[61] the *yetzer hatov*, the altruistic inclination to do good and to fulfill God's will the side of life, and the *yetzer hara*, the side of death. When misused, it turns into a self-seeking, and ultimately self-destructive impulse to do evil.[62]

(*Zohar I,* 27a;*III,* 46a)

וייצר with two *yuds* indicates that only now was man complete, having both right and left. This means that he was given a *yetzer tov* from the moment that he was created. Now, since the verse states וייצר ה' אלקים this indicates the he was endowed with a *yetzer hara* as well. The *yetzer tov* and *yetzer hara* are indicated by left and right, as the verse states, "A wise man's heart is on his **right** side, and a fool's heart is on his **left**" (*Kohelet* 10:2). Elsewhere the *Zohar*[63] and the *Midrash*[64] explain that this refers to the *yetzer tov* and the *yetzer hara* respectively.[65] The *Zohar* now asks: Why does man need two *yetzers*? It answers: The *yetzer tov* is for himself – it urges him to serve his Creator and gain entry into the World to Come,[66] and the *yetzer hara* for the sake of his wife, as our Sages state: "If not for the *yetzer hara*, a man would not build a home or marry a wife. . . ."[67]

(*Zohar I,* 49a)

"The Lord God formed man" – this refers to Israel – i.e., the Jewish people.[68] At that time the Holy One blessed be He endowed

---

61. See also *Berachot* 61a.
62. For a detailed explanation of the purpose of the *yetzer hara* see *Pardes, sha'ar* 25, chap. 3; *Tomer Devorah* chap. 6.
63. Vol. *III,* p. 263a.
64. *Bamidbar Rabbah* 22.
65. See also Rabbi Yitzchak Luria, *Sha'ar HaKavanot, drush "Shevi'i shel Pesachap."*
66. As will be explained in the following extract. *Pardes, sha'ar* 25, chap. 3; *Tomer Devorah* chap. 6.
67. *Bereishit Rabbah* 9.
68. Cf. *Yevamot* 61a; *Bava Metziah* 114b. See also *Zohar I,* 20b; *Zohar II*, 25b.

them with the form of this world and the form of the World to Come. For this reason, the word ויצר has two *yuds;* one signifying this world, the other signifying the World to Come.

(*Zohar I,* 26a)

Happy is the lot of the Jewish People, more than any other nation, for when God created the world, He did so only for the sake of Israel. For they would accept the Torah on Mount Sinai, after all the other nations of the world had refused it.[69] At that time they would become completely purified,[70] and be found righteous before Him.

Come and see what can be deduced from our verse: When the creation of this world was completed with the creation of the Jewish People, so that the lower worlds were just like the higher worlds, as the *Midrash*[71] states "God desired a dwelling place in the lower worlds in exactly the same way as in the higher worlds. For this reason He created man, a composite of body and soul, so that although man was placed on earth, his spiritual stature reached the highest levels of heaven – thus man contains all levels, from the very highest to the very lowest.[72] God wanted to grant the Jewish People with perfection by endowing them with a holy soul from above and a body from below,[73] so that they would unite and bind with one another – the soul with the body, and the body with the soul.[74] This is the meaning of the verse "The Lord God formed (וייצר) man of dust of the earth, the lowest possible level, and blew into his nostrils a living soul" – the highest possible level, for the soul is "part of God Above" (*Iyov* 31:2). They – the soul and the body – would bond with one another, and thus be complete as Above, where the Infinite Light is contained in vessels like a soul to a body. Thus he would be able to perfect himself by fulfilling the commandments,[75] which is possible only as a soul within a body.[76]

---

69. See commentaries to *Devarim* 33:2.
70. See *Shabbat* 146a; *Yevamot* 103b.
71. *Tanchuma, Nasso* 16.
72. *Matok MiDevash* citing *Or Yakar, Mikdash Melech,* R. Chaim Vital.
73. *Matok MiDevash.*
74. *Sulam.*
75. *Matok MiDevash.*

For this reason He created him male and female (see above, 1:27) so that he would be complete. For when is a man complete with the wholeness which is found Above? When he unites joyfully with his willing soul-mate and they produce a son and daughter.[77] Then man is whole just as Above, for he and his wife correspond to *abba (chochmah)* and *imah (binah)* above, and their son and daughter correspond to the six *sefirot* of *zeir anpin (ben)* and the *sefirah* of *malchut (bat)* respectively, thus forming a complete visage.[78] He causes a revelation below, similar to that of the Holy Name above י-ה-ו-ה the letters of which correspond to the *sefirot* just mentioned[79] which is therefore attributed to him[80] because the Tetragrammaton is not mentioned unless there is completeness.[81]

(*Zohar III,* 7a)

"Of dust of the earth." This is the dust of the Holy Land, from which he was created. More specifically – from the site of the *Beit HaMikdash*, where the Holy Temple would be built.

(*Zohar III,* 46b)

The Soul Within

2:7 ויפח באפיו נשמת חיים – And He blew into his nostrils a living soul

Rabbi Yitzchak said: Come and see that when the Holy One blessed be He created Man, He gathered dust from all four corners of the earth. He made his body from the site of the *Beit HaMikdash* below, and drew down a living soul into him from the *Beit*

---

76. See *Shabbat* 88b.

77. The commandment "be fertile and produce offspring" is fulfilled when one has a son and a daughter. See *Tur* and *Shulchan Aruch, Even Haezer* 1; Maimonides, *Code, Ishut* 15:5.

78. *Or Yakar; Matok MiDevash.*

79. *Sulam.*

80. Cf. *Yevamot* 63b.

81. *Zohar II,* 88a.

HaMikdash above.[82] This soul comprises three levels,[83] therefore it has three names:[84] *nefesh, ruach, neshamah*, just like the mystery of their source above.[85] *Nefesh* is the lowest level of them all. *Ruach* is the level of existence which has mastery over *nefesh* and animates it, since it is on a higher level. *Neshamah* is the highest level of existence among these three levels, and it has mastery over all of them.

These three levels are incorporated within man i.e., within the soul of those who have the privilege of serving their Master. Although all three levels are incorporated in **every** soul, nevertheless they are not revealed initially, until a person becomes worthy of each succeeding level through his Divine service.[86] Initially, he is endowed with the level of *nefesh,* as our verse states, "And He blew into his nostrils a living soul" – a living ***nefesh*** which is a holy means of self-restoration by which man can rectify himself. Thus, when a person purifies himself on this level, he rectifies himself sufficiently to be crowned with the next level of soul – *ruach,* a higher level of holiness which alights upon the *nefesh* when a person is worthy of it.

---

82. Cf. "The Temple below is situated in correlation to the Temple above" (*Midrash Tehillim* 30:1).

83. In fact, the soul is a single indivisible essence concealed within the *Ein Sof* – the Infinite One (*Pardes, sha'ar* 4, chap. 7). It emanates from Above via the ten *sefirot*. Thus the three levels of the soul – *nefesh, ruach, neshamah* – each derive their character and path in Divine service from the *sefirah* via which they emanate: *Neshamah* from *binah*; *ruach* from the six *sefirot* of *zeir anpin*; and *nefesh* from *malchut* (*Pardes, sha'ar* 31, chap. 1). See *Introduction*.

84. Cf. *Beresishit Rabbah* 14:9 – "The soul has **five** names: *nefesh, ruach, neshamah, chaya, yechidah.*." R. Yitzchak Luria (the *Arizal*) explains that the first three levels are connected to the physical body in one way or another., whereas the other two transcend the physical body. Accordingly, there is no disagreement between the *Zohar* and the *Midrash*. Here the *Zohar* discusses those aspects of the soul which are attached to the body. Elsewhere the *Zohar* also refers to the higher levels of soul – see *Zohar II,* 158b (*Raya Mehemna*); vol. *I,* 267a (*Hashmatot*). See also *Zohar I,* 103b; *II,* 118b, and numerous other places where the *Zohar* refers to the "soul of the soul."

85. Each of the three levels of soul also corresponds to each of the three worlds, *Asiyah, Yetzirah, Beriah* – *Pardes, sha'ar* 31, chap. 2. See *Introduction*.

86. See *Pardes, sha'ar* 31, chap. 2-3 at length.

After a person has risen to these two levels, and he elevates himself further through serving his master fully, then the level of *neshamah* (which is the most elevated level of holiness among these three), settles upon him, so that he becomes crowned with the highest level of holiness. He becomes whole and complete in every way. He acquires the World to Come and is regarded as God's beloved, as the verse states, "I will give those who love Me the inheritance of True Being" (*Mishlei* 8:21). Who loves Me?

(*Zohar I,* 205b-206a)

Rabbi Yose and Rabbi Chiyya both said: See to what extent a person must introspect and account for himself each and every day, examine his deeds and make a precise reckoning of all matters which concern him. He should consider that the Holy One blessed be He created him and gave him a supernal soul and superiority over all other creations only so that he will occupy his mind with serving Him i.e., by learning Torah and cleave to Him by way of His commandments, and not run after idle pursuits. For as Rabbi Yose said in the name of Rabbi Chiyya: When the Holy One blessed be He created man, he produced him in His image and instructed him saying, "I have created you for My sake – so that you will be the ruler and king over everything on My behalf. I above, and you below.[87] Furthermore, I will place a soul within you so that you can acquire understanding and wisdom which has not been granted to other creatures. Take care to gaze upon My glory, and be careful to fulfill My commandments. Besides Me, no one else will have dominion to the same extent as you." How do we know that God informed him of his special status, and warned him regarding the fulfillment of His commandments? Because the verse states, "Indeed, the awe of God is wisdom, and turning away from evil, understanding" (*Job* 28:28). That is, when awe of God is upon you, then you will achieve wisdom, which is above all things, since it corresponds to *chochmah*, the highest level of revelation.[88] However, when Adam saw that he was the most honored ruler of all, He forget the behest of his Creator, and did not do as he was commanded.

---

87. See *Bereishit Rabbah* 21:5.

88. See *Introduction*.

Rabbi Tanchum said in the name of Rabbi Chanilai: God made man solely for His glory, as it is written, "All those who are called by My Name, and for the sake of My glory – I created them. . . ." (*Yeshayahu* 43:7, Rashi). What is the meaning of "for the sake of My glory?" That one must make the effort to know My glory, and weigh one's actions, so that one can acquire a fitting portion in the World to Come.[89]

Rabbi Yehudah said: Every day a Voice issues forth from Above. When? At sunrise. It says, "What a pity for those who do not see My glory, and do not look into knowing and fathoming My glory. These statements can be interpreted as an exhortation to delve into the secrets of the Torah.[90]

(*Midrash HaNe'elam, Zohar Chadash* 17c-d)

This extract discusses the purpose of the descent of the soul into a physical body in this world

Rabbi Elazar posed the following question to Rabbi Shimon: "Since the Holy One blessed be He knows full well that a man will eventually die, why does He send souls down into this world? What purpose does this fulfill?"[91]

He replied: "This question has been posed to the Rabbis by several students in the following way – the Holy One blessed be He, sends souls down to this world to make His glory known, but afterwards He takes them back. If so why did they descend to this world which is full of negative forces which are liable to harm the soul? Would it not have been better for them to remain above, where they already delighted in the revelation of the Divine Presence in *Gan Eden*? What benefit is there in this descent?[92]

---

89. Regarding the concept of the World to Come, see *Introduction*.
90. See R. Chaim Vital's Introductin to *Eitz Chaim*.
91. See *Damesek Eliezer*.
92. See R. Shneur Zalman, *Likkutei Torah, Bamidbar* 2a.

However, the secret is this: The verse states, "Drink waters from your own well, and running waters from your own spring" (*Mishlei* 5:15) – from the words, "your **own** well, your **own** spring" we infer that this means the well and the spring **within you**, thus, "well" and "spring" are metaphors for levels of the soul.[93] We explain this as follows – a well does not flow, nor produce its own water, whereas a spring does. The level of sanctity of the soul above, before its descent into this world, is maintained but does not increase in and of itself. It is therefore compared to a well. When does water flow forth? When the soul achieves wholeness and completion **in this world** – i.e., precisely through its descent into this world, the soul ascends to an even higher level than it did previously,[94] so that when a righteous person[95] dies and his soul leaves the body, and rises up to the place where it is attached Above, then it is whole and complete, comprising all aspects – below and above, for the soul of a *tzaddik* rises up with all the *mitzvot*[96] he fulfilled in this world with his physical body. Accordingly, his soul is compared to a spring.

When his soul rises up, and the female aspect returns to the male aspect[97] – i.e., when the soul which was clothed in a physical body, ascends and returns to cleave to its Source above, then the water flows from below to above, and what was previously a well, now becomes a spring of flowing water. Since the Torah and *mitzvot* are infinitely higher and greater than the *nefesh, ruach* and *neshamah* themselves,[98] through them the soul is able to cleave to God on a far higher level than before its descent into this world. Then unity and oneness, repentance and goodwill are found, for the souls of the righteous perfect that aspect of the soul which descended

---

93. Compare *Avot* 2:8 – R. Eliezar ben Horkenus is compared to a well which does not lose a drop, whereas R. Elazar ben Arach is compared to a spring which flows with ever increasing strength. The *Mishnah* concludes that if all the Sages of Israel including R. Eliezer ben Horkenus were on one side of the scale, and R. Elazar ben Arach were on the other, he would outweigh them all.
94. See *Likkutei Torah* op. cit.
95. *Damesek Eliezer.*
96. The practical commandments.
97. See *Zohar I*, 85b.
98. See *Zohar I,* 24a; *II*, 60a. Explained in *Tanya* chap. 4.

below, and thus arouse love and goodwill Above, so that the soul unites with God as one.[99]

(*Zohar I,* 225a)

The Garden of Eden

2:8 ויטע ה' אלקים גן בעדן מקדם – The Lord God planted a garden in the Eden of old

Rabbi Yochanan ben Zakkai[100] said in the name of Rav: In reference to *Gan Eden* (the Garden of Eden), the verse states, "I descended into the nut-garden to see. . . ." (*Shir HaShirim* 6:11). To see what? Those occupied with Torah. Our Sages explain that this is the entire occupation of souls in *Gan Eden*.[101] In this way the souls are unified with, and absorbed into the light of God.[102]

Rabbi Yitzchak asked: "Is *Gan Eden* the nut-garden mentioned in the verse?"

"Yes," replied Rabbi Yochanan. "It is compared to a nut-garden because just as a nut is closed in on every side, and is surrounded by a number of shells, so too, *Eden* above i.e., the higher level of *Gan Eden* – is closed from every side, and is guarded in a number of ways so that none can see it; not angels, not *seraphs*, *chashmals*,[103] nor the eye of a prophet or a seer, as the verse states, "No eye other than Yours has seen. . . . *Gan Eden* (*Yeshayahu* 64:3).

Rabbi Shimon said: I was once a student sitting before Rabbi Beroka, and he said, "Now I will be worthy of the level of the nut-

99. See *Tanya* chap. 23, chap. 35. See also *Or HaChamah*.

100. As will be seen from the continuation.

101. See *Berachot* 17a; *Zohar I,* 135b (*Midrash HaNe'elam*); *Zohar Chadash, Noach* 21a, *Balak* 53b.

102. See *Tanya* chap. 41 (p. 58a), and chap. 5.

103. Different categories of angels.

garden, together with the pious ones of Israel." I did not know what he meant until I heard this explanation of Rabbi Yochanan ben Zakkai, that the Holy One blessed be He called *Gan Eden* the nut-garden, alluding to the fact that just as a nut is enclosed in shell after shell, and the fruit is inside, so too, *Eden* is world beyond world and it is within.

(*Midrash HaNe'elam, Zohar Chadash* 18a)

Gan Eden on earth is among those plantings that the Holy One blessed be He planted Himself, as it is written, "The Lord God planted a garden in the Eden of old." "Planted" in this context may be understood metaphorically, signifying God's instruction to Adam[104] when He placed him in *Gan Eden* "to work it and guard it" (ibid. 2:15), referring to the positive commandments ("work it"), and the negative commandmentand ("guard it"),[105] so that it would grow and produce fruits.[106] He planted it with His complete Name ה' אלקים – the Lord God just as in the upper *Gan Eden* above. The former of the two Names, the four-letter Tetragrammaton, signifies the eternal, transcendent revelation of God, incorporating past, present and future, whereas the latter signifies the immanent revelation of God within creation[107] – both of these levels are revealed in *Gan Eden,* and all the supernal formations of the *sefirot* in the higher worlds are woven and depicted in *Gan Eden* below. In general, there are two level of *Gan Eden*, referred to as the upper and lower *Gan Eden,*[108] corresponding to *binah* and *malchut* respectively.[109] However, in a more specific sense, the highest level of each of the four worlds is called the *Gan Eden* of that world. All the supernal forms are woven and depicted in *Gan Eden* below, and this is where the *keruvim* ("cherubs" – a category of angel which guards the entrance to *Gan Eden)* are. Now these are not the man-made *Keruvim* on the Ark (see *Shemot* 25:18) formed of gold or of some other substance. Rather, they are all entirely supernal illuminations engraved and formed in a skillful interlacing of the letters of the complete Name of

104. See *Zohar I,* 216a.
105. *Zohar II,* 165b.
106. Cf. *Zohar II,* 4a.
107. See *Pardes, sha'ar* 19, 20. See our *Introduction.*
108. Cf. *Zohar III,* 182b; *Midrash HaNe'elam* in *Zohar Chadash* 18a.
109. *Pardes, Arachei HaKinuim* s.v. גן.

God. Everything i.e., every created being in the world below is engraved there. All forms and representations[110] in this world are all depicted, engraved and carved out there, just as they are down here.[111] Now this place, *Gan Eden*, is the dwelling place of holy souls, both those which have already descended to this world, and those which do not descend to this world, as well as those which will descend into this world in the future.

(*Zohar II*, 150a)

2:8 וישם שם את האדם אשר יצר – There He placed the man whom He had formed

The Holy One blessed be He chose this place in which to reveal His *Shechinah*[112] and prepared it so that man could be there forever. God attends it, and waters it with His goodness, with the goodness which flows down from *Eden* above from the level of *chochmah* which is called *Eden*. Rabbi Chaggai asked Rabbi Yehudah: What is the need for *Gan Eden* on earth, since there is a higher level of *Gan Eden* above? He replied, "The upper level of *Gan Eden* is for the delight of the soul which is sufficiently elevated and purified to receive from the upper *Gan Eden*. But if you thought that this is for every soul, we learn that those who do not have permission to ascend above to the higher level of *Gan Eden*, enjoy and delight in that which the lower *Gan Eden* receives from above.

(*Midrash HaNe'elam – Zohar Chadash* 18b)

---

110. The inhabitants of the lower worlds are merely reflections and representations of spiritual formations in the upper worlds. See *Introduction*.
111. Since this world is a reflection of the world above.
112. See *Bamidbar Rabbah* 13:2; *Midrash Tanchuma, Nasso* 16.

2:9 ועץ החיים בתוך הגן ועץ הדעת טוב ורע – The Tree of Life in the center of the garden, and the Tree of Knowledge of good and evil

Elijah the Prophet, the Master of the secret teachings,[113] was speaking to Rabbi Shimon bar Yochai and his colleagues and disciples. He declared: "And they who are wise, shall shine as the splendor of the firmament" (*Daniel* 12:3) – those who are wise through this work of yours, which is the *Sefer HaZohar* (the *Zohar* – literally, the Book of Splendor) which derives from the radiant splendor of *imah ilaah* – the *sefirah* of *binah*, which is the higher level of repentance.[114] Therefore, those who study the *Zohar* will not have to undergo trials to test their faithfulness, for their righteousness and fidelity will shine forth from them.[115]

In the future Israel will taste of the Tree of Life, which is the book of the *Zohar,* and because of it they will leave their exile in a compassionate way. I.e., in the merit of those who study the *Zohar,* all of Israel will be redeemed from the exile.[116] And through them shall be realized that "God alone will lead him, and there is no strange god with Him." (*Devarim* 32:12).[117] The Tree of knowledge of good and evil – i.e., *kelipat nogah,*[118] the source of what is forbidden and what is

---

113. Cf. *Zohar I,* 217a; *Sanhedrin* 98a.

114. See *Zohar III*, 122a ff.; *Tikkunei Zohar, Tikkun* 6, p. 22a; *Tanya, Iggeret HaTeshuvah* chap. 9.

115. This interpretation is based on the context of the previous section which discusses the test which is administered to a *sotah* – a woman suspected of infidelity to her husband (see *Bamidbar* The analogy here is obvious – Israel is regarded as the "bride" of the Holy One, blessed is He. If they display any infidelity by defiling themselves with "strange gods," they are required to re-establish their fidelity through the trials and tribulations of exile, as the foregoing section of the *Zohar* explains.

116. *Damasek Eliezer*.

117. Cf. *I Kings* 18:21.

118. One of the four *kelipot*, or "husks" which conceal Godliness. *Kelipat nogah*, unlike the other three *kelipot*, is an intermediary between holy and unholy, between good and evil. It pertains to those matters which are permissible, but have not been commanded or prohibited. See *Introduction*.

permitted, impurity and purity, will no longer dominate Israel.[119] During the time of the exile of the *Shechinah*,[120] the principal service of man and the purpose of his occupation with Torah and the commandments, is to release and elevate sparks of holiness.[121] Therefore, the principal mode of study is the deliberation and argumentation of the laws of forbidden and permitted, impurity and purity, in order to disencumber the permitted and pure from the forbidden and impure by means of the deliberation and argumentation of the law. However, when the *Shechinah* will emerge from *kelipat nogah*, after the extraction of the sparks shall be completed and the evil shall be separated from the good, then the Tree of good and evil will no longer dominate. Rather, their sustenance will be from the side of the Tree of Life alone. . . . When the Tree of Life will dominate, the Tree of good and evil will be suppressed. . . .Then the occupation with the Torah and its commandments will not be for the purpose of disencumbering the sparks, but to achieve more sublime *yichudim*,[122] in order to elicit more and greater[123] light. This will all be achieved by means of the esoteric teachings of the Torah, by performing the commandments with the supernal intentions known as *kavanot*, which are directed towards eliciting lights from the highest levels. . . ..[124]

(*Zohar III*, 124b-125a, *Raya Mehemna*)

When man strives in Torah study and cleaves to it, i.e., even at times when he is not occupied with studying it,[125] he becomes worthy of being strengthened by the Tree of Life, for it is written "It is a Tree of Life for those who hold fast to it" (*Mishlei* 3:18). Come and see! When man is strengthened by the Tree of Life in this world, he is strengthened by it in the World to Come as well, for when souls leave this world then levels are prepared for them in the World to Come, according to their achievements in this world.

Come and see! The Tree of Life comprises a number of levels, each different from the other, and yet they are all one. For in the Tree of Life there are a number of levels, one above the other

---

119. See *Eitz Chayim* 49:2 ff.
120. I.e., the clothing of *malchut* of *Atzilut* in *kelipat nogah*. See *Introduction*.
121. See *Introduction*.
122. Unifications. See *Introduction*.
123. I.e., transcending the world of *Atzilut*.
124. *Tanya, Igeret HaKodesh* chap. 26.
125. *Or HaChamah*.

comparable to the branches, leaves, bark, the trunk and roots of a tree. These correspond to the five levels of the soul – *nefesh, ruach neshamah, chaya, yechidah.*[126] Nevertheless, all of them are the tree. Similarly, all those who strive in Torah study are rectified and strengthened by the Tree of Life. Commentaries explain that when a person studies Torah his intention should be to draw down holiness upon himself, and attach his soul to its very highest level.[127] Accordingly, each person acquires the level of soul of which he is worthy.[128]

Israel, the faithful ones, are all strengthened by the Tree of Life, and all of them are attached to the Tree. However, some of them are attached to its trunk, some of them to its branches, some of them to its leaves, some to its roots. We find nevertheless that all of them are attached to the Tree, as the *Zohar* states explicitly elsewhere – "Israel is attached to the Torah, and the Torah to the Holy One blessed be He."[129]

(*Zohar I,* 193a-b)

"The Tree of Knowledge of good and evil:" This is a mixture of good and evil called *kelipat nogah*[130] and is therefore referred to as the "Tree of Deception" intending one thing and saying another.

(*Tikkunei Zohar, Tikkun* 59, p. 93a)

The secret of the Tree of Knowledge of good and evil will not be revealed to the world by the Holy One blessed be He until the Messiah comes, but only to the *chevraya* – the colleagues and disciples of Rabbi Shimon and those who learn his teachings.

(*Tikkunei Zohar, Tikkun* 66, p. 97a)

---

126. *Mikdash Melech.*

127. *Ashmoret HaBoker* in the name of the Arizal in *Sha'ar HaMitzvot.*

128. Ibid.

129. *Zohar III,* 73a.

130. *Tanya, Igeret HaKodesh* chap. 26. For a brief explanation of *kelipat nogah*, see previous extracts. A more detailed explanation can be found in the *Introduction.*

2:10 ונהר יצא מעדן להשקות את הגן ומשם יפרד והיה לארבעה ראשים – A river emanates from Eden to water the garden, and from there on, it divides and becomes four sources

In numerous places in the Zohar, the natural order is used as a mirror for the mystical order. Analysis of the former can give us an understanding of the latter. In this selection, the river which flows forth from Eden mirrors the path of Infinite Light from the very highest sefirah downwards. It also mirrors the path of man's Divine service.

Rabbi Chizkiyah began expounding: The verse states, "A song of ascents. From the depths I called out to You, O God" (*Tehillim* 130:1). Unlike other Tehillim[131] which begin with the same words, this psalm states simply "A song of ascents," without specifying who said it. However, the explanation is as follows: This psalm is a song of ascents which everyone will recite in the future, for this song will be recited by all future generations. Therefore, the verse does not specify who said it – because it is everyone's song.

What is the meaning of "from the depths I called out to You?" This is what we have learned. When any person utters his prayers before the Holy King, he must make his request and pray from the depth of his heart, directing his heart and will with absolute devotion towards the Holy One blessed be He. This is the meaning of "from the depths I called out to You." I.e., "the depths" refers to the depths of **man**.

This interpretation is now questioned on the basis of another verse: Is this what King David was saying? Is it not written, "I have sought You with all my heart?" (*Tehillim* 119:10). This latter verse is sufficient to exhort a person to pray to God from the depths of his heart. Accordingly, why is it necessary to state, "from the depths?"[132]

---

131. Such as Tehillim 122, 124, 127, 131, 133.
132. See *Or HaChamah*.

This is what we have learned: Anyone who presents his request to the King must concentrate his mind and will upon the root of all roots, in order to draw down blessing from the depths of the well *chochmah* as it flows into *binah* so that blessing will flow forth from the fountainhead of all from the *Or Ein Sof* (the Infinite Light) which is first revealed in the *sefirah* of *chochmah,*[133] for "the *Or Ein Sof* does not become unified even in the world of *Atzilut*, unless it clothes itself first in the *sefirah* of *chochmah*. This is because the blessed *Ein Sof* is the true One who is Alone and apart from whom there is nothing. This is the level of *chochmah*[134] (which is called *Eden*[135]). And what is this Fountainhead of all? That place from which originates and issues forth the river regarding which it states, "A river emanates **from Eden**." But it is also written, "There is a river whose streams gladden the city of God?!" (*Tehillim* 46:5). Why is it necessary to reach the very Fountainhead, when the outflow from Above (the river – *binah*) comes to "the city of God" (*malchut*) via streams (the *sefirot* of *netzach* and *hod*) which are much closer to the recipient, and therefore easier to reach?[136] And yet here it states, "from the **depths**," in the plural, indicating the very deepest of all things, the depths of the well from which rivers emanate and are drawn down to bless all. However, this is the very beginning of blessing being drawn down from Above to below. Accordingly, the depths referred to in the verse are the depths **above** in the *sefirot*, not below, in man.[137]

Rabbi Chizkiya explains that the two interpretations are not contradictory, but complement each other: "When the Ancient most Hidden One, the Source of all things, (technically referred to as *Atik Yomin*[138]) wishes to grant blessing to the world, He fills and merges everything into that supernal depth. From here He is drawn and flows down that river from which streams and fountains derive, and by way of them everything becomes watered. But when does this take place? When a person prays and directs his heart and will to drawing down blessing from the deepest of all depths, with absolute self-negation,

---

133. Ibid.
134. Note in *Tanya* chap. 35.
135. *Zohar III,* 290b (*Idra Zuta*).
136. Ibid.
137. *Or HaChamah.*
138. See *Introduction.*

through deep meditation,[139] then his prayers are accepted and his will is carried out.[140]

(*Zohar II,* 63a-b)

Rabbi Yitzchak said: It is written, "A river emanates from Eden to water the garden." This river is the pillar upon which the world stands. As explained above, the river alludes to *binah,* which draws down the *Or Ein Sof* from *chochmah* (Eden) into *malchut* (the garden). Without it, the world would not be able to exist. It waters the garden, and the garden is watered by it,[141] thereby producing fruits which fly forth into the world and sustain the world and the Torah. What are these 'fruits?' The souls of the righteous, who are the fruits of God's labor. And for this reason, every night the souls of the righteous rise up to *Gan Eden*, and at midnight the Holy One blessed be He comes to *Gan Eden* to delight in them. And this is the reason for the midnight prayer called *Tikkun Chatzot.*

The question was asked: In which souls does He come to delight, those of the living or those of the dead? Rabbi Yose replied: In both – whether they live in that world, i.e., *Gan Eden,* or this world, the Holy One blessed be He delights in them at midnight.

(*Zohar I,* 82b)

Rabbi Elazar said: When the Holy One blessed be He created the world, He supported it with a single pillar. The name of the pillar is *Tzaddik*, the righteous man who is referred to in numerous places[142] as the "*Tzaddik yesod olam,*"[143] the righteous man who is the foundation of the world. He supports the entire world. He is the one who provides water and sustenance for all, as the Talmud states regarding the Sage Chanina ben Dosa

---

139. Technically, in terms of the soul, "well" is a metaphor for *binah* – meditation; the **depths** of the well, *chochmah*, self-nullification, in which state a person merges into the *Or Ein Sof.* Explained at length in *Sha'ar HaYichud* chap. 1 (R. Dovber of Lubavitch). See also *Or HaChamah*.

140. Cf. *Avot* 2:4 – "Fulfill His will as you would your own will, so that He may fulfill your will as though it were His will..."

141. This repetition is necessary in order to inform us that not only does divine energy flow down to *malchut*, but that it is also **received** by *malchut.*

142. *Zohar I,* 82a, 186a; vol. *II,* 116a; *Chagiga* 12b, Commentaries.

143. *Proverbs 10:25.*

in his generation,[144] as it is written, "A river emanates from Eden to water the garden, and from there on it divides and becomes four sources." What does "from there on it divides" mean? All the sustenance and water is initially taken by the garden, but after that it is distributed to all four corners of the world. Many are those who wish to drink and be fed from there, as it is written, "the eyes of all all Look expectantly to You, and You give them food at their proper time" (*Tehillim* 145:15).

(*Zohar I,* 208a)

"It divides and becomes four sources." These are the four *sefirot* – *chesed* (kindness), *gevurah* (severity or strict judgment), *netzach* (victory, endurance, eternity), *hod* (majesty, splendor), which also correspond to the division of the twelve tribes into four directions, three tribes in each direction. Each of the four divisions was headed by one tribe.[145] This arrangement also corresponds to the "camp of the *Shechinah*" in the higher worlds, headed by one of the angels:[146] *Chesed* is symbolized by the right arm,[147] so that at that time – when the Messiah comes and redeems Israel from exile – one who wishes to be wise should face southward, i.e., somewhat to the right of the direction one faces during prayer.[148] The camp of the angel Michael is also irrigated by it, alongside of the tribe of Yehudah (Judah) and the other two tribes, Issachar and Zevulun. *Gevurah* is symbolized by the left arm, so that at that time one who wishes to be wise should face northward, i.e., somewhat to the left of the direction one faces during prayer. The camp of the angel Gavriel (Gabriel) is also irrigated by it, alongside of the tribe of Dan and the other two tribes, Asher and Naftali. *Netzach,* symbolized by the right leg. The camp of the angel Nuriel is also irrigated by it, alongside of the tribe of Reuven (Reuben) and the other two tribes, Shimon and Gad. *Hod,* symbolized by the left leg. The camp of the angel Rafael, who is appointed over

---

144. *Berachot* 17b; *Taanit* 24b.
145. See *Bamidbar* 2:2 ff.
146. See *Zohar III,* 118b.
147. See *Patach Eliyahu – Tikkunei Zohar,* Introduction II, as cited in our *Introduction.*
148. See also *Bava Batra* 25b. Interestingly, this is cited as present day practice in *Shulchan Aruch, Orach Chaim,* 94:2, Ramah.

health during the time of exile is also irrigated by it; alongside of the tribe of Efraim and the other two tribes, Menashe and Benjamin. These are the four sources among whom the outflow from the *sefirah* of *malchut* (the garden) is divided as it proceeds from the world of *Atzilut* to the world of *Beriah*.

(*Zohar I,* 26b)

2:11 שם האחד פישון – The name of the first is Pishon

The river Pishon is to the right, corresponding to *chesed,* as explained above, and flows down to Egypt. When Avraham who also corresponds to the attribute of *chesed*[149] reached the level of complete faith, he wished to realize all those levels which are attached below in this world, so that he could bring the world closer to God[150] and elevate the sparks of holiness buried there.[151] For this reason he traveled down to Egypt (see *Bereishit* 12:9-10), for Egypt took spiritual sustenance from the right side. Come and see the proof of this from the Torah – famine is not generally found in that land, unless compassion is removed from judgment.

(*Zohar I,* 81b)

2:15 ויקח ה׳ אלקים את האדם וינחהו בגן עדן לעבדה ולשמרה – The Lord God took man and placed him in Garden of Eden, to work it and to guard it

Rabbi Shimon said: "What is the meaning of "God **took** man. . . ." From where did He take him? He took him away from the four elements regarding which it states, "and from there on, it divides and becomes four sources." He separated man from them from division and disunity and placed him in the Garden of Eden in the world

149. As the verse states: "Give *chesed* to Abraham" (*Michah* 7:20). In numerous places the *Zohar* explains that Abraham corresponds to the attribute of *chesed*, e.g. *Zohar I,* 96a; *III*, 262b.

150. Cf. *Sotah* 10b: Do not read, "Abraham called out in the name of God," (*Bereishit* 21:33), but "Abraham made others call out in the name of God."

151. *Sulam.* See our *Introduction.*

of *Atzilut* – the world of oneness and unity.[152] The Holy One blessed be He does the same thing for all men, who are created as composite creatures from the four elements – earth, water, fire, and air. When a person returns to God[153] and occupies himself with Torah, the Holy One blessed be He takes him away from that of which its says "from there on, it divides." That is, He separates his soul from the lust for them. Each of the four natural elements give rise to different negative characteristics. These are: anger and pride which emanate from the element of fire; the lust for pleasures – from the element of water; frivolity and scoffing, boasting and idle talk – from the element of air; and sloth and melancholy from the element of earth.[154] He places it in His Garden, which is the holy *Shechinah.*[155] "To work it" means the positive commandments, "and to guard it" signifies the prohibitions. If he is worthy of guarding it, he becomes the master of the four elements, and becomes a river from whom others drink. Then it is clearly recognized that he is lord and master over them.[156] But if he transgresses the Torah, then he drinks from the bitterness of the Tree of Evil, which is the evil inclination.[157]

(*Zohar I,* 27a)

Rabbi Shimon said: Come and see – when the Holy One blessed be He placed Adam in *Gan Eden*, he looked and saw from there all the secrets of the higher worlds and all forms of wisdom, so that he could understand and gaze upon the glory of his Master. . . . But after he was driven out of *Gan Eden*, the Holy One blessed be He

---

152. See *Sulam.*

153. Sin is the cause of separation and self-alienation, as the verse states, "Only your sins have separated between you and your God" (*Yeshayahu* 59:2). Through repentance a person returns his soul to its former state of unity. See *Zohar III,* 122a – *Raya Mehemna*. The *Zohar* goes on to say that *Teshuvah* does not necessarily mean repentance following sin. It also means returning to one's Source, via Torah study based on love and awe of God, whereby the soul *returns* to its highest level and cleaves to Him who emanated it. See at length, *Tanya, Igeret HaTeshuvah* chap. 5-10

154. *Tanya* chap. 1.

155. The indwelling Divine Presence, as explained previously.

156. See Maimonides *Code, De'ot* chap. 5.

157. The *yetzer hara.*

prepared all the various levels of *Gan Eden* for the souls of the righteous, so that they could delight in the radiance of the supernal glory, as befits them.

(*Zohar I,* 38a)

1:16 מכל עץ הגן אכל תאכל – Of every tree of the Garden you may eat

Since the verse states "from **every** tree," we see that He permitted him to eat from **all** of them, including the Tree of Knowledge. However, there was a condition; that he eat them together with the other trees, and not separately. For we see that Avraham, Yitzchak and Yaakov, and all the prophets ate from the Tree of Knowledge, and they nevertheless lived. But it is a Tree of Death, for if anyone takes from it on its own, he will die; for he takes the elixir of death. Regarding this the following verse states, "for on the day you eat **of it** – i.e., of it alone – you will definitely incur death," for this is "cutting down the plants" – an expression meaning making a distinction between God as He is in Himself, and His revelation of Himself in this world, as if there were two domains. This is regarded as idolatry, and is punishable by death.

(*Zohar I,* 35b)

Rabbi Shimon said: "God placed him in the Garden to work it and guard it" – what kind of work is referred to as regards all men, for the verse does not only refer to Adam?[158] This is work to perfect his soul and complete that which it did not complete in this world.

Rabbi Shimon also said: The Holy One blessed be He placed man in *Gan Eden* and gave him His Torah, to work it and keep its commandments, as it is written "the Tree of Life in the center of the Garden," and it is also written in regard to the Torah, "It is a Tree of Life for those who hold fast to it" (*Mishlei* 3:18). Hence, the Tree of Life is the Torah. But Rabbi Abba said in the name of Rabbi Chiyya: It was literally a tree, and there were actually two of them. One,

---

158. This is understood from the context.

which gives life to man, and enables him to know the good and straight path which perfects him. The other evil path destroys him. For this reason the Holy One blessed be He commanded him not to eat from the latter, lest the good be pushed away and the evil strengthened.

(*Midrash HaNe'elam, Zohar Chadash* 18c)

2:17 ומעץ הדעת טוב ורע לא תאכל ממנו כי ביום אכלך ממנו מות תמות – But of the Tree of Knowledge of good and evil you may not eat, for on the day you eat of it you will definitely incur death

The Holy One blessed be He revealed to them that on the day they would eat from the Tree of Knowledge, they would cause the destruction of the First and Second Temples. For this reason the verse mentions death twice מות תמות (literally, "die, you will die"), corresponding to the two Temples.

(*Zohar I,* 26b)

The following extract tells about Rabbi Akiva's adivce to his students before entering the Pardes[159] *(i.e., meditating on the deepest secrets of the Torah)*

Rabbi Elazar said to his father Rabbi Shimon bar Yochai: Father, one day I was in the house of study, and the *chevraya* – the colleagues and disciples of Rabbi Shimon – asked about the meaning of Rabbi Akiva's statement to his disciples, "When you come to the place of pure marble stones to the world of *Atzilut*, the world of absolute unity[160] do not say, 'Water, water,' as if there were two types of water,[161] lest you endanger yourselves, as it is written: 'A teller of untruths shall not remain in My sight' (*Tehillim* 101:7). Do not say "water, water," even though an earlier verse (1:6) states: "God said, 'There shall be a firmament between the waters, and it shall divide between water and water'" – thus forming the upper waters and lower waters.[162] Just then, a hoary-headed elder[163] descended and said to them, "Rabbis, what are you presently studying?" They replied, "That which Rabbi Akiva said to his students, 'when you come to the place of pure marble stones. . . .'"

The old man then replied, "It is clear that there is a deep secret here. But this has already been explained in the Heavenly Academy.[164] Now, so that you do not err in this matter, I have descended to you from the Heavenly Academy, in order to explain it you. Moreover, I am

---

159. The word *Pardes* is an abbreviation of the words *peshat, remez, drush, sod* – the interpretation of the Torah according to the plain meaning of the text, allusion to deeper meanings, the homiletical explanation, and the secret explanation respectively. These correspond to the four worlds, *Asiyah, Yetzirah, Beriah, Atzilut,* which are attained through the various stages of meditation. See *Introduction.*

160. *Damesek Eliezer.*

161. *Pardes, Arachei Hakinuim,* s.v. מים. A comprehensive commentary on this selection can be found there.

162. An alternative version of this passage is found in *Tikkunei Zohar, Tikkun* 40 (p. 80b), where these words are part of the text. See also *Chagiga* 14b.

163. Literally, "a grandfather of grandfathers." This refers to a very elevated level of *Keter,* namely, *Atik Yomin* – literally, "the Ancient of Days" *(Mikdash Melech).* In terms of man's soul this indicates a revelation of the level of soul called *yechidah* (*Sulam*). See *Introduction.*

164. The souls of the righteous learn Torah in *Gan Eden* from the Holy One Himself. See *Sitrei Torah, Yitro* in *Zohar Chadash* 36b.

justified in revealing this matter, which is hidden from the generation, even though this is generally forbidden,[165] since the secret has already been discovered by you: Certainly from these pure marble stones, pure water flows. They are alluded to in the letter א which is composed of three parts, the upper י (*yud* – the upper arm of the letter on the right), the lower י (*yud* – the lower leg of the letter, on the left), and the ו (*vav*) which is stretched between them, which is the Tree of Life. One who eats from it will live forever, for it is the Tree of **Life.** The upper and lower *yuds* both represent the Holy One blessed be He of whom it states, "I am first, and I am last, and besides Me, there is no god" (*Yeshayahu* 44:6). The former indicates God as He is in Himself, transcending all of creation, whereas the latter represents the immanent aspect, God as He is within creation. Both aspects are connected by the Torah, the Tree of Life, which informs us of God's inseparable Oneness in the higher and lower worlds. Thus, do not think that there are two levels, separated by the firmament. This is not true. Rather, what appear to be two separate aspects, the transcendent and the immanent, are in reality one.[166]

The two *yuds* are alluded to in the word וייצר – "The Lord God formed (וייצר) man. . . ." (above, 2:7), implying two formations; the formation of the higher worlds, and the formation of the lower worlds,[167] *chochmah* at the top (i.e., the upper *yud*, on the right), and *chochmah* at the bottom (i.e., the lower *yud*, on the left). These are *chochmah* and *malchut*, respectively.[168] And they are called the hidden supernal wisdom (*chochmah*), concealed below the supernal *keter*. *Keter* is the most sublime and hidden of all the *sefirot*,[169] and is also referred to as *ayin*, nothingness.[170] *Chochmah* is God's first creative activity, and the initial

165. Cf. *Shabbat* 88a: "Who revealed this secret which only the ministering angels know..?" *Megillah* 3a: "Who revealed these secrets to my son?"; *Otzar HaMidrashim* 181:10.

166. *Pardes,* ad loc.

167. In this context the verse is interpreted as referring to the formation of the *sefirot*, rather than to the formation of man. See *Pardes, Arachei Hakinuim* s.v. אדם; *Eitz Chaim, sha'ar* 26, chap. 1; *sha'ar* 31, *drush* 1; *sha'ar* 42, chap. 13; *sha'ar* 50, chap. 1.

168. *Damesek Eliezer.*

169. *Zohar I,* 147a; *Pardes, sha'ar* 5, chap. 4.

170. *Zohar III,* 256b. Regarding the above, see also *Eitz Chaim, sha'ar Atzilut* in the synopsis of chap. 2 (p. 11b).

momentary revelation which flashes forth from *keter*.[171] In this sense it is the beginning from which everything else derives.[172] Nevertheless, *chochmah* is not perceptible until it takes form within *binah*.[173] Similarly, to the lower worlds, *malchut* of *Atzilut* is also concealed in the process of becoming *keter* of *Beriah*.[174]

These two *yuds* – *chochmah* and *malchut*[175] – correspond to the two eyes[176] from which two tears roll down to the great sea (*malchut* in the lower worlds[177]). Why did tears roll down? Because Moshe (Moses) brought the Torah down from these two tablets, but Israel was not worthy of them and they broke and fell, causing the destruction of the First and Second Temples.[178] Why did the tablets fall? Because the *vav* of וייצר which was between them i.e., between the two *yuds*, joining them flew off. The explanation is as follows: The *vav* represents the Tree of Life, as explained above, and the two *yuds* represent the first set of the Tablets of Stone on which the Ten Commandments were engraved. When Israel had rectified the sin of the Tree of Knowledge of Good and Evil through their servitude in Egypt, the poison of the sin of the Tree of Knowledge was neutralized, and they were ready to receive the Ten Commandments. Thus they were worthy of receiving the Tree of Life, which means freedom from the Angel of Death.[179] Through the sin of the golden calf, though, what they had rectified was annulled. The Tree of Life once again soared aloft, and the blemish of the Tree of Knowledge returned. Thus they were again under the domination of the Angel of Death. The tablets which derived from the Tree of Life broke and fell.[180]

Then He gave them the other tablets of stone on which the Ten Commandments were engraved, but this time from the side of the Tree of

---

171. See *Pardes, sha'ar* 5, chap. 4; *Targum Yerushalmi, Bereishit* 1:1.
172. *Zohar I,* 15b.
173. Cf. *Zohar I,* 15b.
174. *Tikkunei Zohar Chadash* p. 115a, 117a; *Tikunei Zohar, Tikkun* 5, cited in *Pardes, Arachei Hakinuim,* s.v. כתר.
175. *Sulam.*
176. And for this reason the *Chachamim* (the Sages) are referred to as "the eyes of the community" (*Bamidbar* 15:24).
177. See *Zohar II,* 12a, *Or HaChamah; Sulam.*
178. Cf. *Lamentations* 1:16; *Tehillim* 119:136.
179. Cf. *Avot* 6:2: Do not read חרות – engraved, but חירות – freedom.
180. *Sulam.*

Knowledge of Good and Evil. Thus the Torah was given to them in the form of the permitted and the forbidden, to the right (permitted) – life, and to the left (forbidden) – death. This is called the Torah of the world of *Beriah*, rather than the Torah of *Atzilut* – which was given with the first tablets.[181]

For this reason Rabbi Akiva told his students, "When you come to the place of pure marble stones to the world of *Atzilut*, do not say, 'Water, water,'" for the Torah of *Atzilut* is absolutely unified. Do not compare the pure marble stones the Torah of *Atzilut* to other stones the Torah as it is in the lower worlds[182] which are life and death, for "A wise man's heart is on his right side, and a fool's heart is on his left" (*Kohelet* 10:2).[183] Moreover, you will endanger yourselves because the stones of the Tree of Knowledge are separated, whereas the stones of pure marble (of the Tree of Life) are unified, without any separation at all. Thus, if you say that the Tree of Life departed from them due to the sin of the golden calf, and there is separation between them in the world of *Atzilut* as well, "A teller of untruths shall not remain in My sight," for Above there is no separation between them, for what broke was only the outer garment, but not the light which they contained.[184]

(*Zohar I*, 26b)

2:18 לא טוב היות האדם לבדו. אעשה לו עזר כנגדו – It is not good that man is alone. I will make him a helper to match him

Regarding man it is written, "It is not good that man is alone. I will make him a helper to match him." Rabbi Yehudah said: This

181. Arizal in *Likkutei Torah, Bereishit,* 1a; *Damesek Eliezer.*

182. *Damesek Eliezer.*

183. Elsewhere the *Zohar* (vol. *III,* p. 263a), and the *Midrash (Bamidbar Rabbah* 22) explain that this refers to the *yetzer tov* and the *yetzer hara* respectively. See also Rabbi Yitzchak Luria, *Sha'ar HaKavanot, drush "Shevi'i shel Pesachap."*

184. *Damesek Eliezer.*

refers to the soul (*neshamah*) which is a helper to man, to lead him in the way of his Master, as we have learned,[185] "If he comes to be purified, he is helped." Our Rabbis taught:[186] When a person goes in the ways of his Master, he is given much help. His soul helps him, the ministering angels help him, the indwelling Divine Presence helps him, and all of them declare before him, "When you go, your steps shall not be restrained, and when you run you shall not stumble" (*Mishlei* 4:12). Rabbi Nathan said: The souls of the righteous help him. If a person does his utmost to purify himself, so that the very root of his soul is revealed to him, he may become "impregnated" with the soul of a *Tzaddik,* living or dead, who will help him to completely transcend himself.[187]

(*Midrash HaNe'elam, Zohar Chadash* 20d)

The verse states, "It is not good that man is alone." But was he alone? Is it not written, "Male and female He created **them**?" (*Bereishit* 1:27). Regarding this we have learned[188] that Adam was created with two aspects. Yet paradoxically it states here, "It is not good that man is **alone**." The explanation is this: He had not utilized his female aspect, so it was not his "helper to match him" (literally, 'opposite him') because she was at his side, and they were as one at the back. Accordingly, Adam was alone.

"I will make him a helper to match him" – what does "to match him" (literally, "opposite him") mean? **Facing** him, so that they could unite face to face. What did the Holy One blessed be He do? He severed the female from him and removed her, as it is written, "He removed one of his sides" (*Bereishit* 2:21). Which one? His female aspect, as it is written, "One is my dove, my perfect one (תמתי)" (*Shir HaShirim* 6:9) do not read תמתי "my perfect one," but תאומתי, "my twin."[189]

---

185. *Shabbat* 104a.
186. Cf. *Sotah* 14a; *Sifri, Eikev.*
187. See Rabbi Chaim Vital, *Sha'arei Kedushah* part III; *Sha'ar HaGilgulim,* Introduction II; *Sefer HaGilgulim* chap. 5.
188. See *Zohar I,* 2b; *II,* 55a; *III,* 117a.
189. *Zohar III,* 296a.

Then he took her to Adam, having adorned her like a bride, and brought her facing him, so that their faces illuminated each other. . .

(*Zohar III,* 44b)

Rabbi Shimon said: It is certainly the case that man was alone – because he did not have help from his female aspect since she was attached to his side. For this reason it is written, "I will **make** him a helper to match him," not "I will **create** a helper to match him, as it is written, "Male and female He created them" (*Bereishit* 1:27). This implies that they had both already been created.

(*Zohar III,* 19a)

The commandment is to redeem the first-born donkey with a lamb, or to break its neck if it is not redeemed, as it is written, "The first issue of a donkey you shall redeem with a lamb or a kid, and if you do not redeem it, you shall break its neck" (*Shemot* 34:20). This is the secret of the *yetzer hara* the self-seeking, and ultimately self-destructive[190] impulse to do evil,[191] which is compared to a donkey. The *yetzer hara* can be brought back and turned into the *yetzer tov*[192] the altruistic inclination to do good and to fulfill God's will. This is as we have explained regarding the verse, if he is worthy, "a helper," i.e., it becomes an additional *yetzer tov* if not, "to match him," i.e., in opposition to him; it remains the *yetzer hara* until he conquers it.[193]

(*Zohar II,* 43a)

---

190. See *Zohar I,* 52a.
191. For a detailed explanation of the purpose of the *yetzer hara* see *Pardes, sha'ar* 25, chap. 3; *Tomer Devorah* chap. 6 – discussed in our commentary to 3:1 below.
192. See also *Berachot* 54a.
193. As is understood from *Zohar II*, 163a.

2:19 וכל אשר יקרא לו האדם נפש חיה הוא שמו – Whatever man would call each living thing, would be its name

Rabbi Yaakov bar Idi said: Adam was wise i.e. wiser than the angels[194] for he recognized and knew how to distinguish between those who had only a living soul (*nefesh* – the lowest level of the soul) and those who had a *neshamah*, the third level of soul.[195] When all the creatures came to him, he recognized the spiritual level of all of them, as it is written, "Whatever man would call each living thing." Read this as: Man would call, "living thing" that which did not know and recognize the service of its Creator. But he named *neshamah* that which did know and recognize the service of its Creator. And so it is to this very day one who does not know and recognize his Creator, and does not occupy himself with Torah, has only a living soul, but not a *neshamah.*

(*Midrash HaNe'elam, Zohar Chadash* 11c)

2:20 ויקרא האדם שמות לכל הבהמה ולכל חית השדה – The man gave names to all the cattle and to all the birds of the sky, and to every wild beast

Rabbi Huna said in the name of Rav: The Holy One blessed be He named three things in creation – the heavens (*shamayim*), earth (*aretz*), and water (*mayim*). From which verse do we learn that He named the heavens? As it is written, "God named the sky 'Heaven'" (*Bereishit* 1:8). From which verse do we learn that He named the earth? As it is written, "God named the dry land, 'Earth'" (ibid. 1:10). From which verse do we learn that He named the water? As it is written, "and the gathering of water He named 'Seas'" (ibid). Why did He Himself name them? So that He could do all His work with them, for everything else was a product of these three, as the previous section of the *Zohar* explains. What derived from the heavens, the earth, and water –

---

194. See *Zohar II*, 55a; *Bereishit Rabbah* 17:4.
195. See *Introduction.*

the Holy One blessed be He left for Adam to name. Thus, according to Rabbi Hunna citing Rav, Adam gave names to the fish also, for they are a product of water.

However, Rabbi Berachya said: Everything which the heavens and earth brought forth, Adam named; as it states, "The man gave names to all the cattle and to all the birds of the sky, and to every wild beast." This excludes the fish, since they are not mentioned in this verse at all.[196]

(*Midrash HaNe'elam, Zohar Chadash* 13a)

2:21 ויפל ה׳ אלקים תרדמה על האדם ויישן ויקח אחת מצלעותיו ויסגר הבשר תחתינה – The Lord God cast a deep sleep upon the man, and while he slept, He removed one of his ribs and filled in flesh in place of it

He began by citing the verse, "The Lord God cast a deep sleep upon the man, and while he slept" – when the Holy One blessed be He created *Adam HaRishon* (primordial man), He created him with two aspects, as explained in the commentary to 1:27. Technically, these are *zeir anpin* and *malchut*,[197] which were joined together, without any separation. . . . It is written, "Male and female He created them" (ibid) – without separation, for "He created **him**" is not written, but "He created **them**."

They were created as one – one equal to the other. What did the Holy One blessed be He do? He separated them, taking the female aspect from him. He prepared her in a number of ways, adorned her with a number of ornaments, and clothed her with a number of garments.[198] Now, where did all this take place? He prepared her in *Gan Eden*. With how many ornaments did He adorn her? Seventy.

196. See *Tosafot, Chullin* 66b, ה כל"ד; *Midrash Chaser VeYatir*; Chizkuni; Radak to *Bereishit* 2:19.

197. Commentaries.

198. See *Eruvin* 18a.

These are the seventy facets of Torah.[199] How many preparations did make for her? Thirteen. These are the "thirteen petals" – Rabbi Yishmael's Thirteen Rules[200] – by means of which the Torah is expounded. With how many garments did He clothe her? Six garments. These are the six orders of the *Mishnah*. . . . The Holy One blessed be He made all of these preparations, ornaments and garments in *Gan Eden,* and afterwards, "He brought her to the man" (2:22). Where was the man? In the quintessential point of *Tzion,*[201] where the Temple is. From there He took them, and brought them up into *Gan Eden*, and blessed them with the seven blessings which a bride and groom are blessed under the wedding canopy.

(*Zohar Chadash* 55c-d)

The following selection interprets the verse as referring to Moshe and the exile of the Shechinah

Rabbi Shimon said: During the exile, there is not found among them the Jewish people a helper for the *Shechinah* (the Divine Presence, technically, *malchut*), nor for Moshe, who is with her the *Shechinah*. For throughout the exile, he does not depart from her.

Rabbi Elazar, Rabbi Shimon's son, said: "How can one interpret matters relating to Adam as referring to Moshe and the Israelites?"

He replied: "My son, how can you say that? Didn't we learn the verse, ". . . .declaring the end from the beginning?" (*Yeshayahu* 46:10) That is, everything which will take place in the future, at the end of days, is alluded to at the very beginning of man's creation. "This is certainly so," Rabbi Elazar replied.

---

199. See also *Bamidbar Rabbah* 13:15.

200. *Sifra, Introduction.*

201. Throughout Scripture, this term is used as one of the names of the land of Israel in general, and of Jerusalem in particular. See *Shabbat* 139a; *Rosh HaShanah* 23a; *Sanhedrin* 98a; *Midrash Tehillim* 9:8 Technically, the *Zohar* explains this term in two ways – it signifies *malchut*; or it signifies *yesod* – *Pardes, Sha'ar Arachei HaKinuim* s.v. ציון.

Rabbi Shimon now continues: Therefore, Moshe did not die,[202] rather, he is with the *Shechinah* in exile, and he is called Adam, since he is "compared to (*adameh*) the One above,"[203] because he perfected himself during his lifetime, and rectified the sin of Adam which brought death into the world. Accordingly Moshe did not die.[204] The verse refers to him, stating that during the final exile, after the destruction of the Second Temple, "Man did not find a helper" (above, 2:20). Rather, everything was "in opposition to him." כנגדו – "opposite him" is interpreted here in a negative sense, in the sense of opposition and conflict. (So too, regarding the middle column *zeir anpin* it states, "But man did not find a helper" to take the *Shechinah* out of exile), as it states regarding Moshe "he turned this way and that, and saw that there was no man" (*Shemot* 2:12). Thus, Moshe was in the exact likeness of Adam, regarding whom it states, "But man did not find a helper opposite him."

Then since he had no helper "The Lord God cast a deep sleep upon the man." "The Lord" (י-ה-ו-ה) indicates the aspect of *abba* (i.e., *chochmah*), "God" (אלקים) indicates the aspect of *imma* (i.e., *binah*). The name of God used here, י-ה-ו-ה the four-letter Ineffable Name of God is associated with the *sefirah* of *chochmah*,[205] also called *abba*[206] (father), and the Name אלקים is associated with the *sefirah* of *binah*,[207] also called *imma* (mother).[208]

"Cast a deep sleep upon the man." "Deep sleep" refers to the exile, regarding which it states, "A deep sleep fell upon Avraham" (*Bereishit* 15:12) at the Covenant between the Pieces, where Avraham was told that his descendants would go into exile, and He cast a deep sleep, i.e., the exile upon Moshe giving him the task of taking the Jewish People and the *Shechinah* out of exile. "And he slept" i.e., Moshe went to Egypt, where the

---

202. See *Sotah* 13b; *Zohar I,* 37b.
203. *Yeshayahu* 14:14. See Rabbi Menachem Azariah DeFano, *Asarah Ma'amarot, ma'amar "Eim Kol Chai"* part 2, chap. 33; *Shelah* pp. 3a, 20b.
204. *Damesek Eliezer.*
205. *Zohar III*, 255b.
206. *Zohar III*, 290a.
207. *Zohar I,* 2a; *Zohar III*, 275b.
208. *Zohar III*, 65a, 290a.

Jewish people had been enslaved. "Sleep" always signifies exile[209] for just as in sleep, the intellectual faculty is suspended; so too, during the exile the aspect of intellect is not manifested among the Jewish people[210] until Moshe comes to redeem them.

(*Zohar I,* 28a)

2:22 ויבן ה׳ אלקים את הצלע אשר לקח מן האדם לאשה ויבאה אל האדם – The Lord God built a woman from the rib that He had taken from man, and He brought her to the man

Rabbi Shimon said: "Here we learn that the father and mother of the bride must bring her into the domain of the groom. Of the two Divine Names used here, י-ה-ו-ה is associated with the *sefirah* of *chochmah,*[211] also called *abba*[212] (father), and אלקים is associated with the *sefirah* of *binah,*[213] also called *imma* (mother).[214] When a bride and groom are brought to the wedding canopy, the father and mother of the bride bring her to the groom, reflecting the Divine order. This is still the practice at Jewish weddings.[215] As it is written, "I gave my daughter to this man as a wife" (*Devarim* 22:16). But from this point on, a man comes to his wife,[216] for their home is her domain, as it is written, "and he came to her" (*Bereishit* 29:23, 30:4); "He came also to Rachel" (*ibid* 29:30). Initially, i.e., under the wedding canopy, she is brought to him as we learn from our verse. Consequently, it is the obligation of the father and mother of the bride to do this. But subsequently he comes to her as we learn from the latter verses.

(*Zohar I,* 49a)

---

209. See *Bereishit Rabbah* 17:5, 44:17.
210. *Sulam.*
211. *Zohar III,* 255b.
212. *Zohar III,* 290a.
213. *Zohar I,* 2a; *Zohar III,* 275b.
214. *Zohar III,* 65a, 290a.
215. *Likkutei Mahariach, Seder Nisuin; Sefer Matamim* s.v. חתן וכלה para. 75; *Matamim Hechadash* para. 48.
216. *Shulchan Aruch,*

2:23 זאת הפעם עצם צעצמי ובשר מבשרי – This time the bone is of my bone, and the flesh is of my flesh

See how pleasantly Adam spoke to her, in order to attract her with love, and draw her towards his will, and arouse love in her. Look how beautiful these words are, and what love they express: "The bone is of my bone, and the flesh is of my flesh." Thus he showed her that they were one, without any split or discord between them in any way. Now he began to praise her: "Therefore, she will be called 'Woman.' She is without peer, the beauty of the home; beside her, all others are like apes before man; she is the perfection of all; she is the one and no other." All these are expressions of love, as it states, "Many daughters have done well, but you surpass them all" (*Mishlei* 31:29). For this reason, "a man leaves his father and mother, and bonds with his wife, and they become one flesh." (2:24)

(*Zohar I,* 49b)

The double expression indicates two levels: "The bone is of my bone," refers to the light of "the luminous mirror," the highest level of prophecy;[217] and "the flesh is of my flesh" refers to the garments Torah and *mitzvot* in which My supernal light is clothed[218]

(*Zohar Chadash* 55d)

---

217. *Pardes Arachei HaKinuim* s.v. אספקלריא; Arizal's *Sha'ar Ruach HaKodesh* 2a, and *Sha'ar HaMitzvot* 18b. This refers to *tiferet.*

218. *Mitzvahs* done in this world enwrap the soul like a garment, enabling it to enter the Divine Presence. *Zohar II,* 210a-b, 229a-b, vol. *III,* 169a. See *Pardes, sha'ar* 31, chaps. 7, 11. The *sefirah* referred to here is *malchut.*

The Sin

3:1 והנחש היה ערום מכל חית השדה – Now the serpent was the most cunning of all the wild beasts

The serpent: Rabbi Yitzchak said: This is the *yetzer hara* – the self-seeking, and ultimately self-destructive[1] impulse to do evil,[2] as explained in the commentary to 2:7. Rabbi Yehudah said: This was an actual serpent. When they came before Rabbi Shimon, he said to them: They are certainly one and the same thing, for this was Samael, who makes his appearance riding on a serpent. The form of the serpent is Satan, which is the *yetzer hara* which entices man to sin, and afterwards rises up before the Heavenly Court to accuse the sinner. Accordingly, they are one and the same thing.

(*Zohar I,* 35b)

"The serpent was the most cunning." Rabbi Yose taught: This is the *yetzer hara* which is the serpent which entices man. Why is it called a serpent? Just as a serpent slithers around in a circuitous fashion, never walking a straight path; so too the *yetzer hara.* It beguiles man to evil paths, and not directly. As our Sages state:[3] Initially, the *yetzer hara* does not tell you to worship idols, even though this is its ultimate intention. Rather, first he tells you to do some minor infringement, and tomorrow to do another minor infringement, until eventually he says, "Go and worship idols."

(*Midrash HaNe'elam, Zohar Chadash* 18c)

---

1. See *Zohar I,* 52a.
2. For a detailed explanation of the purpose of the *yetzer hara* see *Pardes, sha'ar* 25, chap. 3; *Tomer Devorah* chap. 6.
3. *Shabbat* 105b; *Niddah* 13b.

"The serpent was the most cunning." This is the *yetzer hara*, the angel of death. Because the serpent is the angel of death, it caused death for the entire world. This is the secret of the words which God said to Noah prior to the flood "the end of all flesh has come before Me" (*Bereishit* 6:11) "the one who ends all flesh (the angel of death) who takes the soul from all flesh, has come before Me."

(*Zohar I,* 35b)

The following selection discusses the benefits and hazards of the yetzer hara

Everything which the Holy One blessed be He made, both above and below is for the sake of revealing His glory,[4] and everything is for the sake of His service. But did you ever see a servant who accuses his Master? For he makes every effort to ensure that the will of his Master will not be carried out and then he becomes the accuser. God's will is that man serve Him at every moment and follow in the ways of truth, so that He can merit much good. Since this is God's will, how can an evil servant come to lay charges against his Master by enticing man to the path of evil, and pushing him off the path of good, making him act against the will of his Master, and turn him to the path of evil?

However, the *yetzer hara* certainly does the will of its Master! This can be understood by way of an analogy: A king had an only son whom he loved greatly. Because of his love for him, he commanded his son never to befriend an evil woman, for anyone who does so is not worthy of remaining in the king's palace. The prince swore that he would lovingly fulfill the will of his father.

Outside of the king's palace lived a harlot of great beauty and charm. One day, the king decided to test the prince's love for him. He sent for the harlot and said to her, "Go and entice my son, so

4. See *Yeshayahu* 43:7; *Avot* 6:11.

that I can see if he obeys me!" What did the harlot do? She followed the prince and began to embrace him and kiss him, and entice him in all other kinds of ways.

If the prince is worthy, he will obey the command of his father and rebuke her, and refuse to listen to her. Then his father, the king, will rejoice in him, and bring him into the innermost chambers, and give him gifts, and bestow great honor upon him. Now who caused him all this glory? That same harlot!

What about the harlot? Is she praiseworthy for her actions or not? Indeed she is praiseworthy in every way, for she fulfilled the command of the king, and was also the cause of the prince acquiring all the goodness and love which the king bestowed upon him. Regarding this it is written, "and indeed it was very good" (*Bereishit* 1:31). "It was good" – this is the angel of life; "**very** good" – the angel of death, which is the *yetzer hara*. It is certainly **very good** for one who fulfills the will of his Master. Come and see: If not for this accuser, the righteous would not inherit the supernal treasure-houses which they are due to receive in the World to Come.

Happy are those who encounter this accuser, and happy are those who do not encounter this accuser. The explanation is as follows: Happy are those who did encounter him refers to those who released themselves from his clutches, for because of him they inherit all the good and spiritual delight and precious things in the World to Come, regarding which it states, "No eye other than Yours has seen it" (*Yeshayahu* 64:3).

Happy as well are those who do not encounter the accuser, for had they done so, they would have inherited *Gehinnom* (hell), and would have been banished from the land of life. Those wicked people who encountered him and obeyed him, were drawn after him. Therefore, the righteous should be grateful to him, for because of him they inherit all the good and spiritual delight and precious things in the World to Come.

The question is now asked what is the benefit of the accuser when the wicked obey him? The answer: Even though there is no direct benefit; the accuser nevertheless carries out the will of his Master. Furthermore, the accuser grows more powerful because of this. Because he is evil, he grows more powerful when evil is done, just like a wicked person whose wickedness does not intensify until he kills a man. But when he kills people, then his evil grows more powerful. He become more addicted to it, and he even enjoys it! So too the accuser, which is the *yetzer hara* (called the angel of death) does not grow stronger until it entices people, accuses them, and kills them. Then it derives enjoyment in doing evil, becomes more powerful and increases in might.

Just as the side of life grows stronger when men are good and go along the straight path, similarly, the accuser becomes more powerful when the wicked obey him, until he rules over them, may the Merciful One save us. Happy are those who succeed in overcoming him and subjugating him.

(*Zohar II,* 163a-b)

Come and see: Because Eisav (Esau) was drawn after that serpent in order to receive the blessing that Yitzchak (Isaac) wished to give Eisav (see *Bereishit* 27:1 ff.), Yitzchak had to use guile, like the cunning serpent who used guile as it states, "and the serpent was ערום – cunning." Therefore Yaakov's (Jacob's) actions concerning Eisav were also cunning like a serpent. But this was necessary, so that Eisav would be drawn after the serpent and would part ways with Yaakov, and he would therefore share neither this world with him nor the World to Come. Moreover, this was perfectly legitimate, as we have learned: If someone is coming to kill you, kill him first.[5]

(*Zohar I,* 138a)

5. *Berachot* 58a, 62b; *Yoma* 85b.

3:1 ויאמר אל האשה אף כי אמר אלהים לא תאכלו מכל עץ הגן – It said to the woman, "Did God perhaps say that you may not eat from any tree of the garden?"

[The wicked Samael (Satan)] came to the woman and said to her: "Did God perhaps say that you may not eat from any tree of the garden?" Of course, he knew[6] that God had told them that they could eat freely of every tree of the garden other than the fruit of the Tree of Knowledge (as verses 2:16-17 state explicitly). His reasoning was this: I will ask about more, **adding** to what was really forbidden, so that she will **subtract**, for "anyone who adds to God's commandments actually detracts from them."[7] She replied, ". . . . of the fruit of the tree which is in the center of the garden God has said, 'You shall neither eat of it nor touch it lest you die'" (3:3). Thus she added two things:

She said, "**Of the fruit** of the tree which is in the center of the garden God said you may not eat," whereas she had been told only, "of the Tree of Knowledge," implying the entire tree and not just its fruits;

She also added, "**nor touch it** lest you die," which God had not said at all.

(*Zohar I,* 263b – *Hashmatot Sefer HaBahir* 35b)

---

6. See *Zohar I*, 36a.
7. As stated explicitly in *Devarim* 4:2: "You shall not add to the word that I command you, nor shall you subtract from it. " See *Sanhedrin* 29a; *Sefer HaChinuch, lo taaseh* 456.

3:5 ונפקחו עיניכם והייתם כאלקים ידעי טוב ורע – Your cognition will become developed, and you will be like God, knowing good and evil

Rabbi Yose said: He said to the woman, "With this tree God created the world – the world of *Assiyah*, which is the lowest world.[8] If you eat of it, you will surely become like God, knowing good and evil, and you too will be able to create[9] worlds." For this is how He created the world, and for this reason He told you not to eat from it, so that you will not become divine like Him.[10]

Disagreeing with Rabbi Yose, Rabbi Yehudah said: The serpent did not say this. For had he said that the Holy One blessed be He created the world by means of this tree, that would have been acceptable, because then it would merely have been like an ax in the hands of the woodcutter. I.e., God is the Creator of the world, but He merely used the Tree of Knowledge as a tool. However, the serpent said that God ate from the tree, and **then** created the world with the power He received from the tree. It follows that the serpent was a rank heretic, for he maintained that the power to create the world was actually possessed by the Tree of Knowledge, and from it God obtained the power to create. The serpent continued: Since every artisan hates competition, He told you not to eat from it. Regarding this it is written, "It is because God knows that on the day you eat from it. . . . you will become like God." And because He knew this, he commanded you not to eat from it.

(*Zohar I,* 36a)

---

8. *Damasek Eliezer.*
9. *Sulam.*
10. *Damasek Eliezer.* This has been translated according to the version in *Or HaLevanah.*

3:6 ותרא האשה כי טוב העץ למאכל וכי תאוה היא לעינים ונחמד העץ להשכיל – The woman acknowledged that the tree must be good for eating, and that it was enticing to perceive, and that the tree was desirable as a means to gain intelligence

Rabbi Shimon said: When the serpent enticed the woman the verse states, "The woman acknowledged (literally, "saw") that the tree must be good." But what is the meaning of "must be good?" Rabbi Elazar bar Shalom said: She **acknowledged intellectually** that it must be good.

"And that it was enticing to perceive." This is the desire which both those above the angels and those below man have to know and understand. And therefore, "she took of its fruit and ate."

(*Midrash HaNe'elam, Zohar Chadash* 18d)

The *yetzer hara* was now incited to seize her, in order to bind her to physical lusts, and arouse other such things which the *yetzer hara* delights in. Thus immediately afterwards it is written, "The woman **acknowledged** that the tree must be good for eating, and that it was enticing to perceive." This indicates that she succumbed to the temptations of the *yetzer hara* willingly.

(*Zohar I,* 49b)

"The woman acknowledged that the tree must be good for eating, and that it was enticing to perceive. . . ." When the Holy One blessed be He created man and honored him with supernal glory, He asked man to cleave to Him with a bond of steadfast faith so that he would be unique, with one heart, and attached to one place. In this way he would not undergo constant change and transformation. In regard to this it is written, "and the Tree of Life in the center of the garden" (above 2:9).

But then they strayed from the path of faith, and abandoned the one tree which surpassed all others, i.e., the Tree of Life, and they went and cleaved to the place where there is constant change and transformation from aspect to aspect from good to evil, and from evil to good, i.e., the Tree of Knowledge of Good and Evil. They plunged down from above, becoming attached to multifarious changes. Thus they left the Supernal One, who never changes, as the verse states, "I am the Lord. I do not change" (*Malachi* 3:6). In this regard it is written, "God made man upright, but they sought out many schemes" (*Kohelet* 7:29). They certainly did seek out "many schemes" – that is multiplicity, which stems from the instability of the Tree of Knowledge. And then their temperament changed accordingly – sometimes good, sometimes bad, sometimes compassionate, at other times harsh, just like that to which they cleaved. They sought out multiplicity, and it clung to them.

(*Zohar III,* 107a)

3:6 ותקח מפריו ותאכל – So she took of its fruit and ate

God had permitted Adam and Eve to eat of every tree of the garden, as verse 2:16 above states: "Of every tree of the garden you may eat freely." However, verse 2:17 qualifies this: "But of the Tree of Knowledge. . . . you may not eat, for on the day you eat **of it**, you will definitely incur death." The words "of it" indicate that something other than the tree is referred to here – i.e., its fruits, which are "**of** it." These were forbidden,[11] or were forbidden to be eaten **separately** from the tree.[12] "The woman acknowledged that the tree

11. See Nachmanides (Ramban); *Kli Yakar* to *Bereishit* 2:17. *Ashmoret HaBoker* explains the reason for this: For the first three years of its growth, the fruits of a tree are *orlah*, and may not be eaten (see *Vayikra* 19:23). However, this prohibition only applies to the **fruits**, not to the **tree** (see *Mishnah, Orlah* chap. 1). Spiritual impurity dwells on fruits which are *orlah* - *Zohar II,* 244b.
12. See *Zohar I,* 35b.

must be good. . . ." She acknowledged and did not acknowledge that it was good. I.e., She acknowledged that the tree **itself** was good, but could not decide regarding its fruits. How does the verse continue? "She took **of its fruit** and ate." It does not state, "She took of **it**" – i.e., the **tree**. Thus, she became bonded to the side of death, and caused death throughout the world.

(*Zohar I,* 36a)

3:7 ותפקחנה עיני שניהם וידעו כי ערומים הם ויתפרו עלי תאנה ויעשו להם חגורות – Then their consciousness was awakened and they realized that they were naked. They sewed together fig leaves, and made themselves loin-cloths

"Then their consciousness was awakened" to the external appearance of this world of which they were not previously aware, for prior to the sin of the Tree of Knowledge, they surveyed and perused everything from above, in the higher worlds, the way everything is in its spiritual root.

(*Zohar III*, 261b)

"Then their consciousness was awakened." Literally, this reads: "Then their eyes were opened." Rabbi Chiyya said: They were awakened to knowledge of the evil of the world, which they had not known until this point. As soon as they became aware of evil, they realized that they were naked; that they had lost the supernal aura which had enveloped them. This departed from them, leaving them naked.

(*Zohar I,* 36b)

"They realized that they were naked." Rabbi Yehudah said: When Adam sinned, the Holy One, blessed is He, removed the holy luminous letters with which He had originally crowned them. Them they were afraid, for they understood that they had been stripped of these letters. . . . They realized that death was calling them; they realized that freedom had been stripped away from them.

(*Zohar I,* 53a)

3:8 וישמעו את קול ה' אלקים מתהלך בגן – They heard the sound of the Lord God withdrawing from the garden

The verse does not state מהלך signifying, "moving about," but מתהלך signifying "withdrawing." Alternatively, מתהלך can be understood as a compound of two words מת and הלך – "death is at large."[13]

(*Zohar I*, 52a)

3:9 ויאמר לו איכה – And He said to him, "Where are you?"

Here God hinted to him that in the future the Temple which is the dwelling place on earth of the Divine Presence,[14] would be destroyed. This is why in the book of *Eichah* (*Lamentations*) (1:1) the same word is used – both words have the identical letters – as it is written, "How solitary (איכה) does she sit. . . ." referring to Jerusalem in general, and to the Temple in particular, after their destruction.

(*Zohar I,* 29a)

---

13. The latter interpretation can be found in *Derech Emet.*

14. *Midrash Tanchuma, Nasso* 16; Discourse באתי לגני"ה 5710 (In *Discourses* 10 *Shevat* 5710).

3:10 ויאמר את קלך שמעתי בגן ואירא כי עירם אנכי ואחבא – And he answered, "I heard Your voice in the garden, and I was afraid because I am naked, so I hid"

Before they sinned, they heard the voice from Above. They knew supernal wisdom (*chochmah*), and were endowed with the knowledge (*da'at*) and understanding (*binah*) of the supernal light, and they were not afraid. These three faculties of the soul – wisdom, knowledge and understanding, correspond to three of the highest *sefirot* of the world of *Atzilut* – *chochmah, da'at* and *binah* respectively.[15] When they sinned, however, they could not withstand even the voice as it is heard below. In Kabbalah in general, a distinction is made between the faculties of sight and hearing. "Seeing" is a function of *chochmah*, and denotes a direct, incontrovertible experience, whereas "hearing" is a function of *binah*, and denotes an indirect experience of a lower level. Prior to the sin, their hearing was on the level of seeing. This level of insight was again granted to the Israelites when they received the Torah on Mount Sinai, as the verse states, "And all of the people **saw** the **sounds**. . . ." (*Shemot* 20:18), as our Sages point out.[16]

(*Zohar I*, 52b)

3:15 הוא ישופך ראש ואתה תשובנו עקב – He will crush your head, and you will crunch his heel

"**He** will crush your head" refers to the Holy One, blessed is He, who will remove the serpent from the world in the future, as the verse states, "He will destroy death for ever" (*Yeshayahu* 25:8); and "I will remove the spirit of impurity from the earth" (*Zechariah* 13:2).

---

15. *Damesek Eliezer*. See *Eitz Chaim sha'ar* 39, chap. 1. See also *Introduction.*
16. See also the continuation of this selection from the Zohar.

An alternative explanation: "Head" signifies the time to come, when the dead are resurrected, for then the world will become "head." The first three *sefirot*, referred to as *mochin* (intellect) will then be manifest.[17] This is the level of the supernal world.

"And you will crunch his heel" – in this world, now, prior to the completion of the world's rectification. At present, the world is on the level of the heel, a symbol of spiritual insensitivity. The world's existence is incomplete, and the serpent continues to bite; to darken the face of its creatures.

(*Zohar I,* 124a)

Rabbi Yitzchak the son of Rabbi Yose asked: According to the view that maintains that the serpent is a symbol for the *yetzer hara* (a person's self-destructive evil impulse) how do we interpret this verse?

Rabbi Yose answered: This teaches us that the serpent, which is the *yetzer hara*, is put to death only by the "head." What is the head? The Head of the Academy – the *Rosh Yeshivah*, whose duty it is to identify and take an active part in destroying the *yetzer hara* of his disciples. And the serpent kills man only via the heel – when a person transgresses the commandments and tramples them with his heels,[18] as it is written, "The sin of my heels surround me" (*Tehillim* 49:6).[19] Rashi (*Devarim* 7:12) explains that these are the so-called "minor" commandments which people take lightly. Ramban (ad loc.) explains that this refers particularly to transgression concerning financial matters.

(*Midrash HaNe'elam, Zohar Chadash* 19b)

---

17. Sulam.
18. See also *Avodah Zarah* 18a.
19. Note that the Zohar interprets the verse literally. A non-literal translation would read: "The iniquity of my pursuers surrounds me."

Eve's Curse

3:16 ואל האשה אמר, הרבה ארבה עצבונך והרנך בעצב תלדי בנים ואל אישך תשוקתך והוא ימשל בך – And to the woman He said, "I will greatly increase your anguish, as well as your childbearing; in pain you will give birth to children. Your husband will be your passion, but he will dominate you"

Rabbi Shimon said: "In pain you will give birth to children." If you ask how this is connected to the entire episode with the serpent, the answer is: This provided the opening for all souls to descend into this world. The negative forces wish to prevent the birth of holy souls in this material world, arguing that if there are holy souls born into this world, they will bring the entire world to a state of righteousness and repentance, thus removing man's free choice. Accordingly, these holy souls must be brought down in a physical body in this world in a devious manner, just like the soul of Avraham, who was born to Terach, an idolater. The negative forces never suspected that Avraham would turn out to be righteous, given the circumstances into which he was born. The same is true of all holy souls. The negative forces do not allow it to descend until they are given some hold upon it.[20] Accordingly, had there not been this opening for souls to descend, the soul would not be able to dwell within the human body. What does the Torah state? "Sin lies in wait at the opening" (*Bereishit* 4:7). What is the significance of לפתח – at the opening? This refers to the opening of *malchut*, which is earmarked for the purpose bringing souls into

---

20. *Damesek Eliezer.*

this world. It (the serpent, or the *yetzer hara*) stands at that opening and does not allow the womb to be opened until it is granted some hold upon the soul. Were it not for this situation, which is the will of God, so that man can have free choice, the *yetzer hara* would never have any hold over the souls of Israel.[21]

He does not stand at the entrance, and he has no authority over all the souls which are about to descend into the holy bodies in this world, prior to their descent. However, when the soul actually descends into a body in this world, the serpent bites, and the opening becomes spiritually contaminated. Accordingly, the soul becomes contaminated by its association with the body. This is the secret meaning of the words, "In pain you will give birth to children." It is the secret of the serpent with which souls are born and descend into bodies. It (the serpent, or *yetzer hara*) is given jurisdiction over the bodies, but *malchut* is given dominion over the souls, and although they are clothed in one another, one claims the body, and the other, the soul. A person therefore has both a *yetzer tov,* deriving from his holy soul, and a *yetzer hara,* deriving from the body. A person's divine duty in this world is to ensure that the former dominates the latter.[22]

(*Zohar II*, 219b)

---

21. Ibid.
22. See *Tanya* chaps. 10-12.

Adam's Curse

3:17 ארורה האדמה בעבורך– The earth is cursed for you

After the Holy One blessed be He cursed the world, as it states "The earth is cursed for you," Adam asked God, "Master of the Universe, for how long will the earth remain cursed?" He replied, "Until you have a descendant who is born circumcised, just as you were." So they waited until Noah was born. When Noah was born they saw that he was already circumcised, and was sealed with the sign of the covenant. For this reason they named him "Noah," signifying God's conciliation with the world.[23]

(*Zohar I,* 58a-b)

3:19 כי עפר אתה ואל העפר תשוב – For you are dust, and to dust you will revert

Regarding this God told the serpent, "Dust you shall eat, as long as you live" (above 3:14). "Dust" – this is man, regarding whom it is written, "For you are dust." Therefore the verse uses the term "dust," rather than "earth" or "clay." It is also written, "The serpent's bread is dust" (*Yeshayahu* 65:25). This will be man's portion until the Holy One blessed be He removes the spirit of impurity from the earth,[24] regarding which it is written, "He will destroy death for ever" (*Yeshayahu* 25:8). It is written regarding the resurrection of the dead, "Awake and sing, you that dwell in dust" (*Yeshayahu* 26:19).

(*Zohar II,* 268b)

---

23. See *Zohar III,* 60a.
24. See *Zechariah* 13:2.

Adam was forbidden to eat from the Tree of Knowledge, as it is written, "But of the Tree of Knowledge of good and evil you may not eat, for on the day you eat of it you will definitely incur death" (above 2:17). Based on this, Rabbi Shimon said: Because he was taken from dust, and nothing in the material world is eternal, it was already decreed that Adam would die, even before he sinned. This we deduce from the words, "**on the day** you eat of it you will definitely incur death" – implying that on the very same day that he ate from the tree he would die, though had he not sinned he would merely have lived for much longer, but not forever. When he sinned, his punishment was that his life was shortened and he was to die that same day. When he repented, however, God granted him His day, which is a thousand years, as the verse states, "A thousand years in Your eyes are like yesterday" (*Tehillim* 90:4) i.e., a single day.[25]

This is a proof that it was originally decreed that Adam would die, for if this were not so, when he repented, God should have nullified the decree and Adam should have lived forever. Since we see that He did not nullify the decree of death, we deduce that Adam was destined to die in any event. Said Rabbi Shimon: When Adam repented, God did indeed nullify the decree. Which decree? The decree that "**on the day** you eat of it you will definitely incur death." He extended his life span to one of **His** days – a thousand years.

(*Midrash HaNe'elam, Zohar Chadash* 18c)

Although man sinned, what was the sin of the rest of the world? Death was decreed on the entire world, not just on Adam. If you argue that all the creatures came and ate from the tree, after Adam and Eve had eaten,[26] and therefore eternal life was taken away from

---

25. See *Sanhedrin* 97a; *Bereishit Rabbah* 8:2.
26. See Rashi, *Bereishit* 3:6.

everything; this is not so. Rather, when Adam first stood on his feet, i.e., immediately after he had been created, all the creatures saw him and feared him, and were drawn after him like a servant to the king. They all bowed down to him, believing that he was their creator.[27] Then Adam said to them, "Come, let you and me bow down and prostrate ourselves before God, who created us" (*Tehillim* 95:6). They all followed his lead. When they saw Adam prostrating himself before the Tree of Knowledge. . . . all of them again followed his lead. This was the cause of his death, and the introduction of death into the rest of the world.

(*Zohar III,* 107b)

3:20 ויקרא האדם שם אשתו חוה כי היא היתה אם כל חי – The man named his wife Chava (Eve) for she was the mother of all the living

The word for "living" in Hebrew is חי (*chai*) According to grammar she should have been named Chaya (חיה), not Chava (חוה). However, Chava and Chaya mean the same thing. The fact that the letter *yud* of Chaya was replaced by the letter *vav* of Chava is proper, for the letter *vav* certainly alludes to life. As explained earlier, in the explanation of the letters of the Hebrew alphabet (commentary to 1:1), both the letter *vav* and the letter *yud* are part of the Divine Name (the Tetragrammaton). Nevertheless, the *yud* is on a much loftier level than the *vav* (the level of *chochmah* as opposed to the level of *tiferet*). Thus it **transcends** the life of this world. Had she not sinned, however, she would have been called Chaya, for the world would have been on a sufficiently elevated level to receive from the level of *chochmah.*[28]

(*Zohar II,* 137a)

---

27. *Or HaChamah.*
28. *Damasek Eliezer.*

3:21 ויעש ה' אלקים לאדם ולאשתו כתנות עור וילבשם – The Lord God made for Adam and his wife garments of skin, and he clothed them

"Garments of skin (עור)" – Originally these were garments of **light** (אור), and not of skin (עור). In Hebrew, certain letters are interchangeable, following the rules of *temurot* (exchange of letters).[29] In this case, the letter *aleph* is replaced by the letter *ayin*, indicative of a spiritual descent – whereas the *aleph* represents God Himself (the numberical value of *aleph* is 1, alluding to the oneness of God),[30] the *ayin* alludes to sin (עון).[31] This was the supernal light which illuminated *Gan Eden*. Therefore, when Adam was about to enter *Gan Eden* for the first time, the Holy One blessed be He dressed him in garments of light, and then brought him into *Gan Eden*. Had he not been wearing that garment, he could not have entered. And when he was driven out of there, he required a different set of garments. Hence, "The Lord God made for Adam and his wife garments of skin (עור), and he clothed them."

(*Zohar II*, 229b)

The following extract renders the words כתנות עור *as "garments **for** the skin"*

After their sin, the Holy One blessed be He dressed them in garments in which the **skin** (עור) i.e., the body, delights, as the verse states, "garments **for** the skin," and not garments for the soul. Originally they had garments of light, which the supernal beings (angels) would use above in the higher worlds. Even the angels would come to Adam to enjoy the light of his garments which was

29. See *Pardes, sha'ar* 30, chaps. 5-7.
30. See *Zohar I*, 2b ff.
31. Ibid.

even more elevated than their own,[32] as it is written, "And You made him (Adam) a little less than the angels, but You crowned him with glory and honor" (*Tehillim* 8:6). Now that he had sinned, he wore garment for the skin – from which the flesh benefits, but not the soul.

(*Zohar I,* 36b)

Banishment

3:22 הן היה האדם כאחד ממנו – Man could have indeed been unique among them

Rabbi Yitzchak said: The Holy One blessed be He wished to make man superior to all His creatures – to be one in this world as He is One Above. But when Man sinned, the Holy One blessed be He said: Adam could have partaken of My Oneness, and this was My intention. . . .

(*Midrash HaNe'elam, Zohar Chadash* 10a)

---

32. *Or HaChamah.*

3:24 ויגרש את האדם וישכן מקדם לגן עדן את הכרובים ואת להט החרב המתהפכת לשמור את דרך עץ החיים – When He banished Adam, He stationed the *keruvim*[33] to the east of the Garden of Eden, and the revolving sword of flame to guard the way to the Tree of Life

Rabbi Bo said in the name of Rabbi Huna: When Adam sinned, and decrees were enforced upon him, the Holy One blessed be He banished him from that spiritual pleasure and delight which he had in Eden, and appointed guards over the gates of *Gan Eden.* Who are they (the guards)? The *keruvim*, a type of angel, as it is written, "He stationed the *keruvim.* . . . and the revolving sword of flame to guard the way and the opening" (*Bereishit* 3:24).

Then it was also decreed that from then on, no man had permission to enter there other than the souls of the righteous who have first been purified by the *keruvim.* If they see that a certain soul is worthy of entering, it may enter. But if not, it is driven away, and receives its punishment, burning by the flame of the revolving sword.

We have also learned that the exact parallel was found in the *Beit HaMikdash* (the Temple) when the High Priest entered the innermost sanctuary once a year on Yom Kippur.[34] It has been taught[35]: Rabbi Abba said in the name of Rabbi Yehudah who said in the name of Rabbi Huna that the innermost sanctuary is the duplicate of *Gan Eden.* When the High Priest entered the Holy of Holies, his soul went in, not his body. Moreover, he entered it in awe and dread, in cleanliness and purity. The *keruvim* stand there on guard, just like the *keruvim* which guard *Gan Eden.* If the Priest is worthy,

---

33. Cherubs. A certain category of angelic beings.

34. The Day of Atonement, the holiest day in the Jewish calendar. See *Vayikra* 16:1 ff.; Rashi.

35. See *Zohar III,* 102a.

he enters in peace and exits in peace. If not, a flame shoots out from between the *keruvim* and he dies.

Rabbi Yehudah said: Happy is the person who is worthy of passing through them in peace.

(*Midrash HaNe'elam, Zohar Chadash* 19a)

The following extract tells about Rabbi Akiva's advice to his students before entering the Pardes[36] *(paradise) by meditating on the deepest secrets of the Torah. From this we see that certain of the Sages entered Gan Eden*[37] *alive.*

Rabbi Akiva said to his disciples, "When you come to the place of pure marble stones, to the world of *Atzilut*, the world of absolute unity[38] do not say, 'Water, water,' as if there were two types of water[39] lest you endanger yourselves, as it is written: 'A teller of untruths shall not remain in My sight' (*Tehillim* 101:7). Do not say 'water, water,' even though an earlier verse (1:6) states: "God said, 'There shall be a firmament between the waters, and it shall divide between water and water" thus forming the higher waters and lower waters.[40] Just

---

36. The word *Pardes* is an abbreviation of the words *peshat, remez, drush, sod* - the interpretation of the Torah according to the plain meaning of the text, allusion to deeper meanings, the homiletical explanation, and the secret explanation respectively. These correspond to the four worlds, *Assiyah, Yetzirah, Beriah, Atzilut,* which are attained through the various stages of meditation. See *Introduction*.
37. The entire extract can be found above, in the commentary to verse 2:17. See also *Chagiga* 14b.
38. *Damesek Eliezer*.
39. *Pardes, Arachei Hakinuim,* s.v. מים. A comprehensive commentary on this selection can be found there.
40. An alternative version of this passage is found in *Tikkunei Zohar, Tikkun* 40 (p. 80b), where these words are part of the text..

then, a hoary-headed elder[41] descended and said to them, "Rabbis, what are you presently occupied with?" They replied, "With that which Rabbi Akiva said to his students, 'when you come to the place of pure marble stones. . . .'"

The old man then replied, "It is clear that there is a deep secret here. But this has already been explained in the Heavenly Academy.[42] Now, so that you do not err in this matter, I have descended to you from the Heavenly Academy in order to explain it you. Moreover, I am justified in revealing this matter, which is hidden from the generation, even though this is generally forbidden[43] since the secret has already been discovered by you. Certainly from these pure marble stones, pure water flows. They are alluded to in the letter א which is composed of three parts, the upper י (*yud* – the upper arm of the letter on the right); the lower י (*yud* – the lower leg of the letter, on the left); and the ו (*vav*) which is stretched between them, which is the Tree of Life. One who eats from it will live forever, for it is the Tree of **Life.** The upper and lower *yuds* both represent the Holy One blessed be He of whom it states, "I am first, and I am last, and besides Me, there is no god" (*Yeshayahu* 44:6). The former indicates God as He is in Himself, transcending all of creation, whereas the latter represents the immanent aspect – God as He is within creation. Both aspects are connected by the Torah – the Tree of Life – which informs us of God's inseparable Oneness in the upper and lower worlds. Thus, do not think that there are two levels, separated

41. Literally, "a grandfather of grandfathers." This refers to a very elevated level of *Keter,* namely, *Atik Yomin* - literally, "the Ancient of Days" *(Mikdash Melech).* In terms of man's soul this indicates a revelation of the level of soul called *yechidah* (*Sulam*) See *Introduction.*

42. The souls of the righteous learn Torah in *Gan Eden* from the Holy One Himself. See *Sitrei Torah, Yitro* in *Zohar Chadash* 36b.

43. Cf. *Shabbat* 88a: "Who revealed this secret which only the ministering angels know..?" *Megillah* 3a: "Who revealed these secrets to my son?"; *Otzar HaMidrashim* 181:10.

by the firmament. This is not true. Rather, what appear to be two separate aspects, the transcendent and the immanent, are in reality one.[44]

(*Zohar I*, 26b)

Cain and Abel

4:1-2 והאדם ידע את חוה אשתו ותהר ותלד את קין. . . . ותסף ללדת את אחיו את הבל – Adam knew[45] Chava his wife. She conceived and gave birth to Cain. . . . she gave birth again, to his brother Hevel (Abel)

Rabbi Abba said: Come and see. When a person goes in the path of truth and draws down supernal holiness upon himself, and he cleaves to it, then he draws this holiness down to the child born to him. The child will then be sanctified with the holiness of his Master, as it is written, "You shall sanctify yourselves and be holy" (*Vayikra* 11:44). But when he goes the opposite way,[46] and draws the spiritual impurity upon himself, then he draws spiritual impurity onto the child he produces. . . . Adam attached himself to the side of impurity to which his wife clung first. . . . and the child they had was from this impurity. Therefore, they had two sons. One was from that aspect of impurity, and the other from the pure side, was conceived after Adam repented. One was from the side of unholiness, and the other, from the side of holiness.

Hevel was in the likeness of the supernal image, as the verse states, "God created man with His image" (*Bereishit* 1:27),

---

44. *Pardes,* ad loc.
45. An expression signifying intercourse.
46. Literally, along the left path.

whereas Cain was of the likeness of the nether image.[47] For this reason their paths diverged.

Because Cain was from the side of the angel of death he killed his brother. I.e., the murder of Hevel paralleled the sin of the Tree of Knowledge, which came about through the enticements of the serpent, who is the angel of death. Just as through the sin of the Tree, the angel of death gained dominion of the world, through Cain he gained the ability to remove the soul of Hevel.[48]

(*Zohar I,* 54a)

Rabbi Yehudah said: Two came upon Eve, the serpent and Adam. She became pregnant from both of them, and bore two sons. The first son was from the poison of the serpent, and the second son was from Adam. One therefore possessed the characteristics of the species of the serpent; the other, possessed the characteristics of the species of man. In spirit they were thus different, one was of the side of holiness, and the other on that side of unholiness. One was similar to **his** progenitor, and the other was similar to **his** progenitor. From Cain's side come all the categories of evil, satanism, and witchcraft. From Hevel's side there is more compassion, but it is incomplete, like good wine mixed with vinegar. And therefore the world was not rectified by him, and it remained without rectification until Seth was born. All the generations of righteous people descend from him; through him the world became stable.

(*Zohar I,* 36b)

---

47. *Ziv HaZohar* surmises that the "nether image" is that of an ape. He goes on to explain that the human form of the gorilla and the orangutan may indicate that those primates were descendants of Cain, and therefore seem to be have some human qualities, animal. He adds that Darwin and others who espouse the theory of evolution drew the wrong conclusion – the ape is descended from man (from Cain), and not vice versa!

48. *Sulam.*

4:3-4 ויהי מקץ ימים ויבא קין מפרי האדמה מנחה לה'. והבל הביא גם הוא מבכורות צאנו ומחלביהן. וישע ה' אל הבל ואל מנחתו – In the course of time, Cain brought of the earth's produce as an offering to God. Hevel also offered of the firstborn of his flock, from the fattest. And God turned to Hevel and his offering

Rabbi Shimon said: What is the meaning of מקץ ימים (*keitz yamim*) (translated here as "in the course of time")? This means "the end (קץ) of all flesh" (*Bereishit* 6:13) stated in connection with the destruction of almost all living things during the Flood. What does this refer to? The angel of death. The verse thus hints that Cain brought his sacrifice from קץ ימים – from the angel of death. For this reason Scripture explicitly uses the term קץ ימים (*keitz yamim*) and not קץ ימין (*keitz yamin* – the end of days). The Book of Daniel states that God said to Daniel as he was about to die: "Go your way till the end (קץ)will be. For you shall rest, and stand up for your allotted portion at the end of days (קץ הימין" with the Resurrection of the Dead (*Daniel* 12:13). Daniel asked God: קץ ימים (*keitz yamim*) or קץ הימין (*keitz hayamin*)? I.e., is the angel of death to be my lot, or the Resurrection of the Dead? God replied: קץ הימין the resurrection. However, Cain brought a satanic sacrifice from קץ ימים, the angel of death.

(*Zohar I,* 54b)

Rabbi Yehudah said: Cain resorted to farming, like Adam, and Hevel became a shepherd. Each of them brought a sacrifice, but Cain's was offered with arrogance, whereas Hevel offered his meekly, as it states, "The offering [desirable] to God is a contrite spirit" (*Tehillim* 51:19). What is written subsequently? "God turned to Hevel and his offering, but to Cain and his offering He did not turn."

(*Midrash HaNe'elam, Zohar Chadash* 19c)

4:7 הלוא אם תיטיב שאת ואם לא תיטיב לפתח חטאת רבץ – If you improve your ways, will you not be forgiven? But if you do not improve you ways, sin lies in wait at the entrance.

Rabbi Yehudah taught: That day was *Rosh HaShanah,*[49] the Day of Judgment when all souls pass before Him. He said to Cain: Why be angry? If you improve your ways, will you not be forgiven? What is the meaning of the word שאת (translated here as "forgiven," but literally meaning, "lifting up?") Rabbi Yehudah explained: If you improve your ways, you will become spiritually **elevated**.

"Sin lies in wait at the entrance" – that is, sin waits at the entrance through which souls pass in order to enter *Gan Eden*. God tells Cain: The transgressions of which you are guilty await you there, and that is where you will receive your punishment, for only those "whose hands are clean, and whose hearts are pure" (*Tehillim* 24:4) will be allowed to enter. Thus, a person's own deeds are the cause of his suffering, for justice is not dispensed arbitrarily, but on the basis of man's actions.[50] The verse states, "Your own wickedness shall torment you, and your failings shall rebuke you" (*Yirmeyahu* 2:19).

(*Midrash HaNe'elam, Zohar Chadash* 19c-d)

What does the word שאת mean? It is as Rabbi Abba said: You will be lifted up above, and you will not fall down. Rabbi Yose said: This is a novel interpretation, and it is indeed fitting. However, I heard a different interpretation שאת also means forgiveness. God said to him, "If you improve your ways, the spirit

49. New year. The first of *Tishrei* in the Jewish calendar.
50. *Sulam.*

of impurity which clings to you as the result of your sin will be removed from you and you will be forgiven.

(*Zohar I,* 54b)

4:8 ויקם קין אל הבל אחיו ויהרגהו – Cain attacked his brother and killed him

Rabbi Yitzchak said: Come and see! When Cain killed Hevel, he did not know that his actions would make the soul leave the body, and that Hevel would die.[51] Commentaries[52] explain that the argument between Cain and Hevel was in fact a spiritual disagreement as to how to re-unite the soul with God after the sin of the Tree of Knowledge. According to Hevel, the best way to achieve the desired result was via repentance, which implies self-purification and elevating oneself to a higher level. According to Cain, however, the only way to do this was to elicit an outflow of Divine energy from above which would rectify all blemishes of the soul in its outflow from Above. (As we saw in the preceding selections, God hints to Cain that the former method, elevation from below to above, is preferable). Cain had no intention of killing Hevel. He was not aware that eliciting Divine energy from above also rouses negative severe judgment when the person below is not ready to receive such communion. This is in fact what happened, and Hevel was killed. The *Zohar continues*: He bit Hevel with his teeth, like a snake, and he died. The explanation[53] of this is as follows: The highest level of union of man's soul with God is called *zivug neshikin* (unification through "kissing"), as referred to in the verse, "May He kiss me with kisses of His mouth" (*Shir HaShirims* 1:2). However, this can only be achieved if a person is spiritually purified and ready to achieve such a level of communion. Cain wished to bring this revelation about by force, using the power of sacrifice. Since the world was not ready for such a revelation, the *zivug neshikin*[54] aroused severe judgements

---

51. *Sulam.*
52. *Sulam.*
53. *Sulam.*
54. זווג נשיקין in Hebrew.

and became instead *zivug neshichin*[55] – *neshichin* means "biting" – with the end result that Hevel was killed.

(*Zohar I,* 54b)

4:12 נע ונד תהיה בארץ – You shall be a vagrant and an alien on earth

Rabbi Yitzchak said: He wandered about in all directions, but no place accepted him until he beat his brow and repented before his Master. Then the level below earth accepted him[56] but no higher than this because his repentance was incomplete.[57]

Rabbi Yose disagreed and said: The earth did allow him to be upon it, as it is written, "God placed a mark on Cain" (below, 4:15) which implies that his repentance was accepted.

Rabbi Yitzchak retorted: Not so! This verse also means that he was only accepted on a level below the earth, as it states, "Today you have driven me away from the face (i.e. surface) of the earth" (4:14). He was driven from the surface of the earth, but not from below the surface.

(*Zohar I,* 54b)

---

55. זווג נשיכין in Hebrew.
56. This does not mean that he lived in some subterranean world, but rather that **spiritually** he was on a lower level than any creature on earth.
57. *Sulam.*

4:13 גדול עוני מנשוא – My sin is too great to forgive

When Cain said, "My sin is too great to forgive," the Holy One blessed be He absolved him of half of his punishment.[58] Initially it was decreed that he would be a vagrant (נע) **and** an alien on earth (ונד). Now he only remained an alien (alienated from God) as the verse states, "Cain left God's presence and settled in the land of Nod (נוד) "[59] (below, 4:16). That is, he was expelled from God's presence and was alienated from Him on earth, though he was not forced to wander from place to place.

(*Tosefta Zohar I,* 54b)

4:14 מפניך אסתר – I have caused Your presence to become hidden from me

A literal interpretation of the verse reads: "I am hidden from Your Presence," seeming to imply that God can no longer see Cain. This interpretation is obviously untenable. Accordingly, the Zohar here offers a different interpretation

Rabbi Elazar said: What does מפניך אסתר mean? My building (i.e., everything I have built up) is demolished (Rabbi Elazar interprets the word אסתר derivative of the word סותר – demolish, rather than a derivative of the word הסתר – concealment.

Rabbi Abba said: As it is said, "Nor did He hide his face from him" (*Tehillim* 22:25) and, "Moshe hid his face" (*Shemot* 3:6). Rabbi Abba interprets the word אסתר as "conceal" or "hide." However, it refers

58. *Bereishit Rabbah* 22:11 and Rashi interpret this verse as a question - "is my sin too great to forgive?" Ibn Ezra and others, agreeing with the *Zohar*, interpret it as a confession of guilt and remorse.

59. Note that (נוד) is a derivative of the word (נד).

to God's concealment of Himself from Cain, and not vice-versa. Cain said: I will be distanced from Your Presence. For You will not protect me, so "Whoever finds me will kill me."

(*Zohar I,* 36b)

4:15 וישם ה' לקין אות – And so God placed a mark on Cain

Why is the word אות "letter" used here? Because it refers to one of the twenty-two letters of the Torah which He placed upon Cain to protect him. Since Cain had lost his Divine image by murdering his brother, he made himself prey to any animal which wished to attack him. Accordingly, God placed a sign on him to protect him.

(*Zohar I,* 36b)

4:25 ותלד בן ותקרא את שמו שת – She gave birth to a son and named him Seth

Rabbi Yehudah said: This is the secret of the soul which was lost i.e., the soul of Hevel, which was now reincarnated and was clothed in another body in this world, as it is written, "God has granted me other seed in place of Hevel." Although the soul was clothed in a new body, it was the same soul as Hevel's.

(*Zohar I,* 55a)

4:26 ולשת גם הוא ילד בן ויקרא את שמו אנוש אז הוחל לקרוא בשם ה' – Seth too, had a son. He named him Enosh. Then they began profaning the Name of God

Rabbi Elazar said: In the days of Enosh, men were very knowledgeable in witchcraft and magic, and knew how to block heavenly influence from affecting the world. From the day that Adam left the Garden of Eden, bringing out with him the knowledge of the fig leaves i.e., the secrets of sorcery and witchcraft[60] there was no one who occupied himself with it. Adam and his wife, and their progeny before Enosh was born, had abandoned this knowledge.

Enosh came and saw those fig leaves, and realized that knowledge of them gave him the power to defy Heaven and destroy holiness.[61] He began to occupy himself with them and perform acts of sorcery and magic. He taught others as well, until this knowledge became widespread during the generation of the flood, when everyone used this knowledge for evil purposes. . . . This is the meaning of "they began profaning the Name of God;" they used the Name of God for sacrilegious purposes.

(*Zohar I,* 56a)

60. See *Zohar I,* 36b, 53b.
61. Explained at length in *Sulam* vol. 3, p. 181-2.

Adam's Descendants

5:1 זה ספר תולדות אדם – This is the book of the descendants of Adam

"This is the book. . . ." This refers to an actual book. When Adam was in *Gan Eden*, the Holy One blessed be He gave him a book via the holy angel Raziel,[62] who is appointed to guard the supernal divine secrets. In it were engraved the supernal letters of holy wisdom, and seventy-two branches of wisdom were explained therein. . . . All of these branches were concealed within that book before it was given to Adam. When he acquired it the supernal angels would gather around him to study it and understand all the mystical secrets contained in that work. The angels then made their request to God, saying, "Be exalted above the heavens, O God, let Your glory transcend the earth" (*Tehillim* 57:6) impart the mystery of Your glory to the angels, not to man.[63]

Then the angel Hadraniel said to Adam, "Conceal the glory of your Master. Do not reveal it to the angels, for only you have been given permission to know the glory of your Master, and not even to the highest of angels. And so it remained concealed with him until he left *Gan Eden.*

At first prior to the sin of the Tree of Knowledge, Adam studied the book and used it to learn the secrets of his Master. Indeed, supernal secrets were revealed to him which even the angels did not know. But after transgressed the commandment of his Master, the book flew away. Then Adam beat his brow and wept. He repented, and in order to purify his sin, he entered the waters of the Gichon River up to

---

62. His name means, "I have the secrets of God."

63. This is possibly the source of Rashi's interpretation of the verse. See also Shabbat 88b ff.

his neck, and he remained there until his body began to disintegrate in the water and change appearance. Then the Holy One blessed be He made a sign to the angel Raphael, the angel of healing, and the book was returned to him. He studied it intensely, and bequeathed it to his son Seth. So it went on, through successive generations until the advent of Avraham, whose knowledge of it allowed him to gaze upon the glory of his Master. . . . This then is the meaning of our verse, "This is the book of the descendants of Adam." According to tradition, this is the extant work known as "The Book of Raziel the Angel."[64]

(*Zohar I,* 55b)

Rabbi Shimon said: It is written, "This is the book of the descendants of Adam. . . ." Did he actually have a book? No. Rather, this must be understood according to the explanation of our Sages: The Holy One blessed be He showed Adam each generation and its preachers, each generation and its Sages. . . . each generation and its leaders.[65] How did He show him generations which did not yet exist? If you maintain that he saw generations which would exist in the future by way of divine inspiration;[66] this is not the case. Rather, he saw them all with his eyes. And he saw them as they would exist in the future in this world – all this he actually **saw**, because from the moment the world was created, all the souls which would live as people in the future all stand before the Holy One blessed be He in the very same form in which they will live in this world. Commentaries[67] point out that this refers to "old souls" which were originally included in Adam. When he sinned, they became divided into 600,000 soul-roots. These souls

64. See *Shem HaGedolim* s.v. רזיאל המלאך.

65. Several versions of this statement may be found in *Midrash*. The version cited here is from *Midrash Rabbah* 24:2.

66. *Ruach HaKodesh.*

67. *Sha'at Ratzon; Matok MiDevash.*

are then re-incarnated in this world so that they can rectify the sin of Adam through Torah and *mitzvot*. However "new souls," which have never before been in existence, were not shown to Adam.

(*Zohar I,* 90b)

5:3 ויולד בדמותו כצלמו ויקרא את שמו שת– He reproduced in his likeness, in his image. He named him Seth

Rabbi Yehudah said: It is written, "He (Adam) reproduced in his likeness, in his image." This implies that his other sons, Cain and Hevel, were not his likeness. Only this one (Seth) was his likeness and image with a properly rectified body and soul, as Rabbi Shimon said in the name of Rabbi Yaiva Sabba: his other sons were contaminated by the poison of the snake and of Samael who rides upon it. For this reason, they were not of Adam's likeness, since he was made in the image of God, as stated explicitly in verses 1:26-7 above. Now if you argue that Hevel derived from the opposite side of Cain, as explained above, this is indeed true. Nevertheless, neither of them was of the form of Adam below.

Rabbi Yose said: It is written, "Adam had known[68] Eve his wife. She conceived and gave birth to Cain" (above 4:1). It is not written that **he** (Adam) conceived Cain. Even in regard to Hevel it is not written, "**he** conceived. . . ." Rather, it is written, "**she** increased her childbearing with his brother, Hevel" (ibid.). This implies that both Cain and Hevel stemmed chiefly from Eve, rather than from Adam. Herein lies the secret of the matter – that neither Cain nor Hevel were born in Adam's likeness. But regarding this one Seth it states, "He reproduced in his likeness, in his image."

(*Zohar I,* 55a)

---

68. A metaphor for intimate relations.

5:24 ויתהלך חנוך את האלקים ואיננו כי לקח רתו אלהים – Chanoch went in the ways of God, and then he was no more, for God took him

Rabbi Yose began expounding this verse on the basis of another verse: "While the king was reclining at his banquet, my spice sent forth its fragrance" (*Shir HaShirims* 1:12). . . . Come and see: this is the way of the Holy One blessed be He. When a person cleaves to God so that His Divine Presence[69] rests upon him, if He knows that later the person will sin – before that happens He plucks him while he gives forth a pleasing scent (i.e., before the person sins) and removes him from the world. This is what the verse states: "The king," referring to the Holy One blessed be He "was reclining at his banquet" i.e., He rested His Divine presence upon the person who cleaves to Him and goes in His ways. The verse continues: "My spice sent forth its fragrance" refers to his good deeds. Because of his good deeds he passes away from the world before his time so that he will not become tainted. . . . Come and see how this applies to our verse: Chanoch was righteous, but the Holy One blessed be He saw that later he would sin, and therefore he plucked him from this world before that happened. This is the meaning of the phrase, "and then he was no more" – he did not live the same long life as the rest of his generation, "for God took him" before his time came.

Rabbi Eliezer said: the Holy One blessed be He removed Chanoch from the earth and raised him to the heavens, placing all the supernal treasure-houses in his charge.[70] What are these? The

---

69. The *Shechinah.*

70. According to *Targum Yonatan ben Uziel* on the verse, Chanoch became the angel Metatron.

keys to the engraved secrets which the supernal angels use. All of these were put in his charge.

(*Zohar I,* 56b)

5:29 ויקרא את שמו נח לאמר זה ינחמנו ממעשינו ומעצבון ידינו מן האדמה אשר ארדה ה' – He named him Noah, saying, "This one will relieve us from our exertion, and from agonizing manual labor on the ground which God has cursed"

How did Lemech, Noah's father, know that his son would in the future bring relief (the name Noah means "relief" or "comfort") to the earth after it had been cursed due to Adam's sin? However, when the Holy One blessed be He cursed the earth, as it is written, "The earth is cursed for you" (above 3:17), Adam said before Him: "Master of the Universe! For how long will the earth remain cursed?" God replied, "Until you have a descendant who will be born circumcised, like you." Elsewhere,[71] the *Zohar* explains that the foreskin is the result of Adam's sin. Adam himself did not have a foreskin prior to the sin of the Tree of Knowledge. So they waited until Noah was born. When he was born they saw that he was already circumcised, sealed with the holy sign. And they saw that the Divine Presence[72] rested upon him. Therefore they named him according to what would take place later.

At first after the earth was cursed due to the sin of Adam, and even more so after the sin of Cain, they did not know how to sow and reap and plow, and so they worked the earth with their hands. When Noah came along, he invented implements and all types of tools needed

---

71. See *Zohar I,* 35b.
72. The *Shechinah.*

to work the earth in order to produce fruits. This is the meaning of, "This one will relieve us from our exertion, and from agonizing manual labor on the ground. . . ."

(*Zohar I,* 58a-b)

6:2 ויראו בני האלהים את בנות האדם – The sons of nobility saw that the daughters of man were comely

Rabbi Yirmeya said: The words בני האלהים mean "sons of nobility." Their fathers, who were the leaders of the generation, did not rebuke them for their immoral behavior, and this caused their eventual downfall.

(*Midrash HaNe'elam Bereishit,* 20b)

The following extract from the Zohar renders the words בני האלהים *as "angels," rather than as "the sons of nobility"*[73]

Rabbi Nechemiah said: "The angels saw. . . ." refers to Azza and Azae-l, two angels[74] who lobbied their Master against creating man.[75] The Holy One blessed be He cast them down from their holy place above. As they descended they acquired human form. For this reason they are referred to as the *nefilim* in verse 4 below – literally, "the fallen ones."

(*Zohar Chadash Ruth,* 81a)

---

73. Rashi cites both views, in the order in which they appear here.
74. See *Yoma* 67b.
75. See *Midrash HaNe'elam, Zohar Chadash* 16a-b.

Man's Decadence

6:3 לא ידון רוחי באדם לעלם – My spirit will not continue to judge man forever

Rabbi Acha said: At that time prior to the Flood the river[76] which flowed out from Eden brought forth an elevated spiritual level from the Tree of Life. This affected the Tree which has a connection to death, i.e., the Tree of Knowledge from which the life-force of man is drawn. For this reason man's life-span was extremely long. Instead of a life-span of seventy, eighty or ninety years, they lived for seven, eight or nine hundred years. But when their days became so filled with evil, that eventually their evil rose up on High and planted itself firmly at the entrance, as the verse states, "sin lies in wait at the entrance" (above, 4:7) then the elevated spiritual level which issued forth from the Tree of Life was revoked. In this context, the "entrance" referred to in verse, "sin lies in wait at the entrance" is interpreted as the entrance to this world, as the soul descends to the body. Thus, regarding the descent of souls to men it is written, "My spirit will not continue to judge man forever." The word "forever," *le-olam* (לעולם) has another meaning as well – "to the world." Rabbi Acha thus interprets the verse as follows: "My spirit will not continue to imbue man in this world for such long periods of time."

(*Zohar I,* 37b)

---

76. Technically, the *sefirah* of *binah.*

6:5 וכל יצר מחשבת לבו רק רע כל היום – The entire disposition of his innermost thoughts was only and constantly evil

Rabbi Yehudah said: They were involved in all types of evil, but their debt only became due[77] when they spilt blood needlessly upon the earth. To whom does this refer? To those who deviate from their line upon earth i.e., to men who waste their seed needlessly. This is the meaning of "only and constantly evil," as it is written with reference to Er and Onan who incurred death because they emitted their seed wastefully: "Er, the firstborn son of Yehudah, was evil in God's eyes" (*Bereishit* 38:7 ff.). The *Zohar* thus makes a *gezeirah shava*[78] based on the common usage of the word רע – evil. Just as evil in the verse concerning Er and Onan refers to wasteful emission, so too in this case.

Rabbi Yose asked: Isn't the word רע synonymous with the word רשע (wicked)? In which case it does not refer only to wasteful emission, but to all types of wickedness!

No, he replied. A person is wicked even if he merely raises his hand against his fellow in a threatening gesture, even if he does not hit him, as it is written regarding Moshe, who rebuked the quarreling Datan and Aviram: "He said to the wicked one, 'Why hit(תכה) your friend?'" (*Shemot* 2:10). It is not written, "Why did you hit (הכית)," in the past tense, indicating that he had already beaten his fellow, but rather תכה in the future tense, indicating that he was only threatening to hit him, but had not actually done so. Someone is called evil (רע) only if he does perverse acts, thereby contaminating himself and the earth, giving vigor and strength to the spirit of impurity, which is called "evil," as it is

---

77. An expression meaning that they overstepped the limit of God's tolerance and forgiveness.

78. The second of Rabbi Yishmael's thirteen rules of Torah exposition states that an analogy between two laws is established on the basis of identical expressions in the Biblical text.

written, "only and constantly evil." Such a person will not enter the palace, and will not behold the countenance of the Divine Presence; for by his actions he causes the Divine Presence to become concealed from the world.

(*Zohar I,* 56b)

6:6 וינחם ה' כי עשה את האדם בארץ ויתעצב אל לבו– But God consoled Himself that He had made man on earth, and in His heart it grieved Him

Rabbi Eliezer said: Come and see that the attributes of the Holy One blessed be He are not like those of man. The nature of man is to act, and then to regret it, and grieve over it afterwards. If you think that the same is true of the Holy One blessed be He it is written, "See, I have placed before you today life and good, and death and evil. And you shall choose life." (*Devarim* 30:19). Thus man has free choice, but he was warned, "choose life, so that you shall live." If he is sinful, this will be the cause of his death,[79] as it states, "The sins of the wicked will trap him" (*Mishlei* 5:22). Thus it is written, "God saw that man's wickedness had increased. . . ." (above 6:5). The Holy One blessed be He said: "I see that everyone is blameworthy. But if they are destroyed by their own evil, My world will be desolate. When Noah and his sons proved to be righteous, and could remain as a surviving vestige in the world, He was consoled and happy. I.e., God's consolation was that some men were righteous.

---

79. In his *Iggeret HaTeshuvah* chap. 6, Rabbi Shneur Zalman of Liadi points out that this applied only in former times, when the vitality of the body derived from the divine soul. However, once the Divine Presence became "exiled," the physical body receives its vitality from *kelipat nogah*, or even from the side of unholiness, and therefore sinners do not die immediately due to their sin.

Rabbi Eliezer said: This word וינחם is an expression meaning "comfort" or "consolation." Similarly, all instances of וינחם in the Torah mean "consolation." One sees the evil and one sees the good, and is comforted by the good.

Rabbi Akiva said to him: If so, why does it state, ויתעצב אל לבו – "in His heart it grieved Him," which seems to imply that God was distressed by the situation, and was not comforted by the fact that Noah and his sons were righteous.

He replied: Come and witness the compassion of the Holy One blessed be He. Even though he was consoled by the fact that Noah and his sons were righteous, He was nevertheless grieved that the wicked would be destroyed. Even though they were wicked, He did not wish their deaths; consequently, He was not joyful.

(*Midrash HaNe'elam, Noah,* 21c)

6:7 אמחה את האדם אשר בראתי מעל פני האדמה – I will obliterate man whom I have created from the face of the earth

The expression "man. . . . from the face of the earth" is deliberately worded in order to exclude supernal "man" i.e., the configuration of the *sefirot* in the higher worlds. Can one maintain that the flood affected only man below, whereas the *sefirot* of the higher worlds were not affected at all? Do not make such a distinction between man below and man above, for one does not exist without the other. The damage below had its effects above as well.[80] As explained previously, this physical world is the consummation of creation, and without it, the entire spectrum of creation lacks this dimension.

(*Idra Rabbah, Zohar III,* 144a)

---

80. *Sulam.*

"I **will** obliterate man. . . . from the face of the earth." This is written in the future tense, because God said, "I will first inform them, via Noah, of what I intend to do if they do not change their ways." He warned them several times, but they paid no heed. Subsequently, He judged them and then removed them from the face of the earth.

(*Zohar I,* 58a)

6:8 ונח מצא חן – But Noah found favor

One of the branches of Kabbalah is known as "chochmat hatzeiruf," the knowledge of letter combination.[81] The letters of a word can be switched around to reveal hidden aspects of that same word, sometimes referred to as "the back" of the word. The reverse combination can often tell even more about the object it refers to than the direct combination, as the following extract shows.

If the letters of Noah's name – נח in Hebrew are transposed, the result is חן – "grace," or "favor." Rabbi Yose said: The names of the righteous is a factor in causing them good, whereas the names of the wicked are a factor in causing them evil. As regards Noah, it is written, "Noah (נח) found favor (חן) in God's eyes," whereas with Er (ער), Yehudah's firstborn, switching the letters of his name brings out the negative aspect רע, "evil." "He was evil in God's eyes."

Nevertheless, the *Zohar* points out, the main factor in causing a person good or otherwise is their own actions: After Noah was born and grew up, he witnessed man's tendency to sin before God. He secluded himself so that he would not be influenced to follow their ways, and he occupied himself with the service of his Master. If you ask what he occupied himself with, the answer is, with the book which had been given to Adam, and which had been passed on to Chanoch.[82]

(*Zohar I,* 58b)

---

81. See at length *Pardes, sha'ar* 30.

82. Explained above in the commentary to verse 5:1.

Noah

Noah

Noah and his Descendants

6:9 אלה תולדות נח, נח איש צדיק תמים היה בדורותיו – These are the descendants of Noah. Noah was a righteous man, wholehearted in his generation.

Why does the verse mention Noah's name twice "These are the descendants of Noah. Noah was a righteous man. . . ." when it could simply have said, "These are the descendants of Noah **who** was a righteous man. . . .?" Every righteous person (*tzaddik*) in this world has two souls, one soul in this world, and another soul in the World to Come. These are really different **levels** of the soul, the main part of the soul remains above in the higher worlds (referred to here as the World to Come), and a mere radiance or reflection thereof is clothed in the physical body in this world.[1] And thus we find with all *tzaddikim,* that God mentions their name twice – "Moshe Moshe;"[2] "Yaakov, Yaakov;"[3] "Avraham, Avraham;"[4] "Shmuel, Shmuel;"[5] etc. However, as regards Yitzchak, his name is not mentioned twice, unlike the others. This is because when he was offered up on the altar (see *Bereishit* ch. 22) his soul as it is in this world left him. Alternatively, about him it is said, "Blessed be He, who brings the dead back to life,"[6] for his soul from the World to Come entered him at that point. . . .

(*Tosefta, Zohar I,* 60a)

---

1. Explained at length in *Likkutei Torah, Ha'azinu* 71d; *Shir HaShirim* p. 16d.
2. *Shemot* 3:4.
3. *Bereishit* 46:2.
4. *Bereishit* 22:11.
5. *Samuel I,* 3:10.
6. This emendation of the text is recommended by *Ziv HaZohar.*

The Zohar cites two opinions Regarding Noah's degree of righteousness.[7]

"Faultless **in his generation**": But, had he lived in any other generation, such as the generation of Avraham, or of Moshe, or of David, he would have been disregarded, i.e., he would not have been regarded as a *tzaddik.* Only relative to his own generation, which was replete with wicked men, was he considered righteous. Another opinion: Look at what he achieved in his generation, which was replete with wicked men. Had he lived in a generation of righteous men, how much more so would he have been regarded as a *tzaddik.*

(*Tosefta, Zohar I,* 60a)

6:9 את האלקים התהלך נח – Noah went in the ways of God

The head of the academy said: Wherever the word תמים, "wholehearted,"[8] is written in Scripture (as in the first part of this verse), it indicates that the person is inscribed with the covenant of circumcision – a sign of holiness. Although Noah was **born** circumcised, as explained above, the *Zohar* does not refer to circumcision *per se*, but to the fact that Noah **guarded** the covenant of circumcision by maintaining the rules of reproduction: Because he kept the covenant, he alone was called "faultless" in his generation, whereas no one else was so, for they had deviated from their line by interbreeding outside of their species.[9] Therefore it is written, "Noah went in the ways of God" – literally, the verse states: "Noah walked with God." Who can walk with God? Only those who guard the covenant![10] Then the Divine Presence unites with him and rests upon him. Regarding this it

---

7. See also *Sanhedrin* 108a in the names of Rabbi Yochanan and Reish Lakish. See also Rashi's commentary on this verse.
8. Or, "faultless."
9. See *Zohar I*, 68a. Cited below in commentary to verse 6:12.
10. Cf. *Avodah Zarah* 20b.

is written, "You shall be wholehearted (תמים) with the Lord your God" (*Devarim* 18:13). Be wholehearted by guarding the covenant and then you will be "with the Lord your God!"

(*Zohar III,* 165b)

6:11 ותשחת הארץ לפני האלקים ותמלא הארץ חמס – The world became depraved before God, and the earth became filled with crime

Rabbi Yehudah said: Since it is written, "The world became depraved," why is it written "before God" is it not obvious that this was revealed to God, since nothing is hidden from Him? The intention is actually as follows: They sinned openly and flagrantly is indicated by the words, "before God."

Rabbi Yose said: I interpret it the opposite way. "The world became depraved **before God**." Initially, they sinned only before God, i.e., in secret. This is "before God," so that only God was aware of it, but not before man. Eventually they came to sin openly. This is why it is written, "and the earth became filled with crime;" for there was not one place on earth where they did not sin openly. Therefore the verse states this in two parts indicating that there were two stages.

(*Zohar I,* 60b)

6:12 כי השחית כל בשר דרכו על הארץ – All flesh had deviated from its way on earth

Rabbi Yose was often in the company of Rabbi Shimon bar Yochai. One day he asked Rabbi Shimon: Why did the Holy One blessed be He destroy all the animals and birds together with wicked men? Although man sinned, what was the sin of the animals and birds, and the other creatures? He replied: As it is written, "**All**[11] flesh had deviated from its way on earth." They abandoned their own species and mated across the species, thus transgressing the boundaries of creation stated in the verse, "The earth shall bring forth living creatures, each according to its kind. . . . in their species" (above 1:24). This may be regarded as moral deviance akin to adultery in human terms, and therefore punishable by death.[12]

(*Zohar I,* 68a)

The Flood

6:14 עשה לך תבת עצי גפר – Make yourself an ark of gopher-wood

Rabbi Shimon said: Come and see! Why did Noah have to build an ark? Couldn't the Holy One blessed be He guard Noah from the flood in some place in the world, making the flood everywhere except that place? Or, could He not have guarded him in the land of Israel, about which it is written, ". . . .nor rained upon in the day of anger" (*Yechezkel* 22:24), for the flood did not come upon on the land of Israel? However, when the destroyer[13] descends upon the world, whoever does not seal himself up in his house, and reveals himself to the destroyer is guilty of his own death. From where do we learn this? From Lot, about whom it is written, "Flee for your life. Do not look back!" (*Bereishit* 19:17). Why shouldn't he look behind him? Because the destroyer was behind him, and if he turned and looked back, and he saw the destroyer face-to-

11. See Ramban (Nachmanides) who explains why this necessarily applies to **all** flesh.
12. Cf. *Or HaChamah.*
13. The forces of destruction, or the angel of death.

face, he could be harmed. And therefore, regarding Noah it is written, "God closed the door of the Ark behind him" (below, 7:16), so that he would not see the destroyer, and have the angel of death rule over him.

(*Zohar II,* 196b)

6:18 והקמתי את בריתי אתך ובאת אל התבה אתה. . . . – But I will give you My pledge, and you will enter the ark, you. . . .

Rabbi Yehudah[14] said: Although Noah himself was righteous, his worthiness alone was not sufficient for the Holy One blessed be He to preserve the world on his behalf. Come and see how this is so: Moshe did not attribute anything to his own merit, but rather to the merit of his predecessors. Noah, however, did not have sufficiently righteous ancestors upon whose merit he could depend, like Moshe. This, of course, was no fault of his own.

Rabbi Yitzchak said: Nevertheless, when the Holy One blessed be He said to him, "I will give you My pledge. . . ." he should have prayed for mercy on their behalf. The sacrifice which he offered after the flood, should have been offered before the flood. Perhaps he might have thereby caused the severe judgments to subside from the world.

Rabbi Yehudah said: What should he have done? The wicked people of the world had angered God. Should he have offered a sacrifice on their behalf? He had to worry about himself – that death would overtake him among the wicked men of the world, for he witnessed their evil deeds all day long, and how they angered the Holy One blessed be He.

---

14. This passage has been interpreted as a continuation of the disagreement mentioned in the commentary to verse 6:9. Although the *Zohar* did not state there who the disagreeing parties were, it may be assumed that Rabbi Yehudah and Rabbi Yitzchak maintained these opposing views, even if they were not the Sages who disagreed in the earlier passage.

Rabbi Eliezer[15] said: Whenever the wicked of the world proliferate, the righteous among them are punished first, as it is written, "Begin the destruction with My Sanctuary (ממקדשי)" (*Yechezkel* 9:6). We have learned: Do not read "with My Sanctuary (ממקדשי) (*mi-mikdashai*)," but "with My holy ones (ממקודשי) (*mi-mekudshai*)" How was Noah then saved by the Holy One blessed be He from among all those wicked men, contrary to the above principle? God spared him because he would produce descendants in the future. This proves that he was a worthy *tzaddik,* contrary to Rabbi Yitzchak's view.

Moreover, Noah warned them every day that their actions would lead to their destruction, but they paid no attention to him. Thus he fulfilled the verse, "If you warned the wicked man, but he did not abandon his wickedness and evil ways; he shall die in his sin, but you have saved your soul" (*Yechezkel* 3:19). From this verse, we learn that one who warns a wicked person, even if the latter does not accept the rebuke, saves his own soul; while the guilty is trapped by his own misdeeds. To what extent is one obligated to warn him? Until he berates you.

(*Zohar I,* 67b-68a)

7:6 ונח בן שש מאור שנה – Noah was six hundred years old

Why does Scripture mention his age? Because if Noah was not six hundred years old, he would not have entered the ark. . . . This age represents a certain level of spirituality.[16] From the day that the sins of the wicked men of the world were had reached their full measure, i.e. when they had reached a level deserving of punishment, the Holy One blessed be He nevertheless waited patiently until Noah fully achieved this level of "six

15. Other versions read: "Rabbi Yitzchak said," but this does not seem to fit with his previous statements.
16. Technically, *yesod*, which is the sixth *sefirah* of *Zeir Anpin.* Thus he was not able to enter the ark - the *sefirah* of *malchut* until he reached this level (*Sulam*).

hundred." Then he became a complete *tzaddik*[17] and entered the ark. This entire episode – Noah entering the ark – was a representation of supernal matters – i.e., relationships between the *sefirot*.

(*Zohar I,* 65b)

7:22 כל אשר רוח חיים באפיו מכל אשר בחרבה מתו – Everything on dry land whose *neshamah* was his breath of life perished

Rabbi Chiyya asked Rabbi Abba: Our Rabbis teach that the level of soul called *neshamah*[18] does not enter a person until he delves deeply into the service of the Holy One blessed be He. Only then is he given the level of *neshamah.* Moreover, since the *neshamah* is holy and is emanated from supernal transcendent levels, why does the verse state, "Everything on dry land whose *neshamah* was his breath of life **perished**? Since they had achieved the level of *neshamah* they should have been spared from the flood along with Noah! He did not know what to answer.

They came to ask Rabbi Elazar, the son of Rabbi Shimon bar Yochai. He said: This is indeed the case – those who had achieved the level of *neshamah* died. This verse proves it, just as my father said: When the flood came, there was no person in whose merit the Holy One blessed be He would show kindness other than Noah. His merit was sufficient only to protect himself and the members of his household. It was not sufficient to protect the entire generation. Those righteous men who preceded Noah, such as Chanoch and Yered, who had acquired holy

17. This is possibly the solution to the apparent disagreement mentioned above regarding Noah's spiritual status (6:9; 6:18) - the view that Noah was a *tzaddik* only relative to his generation applies to the period prior to his 600th birthday, whereas the view that he was a perfect *tzaddik* refers to the period after he turned 600.

18. The third of the levels of the soul. See *Introduction.* See also *Zohar I,* 206a.

neshamot, and were sufficiently worthy for the Holy One blessed be He to do kindness on their behalf, **had already died** on dry land – i.e., prior to the flood, when the earth was still dry.[19] This is why it states, "Everything on dry land whose *neshamah* was his breath of life. . . ." Do not maintain that this refers to those who lived at the time of the flood. Rather, it refers to an earlier era. Therefore Scripture states, "Everything (whose *neshamah* was his breath of life) on dry land i.e., prior to the flood had **already** perished."

(*Zohar I, Hashmatot* to p. 206 – *siman* 20)

8:4 ותנח התבה בחדש השביעי בשבע עשר יום לחדש על הרי אררת – The ark came to rest on the seventeenth of the seventh month on the mountains of Ararat

Rabbi Elazar said: How beloved are the words of Torah, for every word contains supernal secrets. The Torah itself in its entirety is called supernal! We have learned in the eighth of Rabbi Yishmael's Thirteen Principles by which the Torah is expounded:[20] "When a particular case that is included in a general law is singled out to instruct us concerning something new, it is singled out to teach not only concerning its own case, but is to be applied to the entire general law." The Torah as a whole is the general law Above. Now, although a particular story is singled out, it certainly does not come to teach only concerning that story itself, but also to teach us supernal matters and lofty secrets. Thus, it is singled out to teach not only concerning its own case, but is to be applied to the entire general law – i.e., the entire Torah. . . .

For example, this incident, mentioned in our verse: "The ark came to rest on the seventeenth of the seventh month on the mountains of Ararat" –

19. *Ziv HaZohar*
20. *Sifra,* Introduction.

indeed, this verse is singled out from the general law of the Torah and is cited as a simple story, whereas the Torah in general is a book of instructions in how to live one's life properly.[21] What difference does it make to us whether the ark came to rest on this mountain or that? It had to land on some spot or another! However, as mentioned above, it is singled out to teach us about the entire law i.e., the entire Torah. . . .

Come and see the proof of this: It is not befitting the honor of a king of flesh and blood to prattle, much less to write about mundane matters. Do you then think that the Supernal King, the Holy One blessed be He had nothing holy to write the Torah about, so that He merely collected mundane matters, such as the words of Eisav, the words of Hagar, the conversations of Lavan and Yaakov, the words of Bilaam and his donkey, the statements of Balak and Zimri, and all the other stories written in the Torah, and made the Torah from them?....

Certainly, the Torah is truth, and God's Torah is perfect. Every word in this "story" alludes to supernal matters. This story is singled out to instruct us not only about itself, but regarding the entire Law the entire Torah.

Come and see how this is so regarding this verse, as well as other verses: "The ark came to rest. . . ." when judgment hangs over the world, when severity abides, and the Holy One blessed be He sits upon the Throne of Judgment to judge the world thereby. . . . which takes place only in the seventh month, the month of *Tishrei* in the Hebrew calendar. This is the time of judgment, when all creatures of the world are examined, passing before His Throne. Regarding this it is written, "The ark came to rest in the seventh month. . . ." Of course this took place in the seventh month, for this is the month of judgment for the world. "On the mountains of Ararat:" The word "Ararat" (אררט) alludes to the word ארור, "cursed," hinting to the powers of severity, masters at causing moaning and wailing. A number of those who protect the world from severe

21. See *Shemot* 24:12; *Zohar Chadash, Chukat 50a; Zohar III,* 53b.

judgments, i.e., *tzaddikim,* are aroused on that day, and all stand at the foot of that Throne as the judgment of the world takes place.

The Children of Israel pray before the Holy One blessed be He on that day Rosh HaShanah, the Jewish New Year which falls on the first and second of *Tishrei* and they beg and entreat Him to judge the world favorably. The blow the *shofar*[22] and the Holy One blessed be He has compassion for them and transforms severe judgments to mercy. . . . Thus the explanation of our verse is as follows: "The ark (תיבה) came to rest" refers to the words (תיבות plural of תיבה) of prayer which the Jewish people utter "in the seventh month" (*Tishrei*). Their prayers come to rest upon "the mountains of Ararat" (severe judgments) in order to transform them into good טוב which has the numerical value[23] of seventeen. Just as we see that this verse alludes to supernal events, and the role of the Jewish people in them, so too, all the "stories" of the Torah.

(*Zohar III,* 149a-b)

The following extracts substantiates the view that the story of the flood is to be interpreted allegorically, referring to major spiritual (and historic) events

8:7 וישלח את העורב – He sent out the raven

Rabbi Chiyya said: Why did he send out the raven, rather than any other bird? Because Noah was terribly distressed at the destruction of the world. He said, "Master of the worlds, I know that You are merciful, but You did not have compassion for Your world, and Your mercy was transformed to harshness. You did not have mercy upon Your children, therefore let this one (the raven) go out, for it does not have mercy on its young, and turns upon them viciously.[24] For this reason, he sent out the raven and no other bird.

---

22. A ram's horn.
23. *Gematria.*
24. See *Eruvin* 22a.

Rabbi Yose asked: Doesn't Scripture attest that "Noah was a righteous man, wholehearted in his generation?" (above, 6:9). How then did he speak so brazenly towards Heaven?

Rabbi Chiyya replied: He spoke out of anguish, and we have learned,[25] "You may not judge a man in his hour of anguish, as it says, "Iyov speaks without awareness, and his words make no sense." (*Iyov* 34:35). Even though he spoke disrespectfully towards Heaven, he is not judged as one who did so intentionally, but rather as one who spoke without being aware of what he was saying because of his anguish.

The raven did not want to fulfill his mission, for it was set aside for another mission, to provide Eliyahu with food. . . .[26]

(*Midrash HaNe'elam, Zohar Chadash Noah* 22b)

8:8-12 וישלח את היונה - He sent off the dove. . . .

Rabbi Pinchas said: The Holy One blessed be He wished to test the Children of Israel, and so He sent them into exile in Babylon, as it states, "He sent off the dove." "The dove" refers to *Knesset Yisrael* the collective souls of the Jewish people. This exile took place after the destruction of the First Temple. Now see what it written in the next verse in regard to this: "But the dove did not find a perch for its foot," for the King of Babylon exacerbated the yoke of their exile by starvation and thirst, and by murdering many of the righteous. Because of the harshness of the exile, "it returned to him in the ark" symbolizing thatthe Jewish people repented, and returned to God, who stretched out His hand "and took it." This means that their repentance was accepted.

Then *Knesset Yisrael* sinned again, and He sent them into exile again, as it states, "Once more he sent the dove out from the ark" this time into the Greek exile, during the era of the Second Temple. . . ..

---

25. *Bava Batra* 16b. See also *Zohar Chadash, Midrash Ruth* p. 75d.
26. See *I Kings* chap. 17.

After the Jewish People suffered great anguish and duress during the Greek exile it is written, "Toward evening, the dove returned." What is the allegorical meaning of "toward evening?" That the hour of relief did not shine as it had done previously. The righteous were killed, the day darkened, the sun set and they could not withstand the tremendous repression, as it states, "Woe to us, for the day wanes, and the shadows of night are lengthening" (*Yirmeyahu* 6:4). "The day wanes." These are the righteous, who shine like the sun; "and the shadows of night are lengthening" – they remained like the dregs. This is the meaning of "toward evening," and not at the time when the righteous shone like the sun.

"In its beak was an olive leaf it had plucked:" Had the Holy One blessed be He not aroused the spirit of the Kohanim who lit the *menorah*[27] using olive oil – Mattityahu and his sons, the Hasmoneans, who fought against the Greek enemy and eventually defeated them, as told in the story of *Channukah* – then the vestige of the Tribe of Yehudah[28] would have been lost. But each time the Jewish people were sent into exile they repented and returned, and their repentance was accepted. . . .

"He waited yet another seven days and sent out the dove:" This refers to the exile of Edom (Rome) after the destruction of the Second Temple. "It did not return to him any more:" Until this very day we have not repented, and our spirit has not been aroused to return to God. Rabbi Pinchas said: If we repent, we would not remain even a single day longer in exile.

Rabbi Eliezer said: Every time the Jewish People were sent into exile, the Holy One blessed be He set a limit to the exile, and they were always aroused to repentance. But this final exile has no set limit, and everything depends upon repentance.[29]

(*Midrash HaNe'elam, Zohar Chadash* p. 23c)

---

27. The candelabrum in the Temple.
28. I.e., the Jewish People.
29. This is also the conclusion Maimonides reaches: *Code, Teshuvah* 7:5.

Rebuilding the World

8:20 ויבן נח מזבח. . . .ויעל עלת – Noah built an altar. . . . and he offered burnt offerings

This was the same altar on which Adam had sacrificed offerings. Why then does it state, "Noah **built** an altar," implying that he built it from scratch? Because prior to the flood the wicked people of the world had caused it to be removed from its proper place – i.e., they removed it from the realm of holiness to the realm of unholiness.[30] Noah then reconstructed it in the realm of holiness.

(*Zohar I,* 70a)

We learned that when Noah left the ark, and he saw to what extent the world had been destroyed, he began to weep before Heaven, and said, "Master of the worlds, You are called 'Compassionate and Gracious.'[31] You should have had compassion upon the work of Your hands!"

The Holy One blessed be He replied, "Foolish shepherd! Only now do you say this? Why did you not say so when I told you, 'For it is you whom I have seen to be righteous before Me' (above 7:1); or when I informed you that, 'I am about to bring a flood of water upon the earth. . . .' (above 6:17); or when I told you, 'Make yourself an ark of gopher-wood' (6:14). I held back for so long, and told you all these things so that you would beg for mercy on behalf of the world. From the moment that you heard that you would be saved in the ark, it did not enter your heart to ask for mercy that the world should be a good place! So you made an ark and you were saved. Now that the world is destroyed you open your mouth and present requests and pleas before

---

30. *Sulam.*
31. *Shemot* 34:6.

Me?!" When Noah realized his error he offered sacrifices and burnt offerings. For a burnt offering atones for improper thoughts.[32]

(*Zohar I, Hashmatot siman* 12, p. 254b)

9:2 ומוראכם וחתכם יהיה על כל חית הארץ – Fear and awe of you shall be upon every living creature on earth

Rabbi Abba said: At the outset, referring to the creation of man, it is written, "With the image of God He created him" (above, 1:27). It is also written, "with the image of God He created him" (ibid.); therefore all the animals were afraid of man. When they sinned, their appearance changed from that supernal image,[33] and man began to fear wild animals. Initially, when all the creatures in the world lifted their eyes and saw the holy supernal form of man, they were afraid and trembled before him. But when man sinned his image was transformed in the eyes of the wild animals. For this reason, man began to fear other creatures and tremble before them. Come and see that the radiant countenance of those people who do not sin before their Master, and do not transgress the commandments of the Torah, does not change. All the creatures tremble and fear before them as we see from the story of Daniel in the lion's den.[34] When people transgress the Torah, though, then their countenance changes and they fear and tremble before other creatures. . . .

Now that the world was renewed after the flood,[35] as it was originally, in the days of Adam, God gave them this blessing: "Fear and awe of you shall be upon every liiving creature on earth." From now

---

32. As the *Zohar* (vol. 1, p. 69b) states explicitly.
33. See above, commentary to 3:6.
34. *Daniel* chap. 6.
35. Cf. *Bereishit Rabbah* 30:8.

on, you will have the form of men just as with Adam prior to his sin. He thus gave them superiority over all creatures.

(*Zohar I,* 71a)

9:1-7 ויברך אלקים את נח ואת בניו. . . .ואתם פרו ורבו – God blessed Noah and his sons. . . . And you shall be fertile and produce many offspring

Rabbi Abba said: Females are not mentioned in the blessings written in verses 9:1-7; only Noah and his sons, as verse 9:1 states, "God blessed Noah and his sons. . . ." but it does not mention the women.

Rabbi Shimon said: The word ואתם ("and you. . . .") in verse 7 is in the plural, including both males and females. Furthermore, the phrase ויברך אלקים את נח(literally, "God blessed **in addition to**[36] Noah. . . .") includes his wife; and ואת בניו (literally, "**in addition to** his sons. . . .") includes their wives. And therefore it is written, "And you (plural) shall be fertile and produce many offspring." At this point, the Holy One blessed be He gave them the seven Noahide laws[37] for themselves and all future generations. The seven laws are: 1) To establish and administer a system of law and punishment; 2) The prohibition against cursing or blaspheming God; 3) The prohibition against idolatry; 4) The prohibition against murder; 5) The prohibition against illicit sexual relations; 6) The prohibition against theft; 7) The prohibition against removing flesh or a limb from a living animal.[38] Some authorities list several other laws.[39] These seven laws applied to all nations of the world, including the descendants of Avraham, Yitzchak and Yaakov (i.e., the Israelites), until the Jewish People stood and Mount Sinai, and were given all the 613

---

36. "All instances of את in the Torah indicate an addition" (*Pesachim* 22b).
37. See *Sanhedrin* 56a-b.
38. Ibid.; Maimonides *Code, Melachim* 9:10.
39. See Maimonides, ad. loc.; *Sanhedrin* 58a. *Sheiltot* (*parshat Zot HaBerachah*) writes that the nations of the world are also commanded to "be fertile and produce many offspring." (See also Tosafot *Chagiga* 3a).

laws[40] of the Torah. From the era of Noah until the present day, all the nations of the world are obligated to observe the seven Noahide laws, and the Jewish people are obligated to observe the 613 laws received at Sinai.

(*Zohar I,* 71a-b)

The Rainbow

9:13 את קשתי נתתי בענן והיתה לאות ברית ביני ובין הארץ – I have placed My rainbow in the clouds, and it shall be a sign of the covenant between Me and the earth

"I **have** placed" already. I.e., The rainbow was not something new which began in the days of Noah. On the contrary, the appearance of the rainbow is a natural phenomenon caused by the refraction of sunlight through clouds or raindrops, which could have occurred at any time in the past. However, at this point the rainbow was chosen as a sign to the world that there would never again be a flood. From this point on the rainbow appears with a specific purpose: to remind the world to follow the ways of Torah.[41]

(*Zohar I,* 18a; 72b)

In Scripture,[42] the flood is referred to as "the waters of Noah." He was the one who caused them to be called this by failing to pray for compassion on the world's behalf, as explained above. Thus the rainbow indicates that there is no one to protect the world by praying for God's compassion. . . .

When the rainbow does not appear at all throughout a generation, this is an indication that there is a righteous *tzaddik* in the generation, and therefore the world does not need a sign that God will not destroy it. Who is such a *tzaddik*? One who prays for compassion for the world,

---

40. See *Makkot* 23b.
41. *Ziv HaZohar.*
42. *Yeshayahu* 54:9.

and who is worthy of protecting it, such as Rabbi Shimon bar Yochai. In his days the world did not need this sign, for the appearance of the rainbow is an indication that only God protects the world because there are no *tzaddikim* righteous enough to do so. In Rabbi Shimon's day there was no negative decree against the world which he would have to annul.

(*Zohar III,* 15a)

Noah's Impropriety

9:20-21 ויחל נח איש אדמה ויטע כרם. וישת מן היין וישכר ויתגל בתוך אהלה – Noah, the man of the soil, debased himself and planted a vineyard. He drank of the wine and became drunk, and he uncovered himself within his tent

Rabbi Yehudah and Rabbi Yose interpreted these verses differently: One maintained that the grapevine was banished from the Garden of Eden for the Tree of Knowledge from which Adam and Even had eaten was a grapevine[43] and he planted it here in the ground – outside of the Garden of Eden. The other one maintains that the grapevine was from the Land of Israel, and he uprooted it and planted it outside of the Land of Israel. On the same day that he planted it, it produced fruits which he squeezed to make wine. He then drank the wine and became intoxicated. According to the opinion that the vine was banished together with Adam from the Garden of Eden, Noah intended to rectify the vine with which Adam had transgressed. However, instead of sanctifying the wine which he made from the grapes, he became drunk on it. He thus debased himself by repeating Adam's sin, as the *Zohar* explains elsewhere.[44] The sin of the Tree of Knowledge was that Adam drank the juice which Eve squeezed from its grapes. According to the second opinion, Noah found the vine outside of the Garden

43. This is one of the views cited in *Bereishit Rabbah* 15:8; *Sanhedrin* 70b.
44. *Zohar I,* 36a; *Zohar II,* 267b. The meaning of this will be explained below.

of Eden, in the Land of Israel. He debased himself by uprooting it from its proper place, and replanting it elsewhere, in a place that was not fitting for it. According to this view, his transgression was not the same as that of Adam.[45]

Rabbi Shimon said: This verse contains the secret of wisdom. When Noah wished to examine the sin that Adam had committed with the intention of avoiding it himself and learning how to rectify it and the world, he was unable to fathom its secret. So he squeezed grapes in order to examine the secret of the vineyard, as the *Zohar* states: Eve squeezed grapes from the Tree of Knowledge and gave Adam to drink.[46] Commentaries[47] explain that this refers to "external" or secular wisdom, i.e., wisdom other than the Torah, such as philosophy, which attempts to examine Divine secrets by way of the intellect; or witchcraft, which attempts to harness the powers of impurity. When he reached this point, he became intoxicated and exposed, and he lost his resistance to the external forces. Thus, the breach in the world which Adam's sin had made became revealed, after it had been sealed against the entry of external forces[48]. . . . This is similar to what happened with the sons of Aaron, regarding whom we have learned[49] that they entered into the Holy of Holies intoxicated with wine.[50] Now who gave them wine to drink there? Do you really think that they were so brazen as to drink wine there in the Holy of Holies? This is not the case! Rather, they became intoxicated with the same wine which intoxicated Noah – i.e., secular wisdom.[51] Here, regarding Aaron's sons, it is written, "They offered strange

---

45. *Sulam.*
46. *Zohar I,* 36a; *Zohar II,* 267b.
47. *Ziv Hazohar.*
48. *Ashmoret HaBoker.*
49. *Vayikra Rabbah* 12:1; *Pesikta d'Rav Kahana* 26:15. See also *Zevachim* 18a.
50. See *Vayikra* 10:1 ff.
51. *Ziv HaZohar.*

fire (אש זרה) before God." Elsewhere it is written, "Beware of a strange woman (אשה זרה)" (*Mishlei* 7:5)[52] – alluding to secular wisdom.

(*Zohar I,* 73a)

Nimrod

10:9 הוא היה גבור ציד לפני ה' – He was an heretical instigator against God

The literal translation of the verse reads: "He was a mighty hunter before God." However, the Zohar's understands this differently

Nimrod was a mighty hunter: He wore the clothes of Adam which he had stolen. These were the garments which God had made for Adam and Eve[53] when He banished them from the Garden of Eden (above, 3:21). With them, he knew how to trap creatures, for all the creatures showed natural obeisance to Adam, the choicest of God's creations. When Nimrod wore Adam's clothes, his outward appearance was that of Adam, and the creatures were humbled before him.

Rabbi Eliezer said: Nimrod beguiled creatures to pursue idolatry. He used the power of those garments to dominate people, and declared himself the ruler of the world – i.e., he declared himself to be God, so that men worshipped him. Why he was he named "Nimrod?" Because he rebelled (*marad*) against the supernal King of the universe, rebelling against the authority of He Who is Above, as well as against the authority of man below.

(*Zohar I,* 73b-74a)

---

52. Here the *Zohar* makes use of a *gezeirah shavah* - identical expressions found in two different verses to establish an analogy between the two incidents they describe.

53. *Sulam.*

The Tower of Babel

11:1-4 ויהי כל הארץ שפה אחת ודברים אחדים. . . . הבה נבנה לנו עיר ומגדל וראשו בשמים ונעשה לנו שם פן נפוץ על פני כל הארץ – The entire earth had one language and a common purpose. . . . Come, let us build ourselves a city, and a tower whose top will reach the sky. Thus we will make ourselves a name so that we will not become scattered over the entire earth

Rabbi Shimon said: Until that time, the world had a single foundation, principle and root: belief in the Holy One blessed be He. What is written subsequently? "When people migrated from *Kedem*. . . ." The word *Kedem* can be understood literally – "the east," or, as in this case, as referring to the Holy One blessed be He who is called *Kadmono shel Olam*, the Primordial and Principle One in whom everyone believed. Thus, the meaning of the verse is: "They abandoned belief in God, and began to worship idols.
(*Zohar I,* 74b)

"The entire earth had one language." The builders of the city spoke the Holy Tongue (Hebrew), which the ministering angels know, and did not speak any other language. For this reason it is written, "Shouldn't they be prevented from accomplishing all their objectives?" (below 11:6). Had they spoken a different language, which the ministering angels do not know, they could not have accomplished their objectives, because witchcraft has no permanence. The meaning of this is as follows: The builders of the city used their knowledge of the Hebrew language in *hasba'at shemot* (the use or manipulation of Divine Names) to force the ministering angels to aid them in their task of building the city and the tower. Had they not known the Holy Tongue, they would not have been able to force the angels to do their bidding. Angels can be manipulated only by using Divine Names which derive from the Hebrew language. Instead, they would have used witchcraft. Since witchcraft has no permanence, whatever they would have achieved thereby would have soon disintegrated of its own accord.[54]

"A common purpose:" The words ודברים אחדים can also be translated as, "a few matters,"[55] for they knew clearly the rank each of the multiple supernal levels without erring between them, as if they were merely a few matters. For this reason, because of their vast knowledge of spiritual matters, they took evil counsel from wisdom, as it is written, "Let us build ourselves a city, and a tower whose top will reach the sky." The "city and tower" refer to extremely elevated levels of esoteric wisdom which they dragged into impurity, as will be explained shortly. This matter is the secret of *chochmah,* wisdom or better, cunning since this refers to *chochmah* of the side of unholiness. They wanted to increase the power of unholiness on earth, and serve the side of impurity, for they knew that from that level all negative aspects descend upon the world. In this way they attempted to drive holiness away.

"A city and a tower": This refers to supernal *chochmah*, for they knew that the Holy Divine Name[56] is not grasped down below other than by way of the "city and tower."[57] They cunningly worked to make the side of impurity dominate on earth and drive away the Master of the earth *malchut of* Holiness from its proper place, and make the powers of impurity dwell upon earth by building the corresponding levels (city and tower) on the side of unholiness. This is the meaning of "We will make ourselves a name;" their knowledge of esoteric matters enabled them to use Divine Names to force the ministering angels to do their evil will, as mentioned above.

(*Sitrei Torah – Zohar I,* 74b)

---

54. *Sulam.*
55. As in ימים אחדים- "a few days" (*Bereishit* 27:44).
56. The Ineffable Four-Letter Name (*Or Yakar*).
57. *Yesod* and *malchut* (*Or Yakar*).

11:5 וירד ה' לראות את העיר ואת המגדל – God descended to look at the city and the tower

This is one of the ten times that the Divine Presence[58] descended to earth.[59] What did He wish to see that He did not know already? In fact, "to see" in this context means to examine the law, as it is written, "May God look upon you and judge" (*Shemot* 5:21) that is, He examined the verdict of the Supernal Court which had passed judgment upon them.[60]

(*Zohar I,* 75a)

Alternatively, the expression "He descended" is used to indicate that He descended from the holy to the profane. "Descent" here is not to be understood as steeping down from one **place** to another, but from one spiritual **level** to another.

(*Zohar I,* 75b)

11:6 הן עם אחד ושפה אחת לכלם – They are a single people, and they all have one language

Because they are united they will succeed in their endeavor. Therefore, the solution is to scatter each of the supernal levels from which each of the nations derive in a different direction. Thus all those down below (each of the nations) will be scattered. Once their roots have been separated and scattered, the branches will follow.[61] What is written immediately afterwards (verse 8)? "From that place, God scattered them over the surface of the entire earth."

(*Zohar I,* 75b)

---

58. The *Shechinah.*
59. See *Avot d' Rabbi Natan* chap. 34.
60. *Damesek Eliezer.*
61. *Sulam.*

Avraham and Sarah

11:28 וימת הרן על פני תרח אביו – Haran died in front of his father, Terach

The words על פני תרח אביו are generally translated as "**in the lifetime** of his father, Terach."[62] The *Zohar*, however, questions this translation: What does this come to teach us? If you say that it teaches us that Terach dies in his father's lifetime, why would the Torah want to inform us of this? Until that day were there no men other than him who died in their father's lifetime? What about Hevel who died in Adam's lifetime? What about Chanoch whom God took during the lifetime of his father Yered? Why then are we informed that Haran died in the lifetime of Terach?[63]

However, the answer is that this is an incorrect translation. The verse should be translated as: "Haran died in front of his father, Terach." The background to this interpretation is as follows: Avraham refused to worship idolatry. He smashed his father's idols and threw them in the fire. His father complained to the king of the Chaldeans,[64] Nimrod, who condemned Avraham to a fiery death in the furnace of their fire-god.[65] When Avraham was thrown into the furnace Haran was killed. . . . Who killed Haran? When Avraham was thrown into the furnace of *Ur Kasdim*, the Holy One blessed be He revealed Himself to Avraham and rescued him. Avraham stepped out of the furnace completely unharmed. Haran was standing there watching the proceedings. When the Chaldeans concluded that Avraham was spared in Haran's merit, a tongue of flame miraculously shot forth from the furnace and burned Haran to a cinder. This is why it is written, "Haran died in front of his father, Terach" who was also watching the proceedings. Other opinions maintain that the Chaldeans surmised that fire did not affect Terach's

62. Rashi, citing *Midrash Rabbah.*
63. *Sulam.*
64. *Kasdim* in Hebrew.
65. As cited in Rashi's commentary.

progeny. To test their hypothesis they suggested throwing Haran into the furnace. "If he does not burn, it is certain that fire has no effect on Terach's progeny," they said. They tossed Haran into the fire and he was consumed in flames. Since his father Terach was standing right there, the verse states, "Haran died in front of his father, Terach."

(*Zohar I,* 77b)

11:30 ותהי שרי עקרה אין לה ולד – Sarai[66] was barren. She had no children

Since the verse states, "Sarai was barren," don't we already know that she had no children? What then is the meaning of "she had no children?" This is what the Head of the Academy answered: She had not given birth to a child, but she had given birth to souls. These two righteous people, Sarah and Avraham, gave birth to the souls of converts throughout their stay in Charan as it is written, "and the souls (*nefesh*) they had made in Charan. . . ." (below, 12:6). "The souls they had made" is meant literally.

(*Zohar III,* 168a)

---

66. Abraham's wife, Sarai, was given the name Sarah only later on, when God promised them a son (below, 17:15).

Lech
Lecha

Lech Lecha

Avraham's Departure

12:1 ויאמר ה' אל אברם לך לך מארצך וממולדתך ומבית אביך – God said to Avram,[1] "For your own sake, go away from your land, from your birthplace, and from your father's house

God said to Avram, "For your own sake,[2] go away. . . ." The words לך לך (*lech lecha*) translated literally mean "Go to you." Rabbi Elazar said: לך לך, for your own sake, go away from here meaning, depart from the present spiritual course you are occupied with and rectify your soul through the *mitzvot* and good deeds you will fulfill in the Land of Israel. There, you will succeed in advancing your spiritual level. It is not fitting for you to be here, among these wicked people. Even though they have not influenced you to emulate them, the evil which surrounds you taints the soul.[3]

(*Zohar I,* 77b)

An alternative translation of the words לך לך *– "Go to your Self"*

"Go". . . . in order to know yourself i.e., to grasp the root of your soul, so that you can perfect yourself through revealing the root of your soul down in this world. Elsewhere,[4] the *Zohar* explains that every righteous person (*tzaddik*) in this world has two souls; one soul in this world, and another soul in the higher spiritual worlds above. These are really different **levels** of the soul – the main part of the soul remains above, in the higher worlds and a mere radiance or reflection thereof is clothed in the physical body in this world.[5] And thus we

---

1. Avraham was the name he was given only later on - see verse 17:5.
2. See Rashi's commentary to this verse.
3. *Or Yakar*; Rabbi Avraham Galanti; *Mikdash Melech.*
4. *Tosefta, Zohar I,* 60a.
5. Explained at length in *Likkutei Torah, Ha'azinu* 71d; *Shir HaShirim* p. 16d.

find that God calls many *tzaddikim* by their name twice – "Avraham, Avraham;"[6] "Yaakov, Yaakov;"[7] "Moshe Moshe;"[8] "Shmuel, Shmuel;"[9] etc., in order to draw the soul down from above into the radiance of the soul below.[10] At this point, Avraham was thus initiated into the journey of revealing the root of his soul as it is above – below in this world.[11]

(*Zohar I,* 78b)

"Go away from your land, from your birthplace, and from your father's house." Why the repetition? Was it not sufficient to say, "Go away from your land?" However, God was speaking to Avraham's soul as it was above, prior to its descent into the body.[12] "Go away from your heavenly abode, i.e., from the Garden of Eden,[13] and from the storehouse of souls above, which is called *Guf* (body).[14] Alternatively, this may be interpreted as referring to the spiritual "body" mentioned elsewhere in the *Zohar.*[15] From the house of your Father in Heaven to the physical body below in this world.

(*Zohar Chadash, Noach* 21b)

"From your land:" This is the lower level of the Garden of Eden.[16]

"From your father's house:" This is the upper level of the Garden of Eden.

"To the land that I will show you:" This is the lowly and dismal earth.

(*Zohar Chadash, Acharei* 46d)

---

6. *Bereishit* 22:11.
7. *Bereishit* 46:2.
8. *Shemot* 3:4.
9. *Shmuel I,* 3:10.
10. See *Introduction.*
11. *Torah Or, Lech Lecha* 11a ff.
12. As stated explicitly in *Zohar I,* 76b (*Sitrei Torah*); *Midrash HaNe'elam - Zohar Chadash* 47a.
13. See following commentary.
14. See *Yevamot* 62b.
15. *Zohar I,* 47a; *II* , 149b-150a.
16. There are many levels in *Gan Eden,* generally divided into the upper and lower. See *Zohar II,* 211b.

The Head of the Academy began his discourse by citing the verse, "God said to Avram,[17] "For you own sake, go away from your land. . . ." for in this way enlightenment would irradiate him. That is, God told him to leave his land and his birthplace etc., for he was unable to receive enlightenment there. A person who does not succeed in one place should pick himself up and go to another place where he may be successful, just like one waves a glowing log so that it will burst into flame. The Sages of the Talmud also state: A change of place brings a change of fortune.[18]

(*Zohar III,* 166b)

With God's Blessing

12:2 ועאשך לגוי גדול ואברכך ואגדלה שמך והיה ברכה – I will make you into a great nation, and I will bless you and make your name great, and you shall be a blessing

This verse corresponds to the previous one

"I will make you into a great nation" because it is written, "Go away."

"And I will bless you" because it is written, "From your land."

"And make your name great" because it is written, "From your birthplace."

"And you shall be a blessing" because it is written, "From your father's house."

(*Zohar I,* 88a)

---

17. Avraham was the name he was given only later on - see verse 17:5.

18. *Rosh HaShanah* 16b; *Bava Metzia* 75b.

12:4 וילך אתו לוט – And Lot went with him

Lot joined Avram in order to learn from his deeds. Despite his good intentions, he did not learn very much. . . . Nevertheless, as long as Lot was with Avram, he did not involve himself with wicked people. As soon as Avram left him, it states, "Lot chose for himself the Jordan Plain. . . . pitching his tents as far as Sodom" (below 13:11-12). Subsequently it states, "The people of Sodom were wicked, and they acted exceedingly sinfully against God" (13:13).

(*Zohar I*, 78b)

12:5 ויקח אברם את שרי אשתו ואת לוט בן אחיו ואת הנפש אשר עשו בחרן – Avram took Sarai, his wife, and Lot, his nephew, and the souls that they had acquired in Charan

"Avram took Sarai, his wife:" This is the body, which is to the soul like a female to a male. Avraham corresponds to the soul, and Sarah to the body.

(*Zohar I,* 79a)

Rabbi Elazar asked: What is the meaning of he "took Sarai, his wife?" Obviously, it cannot be interpreted literally, that he picked her up and took her with him. Rather, he persuaded her verbally, in a pleasant way, for a man has no right to take his wife away from her home to go to another country against her will. . . . He explained to her how evil the ways of their fellow citizens of Charan were, and she agreed wholeheartedly to leave Charan.

"And Lot his nephew": What did Avraham see in Lot that he took him with him? He saw with divine inspiration (*ruach hakodesh*) that David would descend from him, via his son Moab, who was the ancestor of Ruth the Moabite, whose son, Oved, was the father of Jesse (Yishai), father of King David.[19]

---

19. *Ruth* 4:17.

"And the souls that they had acquired in Charan": These are the male and female converts whose souls they secured. Avraham converted the men, and Sarah, the women. It is therefore regarded as if they actually made them. Elsewhere,[20] the *Zohar* explains that Sarah and Avraham "gave birth" to the **souls** of converts throughout their stay in Charan. Thus the above verse may be translated as, "The souls they had **made**."

(*Zohar I,* 79a)

12:7-8 ויבן שם מזבח לה' הנראה אליו.... ויבן שם מזבח לה' ויקרא בשם ה' – He built an altar there to God who had appeared to him. . . . He built an altar there to God, and prayed with God's Name

Since the verse already states, "To God," why is it necessary to add, "who had appeared to him?" Here the spiritual level which reigns over the Holy Land, and which was previously hidden from him,[21] was now **revealed** to him.

(*Zohar I,* 80a)

The first verse refers to the altar which he built "to God who had appeared to him," whereas the second verse refers only to "an altar to God"

These were two different altars. . . . one corresponding to the level which was revealed to him, and one to the level which was still hidden from him.[22]

(*Zohar I,* 80a)

---

20. *Zohar III,* 168a.
21. As stated in the preceding paragraph of the *Zohar,* and in *Zohar I,* 78a.
22. Technically, these are respectively the aspect of *nukvah* of *ze'ir anpin* from *tiferet* down (also called the *partzuf* of Rachel), and the aspect of *nukvah* of *ze'ir anpin* from *tiferet* upward (also called the *partzuf* of Leah).

12:9 ויסע אברם הלוך ונסוע הנגבה – Then Avram journeyed on, traveling south

South is the portion of Avraham his defining attribute, which is *chesed*[23] (loving-kindness), as the verse states, "Avraham, My beloved" (*Yeshayahu* 41:8).

"Journeyed on, traveling. . . ." from level to level until he reached the south the attribute of *chesed.* There, in the Land of Israel, he became fully attached i.e., he attained this level permanently.

When Avraham became crowned with his level in the Holy Land, what does the Torah write? "There was a famine in that land" (below 12:10). They did not know how to bring themselves closer to the Holy One blessed be He as in, "Not a famine for bread, nor a thirst for water, but for hearing the words of God (*Amos* 8:11). Closeness to God comes about through the attribute of *chesed,* loving-kindness, as the verse states, "His right hand (a symbol of love and kindness) embraces me" (*Shir Hashirim* 2:6).

(*Zohar I,* 80a)

Encounter with Egypt

12:10 וירד אברם מצרימה לגור שם – So Avram went down to stay in Egypt

Why Egypt rather than any other country? . . . .He sought to understand all those levels which are bound below in unholiness, in order to avoid them, as will be explained shortly. Egypt tends to the right. Avraham's attribute was that of *chesed*, corresponding to the right side, and so was that of Egypt. However, Egypt was *chesed* of *kelipah* (impurity). This is why he went down specifically to Egypt.

(*Zohar I,* 81b)

---

23. See *Introduction.*

12:11 ויהי כאשר הקריב לבוא מצרימה – As he approached Egypt

Rabbi Elazar said: Why does the verse state כאשר הקריב, in the causative form, implying that he brought **others** closer. It should have said, כאשר קרב "as he approached!" However, it is written ופרעה הקריב – "And Pharaoh brought (others) closer" (*Shemot* 14:10) for he made the Israelites turn to God through fear of him, they turned to God in prayer, as the verse continues, "they cried out to God." Similarly, in our verse he brought himself closer to God as he approached Egypt with the intention of examining those levels (*chesed* of *kelipah*, as explained above) in order to avoid them and the deeds of the land of Egypt which was the most decadent land in the world at that time.

Rabbi Yehudah said: Because Avraham went down to Egypt without permission, his descendants were enslaved in Egypt for 400 years. It is written, "Avram went down to Egypt," of his own accord, not "Go down to Egypt," a command from God.

(*Zohar I,* 81b)

12:11 הנה נא ידעתי כי יפת מראה את– Now I see that you are a beautiful woman

Did Avraham not know until now that his wife was a beautiful woman? This is the explanation: Until that moment Avraham had never looked at Sarah's features because of the great modesty and propriety between them. As they approached Egypt her face became uncovered[24] and he saw her. This may also be interpreted as follows: Avraham was one who looked at the **inner** qualities of a person, and not at the outer features; thus he only saw her internal beauty. In order to plan for their descent into the decadent Egypt, he looked at Sarah as one of the Egyptians would have looked at her, i.e., at her external beauty.

---

24 . *Ziv HaZohar* suggests that Sarah's face was always covered by a veil, as was common in those days, and a sudden wind blew the veil aside.

An alternative explanation: How did he know that she was beautiful? The rigors of travel generally spoil a person's beauty, but she remained just as unchangingly beautiful.[25]

Another explanation: "Now I see. . . ." He saw the *Shechinah*[26] with her. For this reason Avraham was confident that she would not be harmed by the Egyptians, and so he called her "my sister." This can be interpreted in two ways: 1) Literally, that she was his sister,[27] 2) As it is written, "Say to *chochmah*,[28] 'You are my sister' (*Mishlei* 7:4) thus "you" in our verse refers to the *Shechinah.*[29]

In the same vein, our verse continues: "So that he referring to the Holy One blessed be He not to Pharaoh will be good to me for your sake,"[30] referring to the *Shechinah.* For your (the *Shechinah's*) sake the Holy One blessed be He will be good to me because Avraham was the only one in a world of idolaters who was given the mission of revealing the Divine Presence in this world.[31] Thus, his preservation and advancement would be to the benefit of the *Shechinah* as well.

Rabbi Yeisa said: Avraham knew that the Egyptians were a decadent people. Consequently, why was he not afraid for his wife's safety? Why did he not turn back from there? This was because he saw the *Shechinah* with her.

(*Zohar I,* 81b)

---

25. See Rashi's commentary to this verse.
26. The Divine Presence.
27. Which was in fact true, as Avraham explains in verse 20:12 below: "She is indeed my sister, my father's daughter [from another wife], but not my mother's daughter."
28. Wisdom. This refers to the first immanent *sefirah*. See *Introduction.*
29. The *Shechinah* is also referred to as *chochmah tata'a* - the lower *chochmah*, as stated explicitly in *Zohar III,* 296a commenting on the verse "Say to *chochmah*, 'You are my sister.'"
30. Usually translated as, "on your account," if the verse is interpreted as referring to Sarah.
31. See below 18:19.

12:13 אמרי נא אחותי את – Please tell them that you are my sister

Rabbi Elazar said: This verse is puzzling. Would Avraham, who was so sin-fearing and so beloved of the Holy One,[32] blessed be He, have said this, especially regarding his own wife so that he could derive benefit from it? The explanation is as follows: Although Avraham was a righteous and sin-fearing man, he did not wish to rely on his own merit. He did not ask the Holy One, blessed be He to benefit him in his own merit but rather that he would acquire great wealth from the nations of the world in the merit of his wife, for the wealth that a man merits is for the sake of his wife,[33] as it is written, "House and riches are the inheritance of fathers, but a pious wife is from God" (*Mishlei* 19:14). One who is worthy of a pious wife merits everything. It is also written, "Her husband's heart trusts in her, and he shall have no lack of gain" (ibid., 31:11). Commentaries[34] explain that Avraham's intention was not to amass **material** wealth, but **spiritual** wealth i.e., the sparks of holiness which fell into creation with the shattering of the vessels of *Tohu*, as explained above in the commentary to *Bereishit* 1:16.[35] Later on, his descendants, the Jewish people, did exactly that during their slavery in Egypt. . . .[36] So Avraham trusted in her merit and was sure that they would not be able to harm him or to sport with her. Therefore he was not at all afraid to say that she was his sister.

Moreover, he saw an angel going before her, who said to Avraham, "Do not be afraid for her. The Holy One blessed be He sent me to extract wealth for her from the nations and to protect her in every way." Thus Avraham had no fear for his wife. He did fear for himself, for he did not see an angel accompanying him, but only accompanying her. He said, "You are protected, but I am not, therefore, please tell them that you are my sister. . . ."

(*Zohar III,* 52a)

---

32. As the verse in *Yeshayahu* 41:8 states explicitly.
33. Cf. Rabba's advice in *Bava Metzia* 59a.
34. *Zohar Chai*; *Matok miDevash*.
35. See also *Introduction*.
36. See Arizal's *Likkutei Torah, Shemot*.

12:15 ותקח האשה בית פרעה – Then the woman was taken to Pharaoh

Rabbi Yitzchak said: Woe to the wicked of the world who are unaware of the deeds of the Holy One blessed be He and take no notice of them! They do not see that everything which happens in the world is from the Holy One blessed be He who knows from the outset what will eventually take place, as it is written, "He declares the end from the beginning" (*Yeshayahu* 46: 10). He foresees all and initiates action that will develop with the passage of time. Come and see the proof of this: Had Sarah not been taken to Pharaoh by his soldiers who found her concealed in a trunk where she had hidden from the view of the lecherous Egyptian border guards,[37] he would not have been struck with plagues on her account as verse 17 below states. These plagues which he suffered on account of Sarah caused plagues later on when the Egyptians were struck with severe plagues prior to the exodus of the Israelites from Egypt.

(*Zohar I,* 82a)

12:17 וינגע ה' את פרעה נגעים גדולים... על דבר שרי אשת אברם – But God struck Pharaoh with severe plagues. . . . on account of Sarai, Avram's wife

The verse uses the expression על דבר שרי *which the Zohar interprets literally,meaning, "At Sarah's command"*

Come and see that the *Shechinah* did not budge from Sarah that entire night. As Pharaoh approached her an angel came and beat him. Every time Sarah said, "Beat him!" the angel struck him. The phrase על דבר שריis thus meant literally.

Avraham trusted in God that Pharaoh would definitely not be able to overpower Sarah. . . . this was one of the ten tests which

37. As the *Zohar* states in the *Hashmatot* to this section.

Avraham underwent and withstood.[38] This particular test was whether Avraham would have doubts about God, but Avraham did not wonder about the intentions and deeds of the Holy One, blessed be He.

(*Zohar I*, 82a)

The Return Journey

13:1 ויעל אברם ממצרים– Avram made the ascent from Egypt

Rabbi Shimon said: Come and see that the interpretation of this verse is all to do with the secret of *chochmah*[39] (wisdom). The verse alludes to the level of *chochmah* and to the levels below it, into which Avraham descended and which he comprehended without becoming tainted by them, and from which he subsequently returned to his Master. He was not lured by them into external wisdom,[40] i.e., wisdom other than the Torah, such as philosophy, which attempts to examine Divine secrets by way of the intellect, or witchcraft which attempts to harness the powers of impurity – as Adam was. When Adam reached that level, he was lured by the serpent and brought death upon the entire world through the sin of the Tree of Knowledge. Nor was he enticed like Noah, for when he (Noah) descended to that level, it is written, "He drank of the wine and became drunk, and he uncovered himself within his tent," (above, 9:21) i.e., Noah had intended to rectify the sin of the Tree of Knowledge, which was that Adam drank the juice which Eve squeezed from the grapes of the Tree, as the *Zohar* explains elsewhere.[41] However, instead of sancitfying the wine which he made from the grapes, he became drunk on it. He thus debased himself by repeating Adam's sin.

---

38. See *Avot* 5:3; *Midrash Tanchuma* 18:25; *Avot d'R. Natan* 33:2; *Pirkei d'R. Elazar* 26; *Zohar III*, 263b.

39. The first and highest of the immanent *sefirot*. See *Introduction*.

40. As explained above in the commentary to verse 9:20-21

41. *Zohar I,* 36a; *Zohar II,* 267b. The meaning of this was explained at length above op cit.

However, regarding Avraham, it is written, "Avram made the ascent from Egypt." He ascended, and did not remain below. Rather, he returned to his place, the elevated level to which he was previously attached. This act the descent into Egypt was to teach wisdom, that he was able to maintain his completeness and strength as is proper, without being enticed by the forces of evil.

(*Zohar I,* 83a)

13:7 ויהי ריב בין רעי מקנה אברם – Discord developed between the herdsmen of Avram's cattle

Rabbi Shimon said: Lot wished to return to the idol-worship in which the local inhabitants were steeped. . . . as it is written, "Lot travelled from *Kedem.*" What does *Kedem* mean? The word *Kedem* can be understood literally – "the east," or, in this case, as referring to the Holy One blessed be He who is called *Kadmono shel Olam* – the Primordial and Principle One. Here it is written, "Lot traveled from *Kedem,*" (below 13:11), and previously it is also written, "When people migrated from *Kedem*. . . ." (above 11:2)[42] Just as in the latter verse they moved away from *Kadmono shel Olam*, so too here – in this verse – the intention is that he abandoned belief in God and began to worship idols.[43]

When Avraham found out that this was the direction in which Lot was inclining, he immediately said to him, "Please separate from me" (below 13:9). You are not worthy of being together with me. So Avraham departed from Lot. He did not wish to keep his company; for anyone who keeps the company of a wicked person will eventually follow him[44] and be punished on his account. Where do we learn this from? From Yehoshafat[45] who kept the company of Achav.[46] If not for his ancestral merit he would have

---

42. See commentary there.
43. As stated in *Zohar I,* 74b.
44. Cf. *Sukkah* 56b.
45. Josephat.
46 . Ahab.

been punished. . . .[47] Therefore Avraham did not wish to go together with Lot.

As soon as Avraham warned Lot that he was about to depart from him, Lot should have repented. However, Lot did not wish to turn back from his shameful behavior. Rather, "Lot chose for himself the Jordan Plain. . . . and traveled from *Kedem*" (below, 13:11). He moved away from *Kadmono shel Olam*, and did not wish to cling to perfect faith, like Avraham.

So "Avram settled in the land of Canaan" (13:12) in order to cleave to the place of faith the land of Israel, which is called "the land of faith,"[48] and understand the wisdom of how to cleave to his Master. But "Lot settled among the cities of the Plain, pitching his tents as far as Sodom" (13:12) with those wicked people of the world who abandoned faith in God, as it is written, "The people of Sodom were wicked and they acted exceedingly sinfully against God" (13:13). Each of them departed along his path, as was fitting.

(*Zohar I,* 84a)

13:10 וישא לוט את עיניו. . . . כגן ה' כארץ מצרים – Lot followed his eyes. . . . it was like God's garden, like the land of Egypt

Until this point we did not know to what "God's garden" refers, whether to Egypt or to Sodom, or if "God's garden" refers to *Gan Eden* the Garden of Eden. The intention is actually as follows: "Like God's garden" refers to *Gan Eden*, which has plenty and delight for all; and so were both Sodom and Egypt. Just as God's garden does not need to be irrigated by man, so too Egypt; no one needed to irrigate it because when the Nile rose, it irrigated the entire land of Egypt. So too Sodom, of which it is written in our verse, "it had water in abundance." All the delights in the world were found there, and for

---

47. See *II Chronicles* chap. 18.
48. *Tehillim* 37:3; *Tanchuma* (Warsaw) *Re'eh* 11.

this reason they did not want anyone else to benefit from it, and therefore they banned all guests and visitors.[49]

(*Zohar I,* 108b)

13:14 וה' אמר אל אברהם אחרי הפרד לוט מעמו שא נא עיניך וראה– God said to Avram after Lot had departed from him, "Raise your eyes and look"

Rabbi Abba said: Come and see! Just as the *Shechinah* is not revealed other than in a place which is fitting, so too it is not seen nor revealed other than to a person who is worthy. For from the day that Lot decided to returned to his former ways of idolatry the spirit of prophecy[50] left Avraham. As soon as Lot parted ways with him, the spirit of prophecy immediately rested in its place, as the verse states, "God said to Avram **after Lot had departed** from him" i.e., only after Lot had departed did Avraham once again experience Divine revelation.

Come and see! As soon as Avraham realized that Lot had returned to his former ways , he was afraid. He said, "Perhaps, God forbid, because of this association with Lot I have forfeited the holiness with which the Holy One blessed be He crowned me?" As soon as Lot departed, He said to him, "Lift up your eyes and look from the place where you are. . . ." What is the meaning of "from the place where you are?" The level to which you formerly clung when you were crowned with complete faith. . . .

Then he was informed that this level of holiness would never leave him and his descendants, Yitzchak, Yaakov and Yaakov's descendants, for it is written, "For all the land which you see I will give to you and your descendants" (below, 13:15). What is the meaning of "all the land which you see?" After all, a person can see for only a few miles, as will be pointed out shortly. It refers to the very first level which was revealed to him, as is written, "to God who had appeared to him"

---

49. See below 18:20 ff.; *Bereishit Rabbah* on those verses.

50. *Ruach HaKodesh.*

(above, 12:7). Therefore it states, "which you see"[51] because this first level comprises all levels, and all levels are reflected in it. Commentaries[52] explain that this refers to the *sefirah* of *malchut.*

(*Zohar I,* 85a)

13:15 כי את כל הארץ אשר אתה ראה – For all the land which you see

Rabbi Abba said: Did Avraham then inherit the land according to what he saw? How far can a person see? Three or four or five parasangs? He said, "**All** the land which you see" rather than "what you see of the land. . . ." The former expression implies that he saw **all** of the land of Israel. However, since he saw all four directions north, south, west and east, he saw the entire land, for these four directions include the whole world.[53] An additional explanation: The Holy One blessed be He raised him up over the land of Israel and showed him that it is bound to all four "sides" of the world, so he saw all of the land. Israel corresponds to the *sefirah* of *malchut.* Since light and energy from all of the *sefirot* flow into this *sefirah, malchut* is regarded as the central *sefirah.* In this sense it is comparable to a mirror in which all the supernal *sefirot* are reflected.[54]

(*Zohar I,* 155b)

---

51. The *Zohar* derives this from the similarity of the words רואה (in the active form) and נראה (in the passive form).

52. *Sulam; Ziv HaZohar.*

53. The four directions correspond to the *sefirot:* south - *chesed;* north - *gevurah*; east - *tiferet*; west - *malchut.* Since all aspects of the physical world stem from these *sefirot*, he was considered to have seen all of the land.

54. *Ziv HaZohar.*

Rescuing Lot

14:1 ויהי בימי אמרפל מלך שנער – In the days of Amrafel, king of Shinar

Rabbi Elazar said: Come and see! When all these kings came together to wage war against Avraham, they made an alliance against him to eliminate him from this world. As soon as they captured Lot, his nephew, they left immediately, as it is written, "They captured Lot. . . . and all his property. . . . and they left" (14:12). What is the reason for capturing Lot, and their subsequent sudden departure? Because Lot's features were similar to Avraham's. For this reason they left suddenly, since the entire purpose of their war was to capture Avraham. When they believed that they had captured him, the purpose of their mission was fulfilled and they left. Why did they wish to capture Avraham? Because Avraham extricated people from idolatry and transferred them to the service of the Holy One, blessed be He. In addition, the Holy One blessed be He aroused them to make war in order to make Avraham's name famous in the world. . . .

(*Zohar I*, 86b)

14:15 ויחלק עליהם לילה הוא ועבדיו ויכם – With nightfall, he and his servants split up against them and attacked them

Why is the word ויכם (literally "**he** attacked them") in the singular? It should have used the plural form ויכום – "**they** attacked them." However, this refers to the Holy One blessed be He who attacked them; therefore this word is in the singular. Only Avraham and Eliezer, his servant, pursued the kings who had captured Lot.[55] Rabbi Yitzchak said: We have learned that where there is danger a person should not rely on a miracle, and in no situation was there more danger than in here, for Avraham and one servant chased after five kings and their armies in order to wage war upon them. Since one may not rely on a miracle, how could he do such a thing?

Rabbi Yehudah replied: When Avraham went after them, it was not to wage war against them, and he did not rely on a miracle. Anguish over Lot made him leave his home, and he took money to redeem him. If he did not succeed, he would die together with him in captivity. But when he set out, he saw the Divine Presence[56] lighting the way before him, and a number of angelic legions surrounding him. Then he pursued the kings and the Holy One, blessed be He killed them.

(*Zohar I,* 112b)

---

55. The *Gemara* (*Nedarim* 32a) explains that although verse 14 mentions 318 men, this is the numerical value (*gematria*) of Eliezer's name. See also Rashi's commentary.

56. The *Shechinah*.

14:15-20 וישמע אברם כי נשבה אחיו וירק את חניכיו ילידי ביתו... וירדף עד דן. ויחלק עליהם לילה הוא ועבדיו ויכם וירדפם עד חובה... וישב את הרכוש וגם את לוט... ומלכי צדק מלך שלם הוציא לחם ויין והוא כהן לא-ל עליון... ויתן לו מעשר מכל – When Avram heard that his kinsman had been captured, he armed his disciples who had grown up in his house. . . . And he pursued them as far as Dan. . . . He and his servants. . . . attacked them, pursuing them as far as Chovah. . . . He brought back all the booty, and his kinsman, Lot. . . . Malki-Tzedek, the king of Shalem, brought out bread and wine. He was a priest of God, the Supernal One. . . . And he gave him a tenth of everything

Rabbi Abba said: "Avram heard" – this refers to the Godly soul.[57] "That his kinsman had been captured" – this refers to the *yetzer hara.*[58] "He armed his disciples who had grown up in his house" – this refers to righteous men who have been educated in the precepts and in the way of good, as Rabbi Abohu said: When a righteous *tzaddik* sees that a wicked person has been deserted by his *yetzer tov* (his motivation to do good) and has become trapped by his sin, he goes and grabs him, for perhaps he can bring him back. Thus, he draws him closer and teaches him, as it is written, "And he pursued them as far as Dan (דן)" – he chases after him to rescue him from the main charges (דינו) against him, and from the sentence (דינה) of Gehinom ("hell").[59] This is the way of the righteous: to chase after the wicked in order to bring them back to the good. . . . "He and his

---

57. *Neshamah* in the *Zohar*. For the term "Godly soul" see *Tanya* p. 5b and ch. 2, citing the Rabbi Yitzchak Luria's *Eitz Chayim sha'ar* 50:2; Rabbi Chaim Vital's *Sha'arei Kedushah*.

58. The self-destructive impulse to do evil.

59. The *Zohar* derives this from the similarity between the words דן, דינו, דינה which all have there root in the word דין - judgment or severity.

servants. . . . attacked them" The Godly soul together with the righteous pursue them, rebuke them and castigate them. "Pursuing them as far as Chovah." They inform them of their evil ("Chovah" literally means "debt" or "guilt") and they chase after them until they reveal their evil and wickedness to them, so that they will be ashamed of their ways. . . . This is what the Godly soul does.

What is written subsequently? "He brought back all the booty, and his kinsman, Lot" – Rabbi Abohu said: Against their will they repent, as it is written, "His kinsman, Lot, together with his property, he brought back." Even the *yetzer hara*, against its will, returns and repents. Rabbi Abohu said: Come and see how great is the reward of a person who makes others come back and repent. From which verse do we deduce this? From that which is written immediately afterwards, "Malki-Tzedek, the king of Shalem," which is interpreted as follows: The great Rabbi Chiya taught that when the soul of a *tzaddik* who brought others back and helped them repent leaves the body, the archangel Michael, who brings the souls of *tzaddikim* before their Creator, goes out to meet the soul of that *tzaddik*. It states, "Malki-Tzedek" this is Michael,[60] the chief guardian of the gates of righteousness; "the king of Shalem" this is Jerusalem above, i.e., the spiritual level above which corresponds to Jerusalem below, as our Sages state, "Jerusalem above corresponds to Jerusalem below."[61] "Brought out bread and wine" he went out to meet Avraham and said, "May you come in peace."

"He was a priest of God, the Supernal One," as Rabbi Yosef taught: Just as there is a High Priest in the Temple below, so Michael, the archangel is the High Priest above. He goes out and blesses the incoming soul of a *tzaddik* first, and then he blesses the Holy One, blessed be He. . . .. as it states: Then he blessed him saying, "blessed is Avram of God, the Supernal One, Maker of heavens and earth." Blessed are you who has merited this. Afterwards he blesses God, saying: "Blessed is God, the Supernal One, who has

---

60. Note that מלכי (Malki) has the identical letters to מיכאל (Michael), although the latter has an additional letter א.

61. *Tanchuma, Pikudei* 1; *Zohar I,* 183b. See also *Taanit* 5a.

delivered your enemies into your hand." This refers to the wicked who have returned in your merit. You have made their soul as the verse states "And the souls that they had made in Charan" (above, 12:5).[62]

"He gave him a tenth of everything." Rabbi Yitzchak said: From the verse we do not know who gave to whom whether Avraham gave a tenth to Malki-Tzedek[63] or to God,[64] or whether Malki-Tzedek offered Avraham a tenth of what he had brought back.[65] However, Rabbi Yitzchak concludes that none of these views is correct. Rather, the Holy One blessed be He gave him (Avraham) a tenth. He took a letter from beneath the Throne of Glory and gave it as a crown to the soul, which is Avram. Which was this letter? The letter ה as it is written, "Your name shall no longer be Avram (אברם), but Avraham (אברהם)" (below, 17:5). Commentaries[66] explain that the letter ה denotes the *sefirah* of *malchut*, which is the **tenth** *sefirah*, and is therefore referred to as a tenth.

"Of everything." Rabbi Yehudah said: What does "of everything" mean? Of the *Shechina,*[67] of the Omnipresent One….

(*Midrash HaNe'elam, Zohar Chadash* 24d-25a)

14:21-2 ויאמר מלך סדום אל אברם תן לי הנפש והרכש קח לך. ויאמר אברם... הרמתי ידי... – The king of Sodom said to Avram, "Let me have the souls, and take the possessions for yourself." And Avram replied. . . . "I raise my hand. . . ."

Arsiel, the prince of *Gehinom* (hell) stands before the souls of the righteous so that they will not pray for the wicked before the

---

62. As stated explicitly in *Zohar I,* 79a; *Zohar III,* 168a.

63. As *Pirkei d'R. Elazar* 27:1, and *Pesikta Rabbati* 25:4 maintain (followed by Rashi).

64. This view is maintained by *Bamidbar Rabbah* 12:11; *Tanchuma, Chaya Sarah* (Buber) 6, adopted by Ibn Ezra.

65. The *Zohar's* words, "we do not know **who** gave to **whom** seem to imply that we do not know **from** whom the tenth came either.

66. *Sulam.*

67. The indwelling Divine Presence.

Holy One, blessed be He. He demands that they be placed under his dominion in order to take them down to the nether world, as it states, "The king of Sodom said to Avram, 'Let me have the souls. . . .'" The king of Sodom is one and the same as the prince of *Gehinom* who stands over the wicked.

What does he say to the soul, which is Avraham? "Let me have the soul which sins," as it is written, "The soul that sins shall die" (*Yechezkel* 18:4). That is, "Give me that soul which lusts for sin, so that it can be sentenced according to its wickedness. Do not take it with your supplications. But you can take the possessions for yourself – those who returned from their evil ways in complete repentance. Take them and rescue them from the condemnation of *Gehinom*.

R. Yehudah said: At that moment, what does the soul say? "And Avram said to the king of Sodom, 'I raise my hand to God, the Supernal One. . . .'" as I make an oath, "I will neither pray for nor take those wicked ones whom I informed in this world of their evil ways, and whom I chastised, exhorting them to repent, and I explained to them all of the laws of *Gehinom*, but they did not listen to me. Therefore, "I will not take anything of yours" for they belong to you, and are under your dominion.

(*Midrash HaNe'elam, Zohar Chadash* 25a-b)

14:24 בלעדי רק אשר אכלו הנערי – Excluding only what the youths have eaten

Rabbi Tanchum said: Come and see how beloved the Torah is before the Holy One blessed be He. For on its account a person merits the life of the World to Come, and anyone who teaches others Torah merits more than anyone else. Come and see i.e., prove this from what is written here: "I will not take anything of yours" meaning the wicked ones who are fit for you. "Excluding only what the youths have eaten" meaning those who teach Torah to others, and to children, for their reward is double.

(*Midrash HaNe'elam, Zohar Chadash* 25b)

God's Promise to Avraham

15:1 אחר הדברים האלה היה דבר ה' אל אברם במחזה לאמר – Soon after these events, Avram received the word of God in a vision, saying. . . .

Rabbi Yehudah said: "Soon after these events" i.e., after Avraham's pursuit of the kings, whom the Holy One blessed be He killed, Avraham had regrets, saying, "Perhaps I have forfeited my reward[68] for returning people to God and for befriending them in order to bring them close to Him, because now people have been killed through me?" Avraham was not worried about his reward *per se*, but rather about the possibility that he had done the wrong thing. This would be evidenced in his loss of reward.

Immediately the Holy One blessed be He said to Avraham, "Have no fear, Avram. I am your Protector. Your reward is very great."

(*Zohar I,* 88b)

Wherever the word "in a vision" (במחזה) is written in the Torah, it refers to the Divine Name which was revealed to the Patriarchs. And which Name is this? ש-ד-י. This Name represents a limited revelation, reaching to the root of creation, whereas the Ineffable four-letter Name (י-ה-ו-ה), the Tetragramaton, represents an infinite vision, transcending creation. The latter Name was revealed to Moshe, as the following verses attest: "The Lord spoke to Moshe and said to him, "I am God (י-ה-ו-ה). I appeared to Avraham, to Yitzchak and to Yaakov as El Shaddai (א-ל ש-ד-י), but with My Name י-ה-ו-ה I did not make Myself known to them (*Shemot* 6:2-3).

(*Sitrei Torah, Bereishit* 88b)

---

68. See *Bereishit Rabbah* ch. 44.

The following extract interprets the words אחר הדברים האלה *as, "after these **words**," rather than "after these **events**"*

"Soon after these words. . . . Your reward is very great": This signifies the words of Torah, as in the verse, "And these words. . . . (הדברים האלה)" (*Devarim* 5:22). Just as the latter signifies the words of Torah, so our verse signifies words of Torah. The intention is that when a person has occupied himself with "these words" (Torah study) in this world, the Holy One blessed be He tells it that He Himself will protect it, and that its reward is very great.

(*Sitrei Torah, Zohar I,* 88a)

15:2 מה תתן לי ואנכי הלך ערירי – What can You give me, since I am childless

How could Avraham say, "What can You give me," making it seem as if he did not believe in God's promise? However, since the Holy One blessed be He had declared, "I am your Protector" in this world, and "Your reward is very great" in the World to Come, Avraham immediately grasped the hint[69] and said, "What can You give me, for I know that a man who has no son will not receive a reward when he goes to the World-to-Come, since the soul receives reward for bringing about the supernal *zivug* which gives birth to new souls in this world. Thus, You can give me nothing, for I am not worthy of it" as proven by the fact that I was not able to bring about the supernal *zivug* and have children.

(*Zohar I,* 90a)

69. God was hinting to him that this was an auspicious occasion to ask for a child. The wise Avraham did not overlook the inference.

15:3 לי לא נתתה זרע – To me you have given no offspring

Avraham did not pray for children, even though Sarah was barren because he did not believe himself to be worthy of a miracle. Another explanation: He did not wish to take his reward in this world, and so he left it up to the Holy One to do as He wished.[70] If you contend that he declared, "To me you have given no offspring. . . ;" this was not a prayer, but rather like a person declaring a fact.

(*Zohar I*, 137b)

15:5 ויוצא אותו החוצה– He took him outside

The Rabbis taught[71]: Children, health and livelihood do not depend upon one's merits and righteousness, but on one's *mazal*. *Mazal* does not mean "luck," as is usually understood. Rather it refers to the *sefirah* of *Keter* from which divine energy flows forth (*nozel*, directly related to the word *mazal*) to the other *sefirot*,[72] and ultimately to the physical world. The practical implications of this outflow can be foretold using the science of astrology (as known to the Sages), which examines the position of the heavenly constellations (*mazalot* – also related to the word *mazal*) at the time of a person's birth. We deduce that Avraham saw in his constellation that he would not have a son. But the Holy One "took him outside," which the Rabbis interpret[73] as meaning, "dissociate yourself from your astrological predictions." He thus raised Avraham above the stars – beyond the realm of reason and nature[74] – and told him, "Now gaze at the heavens and count the stars. . . ." promising him that his offspring would be as numerous as the stars. We must now explain these words of the Rabbis: Before the Torah was given to Israel all creatures were dependent upon their *mazal*, including children, health and

---

70. Rabbi Avraham Galanti.
71. See *Mo'ed Katan* 28a.
72. See *Tikkunei Zohar, tikkun* 10, p. 24; *Pardess, Arachei Hakinuim* s.v. מזל.
73. *Shabbat* 156a.
74. See *Pesikta Zutreta* on the verse.

livelihood. But when God gave the Torah to Israel, He removed the control of the stars and constellations over them for the Torah itself transcends the world. This we learn from Avraham, for his descendants would in the future receive the Hebrew letter ה from his name, alluding to the five books of the Torah. Originally, Avraham was called Avram (אברם). Later the letter ה was added to his name making אברהם. The numerical value of the letter ה equals five. Regarding this the verse states, "These are the products of the heaven and the earth when they were created (בהבראם)" (*Bereishit* 2:4) This word has the identical letters as the identical letters as באברהם "with Avraham," as explained above 2:4. He said to Avraham: Because of the ה which has been added to your name the heavens will be in your control and all the stars and constellations which give forth light will be subjugated to you!" Accordingly, anyone who studies Torah in order to fulfill the commandments nullifies the power and influence of the constellations over himself. If he does not study Torah in order to fulfill the commandments it is as if he did not study at all, and he remains subject to the influence of the stars and constellations.

(*Zohar III,* 216b)

15:5-6 ויאמר לו כה יהיה זרעך. והאמן בה' ויחשבה לו צדקה— And He said to him, "So shall your offspring be!" And he trusted in God and he regarded it as righteousness

Rabbi Zeira asked Rabbi Abba whether the verse, "he regard it as righteousness" means that the Holy One reckoned it to Avraham as righteousness for his faith in Him,[75] or that Avraham regarded it as God's righteous kindness in promising him offspring unconditionally, without regard to Avraham's future merit. Rabbi Abba replied: I have heard it explained by the Sages that the Holy One reckoned it to Avraham. This does not sit well with me. It seems to me that the proper explanation is that Avraham regarded it as God's righteous

75. As Rashi explains in his commentary to this verse.

kindness. Rabbi Abba then explains that if the Torah had intended us to understand the verse according to the first explanation, it would have expressed this differently: Look here, it does not state ויחשוב לו [and he reckoned it to him] but rather ויחשבה לו in the feminine form, indicating that Avraham reckoned it to the Holy One who had removed him and his future descendants from the influence of the stars and constellations. The Torah states, "the Holy One 'took him outside,' and told him 'dissociate yourself from astrological predictions, for this is not the way to know My Name. You perceive one thing and I perceive something different. Avram will not have children, but Avraham will. From now on strive to follow a different path, and so (כה) shall your offspring be!'" What does כה mean? It signifies the tenth holy crown of the King, *malchut*, the tenth *sefirah* of the world of *Atzilut,* through which His Name is known.[76] This is the crown in which severe judgments are generally aroused. However, Avraham regarded it as a source of Divine Compassion, for through him the severities were sweetened.[77] This is what is taught: "So shall your offspring be!" This may be interpreted literally – his offspring would be *malchut*, for his son Yitzchak initially embodied this quality, although he subsequently ascended to the level of *gevurah*.[78] Accordingly, Avraham regarded the severity of *malchut* as an expression of Divine Compassion. . . . That is why the verse states ויחשבה לו in the feminine form, for it refers to the feminine attribute of *malchut*.[79]

(*Zohar III*, 148a)

---

76. Each of the ten *sefirot* is associated with one of the Divine Names and with several appellations and cognomens, as is explained at length in Rabbi Yosef Gekatilia's *Sha'arei Orah*.
77. *Mikdash Melech;* R. Chaim Vital.
78. As the *Zohar* explains below, p. 96a.
79. *Or Yakar; Mikdash Melech.*

15:14 ואחרי כן יצאו ברכש גדול – And afterwards they shall leave with great wealth

Rabbi Yose asked Rabbi Shimon bar Yochai: Why is it that the Holy One reminds us in several places in Torah,[80] "I am the Lord your God who took you out of the land of Egypt?" What additional insight does it the fact that the exodus is mentioned several times teach us?" Each time this is mentioned it must be in order to teach a new insight, otherwise it would have been sufficient to mention it once only.[81] Rabbi Shimon replied: "This is an explicit teaching, as God said to Avraham: 'Your offspring shall be aliens in a land not their own, they will serve them. . . . and afterwards they shall leave with great wealth.'" (*Bereishit* 15:13). Rabbi Abba asked again, "But why does He remind them of this time after time?" Rabbi Shimon replied: "My son, the Holy One promised Avraham only that He would deliver the Israelites from slavery in Egypt. But He did not promise them that He would deliver them from spiritual servitude. When the Israelites were in Egypt the Israelites undoubtedly debased and sullied themselves with all types of impurity, until they sank to the forty-ninth level of impurity.[82] But the Holy One extracted them from spiritual servitude to Egyptian idolatry. Moreover, He raised them up through the forty-nine gates of purity,[83] which He had not promised to Avraham. He did this out of His goodness and kindness towards them. It is for this reason that your will find the exodus from Egypt mentioned fifty times in the Torah.[84] The fifty times the exodus is

---

80. *Shemot* 20:2; *Devarim* 5:6; see also *Shemot* 6:26, 7:4, 12:17, etc.

81. One of the rules of biblical exegesis is that a matter is stated only once. Every subsequent mention of the same idea is in order to provide a further rule or insight.

82. There are fifty degrees of impurity (See *Tikkunei Zohar Intro.* 14a). The lowest rung is the point of no return.

83. *Ibid.*

84. See also *Zohar II,* 83b, 85b; *Tikkunei Zohar Tikkun 6,* p. 22a. In fact, however, the exodus is mentioned far more than fifty times. Rabbi Moshe Cordovero (the RAMAK) explains that the *Zohar* reckons only the fifty which point out the miracle of the exodus, but not those which simply mention it as

mentioned is the fifty gates of understanding.[85] This wealth of **spiritual** knowledge is the "great wealth" to which the verse alludes.

(*Zohar Chadash, Yitro* 31a)

The Covenant

15:17 והנה תנור עשן ולפיד אש אשר עבר בין הגזרים האלה – And there was a smoking furnace and a torch of fire which passed between these pieces

The concept of covenant is mentioned in connection with five things: 1) The covenant of circumcision, as the verse states: "My covenant shall be in your flesh for an everlasting covenant" (*Bereishit* 17:13); 2) The covenant of the rainbow, as it states: "I have set My rainbow in the cloud, and it shall be a sign of the covenant" (*Bereishit* 9:13); 3) The covenant of salt, as the verse states: "It is an eternal covenant of salt. . . ." (*Bamidbar* 18:19); 4) The covenant of suffering, as it says, "These are the words of the covenant. . . ." (*Devarim* 28:69); 5) The covenant of priesthood, as the verse states, "And it shall be for him and his offspring after him a covenant of eternal priesthood" (*Bamidbar* 25:13). Before these five covenants were made, the covenant was exclusively of fire, as the verse states, "There was a smoking furnace and a torch of fire which passed between these pieces. On that day God made a covenant with Avram. . . ." This covenant preceded all of them, as the *Zohar now explains*: This is deduced from the word בראשית (*Bereishit*), for

---

an historical event (*Pardes, Sha'ar HaSha'arim* ch. 1). Rabbi Elijah of Vilna (the *GRA*) explains the *Zohar* counts only those which God told Moshe to convey to the Israelites (*Biur HaGRA l'Tikkunei Zohar* p. 84b). See at length *Nitzutzei Zohar, Miluim*, to *Zohar Chadash, Yitro* 31a.

85. *Rosh HaShana* 21b; *Nedarim* 38a.

if you remove the letters אש (*esh* – fire) from בראשית the word ברית (*brit* – covenant) remains, that is ברית אש – "a covenant of fire." Rabbi Yochanan said: This is the covenant which God made with the world which would continue in Avraham's merit, as the verse states, "These are the products of the heaven and the earth which were created (בהבראם) on the day. . . ." (*Bereishit* 2:4). Do not read בהברם "which were created," but, באברהם "with Avraham," as explained above (*Bereishit* 2:4).

(*Zohar Chadash, Midrash Hane'elam* 4d)

16:12 והוא יהיה פרא אדם ידו בכל – And he [Ishmael] will be a wild man, his hand against everyone

Rabbi Shimon bar Yochai taught: Happy are the Jewish people, for the Holy One called them "man," as in the verse, "You, My flock, the flock of My pasture are men" (*Yechezkel* 34:31); "When a man offers a sacrifice to God. . . ." (*Vayikra* 1:2). Why are they called "man?" Because it is written, "And you who cleave to the Lord your G-d. . . ." (*Devarim* 4:4). You the Jewish people cleave to God, but other idolatrous[86] nations do not. The Hebrew word for "man," *adam*, is a cognate of the word *ledamot* – to compare or match, as in "I will be like the Supernal" (*Yeshayahu* 14:14), for he has the potential to mirror divinity.[87] For this reason you are men and are called men, but the idolatrous nations throughout the world are not called men.[88] Rabbi Shimon bar Yochai taught: When a Jew is circumcised, he enters the covenant which The Holy One made with Avraham, as it is written, "And God blessed Avraham with everything [*ba-kol*]" (*Bereishit* 24:1), alluding to the *sefirah* of *yesod*, which corresponds to the sign of the covenant in the flesh – i.e., circumcision.[89] "And kindness to Avraham"

---

86. As in the version found in *Yevamot* 61a; *Bava Metzia* 114b.
87. Cf. *Noam Elimelech, Vayeishev*.
88. *Yevamot* 61a; *Bava Metzia* 114b.
89. *Ziv HaZohar*.

(*Micha* 7:20), by circumcising himself Avraham earned God's benevolence.[90] Avraham had begun to attain the stature of man, because he had fulfilled the commandments of the Torah. Except for circumcision,[91] Avraham kept all the commandments of the Torah even before it was given.[92] When he was commanded to circumcise himself (see *Bereishit* 17:9 ff.), and did so, he consummated all of the commandments and thus attained a much higher level the status of "upon the likeness of the throne was the likeness as the appearance of man above" (*Yechezkel* 1:26), which refers to the supernal Divine revelation in the higher worlds (see *Zohar II*, 217a).[93] After circumcision, he attained the level of "man" to an even greater degree, and he cleaved to the King Himself fulfilling the verse, "And you who cleave to the Lord your G-d. . . ." And therefore he was called a man, and his descendants, the Jewish people, are also called "man."

However, look at what was written regarding Ishmael, the son of Avraham's concubine, Hagar: "And he will be a wild man" – a wild man, but not a man. "A man," because he was circumcised, and the beginning of manhood was thus manifested in him, as it states, "Ishmael was thirteen years old when he was circumcised" (*Bereishit* 17:25), but "a wild being" rather than a man, with "his hand against everyone [*ba-kol*]" – his hand certainly, but no more, for he did not accept the commandments of the Torah. The word *ba-kol*, as mentioned previously, alludes to circumcision, which Ishmael did at the age of thirteen. However, this is also the age at which a Jewish boy is expected to begin observing all the commandments, which Ishmael did not do. He attained the beginning but no more, for he did not complete the remainder of the commandments of the Torah. Accordingly, he is called a wild, unrestrained being, not a man.

The Jewish people who do observe all the commandments are called man in an unqualified way.

(*Zohar II*, 86a)

---

90. Rabbi Avraham Galanti.
91. Riva to *Bereishit* 17:26.
92. *Yoma* 28b.
93. *Ziv HaZohar*.

Avraham's Circumcision

17:1 ויהי אברם בן תשעים שנה וירא ה' אל אברם – When Avram was ninety-nine years old, God appeared to Avram

This verse needs examination, for it presents several difficulties. Had the Holy One not revealed Himself to Avraham until now? Did God reveal Himself to him only when Avraham reached this age? It is written previously "God spoke to Avram (12:1) "God said to Avram" (13:14); "And He said to Avram, 'Know for sure..' (15:13), and so on! Moreover, now a specific age is mentioned in connection with which the verse states that God appeared to Avram implying that **only** when Avram was ninety-nine years old, did God appear to him.[94] From this we understand that until this point God did not appear to him. . . . However, this is what we have learned: Prior to this it was not written that God **appeared** to him, for as long as he was uncircumcised the Holy One did not appear to him fully.[95] Now He appeared to him because He wished to reveal the crown of holiness circumcision in him, and the Holy One wanted to produce holy seed [Yitzchak] from him. Although holiness does not dwell upon a person while he is uncircumcised, now that he was ninety-nine years old, and would soon produce holy offspring, God wanted Avram himself to be holy, prior to producing holy offspring.

(*Zohar I*, 95a)

---

94. Since the words "And God appeared to Avram" are not mentioned at the beginning of the verse, as almost everywhere else, but in the middle of it, after his age was stated, this indicates that Avram's age was the reason that God was revealed to him (*Ziv HaZohar*).

95. Although the identical phrase is used prior to this (see 12:7), nevertheless, this was a lower level of revelation, from the *sefirah* of *malchut*. Here, however, the five aspects of *chesed* were revealed, as will become evident in the text further on. These are alluded to in the additional letter "ה" (having the numerical value of 5) which was added to Avram's name, making Avraham. Accordingly, this was the first **full** revelation (*Mikdash Melech*).

17:1 התהלך לפני והיה תמים – Walk before Me and be perfect [*tamim*]

Avraham is called "My beloved" (Yeshayahu 41:8), for he exemplified the attributes of love and kindness. Prior to his circumcision, however, these attributes were not revealed to their fullest degree. The following section discusses how Avraham attained perfection in these attributes

The second *mitzvah*[96] with which the fear of God is united and from which it is never separated, is the *mitzvah* of loving God. (Elsewhere the *Zohar* explains that love and awe of God are inseparable, for they are compared to the two wings of a bird. The bird cannot soar aloft with only one wing[97]) A person should love God with an absolute love which is called "infinite."[98] Regarding this God told Avraham, "Walk before Me and be *tamim*" which means perfect or complete. After fulfilling the *mitzvah* of circumcision Avraham would attain the level of absolute, perfect love. Regarding this it is written, "And God said, 'There shall be light'" (*Bereishit* 1:3). This absolute love, called "infinite love," is a *mitzvah*; that a person should love his Master fully. There are two kinds of love – conditional and unconditional love. The former is a response to the goodness with which God endows a person. This was the type of love which Noah had for God. It was a direct result of the goodness and kindness which God showered upon him. Regarding this the Torah states, "Noah walked **with** God" (*Bereishit* 6:9) i.e., with God's help.[99] This love is regarded as incomplete and conditional, for it depends on God's display of magnanimity. Avraham's love for God, by contrast, was not a product of God's benevolence. It was perfect and unconditional love. Accordingly the verse states, "Walk **before** Me [without My help] and be perfect [in your love for Me]."[100]

(*Zohar I*, 11b)

---

96. In his *Introduction* to the *Zohar*, Rabbi Shimon lists and discusses the 613 commandments. The first commandment is awe or fear of God; the second, love of God.
97. *Tikkunei Zohar* p. 82b. See *Tanya* chap. 41 ff. (p. 57b ff.)
98. Literally, "great love."
99. *Bereishit Rabba* ch. 30. See also Rashi's commentary on the verse.
100. *Sulam*.

"If not for My covenant [of circumcision], I would not have established day and night, and the laws of heaven and earth (*Yirmeyahu* 33:25). . . . One who succeeds in guarding his circumcision properly by not indulging in illicit sexual activities and does not transgress with it throughout his life, thereby unites day and night. These are the attributes of kindness (Divine **revelation**, as in the verse, "God commands His Kindness in the daytime" [*Tehillim* 42:9]), and severity (Divine **concealment**), "in the night His song [i.e. prayer[101]] will be with me" (ibid.). Through this he is worthy of both worlds, this world and the World to Come. It was in this regard that Avraham was called perfect in the sense of complete, as it is written, "Walk before Me and be perfect." He achieved this perfection only after circumcising himself.

(*Zohar III,* 14a)

17:3-4 ויפל אברם על פניו וידבר אתו אלהים לאמר אני הנה בריתי אתך – Avram threw himself upon his face and God spoke with him saying, "As for Me, this is My covenant with you"

From this we understand that until he was circumcised he would prostrate himself when God spoke to him. But after he was circumcised he stood upon his feet and was not afraid.[102] Moreover, it was precisely at this point that Avraham's circumcision took place, for immediately after he threw himself upon his face it states, "As for Me, this is My covenant with you. . . ." When he arose, he found himself already circumcised.[103]

(*Zohar I*, 96b)

---

101. *Ibn Ezra; Metzudat David.* Prayer is effective especially at times of trouble when Godliness is concealed. See *Sotah* 5b.

102. See also *Pirkei d'R.abbi Elazar* ch. 29.

103. Rabbi Levi said: "It is not written here that Avraham circumcised himself, but rather that he was circumcised [by the Holy One]" (*Bereishit Rabbah* chap. 47, 9. See below verse 17:26.

17:4-5 וידבר אתו אלהים לאמר אני הנה בריתי אתך ולא יקרא עוד את שמך אברם והיה שמך אברהם – And God spoke with him saying, "As for Me, this is My covenant with you. . . . And You shall no longer be called Avram. Your name shall be Avraham"

Rabbi Abba said, "Come and see. After Avraham was circumcised and he was no longer an *arel*,[104] he entered the holy covenant, became crowned with holiness and entered the foundation upon which the world stands i.e. he became the righteous person upon whose merit the entire world exists, as in the verse, "And a righteous man is the foundation of the world" (*Mishlei* 10:25). Then the world was sustained in his merit, as it is written "If not for My covenant [the covenant of circumcision], I would not have established day and night, and the laws of heaven and earth (*Yirmeyahu* 33:25). Therefore concerning creation it is written, "These are the products of the heaven and the earth when they were created (בהבראם)" (*Bereishit* 2:4). The word בהבראם has the identical letters as באברהם "with Avraham,"[105] for in his merit the world was sustained.[106]

(*Zohar I*, 91b)

---

104. One who has a foreskin. Note that circumcision comprises two parts – to be circumcised and not to be an uncircumcised. Accordingly, one who was born naturally circumcised is still regarded as an *arel* and requires a procedure known as *hatafat dam brit.* See *Yerushalmi, Shabat 87b; Yerushalmi, Yevamot* 45a. See also *Ran, Nedarim* 31b.

105. As explained above 2:4, 15:5

106. See also *Shabbat* 137b.

17:10 זאת בריתי אשר תשמרו... המול לכם כל זכר – This is My covenant which you must keep. . . . Every male among you shall be circumcised

Rabbi Abba said: Happy are the Jewish people whom God chose from among all the nations and gave them this sign of the covenant. Whoever has this sign sealed in his flesh will not descend to Gehinom[107] if he guarded it properly and did not place it in another person's domain.[108] Rabbi Abba also said: When a man brings his son into the covenant of circumcision The Holy One calls His heavenly entourage of angels and says to them, "Come and look at what my sons are doing in the world." At that time Eliyahu [Elijah] the angel of the covenant,[109] swoops down there in four leaps.[110] Eliyahu did not die but rose up in a whirlwind to heaven (*II Melachim* 2:11) and became the angel of the covenant. For this reason we have been taught[111] that he must prepare a chair in Eliyahu's honor,[112] and should say, "this is the chair of Eliyahu." If he does not do this, then Eliyahu does not dwell there. Then he Eliyahu ascends to the Holy One and testifies before Him. See now that first it is written (*I Melachim* 19:9 ff.) that God says to the Prophet Eliyahu, who was secluded in a cave, "Eliyahu, what are you doing here, instead of remaining among the people,[113] where you belong?" Then it is written "I have been very zealous for the Lord, God of Hosts, for the children of Israel have forsaken Your

---

107. "Hell." *Zohar II* p. 150b explains that "the fires of hell" are none other than the person's own burning passions and desires which consume him.
108. Apparently a euphemism for adultery. However, other interpretations may [also] be intended. See *Eruvin* 19a.
109. Liturgy of the circumcision ceremony.
110. See *Berachot* 4b.
111. See also *Pirkei d' Rabbi Elazar* ch. 29; *Tur, Yoreh De'ah* 265.
112. In the circumcision ceremony, the baby is placed on a chair which has been set aside as "the Chair of Eliyahu" just prior to the circumcision. In most communities today the *mohel* (person performing the circumcision) designates the chair and says out loud, "this is the chair of Eliyahu" as he places the baby upon it for a few seconds.
113. Malbim on the verse.

covenant. . . ."by failing to circumcise their sons.[114] God replied, "I vow that whenever My children make this sign in their flesh i.e., whenever there is a circumcision, you will be present, and the mouth which testified that the Jewish people have abandoned My covenant will testify that they are keeping it." Thus we learn[115] that Eliyahu was punished by the Holy One for vilifying the Jewish people, and he was given the opportunity to rectify his error by testifying in their favor and to their credit; namely, that they keep the covenant.[116]

(*Zohar I*, 93a)

17:12 ובן שמונת ימים ימול לכם – Every male shall be circumcised when he is eight days old

Rabbi Shimon bar Yochai said: When a man has a son and he enters the child into the covenant of circumcision he becomes bound to the *Shechinah* (the Divine Presence), not as manifested below, but as it is above the entrance to all supernal doors. The *Shechinah* is the attribute of *malchut,* from which all the other supernal attributes are accessed. *Malchut* is associated with the Name א-ד-נ-י which is bound to the ineffable Holy Name י-ה-ו-ה. The latter Name, the Tetragrammaton, denotes the utter transcendence of God,[117] where past, present and future are all one.[118] It therefore cannot be uttered.[119] Instead, it is cloaked in the Name א-ד-נ-י, so that it is not read as written.[120] When severity is aroused upon the world, the Holy One gazes upon the blood of circumcision and redeems the world from the severe judgments which threaten it.[121] Therefore it is written, "Every male shall be circumcised when he is eight days

114. Cf. *Radak.*
115. See also *Shir HaShirim Rabbah* ch. 1.
116. Ramak in *Or HaChamah.*
117. *Kuzari* 2:2; *Moreh Nevuchin* 1:63.
118. *Tur, Orach Chaim* ch. 5; Rabbi Eliezer of Garmiza on *Sefer Yetzira* 1:1.
119. See *Sanhedrin* 90a.
120. See Rashi to *Shemot* 3:15; *Sha'arei Orah, sha'ar 1.*
121. See also *Shabat* 137b: "If not for the blood of circumcision the laws of heaven and earth would not endure."

old." And, as mentioned previously (verse 17:1), this will cause a revelation of Divine kindness and compassion.

(*Zohar III*, 14a)

17:19 וקראת את שמו יצחק – You shall name him Yitzchak / You named him Yitzchak

The letter vav before the verb in this sentence functions in two ways: It makes the verb an imperative, so that וקראת *is rendered as "you shall name," referring to Avraham; or it changes the verb to the past tense, "You named him," referring to God who gave Yitzchak his name. This section uses the second interpretation.*

Rabbi Elazar once asked Rabbi Shimon bar Yochai his father: Since the Holy One Himself named him Yitzchak, as it is written, "You named him Yitzchak" even before he was born, then his name is not because of the joy and laughter which his birth brought about, as seems to be implied by the verse "God has made laughter for me" (*Bereishit* 21:6). Rabbi Shimon replied: We have learned that fire signifying the attribute of strict justice (*gevurah*) absorbs water the attribute of kindness (*chesed*), so that the water can now come from the aspect of severity. Just as when water and fire combine to form wine, in which both God and man rejoice (*Shoftim* 9:13);[122] so too combining *gevurah* and *chesed* gives rise to laughter. Further proof of this can be adduced by investigating the Levites, who also derive from the aspect of *gevurah,* for they "cheer up" the aspect of *gevurah* with their musical instruments and songs of praise (the assignment of the Levites in the Temple was to sing and make music). Thus we see that the aspect of sweetened *gevurah* is inherently associated with laughter. Accordingly, Yitzchak was not given his name because of the joy and laughter his birth **caused**, but rather Yitzchak himself is laughter, since he derives from that aspect and clings to it. This is further substantiated by several verses regarding Yitzchak: When Avraham was told that he would have a son in his old age the verse states, "Avraham fell upon his face and laughed with joy" (*Bereishit* 17:17); similarly, after the birth of Yitzchak Sarah declares, "God has made laughter for me; whoever hears will laugh for me" (*ibid.* 21:6).

(*Zohar I*, 103b)

---

122. *Sulam.*

Vayera

Vayera

Divine Revelation

18:1 וירא אליו ה' – God appeared to him [Avraham]

Until Avraham was circumcised, only a minor level of prophecy from the Holy One blessed be He communicated with him, indicated by the Name *Elokim* or *Shaddai*.[1] These Names signify a limited prophetic revelation. Superior levels of revelation do not exist on that plane of prophecy. However, after he was circumcised it is written that "God appeared to him." The verse uses the Ineffable Name, י-ה-ו-ה, indicating a far superior level of revelation.

Now why doesn't the verse also state to whom He appeared, for it is not written, "And God appeared to Avraham," but merely, "God appeared to **him**?" Had it stated that "God appeared to Avraham," this would not have been more noteworthy than before his circumcision, where it was stated that "God appeared to Avraham?" (as in *Bereishit* 12:7, 17:1-3, which also mention the Ineffable Name). However, this is a deep secret – now the Voice of God was revealed in his speech as He spoke to him. Thus Avraham became a full-fledged prophet and "the Divine Presence (*Shechinah*) spoke from his throat."[2] Prior to his circumcision, his prophetic experience was merely visionary. Now the voice of prophecy issued forth from his lips.[3]

(*Zohar I*, 97b-98a)

This verse can also be rendered as, "God showed him. . . ." Rabbi Shimon bar Yochai said: The intention here is that just as the Holy One had shown Adam each generation and its heads and leaders,[4] He also showed the future generations to Avraham, and told him,

1. As God Himself testifies in *Shemot* 6:3.
2. This is actually stated in regard to Moshe. See *Zohar III*, 232a, 306b; *Tikkunei Zohar*, end *Tikkun* 38.
3. *Ziv HaZohar*.
4. *Avodah Zara* 5a.

"This will be a generation of righteous people. That generation will be one of intermediate stature; this other one, of evil people," and so on.

Rabbi Yose asked: Holy Light![5] Don't our sages teach that everything is in the hands of Heaven, other than the fear of Heaven?[6] As the verse states, "And now, Israel, what does God ask of you other than to fear Him" (*Devarim* 10:12). It is written, "Neither evil nor good is decreed by the Supernal One" (*Eichah* 3:38). Thus man is granted free choice. Accordingly, if you say that it has been pre-ordained that a person will be righteous or of intermediate stature or evil, is it not inappropriate to punish or reward him for his actions? The prophet should have told us that evil and good are not decreed on high! Nor should the sages have declared that everything is in the hands of Heaven, other than the fear of Heaven, since the fear of Heaven also seems to be pre-ordained.

Rabbi Shimon replied: This question is very deep, and is a subject of disagreement among the sages of earlier generations. Moreover, many of them erred in this matter because they did not get to the depth of this abstruse matter.[7] Regarding a prophet the verse states, "Before I formed you in the womb, I knew you" (*Yirmeyahu* 1:5). This is the secret of the statement in the *Mishnah*, "Everything is foreseen, but free choice is given." God foresees all of a person's actions, but since the person himself is not aware of God's foreknowledge, his free choice is not affected.[8] This matter is abstruse and can only be understood according to the statement of the sages that, "The Holy One joins a good thought to deed, but not a bad thought."[9] This is what it teaches us: Before a child is conceived, if the father prays that the child will be righteous, and he keeps his mind on this at the time of union,[10] the child will be affected by his positive thoughts. This applies to the mother's thoughts and prayers as well. This then is the meaning of "The Holy One joins a good thought to deed," the parents'

5. A common way of referring to Rabbi Shimon.

6. *Berachot* 33b.

7. Or, "the depth of this secret."

8. *Avot* 3:15. See also Maimonides' *Pirush HaMishnah* to *Avot* ad loc.; Rabbi Saadia Gaon's *Emunot v'De'ot* 4, 4; *Kuzari* 5; *Moreh Nevuchin* 3, 20-21.

9. *Kiddushin* 40a. See also *Zohar I,* 28b; *ibid., Sitrei Torah Vayetze* 155a; *Zohar II, 150*b;

10. See *Shvuot* 18b; *Tanya* end chap. 1.

holy thoughts ordain that the child born will be a prophet, a sage, or will be divinely inspired, and so on. It does not decree that he will be righteous or wicked.[11] Accordingly, the future of the child is decided by the parents even "before I formed you in the womb. . . ."

18:1 באלני ממרא – In the plains of Mamre

Why in the plains of Mamre and not elsewhere? Because Mamre one of Avraham's allies and confidants had advised him to perform the circumcision. When the Holy One commanded Avraham to circumcise himself, Avraham went to consult his allies Aner, Eshkol and Mamre,[12] as to how to how to go about circumcising himself; whether he himself should do the operation or get someone else to do it upon him. (It was more dangerous for him to do the operation himself than to have another do it for him). Consequently, he was in doubt as to whether the principle of "it is better to fulfill a commandment oneself than through an emissary"[13] applied in his case. Furthermore, since there is a law which states that "only a person who is circumcised can circumcise,"[14] Avraham was not sure that his circumcision would even be valid if done by anyone else. Mamre advised him to trust in God and do the operation himself.[15] Aner said, "You are ninety years old. You will hurt yourself!" But Mamre argued, "Remember the day that Nimrod, the king of the Chaldeans, threw you into the furnace![16] And the famine which everyone endured, as it is written, 'There was a famine in the land, and Avram went down to Egypt' (*Bereishit* 12:10); and those kings whom you pursued and defeated in order to save Lot, whom they had captured (*Bereishit* 14:14). The Holy One saved you every time, and no man could harm you! Arise, and fulfill the commandment of your Master!"

The Holy One then said to him, "Mamre, you advised him to circumcise himself. I promise that I will reveal Myself to him only in your territory." Thus the verse states, "God appeared to him in the plains of Mamre."

(*Zohar Tosefta*)

---

11. *Leket Shmuel.*
12. See *Bereishit* 14:13.
13. *Kiddushin* 41a.
14. *Avodah Zara* 27a; *Menachot* 42b.
15. *Ziv HaZohar.*
16. See *Bereishit Rabba* 38:13; *Tanchuma* 118:11; Rashi to *Bereishit* 11:28.

In the following segment, the Zohar discusses the episode of the visitation of the angels to Avraham

18:1 וירא אליו ה׳ באלני ממרא והוא ישב פתח האהל כחום היום.
וישא עיניו וירא והנה שלשה אנשים נצבים עליו וירא וירץ לקראתם

God appeared to him in the plains of Mamre while he was sitting at the entrance of the tent in the heat of the day. He lifted his eyes and suddenly noticed three men standing nearby him. He looked again, and ran out from the entrance of his tent to greet them

The Rabbis interpret this verse as referring to the demise of a person, as Rabbi Yehudah taught: The day on which a person dies is the day of his judgment, when the soul parts from the body. A person does not pass away from this world until he sees the *Shechinah* (the Divine Presence) as the verse states, "A man shall not see Me and live" (*Shemot* 33:20) – i.e., when a person is about to die, he sees the *Shechinah*. The *Shechinah* is accompanied by three ministering angels these are the three "men" mentioned in the verse which receive the soul of a righteous person. This is the meaning of the verse, "God appeared to him.... in the heat of the day." This refers to the Day of Judgment which is compared to a burning oven[17] which separates the soul from the body.

"He suddenly noticed three men:" This refers to the three angels who examine the deeds which a person does during his life, and which a person must acknowledge. As soon as the soul sees them the angels it ascends to the opening of the throat this is alluded to in the words "and [he] ran out from the entrance of his tent to greet them" and remains there until the person has confessed all that the body has done with the soul in this world. Then the soul of a righteous person rejoices in its parting from this world, as Rabbi Yitzchak taught: The soul of a righteous person longs for the moment when it can depart from this worthless world in order to delight in the World to Come.

(*Midrash HaNe'elam, Zohar I*, 98a)

---

17. In the verse *Malachi* 3:19.

18:4-7 יקח נא מעט מים... ואקחה פת לחם... וימהר אברהם האהלה אל שרה ויאמר מהרי שלש סאים קמח סלת לישי ועשי עגות. ואל הבקר רץ אברהם – Some water will be brought. . . . I will get bread. . . . Avraham rushed off to Sarah in the tent and said, "Hurry! Get fine flour. Knead three measures of meal and make cakes." Then Avraham ran to the cattle and chose a tender, choice calf

When Rabbi Dimi came to Babylon from Israel, he explained: This entire passage alludes to the soul and the body. The soul does not find anything worthier for the body than the sacrifices which are alluded to here. Although the sacrifices went into abeyance when the Temple was destroyed, the teachings of the Torah about these sacrifices did not go into abeyance. One who cannot occupy himself with the sacrifices because the Temple is destroyed should occupy himself with Torah.[18] From this he will derive great benefit.

Rabbi Cruspedai said: One who mentions out loud in the Houses of Worship and Houses of Study matters pertaining to the sacrifices, and the order in which they were offered, and he has the proper intentions while doing so, makes a covenant between himself and those prosecuting angels which disclose his misdeeds. By mentioning the sacrifices etc., he ensures that they will only be of benefit to him. From where do we learn this? From this section, as the verse states, "and [he] suddenly noticed three men standing nearby him (נצבים עליו)." This hints to us that the three angels were standing there in order to examine his case. (The same word נצב is used in connection with judges and judgment, as in *Tehillim* 82:1) As soon as that righteous man (Avraham) noticed this, the verse states that "Avraham rushed off to Sarah in the tent" alluding to the soul which rushes off to the 'tents of Torah,'[19] to the House of Study. Following this the verse states, "Get fine flour. Knead three measures of meal and make cakes," alluding to the subject of his study – the laws of sacrifices,

18. See *Menachot* 110a: Reish Lakish said, "One who occupies himself with the Torah of the sacrifices is regarded as having sacrificed a burnt-offering..."
19. *Bereishit* 25:27, Rashi.

one of which is the *mincha* offering of baked unleavened bread.[20] If the person also has the proper intentions while studying the laws of sacrifices this is pleasing to God[21] and nothing can harm the person. This is the reason that verses dealing with the sacrifices are recited before praying.

(*Midrash HaNe'elam, Zohar I*, 100a-b)

18:4 יקח נא מעט מים– Some water will be brought

Rabbi Elazar said: Come and see that everything that Avraham ate, he ate in a state of ritual purity, because he had water brought before them, and only then did they eat. From the fact that he insisted that even his guests wash themselves ritually before eating we deduce that Avraham kept the laws of purity and impurity in his house. Moreover, he would not serve a ritually impure person in his house until the latter immersed himself in a *mikveh* a ritual pool containing a certain measure of rainwater or water from a spring sanctioned by the Torah to remove spiritual impurity.[22] The implication is not that Avraham prevented the person from approaching, but rather that the person himself could not come closer due to the sanctity of the place. Thus Avraham knew that he was impure, and he arranged from him to immerse himself in a *mikveh*, or to keep seven days of purity, as is required.[23]

Avraham and Sarah both arranged immersion in a *mikveh* for everyone; he for the men, and she for the women. Why did Avraham busy himself with purifying people? Because he was pure and is called pure, as the verse states, "Who can bring the pure out of the impure?" (*Iyov* 14:4) "Pure" refers to Avraham; "impure" refers to Terach, Avraham's father, who was an idolator.

Rabbi Shimon said that the reason why Avraham busied himself with purifying people was in order to manifest his spiritual level, which was the aspect of water *chesed*,[24] or kindness. For this reason he built a

---

20. *Vayikra* 2:1.
21. As stated in numerous places concerning the sacrifices, "A pleasing scent to God..." e.g. *Vayikra* 1:13, 17; 3:5.
22. See *Vayikra* 14:9; Maimonides *Sefer HaMitzvot, Aseh* 109; *Chinuch* 175.
23. Ibid.
24. Commentaries.

mikveh in order to purify people with its waters. Thus, when he invited the angels to his tent, the first thing he said to them is as it is written, "Some water will be brought" – in order to strengthen the spiritual level manifested in water, *chesed.* Therefore he purified all the people with whom he came into contact from those aspects of idolatry and impurity. And just as he purified the men, so too Sarah purified the women. Accordingly, all those who came to them became completely purified.

(*Zohar I,* 102a)

18:4 והשענו תחת העץ – Rest under the tree

Why under **the** tree – signifying a specific tree? Come and see: Avraham planted a tree in every place which he lived.[25] However, the tree did not always grow properly, other than when he lived in the Land of Canaan i.e. the Land of Israel. It was by way of the tree that he could detect who cleaved to the Holy One, blessed is He, and who clung to idol worship. When a person cleaved to the Holy One the tree spread out its branches over his head, providing him with pleasant shade. But the tree would recoil from one who clung to the side of idolatry, and its branches would lift up stretch upwards, so that the person would not be shaded by them. In this way Avraham knew the person's spiritual commitment, and he would rebuke him. The person wouldn't leave until he had devoted himself to faith in the Holy One. . . . The secret of this matter is that the Holy One Himself had decreed this for the tree was none other than the Tree of Life. It is for this reason that Avraham told his guests, "rest under the Tree," under the Tree of Life, not under the tree of idolatry (called an *ashera* in Scripture[26]). Come and see: When Adam sinned with the Tree of Good and Evil he caused death in the world. Therefore it is written, "Now he might stretch out his hand and take from the tree of life as well, and eat and live forever" (*Bereishit* 3:22). But Avraham rectified with world with another tree, the Tree of Life; and he made known the true faith to the entire world. Thus,

---

25. Cf. *Bereishit* 21:33.
26. See *Devarim* 16:21; *II Melachim* 32:15.

regarding the Torah the verse states, "It is a Tree of Life for those who grasp hold of it (*Mishlei* 3:18).

(*Zohar I,* 102a)

18:7 ואל הבקר רץ אברהם – Then Avraham ran to the cattle

"Then Avraham ran to the cattle" can also be rendered as "Then Avraham ran after the cattle," for the "tender, choice calf" which he had selected ran away from him and he chased after it. The calf ran to that cave which is known as the Cave of the Machpela, where Adam and Eve had been buried, and where he and Sarah, Yitzchak and Rebecca, and Jacob and Leah would be buried. He saw what he saw the sanctity of that place, and who was buried there.

(*Zohar I,* 127b)

18:9 ויאמרו אליו איה שרה אשתך – They said to him, "Where is Sarah your wife?"

Didn't these angels from on high know that Sarah was in the tent? Why then is it written, "Where is Sarah?" However, in fact the angels know about this world only that which they have been informed. All the more so are they unaware of the thoughts of man. The *Zohar's* view here seems to disagree with that of some Talmudic commentaries.[27] However, it is possible that the *Zohar* is talking only about when angels descend into this world.[28]

(*Zohar I,* 101b)

18:8-9 ויאכלו ויאמרו אליו איה שרה אשתך – They ate. Then they said to him, "Where is Sarah your wife?"

Come and see an example of proper decorum from the conduct of the angels: Before Avraham invited them to eat, the angels said nothing

27. See e.g. *Tosafot, Shabbat 12b* ד"ה שאין.
28. Commentaries.

to him, so that it should not appear that he only invited them to eat because of the good news they had brought him regarding the birth of a son. Rather, only after they ate, did they give him the good news.

(*Zohar I,* 102a)

18:10 ויאמר שוב אשוב אליך כעת חיה – He said, "At this time next year, when you are all in good health, I will certainly return to you"

Rabbi Yitzchak said: The statement, "**I** will certainly return" is difficult to understand. The verse indicates that when the angel will return Sarah will conceive a son. It should rather have said, "**He** will certainly return," referring to the Holy One since the key to make a barren woman fruitful is exclusively in the possession of the Holy One, blessed is He, and not in the control of any messenger.[29] As we have learned:[30] There are three keys which were never given over to an emissary – birth, resurrection, and rain.[31] Why then does it state "I (the angel) will return? It was undoubtedly the Holy One Himself who stood over them and said this, not the angel, which was merely a messenger for the words of the Holy One. For this reason it is written, "He said, 'I will certainly return. . . .'" Come and see the proof: Every time Scripture states simply, "And he said,"[32] or, "And he called,"[33] without any accompanying indication as to who said or called, it refers to the Angel of the Covenant speaking in the name of the Holy One, and none other. For example: "And He said, 'If you hearken diligently to the Lord your God,'"[34] without saying who said it; "And He called to Moshe,"[35] but it does not mention who called; "And to Moshe He

---

29. Cf. Rashi's commentary to this verse.
30. *Ta'anit* 2a in the name of Rabbi Yochanan
31. Note that the Talmud *ibid.* also mentions a view that there is a fourth key – livelihood. However, Rabbi Yochanan argues that rain and livelihood are one and the same.
32. ויאמר.
33. ויקרא.
34. *Shemot* 15:26.
35. *Vayikra* 1:1.

said, 'Go up to God,'"[36] but it does not state who said this. And similarly in our verse, "He said, '. . . . I will certainly return to you,'" without identifying the speaker. All of these indicate therefore that this was the Angel of the Covenant relaying the words of the Holy One blessed be He. The verse therefore states, "I will certainly return" "I," God, being the sole possessor of the power to make a barren woman fruitful.

(*Zohar I*, 102b)

18:10 ושרה שומעת פתח האהל והוא אחריו – Sarah was listening at the entrance of the tent, which was behind him

What is the meaning of "which was behind him?" It should have said, "she was behind him." This indicates a hidden teaching: "And Sarah heard what the Entrance of the Tent was saying." That is, Sarah heard the announcement of the *Shechinah*, which is referred to here as "the Entrance of the Tent,"[37] that she would have a son.[38] This is a lower level of the revelation of the *Shechinah*, merely the beginning of faith, whereas Avraham was privy to a higher level. Therefore the verse states, "the entrance of the tent. . . . was **behind** [i.e., **below**] him. Now this presents a difficulty, for Sarah actually achieved a greater level of prophecy than Avraham, as we see from the verse (Bereishit 21:12), "And God said to Avraham. . . ., 'Everything which Sarah tells you, obey her words,'" upon which Rashi comments: "This teaches us that Avraham was subordinate to Sarah in prophecy." Moreover, being a woman, she did not require circumcision prior to receiving prophecy, as Avraham did.[39] The reason for this is that from the day Sarah was born, she never before heard the word of God Himself, and since this was the first time, only a lower level of prophecy was revealed to her. Sarah was the only woman to whom God ever spoke directly.[40]

(*Zohar I*, 103a)

Rabbi Shimon commented: "Sarah was listening at the entrance (*petach*) of the tent" – this was the gate of righteousness, as the

36. *Shemot* 24:1.
37. See *Sha'arei Orah*, Rabbi Yosef Gikatilia, *sha'ar* 1, chap. 10.
38. *Ziv HaZohar*.
39. *Or HaChamah*.
40. Jerusalem Talmud *Sotah* 29a.

verse states, "Open (*pitchu*) for me the gates of righteousness" (*Tehillim* 118:19). This is the first opening through which a person must enter, and at this opening are seen all the other supernal openings. Whoever is worthy to achieve this opening will be worthy of understanding it, and through it, all other openings; for all of them rest upon it. Technically, this refers to the *sefirah* of *malchut*, the first level one must master in the spiritual journey upwards. Once one has achieved mastery of this level, all other levels become accessible.[41]

(*Zohar I*, 103b)

18:11 ואברהם ושרה זקנים באים בימים – Now Avraham and Sarah were old, coming on in days

What is the meaning of "coming on in days?" They were approaching the number of days then befitting them, for one – Avraham – one hundred years, for the other – Sarah – ninety years. One of the blessings of the righteous is stated in the verse, "I will fill the number of your days" (*Shemot* 23:26). This means not only that a righteous person will live out the entire span of his years, but also that each and every day will be filled with good deeds and knowledge of God. Thus, instead of interpreting the words באים בימים as "coming on in days," the *Zohar* offers a new interpretation: "coming **together with** their days," which is also a valid translation of the words. Avraham and Sarah had now achieved such perfection in their lives that all of the achievements of their days would accompany them.[42] Since they were entering the measure of those days befitting them, the verse states, "coming on in days," as is written, "And the sun went down" (*Bereishit* 28:11), bringing the day to its completion, for the new day starts with nightfall, as in the verse, "It was night, and it was morning, one day" (*Bereishit* 1:5).

(*Zohar I*, 103a)

---

41. Commentaries.

42. *Eitz Chaim, Sha'ar HaTzelem* p. 78c; *Damesek Eliezer*.

18:12 אחרי בלתי היתה לי עדנה ואדני זקן – Now that I am wizened, shall my flesh be sleek again? But my master is old!

The word עדנה means sleek or delicate flesh, a sign of youth, according to the traditional interpretation. The Zohar, however, interprets the word as a derivative of עדן – Eden or Paradise

The Head of the Yeshiva began speaking: Sarah was revitalized by Eden, the level which is known in Kabbalah as *keter*.[43] Up until this time, she did not have children because the primary function of her level *malchut* was to generate the souls of converts, as the verse states, "and the souls which they made [literally] in Charan" (*Bereishit* 12:5).[44] This verse refers to the converts which Avraham and Sarah made.[45] Thus it is written here, אחרי בלתי היתה לי עדנה – literally, "after I was wizened, I attained *Eden*!" Why is *Eden* spelt here with a *hey* suffix, עדנה, indicating a feminine form? To signify an emanation from the higher Eden *keter* into the lower *Eden, malchut.* There are many levels of *Eden* mentioned in the *Zohar*. However, they may be divided generally into the higher and lower *Eden*.[46] Since she received from the aspect of the feminine *malchut*, the lower *Eden* it is written as עדנה, rather than עדן. This is why the verse also states היתה לי – in the feminine form – indicating that the subject of the sentence, *Eden*, was specifically the lower level, *malchut*.

But my master is old! Most commentaries maintain that the word אדוני (literally, "my master") refers to Avraham. However, this raises a serious question: Even though he was old, was he not able to conceive? Many men even older than Avraham conceive. Moreover, Avraham himself subsequently had several more sons with a concubine, Ketura (*Bereishit* 25:1-2). Accordingly, he was clearly not too old to conceive. It must mean that Sarah was not talking about Avraham. Rather, she was blaming herself for not being able to give birth, because of her own lack of worth, she must

43. As explained in *Tikkunei Zohar, Intro.*, p. 11a; ibid. *Tikkun* 55, p. 85a; *Pardes, Sha'ar Archei HaKinuim*, s. v. עדן. However, *Matok MiDevash*, citing other commentaries, interprets this as referring to *chochmah,* while *Damesek Eliezer* interprets it as referring to *binah*.
44. *Damesek Eliezer* to *Zohar III*, p. 170a.
45. As *Zohar I,* p. 89a explains. See also Rashi's commentary to that verse.
46. See *Pardes, op. cit.*

(inadvertently) be clinging to the "old and foolish king"[47] the powers of evil which are not renewed,[48] i.e., they have no intrinsic vitality, and do not produce descendants. For if the powers of evil had descendants, they would destroy the world. Further proof that this is the intention of the verse is as follows: When the Holy One repeated Sarah's words to Avraham (in the following verse) He quoted her as saying, "I am old," not, "My husband is old," because she was referring to herself, not to him.[49] Now, if you counter that it is also written that "Avraham. . . . was old" (above, 18:11); nevertheless, he was also "coming on in days," in those days in "in which your youth is renewed like the eagle's" (*Tehillim* 103:5). An eagle sheds and renews its feathers annually. A *Midrashic* source explains that a certain type of eagle is rejuvenated after it gets old.[50]

(*Zohar III*, 170b)

The Destruction of Sodom

18:16 ויקמו משם האנשים וישקפו על פני סדום ואברהם הלך עמם לשלחם – The men rose from their places and gazed down upon Sodom. And Avraham walked with them to escort them

Rabbi Elazar said: Come and see the Holy One's kindness towards His creatures, and how much more so towards those who go in His ways. For even at a time that He wishes to mete out severe judgment in the world, He arranges that the merit of good deeds performed by those who love Him will mitigate the severe judgments before they are meted out to the world. We have learned

---

47. Kohelet (*Kohelet*) 4:13, commentaries.
48. Following the Mantoba text. This is also the version approved by Rabbi Eliyahu of Vilna.
49. Rashi, for example, maintains that the Torah changed her words for the sake of peace between her and Abraham.
50. Rashi to *Tehillim* ad. loc.

that when the Holy One loves a person He gives him a gift. What is the gift? A beggar, so that he who the Holy One loves will have the merit of giving charity to the unfortunate fellow. In the merit of this charitable act he draws upon himself a thread of *chesed* (supernal kindness) from the right side which is called *chesed,* the right arm.[51] He spreads it over his head and makes a mark so that when severe judgment comes upon the world the destroyer (Satan[52]) will be careful not to harm him. When the destroyer lifts up his gaze and sees that mark, he will avoid him and take care not to harm him. For this reason the Holy One gives him the prior opportunity to earn merit. As an example of this, come and see: When the Holy One wished to bring severe judgment on Sodom, He first gave Avraham the opportunity to earn merit. So He sent him a gift with which to gain merit, in order to save Lot, Avraham's nephew, from there (from the destruction of Sodom). This is the meaning of the verse "God called Avraham to mind, so He sent Lot from amidst the upheaval when He overturned the cities in which Lot had lived" (*Bereishit* 19:29). It is not written "God called Lot to mind," because he was saved in Avraham's merit. Now, what was it that "[God] called to mind?" The merit Avraham had acquired by serving the three angels. Similarly, when a person acquires merit through charitable acts with his fellow man, when harsh judgment prevails in the world, the Holy One calls to mind for that person's benefit the charitable acts that he did. This is because whenever a person acquires merit it is recorded on High to his credit, so that even when harsh judgments descend upon him, the Holy One recalls to the person's benefit those good deeds he did with others, as the verse states, "Acts of kindness deliver from sin" (*Mishlei* 11:4). For this reason then, that prior to bringing harsh punishment upon the world, the Holy One first gave Avraham the opportunity to save Lot and earn merit. Even though Avraham had performed many other acts of kindness, nevertheless, the degree of kindness he exhibited here was sufficiently effective to sweeten the harsh judgments and save Lot.[53]

---

51. See *Patach Eliyahu, Tikkunei Zohar* 17a.
52. *Bava Batra* 15a: "Satan, the Evil Inclination and the Angel of Death are all one."
53. *Mikdash Melech.*

Come and see how these verses illustrate the point: "The men rose from their places:" from the meal which Avraham had served them, and through which he gained merit. Even though they were angels who do not require food he still earned merit by feeding them. Moreover, not a morsel of food remained from that meal, so that Avraham would earn the fullest possible merit. Thus it is written, "and they ate" (*Bereishit* 18:8) that is, the food was consumed by their fire. Now if you should ask, "weren't there three angels, one of the element of fire (the attribute of *gevurah*), one of the element of water (the attribute of *chesed*), and one of the element of air (the attribute of *tiferet*)? How did the angels of the element of fire and the element of air derive nourishment from an attribute which was not their quality at all, from Avraham, who was *chesed*? The answer is that each one comprises the others, for "the first day (*chesed*) goes together with all of the other days"[54] (all of the Divine emanations). Therefore, "they all ate" means they all derived nourishment from the aspect of *chesed*.

The *Zohar* still needs to clarify what is meant by "eating." Angels obviously do not need physical nourishment. However, this can be understood by way of analogy to the following verse "they gazed at God, and they ate and drank" (*Shemot* 24:11). The context of the verse is this: After hearing the Ten Commandments, before Moshe ascended Mount Sinai to receive the two Tablets of Stone, the Elders ate and drank. Some commentators (*Midrash Tanchuma, Rashi*) view this negatively; others view it positively (*Targum Onkelos, Ramban*). The *Zohar* clearly favors the latter view but interprets their "eating" in a spiritual sense, as deriving nourishment from the *Shechinah*. On that occasion they actually ate, and yet they were sustained by the *Shechinah*. So too, here: They consumed the food although not physically but they were sustained by that aspect to which Avraham adhered, the side of *chesed*. Even though they were angels, they were inferior to Avraham's spiritual level, and they were therefore able to derive spiritual nourishment from "partaking" of the food he offered them.[55] Therefore they did not leave even a morsel of what Avraham gave them, just as a person ought to drink from "the cup of blessing,[56]" so that he will merit blessing from Above. Similarly, the angels "ate" from that which Avraham

54. *Zohar I*, 46a.

55. *Mikdash Melech*.

56. "A cup of blessing" is the cup over which Grace after Meals has been recited. The blessing over wine is then said and the person reciting grace drinks from it. The remainder of the wine is then generally distributed among other participants at the meal.

had prepared for them, so that they would merit sustenance from the aspect of Avraham the *sefirah* of *chesed.* In fact, it is from this aspect that nourishment flows forth to all the angels.

. . . .and gazed down upon Sodom: The expression וישקיפו – they gazed down upon indicates the arousal of Divine compassion in order to rescue Lot. וישקיפו is written in this verse, as in the verse, "Gaze down השקיפה from Your holy abode, from the heavens, and bless your people Israel" (*Devarim* 26:15). Just as the latter verse is an expression of Divine compassion, so too the former verse.

And Avraham walked with them to escort them to fulfill the *mitzvah* of escorting a guest. Rabbi Yaisa said: If you say that Avraham knew they were angels, why did he escort them? Although it is a *mitzvah* to escort a guest on his way, doesn't this only apply to human guests, not heavenly ones? Rabbi Elazar answered: Even though he knew that they were angels he accorded them the same treatment he was accustomed to give men. He accompanied them on their way because that is what a person is required to do for human guests. Everything depends on this, for after Avraham accompanied them, the Holy One appeared to him, as it is written, "And God said, 'Shall I conceal from Avraham what I am about to do?'" Now, why does the verse begin "*And* God said," rather than simply, "God said?" To indicate that this God appeared together with His Heavenly Court. For whenever God metes out punishment to the world, it is not He alone, but He together with His Heavenly Court. Thus He was (so to speak) going with them. Come and see from these verses that when a person accompanies his guest upon the way, he draws down the *Shechinah,* the Holy Presence, which unites with him and accompanies him on his way to rescue him from trouble. Accordingly, a person is obligated to accompany his guests.

(*Zohar I*, 104a)

18:17 וה׳ אמר המכסה אני מאברהם אשר אני עושה – And God said, "Shall I conceal from Avraham what I am about to do?"

Rabbi Yehudah said: The Holy One gave the entire land to Avraham as an eternal inheritance as is written, "All the land that you see I will give to you and to your descendants forever" (*Bereishit* 13:15). It is also written, "Raise your eyes, and from the place where you are, gaze to the north and to the south, to the east and to the west. . . ." (*ibid.* 13:14). Thus the entire land of Israel had been promised to Avraham eternally. When the Holy One decided to uproot these places Sodom and Amora[57] He said, "I have already given this land to Avraham, and he is the father of all the people who live there," as it states, "I have made you the father of many nations" (*Bereishit* 17:5). "It is not proper for me to obliterate the children without informing the father! For I called him 'Avraham My beloved' (*Yeshayahu* 41:8). Therefore I must inform him." This then is the meaning of the verse "And God said, 'Shall I conceal from Avraham what I am about to do. . . .?'"

Rabbi Abba said: Come and behold Avraham's humility. Even though the Holy One said to him, "The outcry against Sodom and Amora has become so great. . . ." (*Bereishit* 18:20), and He spoke to him at length, informing him that He wished to punish Sodom; nevertheless, Avraham did not ask Him to spare Lot and forego punishing him. Why not? He did not wish to claim reward for his good deeds! The Holy One thus sent the angels to Lot to rescue him, all in the merit of Avraham, as it is written, "He remembered Avraham and He allowed Lot to flee from amidst the upheaval when He overturned the cities in which Lot had lived" (*Bereishit* 19:29).

(*Zohar I*, 104b)

Rabbi Chiyya began his discourse and said: "The Lord God will not do anything without revealing His secrets to His servants, the Prophets" (*Amos* 3:7). Fortunate are those meritorious ones whom the Holy One visits. He does not conceal from them at all everything that He does in the heavens and will do in the world because of their righteous deeds. The Holy One wants the righteous

57. The word is often (incorrectly) transliterated as "Gemorra."

to join Him, for they will come and warn mankind to repent for their sins. Then they will not be punished with supernal harsh judgments, and there will be no complaints against Him. For this reason the Holy One informs them that He is about to pass judgment so that none can say He punishes unjustly.

(*Zohar I*, 104b)

If you should say, "Didn't the Holy One know that they could not be saved? Why then did he reveal to Avraham that He was about to destroy Sodom, knowing that Avraham's pleas could not save the wicked cities? This was in order to gain Avraham merit for his efforts. On this basis our Sages teach that one who comes to purify himself is given help from Above, whereas one who comes to desecrate himself – they open the doors for him.[58] What is the meaning of the doors are opened for him? Surely God's emissaries do not help a person to transgress His will? Rather the meaning is that they let him go through the doors that are always open. A person is actually helped from Above to do the right thing, whereas if he wishes to sin, he is merely given the opportunity.

(*Hashmatot* 264b)

18:18 ואברהם היו יהיה לגוי גדול ועצום – And Avraham will become a great and mighty nation

What is the reason for this blessing in here when Sodom is just about to be punished? To inform you that even when the Holy One sits in judgment upon the world He does not change. For while He judges one, he shows compassion for another at the very same moment. When the attribute of *gevurah* prevails in one context, for those deserving harsh judgment, at the same time, the attribute of compassion is focused upon those who merit it.

Rabbi Yose asked: Is it not written, "As for me, may my prayer to You be at an auspicious time,"[59] implying that there are times which are favorable and times which are not? There are times when

58. *Shabbat* 104a.
59. *Tehillim* 69:14.

He listens to prayers and times when He does not;[60] times when He is accessible and times when He is not, as is written, "Seek God when He is to be found?" (*Yeshayahu* 55:6).

Rabbi Elazer replied: This statement that there are times which are favorable and times which are not is as regards the individual. But the statement that He does not change, but remains compassionate and is always accessible through prayer is in regard to the community. That He is not always accessible is in regard to a single place, but that He remains compassionate and is always accessible through prayer is in regard to the rest of the world. Therefore He blessed Avraham, since he was equal to the entire world as it is written, "These are the products of the heaven and the earth which were created" (בהבראם), as we have learned[61] do not read it as, בהבראם (*b'hibaram*) – "which were created," but rather as באברהם (*b'Avraham*) – "with Avraham." The latter word has the identical letters of the former, but in a different order. For the world is sustained through Avraham.[62]

(*Zohar I*, 105b)

18:19 כי ידעתיו למען אשר יצוה את בניו ואת ביתו אחריו ושמרו דרך ה׳ לעשות צדקה ומשפט – For I am attached to him because he commands his children and his household after him: "Keep the way of God, making charity and justice. . . ."

Since it is written, "he commands his children and his household after him, 'Keep the way of God,'" why does it then state, "making charity and justice"? Aren't charity and justice included in "the way of God"? However, this is to inform us that one who guards the way of Torah "makes" charity and justice. The expression used here for doing charitable acts is לעשות צדקה ומשפט. The word לעשות also has the connotation of "making" or "creating," as in the verse, "God blessed the seventh day. . . . because on it He abstained from all His work which God created, [for man] **to**

---

60. As in the verse "Why do you cry out to Me [now]?" (*Shemot* 14:15). "Now is not the proper time for prayer" (*Rashi*).

61. *Zohar III*, 31a.

62. As was explained above in the commentary to verse 2:4.

make (לעשות)" (*Bereishit* 2:3). This implies that there is an ongoing process of creation which man has the duty and privilege of fulfilling, through his observance of the Torah and the commandments.[63] What do charity and justice signify? The Holy One, blessed is He! By doing charity and justice a person fashions the Holy Name, as will be explained below.

Rabbi Shimon bar Yochai wept: "Woe to those who do not have knowledge, and who do not gaze upon the glory of their Master. Who makes the Holy Name every day? One who gives charity to the poor! Come and see: A poor person is bound to the attribute of *din* (limitation, strict justice). All the food which he eats is severely restricted. This is the level called *tzedek*– literally, righteousness, indicating here strict justice which gives only to those who have earned it. Now *tzedek* (צדק)is also the root of the word *tzedaka* צדקה, but with an additional *hei* on the end of the word. However, with the addition of the *hei* the word now indicates charity, even to the undeserving. Thus, when one gives charity to a poor person, he causes the Holy Name to become complete. For *tzedaka* is the Tree of Life (the *sefirah* of *tiferet)*, which pours forth to *tzedek* (*malchut*). And when this happens they unite, and the Holy Name is completed.

The explanation is as follows: On the verses, "David made a name. . . . And David performed justice and *tzedakah* with all his people" (II *Shmuel* 8:13,15) the *Zohar* here comments: By doing justice and charity "David made a name," the Divine Name signified by the Tetragrammaton (י-ה-ו-ה – *yud-hei-vav-hei*). Through charity and justice he aroused the quality of *chesed* above to elicit an infinite light from the level of *chochmah*, which is the letter *yud*, the first letter of the Tetragrammaton, to the letter *hei*, the second letter of the Tetragrammaton. This diffuses through the various spiritual worlds (signified by the letter *vav*) to the world below (signified by the final letter *hei*),[64] thus completing the Divine Name. This is also the explanation of our verse: Avraham commanded his children to do acts of justice and charity in this world, and this elicits the light of God from above to suffuse this world, which is the meaning of the first part of our verse, "I am attached to him."

(*Zohar III*, 113a-b)

---

63. See above, *Zohar* to *Bereishit* 1:1; 1:3; 2:1, etc.

64. See *Tanya*, Igeret HaKodesh chap. 6 for a lengthy exposition of this section.

18:20 ויאמר ה׳ זעקת סדום ועמרה כי רבה וחטאתם כי כבדה מאד – So God said, "The outcry against Sodom and Amora has become so great, and their sin has become so very grave. . . ."

The Zohar addresses the magnitude of the sins of Sodom and Amora. In contrast to the conduct of Avraham, who constantly invited guests into his house, the Sodomites and their neighbors repulsed strangers and treated them with great cruelty

Rabbi Elazar said: Come and see the meaning of the verse "The Holy One said to Avraham, 'The outcry against Sodom. . . .'" There arose before Him what they (the Sodomites) were doing to the entire world: they prevented people from entering Sodom and Amora, as it is written, "He breaks open a stream in a place far from inhabitants. They are dried up, they are gone away from men" (*Iyov* 28:4). "He breaks open a stream in a place far from inhabitants" – the stream was "broken" when people entered there, into Sodom and Amora. For when they saw that one of the inhabitants had given a visitor food and drink, they would throw him into the depths of the river. Then they did the same to the person to whom he had given the food. Accordingly, people began avoiding the place, and it became "forgotten by wayfarers." The few who did still go there "are gone away from men," for the inhabitants starved them, and would not give them food and drink, until they lost their human form. Another interpretation of the words, "are gone away," is as it is written, "her paths wander" (*Mishlei* 5:6). For people would walk in a roundabout fashion in order to avoid going through there. Even the birds of the heavens no longer went there, as it is written, "the path which even the eagle knows not" (*Iyov* 28:7). Accordingly, the entire world cried out against Sodom and Amora and the other cities of that area. For the inhabitants of those areas were all of the same ilk. Therefore, "The outcry against Sodom has become so great."

(*Zohar I*, 105b)

18:21 ארדה נא ואראה הכצעקתה הבאה אלי– I will descend and see. If they are still acting in accordance with its outcry which comes to Me

Rabbi Shimon said: What is the meaning of, "I will descend and see?" Did the Holy One not know of what taking place in Sodom and Amora that He had to say, "I will descend and see?" Everything is revealed openly revealed before Him! However, this is what it means: "I will descend from the level of compassion to the level of strict justice." This is a descent because the will of the Holy One is to do only acts of kindness and compassion. When the attribute of strict justice overcomes the attribute of compassion this indicates a decline.[65]

"And [I will] see." This "seeing" is an investigation by which to judge them. We have found expressions of seeing with positive results and expressions of seeing with negative results. We have seen positive results as in, "God saw the children of Israel, and God knew" (*Shemot* 2:25) that is, He took note of the suffering of the Jewish people in Egypt.[66] Negative results, as in this case, "I will descend and see" in order to pass judgment upon them. Therefore the Holy One said, "Shall I conceal from Avraham what I am about to do?

In accordance with its outcry: The *Zohar's* commentary to the previous verse understood the words זעקת סדום ועמרה as meaning, "The outcry *against* Sodom and Amora." This commentary renders the verse differently, as, "The outcry of Sodom and Amora." Therefore, it should have said, "In accordance with *their* outcry," since there were two cities. Why then does it state, "In accordance with *its* outcry" in the singular? The meaning of "its outcry" is the decree of strict justice that demands judgment. As we have learned in the case of Yosef, for example, justice stood for many years before the Holy One and demanded its due for the sale of Yosef by his brothers. This is why it is written, "In accordance with its outcry," the outcry of strict justice.

Which comes to Me: What is the meaning of "which comes to Me?" Shouldn't the verse have stated, "which came to Me," in the past tense? This is the mystical explanation of, "In the evening she comes, and in the morning she returns," (*Esther* 2:14). It is constant, alluding to the

---

65. *Ziv HaZohar.*

66. See Rashi, commentaries.

Accuser who rises up before the Holy One every night to indict the Jewish people.[67] Similarly, "The end of all flesh comes before Me" (*Bereishit* 6:13). This too is in the present tense and indicates the constant accusations leveled against the Jewish people.

(*Zohar I*, 106a)

18:21 עשו כלה – Then destroy

The *Zohar* understands the word עשו as an imperative in the plural form. To whom was this said? If you maintain that this was said to the angels, who ever saw that the Holy One would be speaking with one, i.e., Avraham, and commanding another (the angels)? Rather, He was speaking with Avraham, since these areas were his property. Alternatively, one can explain that He was indeed talking to the angels. According to the view that He was speaking with Avraham, we need and answer to the question why is עשו in the plural form? It should have said, עשה – the imperative in the singular form. Why then עשו? This refers to Avraham and the *Shechinah*, the indwelling Divine Presence, which had not left him. The Holy One was asking them to agree to the destruction of Sodom, since these areas were his property and responsibility. According to the view however that He was speaking with the angels, we have to answer the other question: How could he be talking with Avraham and commanding the angels? This is because the angels were there with Avraham waiting to carry out Sodom's sentence, if Avraham would not succeed in procuring mercy for them. This is why עשו is in the plural form.

Alternatively, עשו can be understood according to its Aramaic translation "They did," referring to the people of Sodom, who had destroyed the basic fabric of society. According to this interpretation the word עשו is not an imperative; it is rather in the past tense.[68]

(*Zohar I*, 105b)

---

67. See *Sulam*.
68. See *Mikdash Melech; R. Avraham Galanti*.

18:23 ויגש אברהם ויאמר האף תספה צדיק עם רשע – Avraham braced himself and said, "Will You also annihilate the righteous along with the wicked?"

Rabbi Yehudah said: Who ever saw a compassionate father like Avraham? Look at Noah, regarding whom it is written, "And God said to Noah, 'The end of all flesh comes before Me. . . . Make for yourself an ark of gopher wood,'" (*Bereishit* 6:13, 14). Noah kept silent and did not say anything on behalf of his fellow men. He did not beg for God's mercy. But as soon as the Holy One said to Avraham, "The outcry against Sodom and Amora has become so great. . . . I will descend and see." Immediately it is written, "Will You also annihilate the righteous along with the wicked?"

Rabbi Elazar said: Even Avraham did not do the completely proper thing. Noah did nothing at all, whereas Avraham demanded a proper judgment, so that the innocent would not die along with the guilty. He began by asking God to spare all five cities of the Sodom and Amora region if there would be fifty righteous people. He bargained with God to save at least one of the cities if there were at least ten righteous people in it.[69] He began the attempt to spare them but did not complete it. He did not ask for compassion in any event, even if there were fewer than ten righteous people, or even none at all. For Avraham said to himself, "I do not wish to claim reward for my deeds;" i.e., he did not believe that he had sufficient merit himself to ask for mercy for Sodom by virtue of that merit. Who, in contrast, did do the completely proper thing? Moshe. As soon as the Holy One said to him, "They have strayed quickly from the way which I have commanded them. They have made themselves a molten calf. . . . I shall annihilate them" (*Shemot* 32:8, 10). Immediately after this it is written, "Moshe pleaded before the Lord his God. . . ." (*ibid.* 11), until he said, "And now, if You would but forgive their sin! But if not, erase me now from this book that You have written" (*ibid.* 32:32). He pleaded for mercy for them even though all of them had sinned. He did not budge from there until He said to him, "I have forgiven them because of you words" (*Bamidbar* 14:20).[70] Avraham, however, only looked to see

69. See Rashi.

70. According to *Zohar III* p. 14b, there are some words missing. The text here should read: And he did not budge from there until "God relented regarding

if there were righteous people among them. But if there were none, then he did not plead further. Accordingly, there was ever one who protected his generation like Moshe, for he was a faithful shepherd.

(*Zohar I*, 106a)

19:1 ויבאו שני המלאכים סדומה בערב – The two angels came to Sodom in the evening

Rabbi Yose said: Come and see what is written above: "God departed when He had finished speaking with Avraham" (18:33). When the *Shechinah* left Avraham, and Avraham returned to his place, only then did the two angels come to Sodom, in the evening. Now what happened to the third angel, the one which had come to announce the forthcoming birth of Yitzchak? It left with the Divine Presence, and only these two remained, one to rescue Lot, and one to destroy Sodom and Amora. Once an angel has fulfilled his duties he returns to whence he came.[71]

(*Zohar I*, 106a)

19:1 וירא לוט ויקם לקראתם – Now Lot saw and stood up to greet them

As soon as Lot saw them, he ran after them. Why? Did he then run after everyone who came there to take them to his home and give them food and drink? Wouldn't his fellow citizens have killed him? This they had already done to his daughter who had given a loaf of bread to a poor person. When the wicked people of Sodom discovered this, they smeared her with honey, placed her on the roof, and left her there until the bees had eaten her alive. However, Lot took a chance because it was at night and he thought that the citizens of Sodom would not notice. Despite his precautions, as soon as he entered

---

the evil which He declared He would do to His people" (*Shemot* 32:14), and He said to him, "I have forgiven them because of you words."

71. See Rashi this verse.

his house, everyone gathered together and converged upon the house.

Rabbi Yitzchak said: Why did Lot run after them, as it is written "Lot saw and stood up to greet them?" This is a matter of disagreement between Rabbi Chizkiya and Rabbi Yeisa. One of them explained that Lot saw Avraham's countenance with them. Since Avraham had fulfilled the *mitzvah* of accompanying a guest on the way, as was his custom, a radiance of the aura surrounding him left its impression upon them. As Lot had grown up in Avraham's house he had learned to recognize this.[72] The other one explained that that he saw the *Shechinah* resting upon them. This second view relies on one of Rabbi Ishmael's thirteen rules of Torah exegesis,[73] called *gezeirah shava,* whereby an analogy between two laws (or situations) is established on the basis of identical expressions in the Biblical text. In this case it is written, "Now Lot saw and stood up to greet them," and previously it is written, "He [Avraham] looked again, and ran out from the entrance of his tent to greet them" (*Bereishit* 18:2). Just as in the latter case, Avraham saw the *Shechinah,* so too here, Lot saw the *Shechinah*.

(*Zohar I*, 106a)

19:2 ויאמר הנה נא אדני סורו נא אל בית עבדכם – And he said, "Behold now, my lords, please turn aside to your servant's house

Why is the expression "turn aside to your servant's house" used? It should have said, "Come to your servant's house." However, Lot wished to lead them a roundabout way to his house, and not directly, so that the other citizens of Sodom would not see them.

Rabbi Chizkiyah said: Come and see. When the Holy One saw the deeds of Sodom and Amora he sent those angels to destroy Sodom. What is written? "Lot saw." He saw the *Shechinah.* Now who could see the *Shechinah*? Rather he saw a shining light that glowed up above their heads. And then he said, "Now, my lords" Although the word א-ד-נ-י can be understood as the plural construct form of אדון

---

72. *Ziv HaZohar.*
73. *Sifra, Introduction.*

, referring to the angels whom Lot called "My lords," it can also be understood as one of the Divine Names. This is the way in which Rabbi Chizkiyah interprets it, and it refers to that same light of the *Shechinah* that shone forth.

(*Zohar I*, 106a, 107a)

19:24 וה׳ המטיר על סדום ועל עמורה גפרית ואש מאת ה׳ מן השמים – And God had caused sulfur and fire to rain down upon Sodom and Amora, from God, out of heaven

"*And* God" indicates something besides God, He and His court below, which receives permission from Above to execute judgment. The verse teaches us that punishment (and reward) in this world are strictly in the hands of the Almighty.[74] However, Rabbi Yitzchak explains that the words "*and* God" uses the Tetragrammaton, which indicates Divine compassion, as distinct from using the Name *Elokim*, which is indicative of strict justice. This teaches us something else regarding reward and punishment: He carries out the verdict with compassion, as it is written at the end of this same verse, "From God, out of heaven." Commentaries explain that the word heaven (*shamayim*) is a compound of two words, *aish* (fire) and *mayim* (water),[75] indicating the working of justice (fire) through compassion of mercy (water). Now, if you will ask where there is compassion here? The verse states, "And so it was when God destroyed the cities of the plain that God remembered Avraham" (*Bereishit* 19:29). Lot was saved in Avraham's merit (as will be explained below), and two whole nations subsequently stemmed from him from Lot. He thus had the privilege of King David and King Solomon descend from him via Ruth the Moabitess who descended from Lot's child, Moab.

(*Zohar I*, 107b)

Why is it written here, "And God rained down. . . ." using the four-letter Ineffable Name י-ה-ו-ה, which is indicative of compassion, whereas in regard to the flood the Name *Elokim* is written throughout? Although sentence was passed upon Sodom, the intention was not to

74. See Rabbi Yosef Albo's *Ikkarim* 1:12.

75. Menachem Recanati, *Commentary on the Torah*.

destroy the world as in the flood, and therefore that four-letter Name is used together with the Name *Elokim*, indicating strict judgment. In the flood the entire world was destroyed, therefore the Name *Elokim* is used throughout. If you will argue that Noah and those with him were saved, indicating that the attribute of compassion was operative, they were shut away in the ark while the entire the world was being destroyed.

Rabbi Yitzchak also explained that in punishing Sodom, God meted out justice with compassion. If you will ask where the compassion is here, it is written: "And so it was that when God destroyed the cities of the plain, that God remembered Avraham" (below, v. 29). Afterwards two entire nations come out from him Ammon and Moav descended from Lot and he had the merit of King David and King Solomon descending from him.

(*Zohar I,* 64b, 107b; *Zohar II,* 227b)

The Resurrection of the Dead

The following section discusses views about the Resurrection of the Dead.

Rabbi Yitzchak and Rabbi Yehudah were traveling together. Their discussion revolved around the similarities between the fate of those destroyed in the flood and those destroyed in Sodom. Rabbi Yitchak then asked Rabbi Yehudah: Will they – the people of Sodom and Amora – arise when the resurrection takes place[76] or have they been destroyed forever? Rabbi Yehudah replied: Since those destroyed in the flood and the Sodomites were punished in similar ways, and the former will not rise at the resurrection,[77] by association we learn that those of Sodom and Amora will not arise. Moreover, a verse proves this, as it is written, "Sulfur and salt, a conflagration of the entire land, it cannot be sown and it cannot sprout, and no grass shall rise up on it like the upheaval of Sodom and Amora. . . . which God overturned in His anger and wrath" (*Devarim* 29:22). The apparently unnecessary expressions "in His anger and wrath" come to

76. See *Ezekiel* 37:3 ff.
77. See *Zohar I* p. 68b.

purvey additional information: "Which God overturned" – in this word; "in His anger" – in the World to Come, which is the Garden of Eden (Paradise). It is called this because it comes after life in this world; "and wrath" – when the Holy One brings about the resurrection of the dead.

Rabbi Yitzchak disagrees: Come and see: Just as their land was destroyed forever, so too, they are annihilated forever. The argument Rabbi Yitzchak presents is this: The definition of "forever" which applies to their land also applies to them. Since their land will remain waste only during the six millenia for which the world as we know it will exist,[78] but will be restored after that time, as the verse states, "Sodom and her daughters shall return to their former state" (*Ezekiel* 16:55), the same is true of their souls – they will be restored with the resurrection.[79] Come and see what can be deduced from this: the Holy One judges precisely measure for measure.[80] Since they did not restore the souls of the poor with food and drink, so too, the Holy One will not restore their souls to them in the World to Come, which is the Garden of Eden, which comes after life in this world. However, their souls will be restored with the resurrection. Come and see a further example of this quality of measure for measure: They shunned giving charity, which is called life,[81] and therefore the Holy One withdrew life from them in this world and in the World to Come. Just as they prevented people from traversing their roads and paths, so too, the Holy One withheld the ways and paths of compassion from them, so that He showed them neither compassion in this world nor in the World to Come.

However, Rabbi Abba maintains: all people will rise for the resurrection and for judgment. But as regards those people of Sodom it is written, "And many of those who sleep in the dust of the earth shall awake, some to everlasting life, and some to shame and everlasting contempt" (*Daniel* 12:2). But since the Holy One is compassionate; once He has passed judgment upon them in this world and they accepted their punishment, they will only be punished partially in the future. I.e., they will be resurrected, but will have to suffer shame and contempt for their actions. The verse states, "**many** of those who sleep in the dust of the earth shall awake," seeming to imply that not **all** shall awake, which

---

78. *Rosh HaShana* 31a; *Sanhedrin* 97a.
79. *Sulam.*
80. See also *Sanhedrin* 90a.
81. Cf. *Mishlei* 11:18, 11:19, 21:21.

directly contradicts Rabbi Abba's view. This can be elucidated according to the *Zohar I* 131a which explains that since many souls were reincarnated several times, there are more dead bodies than souls. Consequently, only some of the bodies will rise, but not all of them. This seems to be Rabbi Abba's view as well.

(*Zohar I*, 108a)

19:17 המלט על נפשך אל תביט אחריך – Flee for your life and do not look behind you

Rabbi Yitzchak said: Come and see. When harsh judgment prevails in the world a person should take care to avoid going out in public. For when severity is about it makes no distinction between those who are good and those who are evil. This is why one should avoid going out. This is why Noah was cloistered in the ark; so that he would not see the world outside when harsh judgment was being executed. Similarly, when the plague which killed the Egyptian first born was about to take place, Moshe told the Israelites, "and as for you, you should not leave the entrance of the house until morning" (*Shemot* 12:22) until the sentence has been carried out. So too, here: "flee for your life and do not look behind you. . . ."

(*Zohar I*, 107b)

19:26 ותבט אשתו מאחריו ותהי נציב מלח – His wife peeked behind him, and she became a pillar of salt

Rabbi Yose said: Why does it say, "Behind him?" It should have said "behind her." However, it means behind the *Shechinah*. She gazed at the destroying angel which was following the *Shechinah*. Rabbi Yose said: "Behind him" means behind Lot, for the destroying angel followed behind him. Did it indeed follow behind him? Hadn't he (the destroying angel) sent Lot forth from there from Sodom while he (the angel) remained behind to destroy Sodom? However, the intention is this: As Lot fled from one place to another, the destroying angel held back from destroying until Lot had passed in safety. Every place that Lot had already left behind him, the destroying angel overturned. For this reason he told him, "Do not look behind you" (19:17), for I am destroying in your wake. So, as it is written, "His wife peeked behind him" and saw the destroying angel "and she became a pillar of salt." For as long as the destroying angel does not gaze upon a person's face, he will not destroy him. But when Lot's wife turned her face to look behind him, then immediately "she became a pillar of salt."

(*Zohar I*, 108b)

19:27 וישכם אברהם בבקר– Avraham arose early in the morning

Come and see from this verse that Avraham established the morning prayer which corresponds to *chesed,* the quality personified by Avraham[82] and he made his Master known in the world. Out of his love for God, which stems from the attribute of *chesed* in the soul, Avraham rose with alacrity early in the morning to pray. In this way he rectified that hour that quality of *chesed* in the proper way. Yitzchak established the afternoon prayer as the verse states, "Yitzchak went out to pray in the field toward evening" (*Bereishit* 24:63), corresponding to the attribute of *gevurah.* In other words, Yitzchak made known in the world that there is justice and that there is a Judge who absolves and condemns in this world. Jacob established the evening prayer, as the verse states, "He prayed[83] in that place and had to stay there overnight, since the sun had already set" (*Bereishit* 28:11).

(*Zohar I,* p. 72a)

82. See *Zohar II,* 38b.

83. Although the usual translation of the word ויפגע is "he happened upon [that place]," the Sages (*Berachot* 26b) explain that the word also means "he prayed."

19:29 ויזכר אלקים את אברהם וישלח את לוט מתוך ההפכה – And God remembered Avraham, so He sent Lot from amidst the upheaval

"God remembered **Avraham**." It is not written, "God remembered Lot!"[84] This is because Lot was rescued only in the merit of Avraham.

(*Zohar I*, 104a)

19:29 בהפך את הערים אשר ישב בהן לוט – When He overturned the cities in which Lot had lived

Rabbi Chiyya said: What is the meaning of, "when he overturned the cities in which Lot had lived." Why "cities," in the plural, and not "the city" in which he lived? Lot had made his dwelling in all of the cities, as is written, "And Lot dwelled in the cities of the plain and pitched his tents as far as Sodom" (*Bereishit* 13:12). But the other cities did not accept him among them, other than the king of Sodom who accepted him in Sodom because of Avraham who had returned the king's people and possessions to him after their capture by Amraphel and his cohorts (see *Bereishit* chapter 14).

(*Zohar I*, 108a)

Rabbi Abba said: What is the meaning of, "when he overturned the cities in which Lot had lived." Why "cities," in the plural, and not "the city" in which he lived? Did he then live in all of the cities? Rather, the intention here is that the cities were still populated because of Lot, and only because of him they had not yet been destroyed. For all of the people of Sodom and its environs were wicked. There wasn't even one amongst them who had any merit, other than Lot. Now shall one say that this was because of Lot's own merit? No! Because of Avraham's merit. The reason for Avraham's merit protecting Lot will be explained in the next paragraph. From this we learn that wherever the wicked settle will be destroyed.

---

84. See *Berachot* 55b; *Bereishit Rabba* chap 51, para. 11.

Rabbi Shimon said: Come and see that the service one gives to a righteous man protects him in this world. This is so, even if he himself is wicked, for he learns from the ways of the *Tzaddik* and emulates him. Come and see: It was because Lot kept Avraham's company, even though he did not learn all of Avraham's ways, he nevertheless learned to do good deeds for others, just like Avraham did. This is the reason why all of those cities continued to exist as long as he was among them. As soon as he had left the cities were destroyed, as the angel said to Lot, "Hurry, flee there, for I cannot do a thing [to destroy the cities] until you arrive there [in Zoar, Lot's city of refuge] (*Bereishit* 19:22).

(*Zohar I*, 105a)

19:30 לוט מצוער וישב בהר הוא ושתי בניתיו עמו – Now Lot went up from Tzoar and settled on the mountain, his two daughters with him

Come and see. Two separate nations, Moav and Ammon, derived from Lot and his two daughters, and were bound to the place fitting for them – the side of spiritual impurity. For this reason the Holy One brings about the circumstances in the world, and turns the wheels so that everything will be done in the proper way, and everything will be attached to its proper source. Come and see how this applies in the present case: It would have been fitting for Lot that the Holy One produce those two nations from Lot and his wife. But matters were maneuvered so that they would be bound to the spiritual place fit for them. Thus, they derived from wine and drunkenness. That night they Lot's daughters found wine in the cave to which they and their father had escaped. This is the secret of what happened to Noah, as well. He "drank from the wine and he became intoxicated" and was castrated by his grandson, preventing him from having any more children. Although Lot also became drunk, God had planned it this way in order to extract the souls of King David and his descendants, including the soul of the Messiah, from where they were bound up in the realms of impurity, into which they had fallen with the sin of the Tree of Knowledge of Good and Evil. Now had Lot and his wife conjoined, this would have been a permissible relationship, and the forces of impurity would not have allowed these holy souls to leave their jurisdiction. However, since these souls derived from a forbidden conjunction, Lot with his daughters, the forces of evil allowed the souls of Moav and Ben Ami to be born.[85]

Come and see the names which Lot's daughters gave their sons, who were the products of the incestuous relations they had with their father: Moab, meaning, "from father." Rabbi Yose said: The older one of Lot's daughters spoke with arrogance by calling her son Moab, "from my father." Whereas the younger one, who also had a son by her father called him, *Ben Ami*, literally, "the son of my people." She spoke modestly, "the son of my people," as if to say, he was born from my people, without saying who his father was.

(*Zohar I*, 110a)

19:31 ותאמר הבכירה אל הצעירה אבינו זקן – And the older one said to the younger one, "Our father is old"

Rabbi Abba said: What is the meaning of "our father is old?" This refers to the evil inclination, the *yetzer hara,* which is called "an old and foolish king" (*Kohelet* 4:13). It is old because it was born together with the person, whereas the good inclination becomes a reality only later in life, when a person reaches the age of religious obligation (twelve for a girl, and thirteen for a boy).[86]

Rabbi Yehudah said in the name of Rabbi Yose: That same passionate soul called the animal soul says to the other intelligent soul, "Our father the evil inclination is old" he has been with us since we were born, and we have become habituated in his ways. So let us pursue him and cleave to him, just like all the other wicked people in this world. "There is no man upon earth to marry us;" there is no righteous man on earth; for no man can rule over his evil inclination. But there are many wicked people on earth, and not only we will be culpable. So let us do what everyone else does; they are culpable, for this is the way of the world to this very day. "Come, let us go and ply our father with wine ," and enjoy this world. Let us eat and drink and satiate ourselves with wine and cleave to our father, the evil inclination, and lie with him. But the spirit of Divine

---

85. *Mikdash Melech* in the name of Rabbi Yitzchak Luria.
86. See *Tanya* chaps. 1, 2.

Inspiration cried out saying, "they erred with wine, and blundered with beer" (*Yeshayahu* 28:7).

(*Zohar I*, 110b-111a)

19:33 ותבא הבכירה ותשכב את אביה ולא ידע בשכבה ובקומה – And the older one came and lay with her father, and he was not aware of her lying down and of her getting up

Come and see: In the first incident when the older daughter lay with her father the verse states, "and he [Lot] was not aware of her lying down with him and of her getting up." The Hebrew word for "her getting up" ובקומה ("*uvekumah*") is spelled with the plene, i.e. with a *vav* between the *kuf* and the *mem*. Moreover, in the Torah itself there is a dot on top of the *vav*, a traditional method of drawing attention to a special interpretation. The classical commentaries interpret this negatively: Lot was not aware of her lying down, but was aware of her getting up after the deed, and nevertheless went through the same experience the following night (*Midrash*, Rashi). The *Zohar* interprets this in a much more mystical sense: This is because there was help from Above for this act, for the Messianic King would descend from this union, via Ruth, the Moabite, the progenitor of King David and King Solomon, from whom the Messiah will descend. This is why it is written with a *vav*, whereas with the second one *uvekumah* is spelt without a *vav* between the *kuf* and the *mem*, for there did not derive from her a portion for the Holy One, as with the first. Therefore only in the first incident with the older daughter is it written *uvekumah,* spelled with a *vav* with a dot on top.

Rabbi Shimon bar Yochai explained: Why does the verse state "and he was not aware of her lying down and of her getting up," and spell *uvekumah* with a *vav* with a dot on top of it? Because he was not aware that in the future the Holy One would bring forth from this union King David and King Solomon, and all of the other kings of the house of David, including the King Messiah. Come and see an alternative explanation, where "getting up" is written in regard to Ruth, as the verse states: "And she got up before anyone could recognize another person" (*Ruth* 3:14). Now she certainly had a "getting up" on that day, for

Boaz had conjoined with her to establish the name of the deceased with his inheritance. According to Torah law, when a man dies without having any offspring, his brother or nearest of kin is obligated to take the deceased man's wife. If they have a son, he carries on the deceased man's name and inherits his property.[87] Thus Ruth had a "getting up," i.e. she was raised into the realms of holiness by her union with Boaz, so that all the kings and nobility of Israel descended from that conjunction. In regard to Boaz, he too did not know that she lay with him, as it is written, "And when Boaz had eaten and drunk, and his heart was merry, he went to lie down at the end of the heap of corn, and she [Ruth] came softly, and uncovered his feet, and laid herself down. . . . until the morning" (*Ruth* 2:7, 13). However, there is somewhat of a flaw with this explanation, since the "getting up" [the change in Ruth's status] actually precedes the "lying down."

Accordingly, a second explanation is offered: "And of her getting up" was also similar to that of Lot in the sense that they were not aware that the Holy One would bring forth King David and King Solomon, and all of the other kings of the house of David, including the Messiah, from this union, as it is written, "And she got up before anyone could recognize another person."

(*Zohar I*, 110b)

20:1 ויסע משם אברהם ארצה הנגב – And Avraham journeyed from there to the region of the south

All of his journeys were to the south, towards the attribute of *chesed* lovingkindness more than in any other direction. When one faces east, the south is to one's right. South symbolizes the attribute of *chesed*, which corresponds to the right hand, as stated in the Introduction to the *Tikkunei Zohar*. Now Avraham was the archetypal model of kindness; nevertheless he continued journeying southward, with the intention of always intensifying his connection to *chesed*. He acted with wisdom, in order to cleave to the right side*chesed*, which was the root of his soul.

(*Zohar I*, 111a-b)

---

87. See *Devarim* 25:5 ff.

20:2 ויאמר אברהם אל שרה אשתו אחתי הוא – And Avraham said of Sarah his wife, "She is my sister."

We have learned that one should not rely on a miracle.[88] Even if the Holy One does perform a miracle for a person once, he should not rely on a miracle another time, because miracles simply do not happen all the time. Now if a person puts himself in a place of open danger, so that a miracle is necessary to rescue him all of his former merits are nullified, as is written, "I have been diminished by all the kindness and by all the truth that You have done for Your servant" (*Bereishit* 32:11). Since God had already shown Jacob great kindness, and had saved him from several dangerous situations, he was afraid that his merits had become diminished and that Esau would find him vulnerable. Since Avraham had already returned from Egypt where he had miraculously been rescued once by asking Sarah to say that she was his sister (see *Bereishit* 12:10 ff. and the *Zohar's* commentary there) why did he again place himself in that same dangerous situation again? Avraham actually did not rely on himself at all. Rather, since he saw the *Shechinah* constantly in Sarah's tent, and it never left there, Avraham relied on the *Shechinah*, and was referring to it when he said "she is my sister," as it is written "Say to *chochmah*,[89] 'You are my sister'" (*Mishlei* 7:4). Here he was referring to the *Shechinah* which is called *chochmah*. *Malchut*, which is the *Shechinah*, is also called *chochmah tata'ah,* the lower *chochmah*, as in *Zohar I,* 31b, 154b; *Idra Zutta* 290a).

(*Zohar I*, 111b)

Rabbi Shimon bar Yochai began: "The lip of truth shall be established forever, but a lying tongue is only for a moment" *(Mishlei* 12:19). "The lip of truth shall be established forever" refers to Avraham, whose words were truth from beginning to end. "A lying tongue is only for a moment" refers to Avimelech. Regarding Avraham it states, "And Avraham said of Sarah his wife, 'She is my sister.'" This is what he said from the beginning, in Egypt, "She is my sister, referring to the *Shechinah* which was with Sarah, and this is what he said here too. Now Avraham spoke with *chochmah* throughout. Why

88. *Pesachim* 64b.
89. *Chochmah* = wisdom.

is the *Shechinah* called his sister? Because Avraham is from the right side as explained above, Avraham embodied the attribute of *chesed*, the root of which is *chochmah,* the first manifested *sefirah*, which has a particularly important relationship with the last *sefirah, malchut*, the final actualization of the *sefirot* as the *Zohar* explains elsewhere.[90] "*Abba* ("father" another name for *chochmah*) establishes *brata* (the "daughter," *malchut*). Therefore he referred to the Shechinah as "my sister." This is the secret of the verse "My sister, my beloved, my dove, my pure one" (*Shir HaShirim* 5:2). *Malchut* is called "sister" when *chesed* acts upon it, and "beloved" when *gevurah* acts upon it. For this reason Avraham always called her "my sister," for he clung to her as the constant actualization of his kindness and the two never separated.

What is written at the end? "Moreover, she is indeed my sister, my father's daughter, although not my mother's daughter" (below, 20:12) i.e., Sarah was his father's daughter from another wife. Was this indeed so? Wasn't she the daughter of Avraham's brother, Haran?[91] All of this refers to the *Shechinah*: At the outset, "She is my sister," as it is written, "Say to *chochmah*, 'You are my sister'" (*Mishlei* 7:4). And after this it is written, "Moreover, she is indeed my sister, my father's daughter." What does "moreover" mean? This is said by way of an additional explanation of the statement that "she is indeed my sister, my father's daughter," *malchut* is the sister of the six *sefirot* of *zeir anpin,* the first *sefirah* of which is *chesed*, the attribute of which Avraham was the embodiment. At the same time *malchut* is the daughter of supernal *chochmah*, for just as Avraham's attribute of *chesed* is a "son" (i.e., a derivative or branch) of *chochmah*, so is *malchut*, for "*abba* ("father," *chochmah*) establishes *brata* (the "daughter," *malchut*), as explained above. For this reason she is called "my sister," as well as *chochmah tata'ah,* the lower *chochmah.* However, "[she is] not my mother's daughter," since *malchut* receives influence more directly from *chochmah,* the beginning of all the *sefirot,* than from *binah*, for the reasons mentioned above.[92]

(*Zohar I*, 112a)

---

90. *Zohar III*, p. 248a in *Raya Mehemna; ibid.* p. 258a in *Raya Mehemna.*

91. Rashi explains that even though she was not his sister in the literal sense of the word, Abraham's statement was nevertheless justified since grandchildren are regarded as children; thus he could call Sarah his sister in the accepted figurative sense of the word.

92. See *Mikdash Melech.*

20:3 ויבא אלקים אל אבימלך בחלום לילה – And *Elokim* came to Avimelech in a dream by night

Does the Holy One appear to the wicked? It is written, "God [*Elokim*] came to Bilaam" (*Bamidbar* 22:8, 9); and "God [*Elokim*] came to Lavan" (*Bereishit* 31:24). All of these incidences have to do with wicked men. Since Divine Revelation depends upon a person sanctifying himself[93] how could these men have merited a Divine Revelation? The *Zohar* answers: It was the angel assigned to them which appeared to them as an emissary. Every nation has a guardian angel assigned to it, and it was the guardian angel of their people which appeared to them, not God. Why then does the verse state that *Elokim,* which is one of the Names used to refer to God, appeared to Avimelech? Because all angels, when they are occupied with a mission given to them by God receive this Name *Elokim*, for they derive from the side of severity, indicated by the Name *Elokim*. For this reason it is written, "And *Elokim* came to Avimelech in a dream by night, and said to him, 'Now you are going to die because of the woman you have taken.'" So too in all the other verses quoted, the Name *Elokim* is used.

(*Zohar I*, 111b)

20:6 ויאמר אליו האלקים בחלום גם אנכי ידעתי כי בתם לבבך עשית זאת ואחשך גם אנכי אותך מחטו לי – And *Elokim* said to him in the dream, "I too knew that in the innocence of your heart you did this, and I too prevented you from sinning against me"

Why the word "too?" Would it not have been sufficient to say, "I knew," and "I prevented you?" It indicates that something else is included. This was the guardian angel speaking, who said as follows: "Even though above me all is known, I also knew of your innocence." Similarly, "and I **too** prevented you" includes his guardian angel.

"[I too prevented] you from sinning against me." The Hebrew word for "from sinning," מחטו is written without the *aleph*. The proper way

93. See Rambam, *Yad, Yesodei HaTorah* 7:1

of spelling the word is מחטאו. Furthermore, why does it say "from sinning against **me**?" Surely the sin would not be against the guardian angel? However, we have learned that when people sin below, a blemish is made above in the spiritual worlds, and the Divine Presence becomes concealed.[94] Furthermore when the people sin below, their guardian angel is removed from his dominion above. Therefore it is written, "and I too prevented you," for even though the matter of your innocence or otherwise depends on something higher than me, "I too prevented you," the angel's own good.

"From sinning against me;" so that it will not be a needle in my flesh, so to speak. Since the word מחטו is written without the *aleph,* it can be read as מחט a needle. I.e., so that your sins will not cause me to be removed from my dominion and become a goad to me.

(*Zohar III*, 8a)

The Birth of Yitzchak

21:1 וה׳ פקד את שרה כאשר אמר – And God caused Sarah to become pregnant, as He had said

Rabbi Shimon said: The expression "and God caused Sarah to become pregnant" indicates that this was not by means of *mazal.*[95] If you will protest that our Sages declare, "children depend not on merit but on *mazal*,"[96] i.e. not on nature;[97] Nevertheless, in Sarah's case it did not depend on *mazal.* Rather, it is written, "and **God** caused Sarah to become pregnant." Since it is written, "**and** God," this indicates that all the supernal attributes were activated in conceiving Yitzchak.[98] If this is so, why

94. See *Midrash Rabbah, Shir HaShirim* 7:1.
95. Although the word *mazal* is usually translated as "luck," it is quite clear from the *Zohar* (vol. *III* 134a) that no such intention is meant in its Kabbalistic usage. Rather, it indicates an outflow of Divine energy from an extremely elevated level – from *keter.* (See *Pardes Rimmonim* s.v.מזל).
96. *Mo'ed Katan* 28a.
97. *Ziv HaZohar.*
98. *Ziv HaZohar.*

is the word פקד ("impregnate") used, since it generally alludes only to the *sefirah* of *malchut*, as opposed to זכירה ("remembering") which alludes to the higher *sefirot,* such as in connection with Rachel's becoming pregnant (*Bereishit* 30:22). Rather, there was definitely זכירה (remembering) prior to this, then the opportunity[99] was given below for זכירה to become actualized in פקידה (for "remembering" to become actualized in "impregnating," or for the higher *sefirot* to become unified with *malchut*). As it is written, "I will maintain My covenant through Yitzchak whom Sarah will bear to you by this time next year" (*Bereishit* 17:21). The covenant is always related to the secret of "remembering,"[100] as in the verses "I will remember My covenant between Me and you" (*Bereishit* 9:15); "to remember the everlasting covenant" (*Bereishit* 9:16); "and God remembered His covenant with Avraham" (*Shemot* 2:24); "I have remembered My covenant" (*Shemot* 6:5); "I will remember My covenant with Jacob and also My covenant with Yitzchak, and also My covenant with Avraham will I remember. . . ." (*Vayikra* 26:42), and so on. After the supernal mystery of remembering the male aspect it states the secret of the female, impregnation, so that they become a single unity.

(*Zohar I*, 159b)

"And God caused Sarah to become pregnant, as He had said." Why "as He had said?" As it is written, "At this time next year, when you are all in good health, I will return to you. Sarah your wife will have a son then" (above 18:10). From the statement, "as He had said," without specifying who said it, it is understood that it was He Himself who removed Sarah's barrenness, and not an emissary such as an angel.

(*Zohar I*, 115a)

21:3 ויקרא אברהם את שם בנו הנולד לו... יצחק – Avraham called the name of his son who was born to him. . . . Yitzchak

Rabbi Shimon bar Yochai said: Regarding Avraham it is written, "Then Abram journeyed on, traveling south" (above, 12:9), and all

---

99. Literally, "key."
100. *Or Yakar*.

of his journeys were towards the south, towards the attribute of *chesed*, as explained above (20:1), to which he bound himself. Nevertheless, he was not elevated completely to his place i.e., to his spiritual root until Yitzchak was born. As soon as Yitzchak was born, he was elevated to his place, and they worked in unison and were bound to one another. I.e., Yitzchak's attribute of *gevurah* was sweetened by Avraham's *chesed*, and Avraham's overflowing *chesed* was tempered by Yitzchak's *gevurah*. This is why Avraham, and no one else, gave him the name Yitzchak, in order to combine water, symbolizing the attribute of *chesed* as epitomized by Avraham, and fire, symbolizing the aspect *gevurah* as epitomized by Yitzchak, so that the two attributes temper each other and harmonize with each other. *Chesed* on its own, untempered by *gevurah*, does not distinguish between deserving and undeserving. *Gevurah* on its own, unmitigated by *chesed*, cannot relate properly to the world. A successful balance of the two is the ideal. Accordingly, the verse states, "who was born to him," fire from water. This can also be rendered as "who was born **for** him," for his benefit, in order to balance Avraham's qualities with those of his son.

(*Zohar I*, 118a)

Instead of stating simply, "Avraham named the son born to him. . . . Yitzchak (Yitzchak)," the verse uses the circuitous expression, "called the name of his son." The *Zohar* now explains the reason for this. Come and see: "Yitzchak" is an expression of joy and happiness, from Hebrew the word צחוק (laughter), as the verse states, "Sarah said, 'God has made laughter for me; whoever hears will laugh for me" (below, verse 6). For water, symbolizing the attribute of *chesed* as epitomized by Avraham, was exchanged for fire, symbolizing the aspect *gevurah* as epitomized by Yitzchak, and fire for water. So he was called by this name, for whenever an unexpected positive event happens, is it a cause for laughter.[101] Therefore the Holy One blessed be He called him this name even before he was born into the world, and he informed Avraham that this should be his name, as it is written, "And God said, 'Your wife Sarah will bear you a son and you shall call his name Yitzchak'" (above, 17:19). This is the explanation of why the verse uses the circuitous expression, "called the name of his son," since his son had already been named Yitzchak by God. Accordingly, Avraham merely called his son what he had already been named. Come and see that this was an unusual situation, by noting what was done in other cases: When other children were born, the

---

101. See above, the *Zohar's* commentary to 17:19.

Holy One let them (the parents) call them whatever names they wished. Not only the men, but also the women gave their sons names, as we see with the sons of Leah and Rachel (see below chapters 29, 30). But in this case the Holy One did not let his mother give him a name; but only Avraham, as it is written, "You shall call his name Yitzchak," you and no other, in order to bring about the exchange of fire and water and to include him (Yitzchak) in his (Avraham's) side, i.e., to sweeten the *gevurah* of Yitzchak with the *chesed* of Avraham.[102]

(*Zohar I*, 103b)

21:7 מי מלל לאברהם היניקה בנים שרה – Who said to Avraham that Sarah would nurse children?

Sarah nursed all their children the children of the scoffers who doubted that she could have borne Yitzchak. They said that he was a foundling that had been brought to her, and so they brought their own children with them, and Sarah took them and nursed them in their presence.[103] This is certainly why it is written, "that Sarah would nurse children," in the plural, and not child.

(*Zohar Introduction*, 10b-11a)

21:8 ויגדל הילד ויגמל ויעש אברהם משתה גדול – The child grew and was weaned. Avraham made a great feast

Avraham made a feast and invited all the great people of the generation.[104] We have learned that the accuser comes to observe every festive meal. If the person making the celebration first acts virtuously towards the poor, by sending gifts to their homes and also by inviting them to the feast, then the accuser goes away and does not enter the house. If he sees, however, that a festivity is

102. As explained above 17:19.
103. See *Bava Metzia* 87a; *Pirkei d'R. Elazar* ch. 52.
104. *Bereishit Rabbah* 53, 10.

unattended by poor people, he rises up before the Heavenly Court and denounces the person making the celebration. Since Avraham had invited all the prominent people of that generation, the accuser descended and stood outside the entrance disguised as a beggar. No one noticed him to invite him in and give him food, not even Avraham, who was inside and did not see him. Of course, had he seen a poor man, he would have invited him in. Immediately the accuser rose up before the Holy One and said, "Master of the World, You called Avraham, 'My beloved!' (*Yeshayahu* 41:8) Look! He made a feast and offered no part of it to You. Nor did he give the poor; nor did he sacrifice even a single dove before You." The accuser did not budge from there until he had thrown the entire celebration into disarray, and the Holy One commanded that Avraham offer Yitzchak as a sacrifice.[105] He also decreed that Sarah would die with sorrow for her son whom she believed had been sacrificed on the altar. This was all caused by the fact that nothing had been given to the poor.

(*Zohar Introduction*, 10b)

105. See also *Bereishit Rabbah* 58, 5.

Yitzchak and Ishmael

21:9 ותרא שרה את בן הגר המצרית – Sarah saw the son of Hagar, the Egyptian

Rabbi Chiyya said: From the day that Yitzchak was born, Ishmael Avraham's son from Hagar who was in Avraham's house, was never again referred to by his name. For where gold is found, the dross is not mentioned, and no importance is attached to it at all. For this reason the verse here refers to Ishmael merely as "the son of Hagar the Egyptian." He is neither referred to by his name, nor as "the son of Avraham."

Rabbi Yitzchak said: "Sarah saw;" she looked upon him with a disapproving eye, for she did not regard him as a son of Avraham, but rather as a son of Hagar the Egyptian. And for this reason the verse emphasizes that Sarah saw; for she, not Avraham, looked at him in this way. Avraham, however, regarded Ishmael as his son.

Rabbi Shimon added: This verse extols Sarah's praises, for when she saw Ishmael playing with idols[1] i.e., engaging in idolatrous acts she said, "this boy cannot be Avraham's son." If he were Avraham's son he would act like Avraham. The intention of the *Zohar* seems to be not that Avraham was not Ishmael's biological father; but that since Ishmael did not follow in Avraham's footsteps, he could not be regarded as his true son. Accordingly she told him, "Drive out this maidservant together with her son." **Her** son, not his, for she saw that his mother Hagar was teaching him the practices and customs of idolatry. So she said, "The son of that maidservant shall not inherit with my son with Yitzchak." That is to say, I know that he (Ishmael) will never inherit a portion of the faith, so that he will not have a portion together with my son; not in this world, and not in the world to come. For this reason the Holy One said to Avraham, "Whatever Sarah tells you, listen to her, for through Yitzchak will offspring be considered

---

1. See also *Bereishit Rabbah* chap 53, 11; Rashi.

yours" (below, v. 12). Through Yitzchak, and not through Ishmael. What is written after this? "She departed, and strayed. . . ." From what did she stray? From the path of Avraham! Here the *Zohar* learns a *gezeirah shava*:[2] It is written here, "and she strayed," and it is written in *Yirmeyahu* 10:15, "They are vanity, the work of delusion." Just as the latter verse is referring to idolatry, so too our verse. Nevertheless, for the sake of Avraham, the Holy One did not abandon her and her son (Hagar and Ishmael) as the verses which follow indicate.

(*Zohar I*, 118b)

21:12 כי ביצחק יקרא לך זרע – Because from Yitzchak offspring will be regarded as yours

From Yitzchak, and not from you. Yitzchak gave birth above, to the quality of truth, the attribute of *tiferet,* as it is written, "You give truth to Yaakov" (*Michah* 7:20), and Yaakov perfected everything. Neither *chesed* (the attribute of Avraham) nor *gevurah* (the attribute of Yitzchak) manages to achieve perfection. Because of his infinite undiscriminating kindness, Avraham gave birth to Ishmael,[3] *chesed* of unholiness, and prayed that he would live.[4] Similarly, Yitzchak gave birth to Eisav, *gevurah* of unholiness, and wished to bless him.[5] However, "Yaakov's bed [offspring] was perfect;"[6] none of his progeny were wicked. Yaakov, who came **from** Yitzchak, is the offspring who continued in Avraham's ways, and can thus be regarded as his. This is also the meaning of the verse, "Yaakov, who redeemed Avraham" (*Yeshayahu* 29:22).[7] See further, *Zohar* to 22:4 below.

(*Zohar I*, 96a)

---

2. An analogy between two laws or statements established on the basis of identical expressions in Biblical texts.
3. *Sifri, Devarim* 32:9.
4. *Bereishit* 17:18.
5. *Bereishit* 27:4 ff.
6. See Rashi to *Bereishit* 47:31; *Ba'al HaTurim* to *Bereishit* 22:17.
7. See *Torah Or* (Rabbi Shneur Zalman of Liadi) p. 12a ff.

21:14 ויתן אל הגר שם על שכמה – He gave them to Hagar; he placed them on her shoulder

Rabbi Beroka said: Since it is written, "He gave them to Hagar;" what is the meaning of, "he placed them on her shoulder?" Since he gave them to her, the verse should have stated, "*she* placed them on her shoulder." However, this teaches that he admonished her regarding the yoke of faith. Here it is written, "he placed them on her shoulder;" while elsewhere it is written, "there he placed[8] a decree and an ordinance for them" (*Shemot* 15:25). Just as the latter verse refers to placing the Yoke of Heaven upon their shoulders, so too the first verse. The *Zohar* uses one of Rabbi Ishmael's thirteen rules of Torah exegesis,[9] called *gezeirah shava,* whereby an analogy between two verses (or situations) is established on the basis of identical expressions in the Biblical text. In this case it is the identical use of the words "he placed."

(*Zohar Chadash, Ruth* 82a)

21:14 ותלך ותתע במדבר באר שבע – She left and strayed in the desert of Beer Sheva

As soon as she saw that she was no longer under Avraham's supervision she strayed from the path of righteousness, and returned to her former idolatrous ways.[10]

(*Zohar Chadash, ibid.*)

Here it is written, "she strayed;" while elsewhere it is written, "They are vanity, the work of error" (*Yirmeyahu* 10:15), referring to idolatry.[11] The *Zohar* again uses Rabbi Ishmael's *gezeirah shava,* rule, whereby an analogy between the two verses is established on the basis of identical expressions in the Biblical text, in this case the use of the root-word תעה signifying the errant ways of idol-worshippers. However, for Avraham's

8. Or, "proclaimed," "instituted," etc.
9. *Sifra, Introduction.*
10. Cf. Rashi.
11. *Ziv Ha Zohar.*

sake, the Holy One did not abandon her or her son. Come and see that this was only for Avraham's sake: What is written the first time Hagar ran away from Sarah? "God has heard your prayer" (*Bereishit* 16:11). Before she returned to idolatry, God listened to her own prayers. However, after she erred and returned to idolatry, even though it is written, "she lifted her voice and wept" (below, verse 16), it is also written, "God heard the cry of the youth." He responded to Ishmael's cry, not to hers since it does not state, God heard **your** cry."

(*Zohar I,* p. 118a)

21:17 כי שמע אלקים אל קול הנער באשר הוא שם – For God has heard the cry of the boy where he is

"Where he is" can be interpreted as "in his present state," meaning that he is not yet liable for punishment before the Heavenly Court. The earthly courts may administer punishment only to a person of the age of thirteen and older, whereas the Heavenly Court administers punishment only from the age of twenty and older. Even though Ishmael was a wicked person, since he indulged in idolatry, as explained above (verse 9), nevertheless, being underage he was not yet liable for punishment, as we have explained. Therefore it is written, "God has heard the cry of the boy where he is" in his present state of unpunishable youthfulness.

(*Zohar I,* p. 118a)

The Covenant with Avimelech

21:23 כחסד אשר עשיתי עמך תעשה עמדי ואם הארץ אשר גרת בה – According to the kindness that I have done with you, do with me and with the land in which you have stayed

Therefore, when the descendants of Avraham left Egypt with Moshe, "God did not lead them by way of the land of the Philistines because it was near" (*Shemot* 13:17 ff.). Why *because* it was near? Shouldn't the verse have stated, "*Although* it was near?" However, the verse intentionally states "because it was near." It signifies the oath which our Patriarch, Avraham, made to Avimelech concerning the kindness which the Philistines had shown to him, as it is written, "according to the kindness that I have done with you, do with me and with the land in which you have stayed." The oath was "near," i.e., still in effect.

(*Zohar II,* p. 45a)

21:28 ויצב אברהם את שבע כבשות הצאן לבדהן – Avraham set seven ewes of the flock by themselves

By doing this he hinted to Avimelech that retribution would not be exacted upon him or his people the Philistines,[12] until the seven righteous men of Israel, Avraham, Yitzchak, Yaakov, Moshe, Aaron, Yosef and David would secure the seven supernal levels *chesed, gevurah tiferet, netzach, hod, yesod, malchut.*[13] As soon as those would be attained, the lower world would correspond perfectly to the higher world, and David, who is the seventh, would gain the supernal Bat-

12. From verse 32 below it is clear that Avimelech was the king of the Philistines.
13. Note that the order is not chronological (chronologically, Joseph follows Yaakov, and Moshe follows Aaron). Rather, it is arranged according to the order of the *sefirot*, whom each of them represents.

Sheva. Bat-Sheva was King David's wife and the mother of King Solomon. Her name means, literally, "the seventh daughter;" thus the "supernal Bat-Sheva" signifies the *sefirah* of *malchut*, which corresponds to King David. Then when the kingdom of David will be established, the Israelites will exact retribution, as the verse states, "And after this, David conquered the Philistines and subdued them" (*II Shmuel*, 8:1). What is the meaning of "and after this. . . .?" After the Jewish People became complete and mirrored the higher world, then "David conquered the Philistines."

(*Zohar III, Tosafot* p. 302a)

21:33 ויטע אשל בבאר שבע – And he planted an *eshel* in Beer-Sheva

Avraham provided food and drink for anybody who came his way. Then he would talk to them heart-to-heart and ask them whom they worshipped. "Worship the Lord, God of heavens and earth," he would urge them. Then he explained the tenets of his faith to them until they returned to the true path of worship.[14]

(*Zohar I, Hashmatot* p. 264b)

An alternative explanation of the word eshel

He planted an *eshel* in Beer-Sheva. That which Adam truncated, the Tree of Knowledge of Good and Evil, Avraham rectified. This took place in Beer-Sheva, literally the seventh well, i.e., the *sefirah* of *malchut*.

(*Zohar Hadash, Ki Tavo* p. 60b)

---

14. As in Maimonides, *Yad, Avodah Zara,* 1:1 – initially all people worshipped God, but with time the generations erred and began to worship idolatry. Thus Abraham merely brought them back to the path which all men originally followed.

The *Akeidah* – the Binding of Yitzchak

22:1 ויהי אחרי הדברים האלה והאלקים נסה את אברהם – And so, after these events, God tested Avraham

Rabbi Shimon bar Yochai said: From the verse "And so, in the days of Achashveirosh" (*Esther* 1:1), we have learned[15] that this expression "and so" signifies calamity. Although this verse states only "and so," without the words "in the days of," it nevertheless indicates that there was a measure of anguish, albeit a lesser measure than that experienced by the Jews under Achashveirosh.[16] What is the meaning of "And so, after these events?" It means after the lowest of all the supernal levels after the *sefirah* of *malchut,* which is called "words."[17] The Hebrew "*devarim*," which we have translated as "events," also means "words," as is written, "I am not a man of words (*devarim*)" (*Shemot* 4:10). Now what came after ("after" in the sense of "lower than") these words? God tested Avraham. . . . The expression "after these words," is thus indicative of a level which is lower than the lowest *sefirah, malchut. Malchut* is called "word,"[18] and thus refers to Satan[19] who came to stage a protest about Avraham to the Holy One, saying: "This matter of testing Avraham's faith in You is not complete until he acts with severity towards Yitzchak. For Satan is the Evil Inclination and he comes to make his accusation "after these words" below the level of the *sefirah* of *malchut.*

(*Zohar I,* p. 119b)

---

15. Babylonian Talmud, *Megillah* 10b.
16. In the Talmud (ibid.) R. Levi (or R. Yonatan) points out that we have a tradition from the Men of the Great Assembly that word ויהי (and so) alone indicates catastrophe, without the word בימי, (in the days of). However, R. Ashi argues that ויהי alone does not necessarily signify anguish, only when followed by the word בימי. The *Zohar* apparently maintains that ויהי alone indicates a lesser level of suffering.
17. See *Tikkunei Zohar* p. 105a, 137a..
18. See *Tikkunei Zohar* p. 11b, 17a, 105a.
19. Other versions state: the *yetzer hara* (the Evil Inclination) instead of Satan.

God tested Avraham

The following excerpt discusses the tikkun, *rectification of the worlds, achieved through the akeidah (the binding of Yitzchak). When the attribute of chesed (kindness – the quality of Avraham) prevails in the world, then evil flourishes, for kindness allows even the wicked to exist. When the attribute of gevurah (strict judgment, Yitzchak's quality) prevails in the world, even the righteous may be viewed as not completely worthy. These two qualities must therefore be balanced and harmonized. However even this is insufficient, for chesed and gevurah may be balanced above in the supernal realms without it affecting this world. Therefore a third quality, (tiferet – truth) was given to Yaakov.*[20] *This restored the proper cosmic balance.*

This text needs to be understood, for it presents us with an apparent difficulty. It should have said, "God tested Yitzchak." Since Yitzchak was thirty-seven years old at the time, his father Avraham was not punishable for Yitzchak's actions.[21] so that if Yitzchak would have protested, and would have refused to cooperate with Avraham, his father would not have been punished on his behalf. Accordingly, this should be viewed as a test of Yitzchak's willingness to be offered as a sacrifice. Why then is it written that God tested Avraham, not Yitzchak? This was indeed Avraham's test, for God wanted to bring Avraham to perfection. Thus he sought to blend Avraham with *din* severity, the *sefirah* of *gevurah,* of which there was no trace at all in Avraham prior to this. Now, once Avraham passed the test water (*chesed*, kindness[22]) would be blended with fire (*gevurah, din*, severity[23]). Thus, after the test, the angel states, "Now I know that you *fear* God" (below, 22:12); fear as well as love. Until this point, Avraham was not complete. Now water was blended with fire Avraham attained the quality of *gevurah*. In addition, fire was blended with water Yitzchak, who was willing to allow himself to become an offering, gained the quality of *chesed*.[24] This is why the verse states that God tested Avraham. He gave Avraham the opportunity

---

20. See *Michah* 7:20.
21. In Jewish Law, a father is held accountable for the actions of his son until the boy reaches the age of thirteen.
22. *Zohar III,* in *Raya Mehemna* p. 235b-236a, 243b, 247a.
23. *Ibid.*
24. *Ziv HaZohar.*

to acquire the quality of *din*, and thus become complete. When Avraham did so, fire blended into water and they complemented each other.

Now come and see the secret of this matter. Even though we have explained why it is written that God tested Avraham and not Yitzchak, nevertheless, note that the verse uses the expression *v'haElokim nisa **et** Avraham*, and not *v'haElokim nisa **l'**Avraham*. The Talmud explains that *et* indicates something in addition to the subject which the *et* precedes.[25] In this way Yitzchak is also included in this verse, in the words *et Avraham*: ***et*** refers to Yitzchak, who at that time remained below within his attribute of *gevurah*. When he was bound by his father and was placed on the altar, thus providing Avraham with the opportunity to acquire the attribute of *din* as explained above he became crowned while remaining in his place together with Avraham. Even though Yitzchak remained within his attribute of *gevurah* without having to acquire the opposite attribute of *chesed*, nevertheless, through his willingness to be offered as a sacrifice he accomplished the blending of fire into water, and both of them ascended to a higher level. Then the division of fire and water was brought into the proper balance. Who ever saw a kindly father (Avraham) acting with such apparent cruelty? This was because of the disharmony of fire and water within Avraham himself,[26] which became balanced in their root above through this action. Until Yaakov, who was the attribute of *tiferet* the quality of truth, came and rectified the situation completely. Until Yaakov's time, the attributes of fire and water (*gevurah* and *chesed*) were only reconciled in their roots above, but not in the world below. Yaakov, by bringing his attribute of truth into this world harmonized and balanced the attributes of Avraham and Yitzchak. The Sages state, "Yaakov who redeemed Avraham,"[27] and the *Zohar* also states[28] in explaining the verse, "You command the salvations of Yaakov" (*Tehillim* 44:5) salvations in the plural which the *Zohar* interprets as the salvation of Avraham and of Yitzchak. Thus the three patriarchs, Avraham, Yitzchak

---

25. See *Chagiga* 12a; *Kiddushin* 57a..
26. *Damesek Eliezer*.
27. *Sanhedrin* 19b.
28. Above, 119a.

and Yaakov, were brought to completion, and the upper and lower realms were rectified.

(*Zohar I,* p. 119b-120a)

God tested Avraham

Rabbi Yehudah said: What is the meaning of the word נסה (translated here as "tested")? It may also be explained as a derivative of the root נס (banner) in the sense of raising a flag as in the verse, "raise aloft the banner" (*Yeshayahu* 62:10) meaning raise His flag throughout the world so that the righteous will flock to it.[29] Similarly, as a direct result of binding of Yitzchak Avraham's flag i.e., what he represented was raised on high for the entire world to see. This is the double meaning of the word נסה here. In order to raise the banner of the righteous, the Holy One tests them. Furthermore, the purpose of testing a righteous person in this world is in order to raise his head throughout the world.

(*Zohar I,* p. 140a)

22:2 ויאמר קח נא את בנך – And He said, "Please take your son. . . ."

Rabbi Shimon bar Yochai said: How could Avraham, who was an old man, take Yitzchak against his will, as implied by the word "take?" If you say that this is because Yitzchak never left i.e., defied Avraham's authority;[30] this is true. However, an alternative explanation may deduced from the verse where Aaron is divested of his duties which are then given to his son Elazar, "Take Aharon and Elazar his son, and bring them up to Mount Hor" (*Bamidbar* 20:25), where the intention is clearly to coax and encourage him (Elazar) with words, and lead them to the fulfillment of God's will. So too here; take him with words of encouragement and support. A third explanation: How could Avraham, who was the pinnacle of

---

29. See Rashi to *Yeshayahu ad loc.*
30. Cf. *Sulam.*

chesed (represented by the image of the old man[31]), also take the quality of Yitzchak, *gevurah*? If you say that this is because Yitzchak never defied Avraham's authority, and would do as his father told him, this is true. However, we can also explain that Avraham's eagerness to fulfill God's will, even at the greatest personal cost, encouraged Yitzchak to follow suit and offer himself willingly. This is the connection with the verse, "Take Aharon and Elazar his son, and bring them up to Mount Hor" which speaks about how Moshe encouraged Elazar to accept God's will and take his father's duties upon himself despite his knowledge that as soon as he was appointed his father would die.

(*Zohar I*, p. 119b)

22:3 ויחבש את חמרו– And he saddled his donkey

He himself saddled the donkey, rather than commanding one of his servants to do so – Rashi.[32]

Because of this Avraham's eagerness to fulfill God's will, to the extent of saddling the donkey himself, rather than have a servant do it the verse states in regard to Mashiach[33]: "He is poor and rides a donkey" (*Zechariah* 9:9). This is in Avraham's merit.

(*Zohar III*, p. 238a, *Raya Mehemna*)

22:4 ביום השלישי וישא אברהם את עיניו וירא את המקום מרחוק– On the third day, Avraham looked up and saw the place from afar

Why does the verse tell us that "on the third day, Avraham. . . . saw the place from afar?" The *Zohar* is asking two questions here: 1) Why is it necessary to mention that this was specifically on the *third* day? 2) Why is it necessary to mention that he saw the place from afar? In answer to the first question, this is because it is written: "From Yitzchak offspring will be regarded as yours" (*Bereishit* 21:12). This refers to Yaakov, who came from him Yitzchak, and not directly from Avraham. This is also the

31. *Damesek Eliezer.*
32. From *Bereishit Rabbah* 55, 8.
33. The Messiah.

meaning of "on the third day" i.e., the third day alludes to the third *sefirah, tiferet,* which is called the third day,[34] corresponding to Yaakov.[35]

In answer to the second question, why the verse states, "[he]. . . . saw the place from afar;" this can be understood from the verse, "from afar, God appears to me" (*Yirmeyahu* 31:2). Even though the *sefirah* of *tiferet* follows *chesed* and *gevurah*, nevertheless, the *tikkun* (rectification) of is from the light of the *sefirah* of *chochmah*,[36] which is distant from the vantage point of Avraham, the *sefirah* of *chesed*.

The Zohar now offers another explanation

"[Avraham looked up] and saw the place. . . ." This refers to Yaakov, of whom it is written, "he took from the stones of the place" (*Bereishit* 28:11). Avraham looked at the third day, which is the third level (the *sefirah* of *tiferet*) and saw Yaakov, who would be his future descendant. This was from afar though, not close up. Rabbi Elazar said to him, "What compliment is this to Avraham that he looked and saw from afar that Yaakov would be his future offspring, when he was on his way to bind Yitzchak upon the altar?" He replied, "Avraham had certainly seen the level represented by Yaakov, for even prior to this he knew this wisdom and he had seen the third day, that is the third level which brings about perfection i.e., that the *sefirah* of *tiferet* perfects *chesed* and *gevurah* by balancing the *chesed* of Avraham, and the *gevurah* of Yitzchak. There he saw Yaakov, as it is written, "[Avraham looked up] and saw the place" which refers to Yaakov. Now this matter stood at a distance from him he did not understand how the perfection of *chesed* and *gevurah* through *tiferet* would be achieved[37] since he was going to sacrifice Yitzchak. Yet he did not entertain doubts about the Holy One.[38] This is why he was praiseworthy.

(*Zohar I,* p. 120a)

---

34. *Zohar III*, p. 247b, *Raya Mehemna.*
35. *Ziv HaZohar.*
36. *Or HaChamah; Damesek Eliezer.*
37. *Leket Shmuel.*
38. See *Sanhedrin* 111a.

22:8 ויאמר אברהם אלקים יראה לו השה – And Avraham said, "God will seek for Himself the lamb for a burnt-offering, my son."

The verse states, "And **Avraham** said," not "and **his father** said," because he did not act towards him (to Yitzchak) like a father in this case. Instead he acted like a foe. Since he was about to slaughter Yitzchak, he could be regarded as an enemy. Alternatively, Avraham acted as an enemy towards **himself** i.e., not in character as the epitome of kindness, but as the epitome of severity.[39]

"God will seek for Himself the lamb for a burnt-offering." Shouldn't the verse have stated, "God will seek for **us** the lamb for a burnt-offering?" However, Avraham's intention was this: God will seek for Himself, when He wishes to do so. For now, my son will be the burnt offering, not a lamb. Immediately, "the two walked on together." Even though Yitzchak understood that he was the intended offering, he went together (consenting wholeheartedly) with Avraham.[40]

(*Zohar I,* p. 120a)

22:9 ויעקד את יצחק בנו– He then bound his son, Yitzchak

Rabbi Abba said: The reason that we read this section about Yitzchak on Rosh HaShanah, the Jewish New Year is that on the day on which Yitzchak was tied up below by Avraham, he was also bound to the corresponding level above, which is called the World to Come, the level of *binah,* as it is written, "He then bound his son, Yitzchak using the future tense **ויעקד** (alluding to the World to Come) rather than the past tense – **ועקד**. By virtue of the *akeidah,* the severities of Yitzchak were sweetened in their source, *binah.*[41]

(*Zohar III,* p. 18a)

---

39. *Damesek Eliezer.*
40. See also Rashi's commentary.
41. *Mikdash Melech.*

22:10 וישלח אברהם את ידו ויקח את המאכלת לשחט את בנו – Avraham reached out and grasped the knife in order to slaughter his son

Rabbi Shimon bar Yochai began his discourse and said: "Indeed the mighty ones shall cry outside; angels of peace shall weep bitterly" (*Yeshayahu* 33:7). "The mighty ones" are the supernal angels. At that time when Avraham was about to slaughter Yitzchak they cried "outside!" They declared: It is written, "He [God] took him [Avraham] **outside** and said, 'Look up at the sky and count the stars, if you are able to count them!' And He said to him, 'That is how your descendants will be'" (*Bereishit* 15:5). Why are You telling Avraham to offer up his son after You took him outside and promised him descendants like the stars? The angels tried to understand what God's intention could be.[42] "Angels of peace" refers to other angels who would in the future go before Yaakov. For Yaakov's sake God promised them peace, as it is written, "And Yaakov went on his way and angels of God met him" (*Bereishit* 32:2). These are the ones called angels of peace. They all cried when they saw that Avraham had bound Yitzchak and was about to fulfill God's command and slaughter him. The higher and lower worlds shuddered over what was about to happen to Yitzchak.[43]

(*Zohar I,* p. 120a)

22:11 ויקרא אליו מלאך מן השמים ויאמר אברהם, אברהם – An angel called to him from heaven and said, "Avraham! Avraham"

Why does the angel repeat Avraham's name? Because every *tzaddik* (righteous person) in this world has two souls, one in this world and one in the World to Come. So one finds with every *tzaddik* – that at one point or another in the Torah, his name is repeated: "Moshe Moshe"[44]

42. *Damesek Eliezer.*
43. *Or Yakar.*
44. See following entry for the reason why Moshe' name is written differently from Abraham's etc.

(*Shemot* 3:4); "Yaakov! Yaakov!" (*Bereishit* 46:2) "Shmuel! Shmuel!" (*I Shmuel* 3:4); "Shem! Shem!" (*Bereishit* 11:10).[45] The only exception is Yitzchak, whose name is not written twice like the others. For when Yitzchak was offered on the altar, his this-worldly soul left him. When Avraham said, "Blessed is the One Who brings the dead back to life," only Yitzchak's soul from the World to Come returned to him. Therefore we find that the Holy One, blessed is He, did not assign His Name to anyone living in this world other than Yitzchak, because he was regarded as dead in this world, and living in the World to Come.

(*Zohar I,* p. 60a)

Wherever a name is mentioned twice in the Torah, there is a *psik ta'ama* a cantillation note which requires the reader to pause between the first and the second mention of the name between them, such as "Avraham! Avraham!" "Yaakov! Yaakov!" "Shmuel! Shmuel!" However, "Moshe Moshe" is written without a *psik ta'ama* between the two. What is the reason? Regarding the verse, "Avraham! Avraham!" the latter is complete i.e., it indicates that Avraham had reached perfection, for he passed all ten trials with which he was tested; whereas the former indicates that he was as yet incomplete. That is why there is a *psik ta'ama* between the names: Now he was not the same as before. Similarly, Yaakov! Yaakov!" the latter is complete, for it was announced that Yosef was alive, after which the *Shechinah* once again[46] dwelt upon Yaakov, while the former is not. Furthermore, now in the land of Israel the Holy Tree (Yaakov[47]) became complete, reflecting the world above *ze'ir anpin* which has twelve dimensions the twelve tribes, corresponding to all the possible permutations of the Ineffable Name[48] and seventy branches, which correspond to the seventy souls which

45. Note that this verse merely repeats his name; his name was not called twice.

46. See Rashi's commentary to 45:27, on the words, "and the spirit of their father Yaakov was revived."

47. *Sulam.*

48. Ibid.

accompanied Yaakov down to Egypt.[49] Yaakov did not have this before. Since the latter name "Yaakov" indicates completion or perfection, whereas the former does not, there is a *psik ta'ama* between them. Also "Shmuel! Shmuel!" has a *psik ta'ama* between the names Why? Because the latter indicates perfection, whereas the former does not. At a certain point, he became a prophet; prior to this he was not. However, "Moshe Moshe" is written without a *psik ta'ama* between the two. From the day that Moshe was born he was perfect, as it is written, "And she Moshe's mother saw that he was good" (*Shemot* 2:2).

(*Zohar III,* 138a)

22:12 אל תשלח ידך אל הנער ואל תעש לו מאומה– Do not lay your hand upon the lad. Do not do anything to him

Rabbi Yehudah said: Yitzchak became purified and was lifted up to find favor before the Holy One just like the scent of the incense which the priests offered up on the golden altar in the inner sanctum of the Temple twice daily. This sacrifice was perfect, despite the fact that Avraham was pained when he was told, "Do not lay your hand upon the lad. Do not do anything to him," because he thought that his sacrifice was imperfect, and therefore could not be offered. Thus he had toiled and arranged the sacrifice and built the altar in vain. This does not mean that he was pained that he had worked in vain, but rather that his sacrifice and his service had apparently been found unworthy. Therefore, God immediately showed Avraham that his service was indeed worthy: "Avraham lifted his eyes and saw a ram trapped in the thicket by the horns. . . ." as will be explained below.

(*Zohar I,* p. 120b)

---

49. See *Shemot* 1:5. It is possible that seventy also represents the state of *tikkun* (full rectification) of the *sefirot* of *ze'ir anpin* and *malchut* – 7 X 10, where each of the seven *sefirot* contains all ten of the other *sefirot*.

22:13 וישא אברהם את עיניו וירא והנה איל אחר נאחז בסבך בקרניו – Avraham lifted his eyes and saw a ram trapped in the thicket by the horns

We have learned[50] that this was the ram created at dusk at the end of the sixth day of Creation, and that it was a year old, as it is written the daily sacrificial lambs had to be "male lambs in their firs year."[51] How then did they say that it was created at dusk at the end of the sixth day of Creation? After all, the binding of Yitzchak took place more than two thousand years later! Furthermore, Yitzchak was not in the world at that time and if we maintain that God created the sacrificial lamb which took was sacrificed in place of Yitzchak, this seems to indicate that Avraham and Yitzchak were preordained to act the way they did. Now, what value is there in action which is not the result of free choice?[52] At dusk on the sixth day only the potential was created for the lamb to be available should it be needed by Avraham. This is also true of all the other things created at dusk on the sixth day; the potential was given for that thing to exist when it would be needed.

(*Zohar I,* p. 120b)

22:14 אשר יאמר היום בהר ה׳ יראה – Today it is referred to as, "On this mountain God will be seen"

Avraham called it[53] the place where Yitzchak was bound on the altar and where the Temple would later be built "mountain," as in this verse. Yitzchak called the same place "field," as in the verse, "And Yitzchak went out into the field towards evening to pray" (*Bereishit* 24:63). Yaakov called that place "house," as in the verse, "How awesome is this place. It is none other than the house of God" (*Bereishit* 28:17). Avraham called it "mountain," to indicate that just as a mountain is accessible to everyone in the world, so too this holy place is accessible to anyone who desires it.

(*Zohar II,* p. 69b)

---

50. *Mishnah Avot* 5:6.
51. *Bamidbar* 28:3.
52. *Ziv HaZohar.*
53. See also *Pesachim* 88a; *Midrash Tanchuma* 81:2.

Bibliography

This bibliography does not include standard Jewish texts

Anatomy of the Soul, Rabbi Yitzchak Ginsburgh, *Gal Einai* Publications (Jerusalem 1995).

Asarah Ma'amarot, Rabbi Menachem Azariah MiPano (DeFano), d. *circa* 1620.

Ashmoret HaBoker, Commentary on Zohar, Rabbi Moshe Castro (Salonica 1852).

Ateret Tzvi, Commentary on Zohar, Tzvi Hirsch of Zhdachov (Lvov 1872, Jerusalem 1966)

Avraham Galanti, Rabbi: see *Zoharei Chama*. Quoted in numerous places in *Or HaChama* and *Or HaLevana*.

Bati Legani, 10 *Shevat* 5710, Rabbi Joseph Isaac Schneersohn, "Kehot" Publication Society (Brooklyn 1950).

Biurei HaZohar, Rabbi Dovber of Lubavitch, "Kehot" Publication Society (Kopust 1916; Brooklyn 1955).

Biurei HaZohar, Rabbi Menachem Mendel of Lubavitch, "Kehot" Publication Society (*Tzemach Tzedek*) (Brooklyn 1968, 1978) 2 vols.

Damesek Eliezer, Commentary on Zohar, Rabbi Eliezer Tzvi of Komarna (Komarna 1902; Jerusalem 1972).

Derech Emet, Commentary on the *Tikkunei Zohar*, Meshulam Feivish Heller of Zabarazh (Jerusalem 1899).

Derech Mitzvotecha, Rabbi Menachem Mendel of Lubavitch, "Kehot" Publication Society (*Tzemach Tzedek*) (Poltava 1911, Brooklyn 1990).

Eilimah Rabbati, Rabbi Moshe Cordovero (*Ramak*) (Lvov 1881; Jerusalem 1974).

Eitz Chaim, Rabbi Chaim Vital (Warsaw 1891; Jerusalem 1910; Tel Aviv 1960).

Hadrat Melech, Commentary on selected passages of *Zohar*, Rabbi Shalom Buzaglo (Jerusalem 1858). See *Mikdash Melech*.

Iggeret HaKodesh (*Tanya* part 4. See *Tanya*).

Ketem Paz, Rabbi Shamon Lavi (Livorno 1795).

Kevod Melech, Commentary on the *Idra*, Rabbi Shalom Buzaglo (Jerusalem 1858). See *Mikdash Melech*

Kisei Melech, Commentary on *Tikkunei Zohar*, Rabbi Shalom Buzaglo (Jerusalem 1899).

Kuntres HaAvodah, Rabbi Shalom DovBer Schneersohn, "Kehot" Publication Society (Brooklyn 1978).

Leket Shmuel, a selection of teachings from Zohar, elucidated by Rabbi Shmuel Kipnis, Jerusalem 1963.

Likutei Amarim, Rabbi Shneur Zalman of Liadi. See *Tanya.*

Likutei Torah, Rabbi Shneur Zalman of Liadi, "Kehot" Publication Society (Zhitomer 1848, Vilna 1904, Brooklyn 1979).

Matok MiDevash, Compendium of commentary on Zohar, Rabbi Daniel Frisch (Jerusalem 1986).

Meditation and the Kabbalah, Rabbi Aryeh Kaplan, Simon Weiser Inc. (Maine 1982).

Mikdash Melech, Commentary on entire Zohar, Rabbi Shalom Buzaglo. (published Amsterdam and London 1750-1755; printed together with the *Zohar* in Leghorn 1858; Zolkiev, 1862, 1864).

Moreh Nevuchin (Guide for the Perplexed) Rambam (Maimonides)

Nefesh HaChaim, Rabbi Chaim of Volozhin (Vilna 1824, Bnei Brak 1958).

Nitzutzei Zohar, Commentary on Zohar, *Tikkunei Zohar* and *Zohar Chadash*, Rabbi Reuven Moshe Margoliot (Jerusalem 1978).

Noam Elimelech: Rabbi Elimelech of Lizhensk (Lvov 1788; New York 1956, Jerusalem 1978).

Or HaChamah, Commentary on Zohar, Rabbi Avraham Azulai (Hebron 1618; Jerusalem 1876).

Or HaLevana, Commentary on Zohar, Rabbi Avraham Azulai (Pshemishel 1899).

Or Yakar, Commentary on Zohar and *Tikkunei Zohar*, Rabbi Moshe Cordovero (Jerusalem 1962-95), 23 volumes.

Pardes Rimonim Rabbi Moshe Cordovero (Ramak) (Koretz 1780, 1786; Munkatch 1906; Jerusalem 1962)

Rabbi Eliezer of Garmiza (Wurms): The *Ba'al Rokeach.* Commentary on *Sefer Yetzirah* (published with *Sefer Yetzirah* Jerusalem 1962).

Ramaz, Commentary on Zohar, Rabbi Moshe Zacuto (c. 1620-1697). Manuscript in British Library. Published in abridged form in *Mikdash Melech.*

Seder HaDorot, Rabbi Yechiel Heilperin of Minsk (Warsaw 1867; Jerusalem 1956).

Sefer HaChareidim, R.Elazar Azikri (Venice 1601; Jerusalem 1981).

Sefer HaGilgulim, Rabbi Chaim Vital (Przemysl 1875).

Sha'arei Emunah, Rabbi M. M. Shneerson, *Heichal Menachem* Publications (Jerusalem, 1990)

Sha'arei Orah, Rabbi Joseph Gekatilia (Warsaw 1883).

Sha'ar HaGilgulim, Rabbi Chaim Vital, (Jerusalem 1903).

Sha'ar HaKavanot, Rabbi Chaim Vital. *idem.*

Sha'ar HaMitzvot, Rabbi Chaim Vital. *idem*

Sha'ar HaYichud, (2nd part of *Ner Mitzvah v'Torah Or*) Rabbi Dovber of Lubavitch (Kopys 1882).

Sha'arei Kedushah, Rabbi Chaim Vital (Amsterdam 1715; Zolkiev 1780; Lvov 1791; Bnei Brak 1973).

Sha'at Ratzon,

Shnei Luchot HaBrit (*Shelah*), Rabbi Yeshayahu Horowitz (Amsterdam 1695).

Siddur With Chassidic Commentary, (*Siddur im Da"ch* or *Tefilot mikol HaShanah*), Rabbi Dovber of Lubavitch, "Kehot" Publication Society (Shklov 1803; Berdichev 1817).

Sulam, Commentary on Zohar and *Tikkunei Zohar*, Rabbi Yehudah Halevi Ashlag (Jerusalem 1946).

Tanya, Rabbi Shneur Zalman of Liadi (Slavita 1796; Vilna 1937; Brooklyn 1982).

Tomer Devorah, Rabbi Moshe Cordovero (transl. Moshe Miller Jerusalem 1993).

Yom Tov Shel Rosh HaShana 5666, Rabbi Shalom Dovber Schneersohn, "Kehot" Publication Society (Brooklyn 1971, 1976, 1984).

Ziv HaZohar A compendium of commentary on Zohar *b'lashon HaKodesh*, Rabbi Y. Y Rozenberg (1923).

Zohar Chai, Rabbi Yitzchak Yehudah Yechiel Safrin of Komarna (Lemberg, 1869, five volumes).

Zoharei Chama, Commentary on *Zohar Bereishit* and *Shemot*, Rabbi Avraham Galanti (Venice 1655, 1882).

Zohar HaRakia, on selected passages of *Zohar*, Rabbi Isaac Luria, *Shaarei Ziv* Institute (Jerusalem n.d.).

GLOSSARY

Abba, an aspect of *chochmah.*

Adam Kadmon, loftiest of the five worlds, or planes of reality. Above *Atzilut.*

Ahavah, love (of God), one of the ten innate powers of the soul, deriving from *chesed.*

Aleph, the first letter of the Hebrew alphabet.

Arich Anpin, the external aspect of *keter.*

Asiyah, lowest of the five worlds or planes of reality.

Atzilut, next to highest of the five worlds, below *Adam Kadmon.*

Avram, Abram. The Patriarch Abraham before the letter *hei* was added to his name to make Avraham.

Avraham, the Patriarch Abraham.

Bamidbar, Numbers. The fourth of the five Books of Moses (the Pentateuch).

Beit HaMikdash, the Temple in Jerusalem.

Beraita, Jewish legal statements of Tannaitic origin not included in the *mishnah.*

Bereishit, Genesis. The first of the five Books of Moses (the Pentateuch).

Beriah, the world below *Atzilut*

Binah, understanding, the third of the ten *sefirot*, below *chochmah* and *keter.*

Chaya, the fourth and next to highest of the five levels of soul. Corresponds to the world of *Atzilut.*

Chesed, kindness, fourth of the ten *sefirot*; corresponds to the right arm and to the first day of creation.

Chochmah, wisdom, the second *sefirah*, below *keter,* corresponding to one of the lobes of the brain.

Da'at, knowledge, the third of the soul powers. It is the key to the emotional attributes. *Da'at* is sometimes counted as the third of the ten *sefirot* – when *keter* is not counted.

Devarim, Deuteronomy. The fifth of the five Books of Moses (the Pentateuch).

Ein Sof, the Endless or Infinite. Frequently used in the *Zohar* to denote God. See *Or Ein Sof.*

Eisav, Esau.

Gan Eden, the Garden of Eden.

Gevurah, severity or restrictive power, the power to limit and conceal the Infinite Light so that each creature can receive according to its capacity. Corresponds to the left arm and the second day of the week.

Halachah, Jewish law.

Hey, the fifth letter of the Hebrew alphabet.

Hod, the eighth *sefirah.* Corresponding to the left leg.

Imma, an aspect of *binah.*

Iyov, Job.

Kabbalah, the esoteric wisdom of the Torah handed down from Moses to Joshua, and down on through the generations. Often divided into *Kabbalah Iyunit* (contemplative or analytical Kabbalah) and *Kabbalah Ma'asit* (practical Kabbalah).

Kelipah pl. kelipot, literally, shell or husk or bark. The *kelipah* conceals within it a spark of holiness, which is the vital force by virtue of which the *kelipah* exists, analogous to a fruit surrounded by a shell or peel. In order to release the holy spark the encumbering shell must be removed. The *Zohar* distinguishes four *kelipot,* three of which are entirely evil. The fourth, *kelipat nogah,* is the shell which actually envelops the spark of holiness.

Kelipat Nogah, the most elevated of the four *kelipot.* Literally means "glowing husk."

Keter, "crown," the first and highest *sefirah*, comprising two aspects – the inner aspect of *keter*, called *atik* or *atik yomin*, and the outer aspect, called *arich anpin*.

Kli, Kelim, vessel(s). The aspect of the *sefirot* which limit and define the expansion of the lights (*orot*) of the *sefirot*.

Knesset Yisrael, the community of Israel, reffering to the collective soul of the Jewish people, the source from which individual souls descend and are sustained.

Kohelet, The Book of Ecclesiastes. Written by King Solomon.

Ma'aseh Bereishit, the Work of Creation. Knowledge of the natural realm (as distinct from the supernatural). divine knowledge, that is, knowledge concerning the existence of God and the Divine Names and descriptions used for Him

Ma'aseh Merkavah, literally, "Work of the Chariot." Divine knowledge – concerning the existence of God and the Divine Names and descriptions used for Him.

Malchut, The tenth and final *sefirah*. Malchut actualizes all the other *sefirot*. *Malchut* comprises two opposite qualities – exaltedness, and its opposite, humility.

Melachim, the Book of Kings.

Merkavah, "chariot." Ezekiel's vision of the Divine Chariot (*Ezekiel* ch. 1) represents the ultimate in submission to God's will.

Middot, the seven emotional attributes of the soul, corresponding to the seven days of creation: *chesed, gevurah, tiferet, netzach, hod, yesod, malchut*.

Midrash, a compilation of homiletical and exegetical teachings.

Mishlei, the Book of Proverbs.

Mitzvah pl. ***mitzvot,*** commandment(s); religious obligation(s).

Moshe, Moshe Rabbeinu, Moses; Moses our teacher.

Nefesh, a generic term for the soul. More specifically, refers to the lowest level of the soul – the vital soul. Manifested in action. Corresponds to the lowest world – *Assiyah*.

Neshamah, also a generic term for the soul. More specifically, refers to the third level of the soul, manifested in intellect. Corresponds to the world of *Beriah.*

Netzach, the seventh *sefirah,* corresponding to the right leg.

Olam pl. ***olamot,*** world(s), plane(s) of reality, including spiritual planes. There are five worlds, from highest to lowest: *Adam Kadmon, Atzilut, Beriah, Yetzirah, Assiyah.*

Or Ein Sof, "Infinite Light." A metaphor for God's infinite revelation.

Or, Orot, light(s). Often refers to the light of the *sefirot,* as opposed to the vessels (*kelim*).

Pardes, literally, "orchard." The word is an abbreviation of *peshat, remez, drush, sod* — the interpretation of the Torah according to the plain meaning of the text, allusion to deeper meanings, the homiletical explanation, and the secret explanation respectively. These correspond to the four worlds, *Assiyah, Yetzirah, Beriah, Atzilut.*

Partzuf, pl. ***partzufim*** (visage) a compound structure of the *sefirot.* A *partzuf* is a metaphorical figure of human likeness, used to represent the expansion of an individual *sefirah* (or group of *sefirot*) into an independent configuration with ten *sefirot* of its own. *Partzufim* include *Atik Yomin, Arich Anpin, Abba, Imma, Zeir Anpin* (*ben*), *Nukva*(*bat*).

Ruach HaKodesh, literally "the holy spirit," or Divine inspiration. A form of prophecy.

Ruach, also a generic term for the soul. More specifically, refers to the second level of the soul, manifested in emotions. Corresponds to the second to lowest world – *Yetzirah.*

Sefirah, pl. ***sefirot,*** ten Divine emanations, through which God creates the world and is expressed in it.

Shechinah, the Divine Presence. Associated with the *sefirah* of *malchut.*

Shema, central Jewish prayer expressing God's oneness. Required Biblically to be recited twice a day.

Shemot, Exodus. The second of the five Books of Moses (the Pentateuch).

Shir HaShirim, the book Song of Songs.

Shmuel, the Book of Samuel.

Shoftim, the Book of Judges.

Sitra Achra, lit. "the other side;" the aspect of unholiness, or the forces of evil.

Talmud, the comprehensive anthology of Jewish teachings redacted in Babylon by Ravina and Rav Ashi. Also called *Gemara.* Comprising the Jerusalem Talmud (*Talmud Yerushalmi*) and Babylonian Talmud (*Talmud Bavli*).

Tanna pl. ***Tannaim,*** sages of the *Mishnah.*

Tehillim, Psalms.

Tetragrammaton, the four-letter Ineffable Name י-ה-ו-ה, signifying the eternal, transcendent revelation of God.

Tiferet, the sixth of the ten *sefirot. Tiferet* harmonizes and blends of *chesed* and *gevurah*, so that a proper mixture of the two will result in a bearable revelation of *chesed* to finite created beings.

Tikkun, rectification, order. Also signifies the world of *Atzilut.*

Tishrei, seventh months of the Hebrew calendar.

Tohu, a prior form of creation which shattered. Therefore it is not included in the five worlds.

Torah, the entire body of Jewish wisdom and teachings. Sometimes refers to the written scroll of the Divine Law (the Five Books of Moses).

Tzaddik pl. ***Tzaddikim,*** A righteous, saintly person. One who has achieved a permanent inner spiritual transformation.

Tzedakah, charity.

Vav, the sixth letter of the Hebrew alphabet.

Vayikra, Leviticus. The third of the five Books of Moses (the Pentateuch).

Yaakov, the Patriarch Jacob.

Yechidah, the highest of the five levels of the soul. Corresponds to the world of *Adam Kadmon.*

Yehoshua, Joshua; the Book of Joshua.

Yetzer Hara, the evil inclination – a person's innate tendency to destroy himself.

Yetzer Tov, or ***yezer hatov,*** the innate altruistic inclination to do good and to fulfill God's will.

Yichud pl. ***Yichudim,*** "unification." A mystical process of uniting forces in the spiritual realms.

Yitzchak, the Patriarch Isaac.

Yonah, the Book of Jonah.

Yud, the tenth letter of the Hebrew alphabet.

Zeir Anpin, the *partzuf* configuration of the *sefirot* from *chesed* to *yesod.*

Zivug pl. ***Zivugim,*** literally finding and marrying one's mate. In kabbalah this signifies the intimate relationship between the *sefirot*, whereby they become united.

Zivug neshikin, the nullification of the soul in communion with God, resulting in physical death.